26⁰⁰

# Adam Smith's Marketplace of Life

JAMES R. OTTESON

*University of Alabama*

CAMBRIDGE
UNIVERSITY PRESS

PUBLISHED BY THE PRESS SYNDICATE OF THE UNIVERSITY OF CAMBRIDGE
The Pitt Building, Trumpington Street, Cambridge, United Kingdom

CAMBRIDGE UNIVERSITY PRESS
The Edinburgh Building, Cambridge CB2 2RU, UK
40 West 20th Street, New York, NY 10011-4211, USA
477 Williamstown Road, Port Melbourne, VIC 3207, Australia
Ruiz de Alarcón 13, 28014 Madrid, Spain
Dock House, The Waterfront, Cape Town 8001, South Africa

http://www.cambridge.org

First published 2002

Printed in the United Kingdom at the University Press, Cambridge

*Typeface* ITC New Baskerville 10/13.5 pt.    *System* LaTeX 2ε   [TB]

*A catalog record for this book is available from the British Library.*

*Library of Congress Cataloging in Publication Data*
Otteson, James R.
Adam Smith's marketplace of life / James R. Otteson.
p.     cm.
Includes bibliographical references and index.
ISBN 0-521-81625-4–ISBN 0-521-01656-8 (pbk.)
1. Capitalism–Moral and ethical aspects.  2. Ethics.  3. Smith, Adam, 1723–1790.
I. Title.

HB501 .O824   2002
174–dc21
2002023867

ISBN 0 521 81625 4 hardback
ISBN 0 521 01656 8 paperback

*To Katie*

*It Could Have Been No One Else*

# Contents

# Preface

This book had its beginnings several years ago as a dissertation in the philosophy department of the University of Chicago. I was and am still interested in the origins of moral judgment, particularly in the commonplace phenomenon of shared standards of moral judgment in human communities. Where did these standards come from? Why did they arise? How are they justified? I first became interested in these questions by reading Hume's second *Enquiry*, which, it seemed to me, contained hints of an evolutionary explanation—but only the hints. When I discovered that Smith was a close friend of Hume's and that Hume read and admired Smith's work, I decided to read *The Theory of Moral Sentiments* (TMS) to see whether there was anything of value in it. I could not believe my eyes: here was a good—indeed, great—work in moral philosophy, and yet so few moral philosophers read it, let alone studied it.

I decided to study it. TMS became the centerpiece of my dissertation, then of several journal articles, and now of this, my first book. I attempt here to give a comprehensive, faithful interpretation of TMS and to relate what I see as its central methodological program to other central parts of Smith's work. Some elements of this book were present in my dissertation, but the majority of it is new, and in any case I have changed my mind about many things since I wrote the dissertation. I do not fancy myself to have now given the final word on the matter; on the contrary, I see this book as only the first step in a long line of much more detailed and particular investigation. But I hope that it is sufficiently suggestive to inspire others—particularly philosophers—to read and study Smith, and I hope that it in some measure indicates just how much Smith's work has to offer.

## Acknowledgments

The first thanks I owe is thus to Hume, who almost single-handedly brought me into philosophy in the first place, and who directed my attention to Smith. I must next thank my dissertation advisor, Daniel Garber, and my other readers at Chicago, Ted Cohen and Ian Mueller. A special thanks goes to Knud Haakonssen, an outside reader from Boston University, who not only helped me convince my committee that one could write a worthwhile dissertation on Smith in a philosophy department, but whose judgment that my dissertation was "excellent and certainly ready for submission" effectively brought to a close my tenure as a graduate student.

I must also thank my eldest son, James, since it was his impending birth that gave me an absolute deadline for finishing the dissertation: my wife told me that she would not have another child while I was still a graduate student.

Since leaving Chicago, a number of people have contributed in various ways to my education in Adam Smith and the Scottish Enlightenment, or have influenced my thinking more generally. They are too numerous to mention, but a few stand out and should be thanked: Hank Clark, John Danford, Doug Den Uyl, Charles Griswold, Knud Haakonssen, Max Hocutt, and Richard Wallace. Of course, none of them is responsible for my stubborn resistance to their counsel.

I also thank Liberty Fund, Inc., of Indianapolis, which not only publishes Smith's works at a price that even a graduate student can afford, but also has generously allowed me to attend and direct several colloquia in which I investigated themes and tested theses relevant to this project and in which I filled in many of the gaps in my educational background generally. Liberty Fund is providing a great service to mankind, and I thank them for it.

I must also thank the editors of several journals in whose pages some of this book's material has appeared: Catherine Wilson, editor of *History of Philosophy Quarterly*, granted permission to use material from "The Recurring 'Adam Smith Problem'" and "Adam Smith's First

Market: The Development of Language"; G. A. J. Rogers, editor of *British Journal for the History of Philosophy*, granted permission to use material from "Adam Smith on the Emergence of Morals: A Reply to Eugene Heath"; and Don Garrett, North American editor of *Archiv für Geschichte der Philosophie*, granted permission to use material from "Adam Smith's Marketplace of Morals." I gratefully acknowledge and thank them.

For the production of this book, I must thank not only those already mentioned, but also Terence Moore of Cambridge University Press, two anonymous referees for the press, and Sara Black for her careful editorial work. Max Hocutt needs to be mentioned again: I often relied on his quiet but firm support, as well as his remarkable grasp of philosophy, history, and ethics. My greatest debt, however, is to my family: Katie, Victoria, James, and Joseph are continual reminders to me of what is truly important, and it was principally their steady and unwavering love and support that encouraged me to bring this book to fruition. For this book, as in everything else I do, they are the sine qua non.

Tuscaloosa, Alabama                                                        JRO

# Abbreviations

1E  David Hume. *An Enquiry Concerning Human Understanding* (1748). Eric Steinberg, ed. Indianapolis: Hackett, 1977.

2E  David Hume. *An Enquiry Concerning the Principles of Morals* (1751). J. B. Schneewind, ed. Indianapolis: Hackett, 1983.

T  David Hume. *A Treatise of Human Nature* (1739–40). L. A. Selby-Bigge, ed. 2nd ed., with rev. text and notes by P. Nidditch. Oxford: Oxford University Press, 1978.

EPS  Adam Smith. *Essays on Philosophical Subjects.* W. L. D. Wightman, ed. Oxford: Oxford University Press, 1980.

LJ  Adam Smith. *Lectures on Jurisprudence* (1762–63, 1766). R. L. Meek, D. D. Raphael, and P. G. Stein, eds. Oxford: Oxford University Press, 1978.

LRBL  Adam Smith. *Lectures on Rhetoric and Belles Lettres.* J. C. Bryce ed. Oxford: Oxford University Press, 1983.

TMS  Adam Smith. *The Theory of Moral Sentiments* (1759). D. D. Raphael and A. L. Macfie, eds. Oxford: Oxford University Press, 1976.

WN  Adam Smith. *An Inquiry into the Nature and Causes of the Wealth of Nations* (1776). R. H. Campbell, A. S. Skinner, and W. B. Todd, eds. Oxford: Oxford University Press, 1976.

# Introduction

The Scottish Enlightenment has received a great deal of scholarly attention over the past few decades, and Adam Smith's work in particular has seen increasing interest.[1] This interest in Smith has been not only from economists but also from political scientists, historians, sociologists, and English professors—but, curiously enough, not philosophers. With only a few notable exceptions (and most of these fairly recent), philosophers have tended to pay little attention to Smith, perhaps believing that anything philosophically interesting Smith might have had to say was probably already said by Hume—and no doubt better. But even putting to one side the influential historical role Smith's work has played, it turns out upon examination that Smith is a surprisingly sophisticated philosopher in his own right, his moral philosophy in particular displaying an impressive subtlety and penetration. Smith hence merits and deserves more attention from philosophers today. This book is one step toward fulfilling that obligation.

Smith's *The Theory of Moral Sentiments* (TMS) is one of the great works in the history of moral philosophy, and although study of it has formed a central part of this recent scholarship, what is still required is a sustained examination of the book's overall argument, of the model it proposes to account for the growth and development of human institutions, and of the relation this model bears to Smith's other principal

---

[1]   In just the last few years, several major studies have appeared, including Brown (1994), Fitzgibbons (1995), Griswold (1999), and Muller (1993).

works. That is what this I propose to do here. I begin by offering a systematic examination and evaluation of TMS as a philosophical work. In the process, I present and build a case for a novel interpretation of Smith's project in TMS, and I then indicate how on my interpretation this project links up with Smith's other work, including in particular his *An Inquiry into the Nature and Causes of the Wealth of Nations* (WN) and an early essay on the origin of languages, suggesting a way to understand these central parts of Smith's corpus as successive steps in a single project. I should note at the outset, however, that the examination of those latter works is not intended to be systematic or complete; it is introduced rather to supplement and illuminate the examination of TMS and the model it proposes. I shall also be less concerned to establish or trace historical precedent or influence, or to situate Smith and his work in his historical or cultural context. I have occasion to discuss a handful of other thinkers—Hume foremost among them, for obvious reasons—but only when the comparison or contrast is instructive in getting at Smith's view; similarly, historical events in or around Smith's lifetime are introduced, but only when they help us understand Smith's argument. Smith wrote TMS as a work of philosophy—not of economics, history, or literature—and it should stand or fall on its merits as such. I think that it largely withstands philosophical scrutiny and that it enables a new, and plausible, understanding of parts of Smith's larger scholarly project. I hope to show not only that TMS deserves to be part of the canon of great eighteenth-century moral philosophy, but also that Smith's work reveals that he was a keener and more systematic social philosopher than he might at first blush seem to be.

## The Recurring "Adam Smith Problem"

In the century after Smith's death, such a number of scholars noted and commented on a particular issue regarding his writings that it became known as the "Adam Smith Problem." The problem was this: how could the same person who wrote *The Theory of Moral Sentiments*, which apparently established a natural "sympathy" as the cement of human society, go on to write *The Wealth of Nations*, which seemed to argue that economic policy should be predicated on the assumption that people are fundamentally self-interested? The problem became quite celebrated, with a number of commentators arguing that the pictures of human nature presented in the two books were simply inconsistent. The explanation usually offered for the inconsistency was that Smith changed his mind in the years between the time TMS was first published (1759) and the time WN was published (1776), probably during the period of the middle 1760s, when he spent time with and came under the influence of a group of free-trade-oriented thinkers in France known as the Physiocrats.

Around the beginning of the twentieth century, however, the scholarly tide turned. August Oncken, Edwin Cannan, John Rae, and a few others argued that the problem those previous commentators pressed was based on several confusions. First, in his two books Smith was discussing two different arenas of human life—moral relations and economic relations—and hence he understandably ascribed different motivations to people in those two different arenas. Smith was not giving two exhaustively independent descriptions of human nature and proper human motivation in the two books, but only describing parts of human nature and motivation in each; that meant the books were not at odds, but, rather, complementary. Second, Smith's examination in TMS includes an extended discussion of the virtue of prudence and its proper role in a virtuous person's life; since prudence is a self-regarding virtue, this shows that Smith was well aware, already in TMS, of the important role of self-interest in some areas of human life. Hence the introduction of self-interest in WN is not a novelty in Smith and does not indicate a change of mind. Third and finally, Smith did not in any case argue in TMS that sympathy for others was a motive to action. The sympathy of which Smith speaks in TMS is rather a "concord" or "harmony" of sentiments between an agent and a spectator to the agent's conduct. Our desire for what Smith terms a "mutual sympathy of sentiments" is indeed a natural human motive to act, but Smithian sympathy itself is not a desire, passion, or motive and hence cannot conflict with other motives to act. After these clarifications are made, it turns out, these later scholars argued, that there was no Adam Smith Problem at all. With only a handful of exceptions, this issue today is generally regarded by Smith scholars as settled in favor of Smith's consistency. Knud Haakonssen, for example, dismisses the topic altogether by calling it an "old hobby-horse."[2]

---

[2] Haakonssen (1981), 197.

Yet at the risk of riding the old hobby-horse again, I would like to suggest that the Adam Smith Problem has not yet been resolved adequately. I agree with twentieth-century scholars that a proper understanding of Smith's project in both TMS and WN, but in TMS particularly, resolves the alleged problem, but I do not think that any of them has yet provided an account that adequately addresses the most challenging aspects of the problem.

### The Familiarity Principle, the Market, and Unintended Systems of Order

I shall argue that both of Smith's great works reveal that he was conscious of a fundamental characteristic of human nature, a characteristic Smith laid out, examined, and defended in TMS and then presumed and applied in WN. The characteristic is this: the natural interest that people have in the fortunes of others is informed and modulated by the knowledge they have of one another. The degree to which I can understand and therefore sympathize with your motives and your actions depends on the degree to which I know what your circumstances, passions, and interests are and whether I judge your motives and actions to be proper in light of them. We know more about the people we encounter in some situations than we know about the people we encounter in others, and our judgments of them reflect our level of familiarity in each case. It turns out that in cases dealing with strangers or near strangers we approve of behavior predominantly motivated by self-interest—as long as it is in accordance with justice, which Smith thinks prescribes the rules of behavior necessary for the survival of any community. In cases dealing with acquaintances, friends, or family members, however, we approve of behavior that not only accords with justice but that also reflects an ascending level of benevolence and hence a descending level of self-interest. Smith argues in TMS not only that the benevolence we naturally feel toward others varies directly with our level of familiarity with them—the more familiar, the more benevolent; and vice-versa—but also that it is morally proper that our behavior toward others should be motivated in this way. I call the combination of these two claims Smith's "familiarity principle."

But how exactly do we determine what motivations are proper in each case? The fact that our judgments of others are affected by our familiarity with them, in conjunction with certain other assumptions about human nature (which will have to be sorted out), leads, according to Smith, to people judging their own and others' behavior from the standpoint of an impartial spectator. Smith argues that people have access only to their own experience; experience is essentially private. Yet they have an innate desire that Smith calls the desire for "mutual sympathy of sentiments." People take pleasure when they recognize that their own sentiments correspond with those of other people, Smith thinks, and this desire for mutual sympathy impels them to find some means to bridge the gap that results from the privacy of their respective bodies of experience. To understand the sentiments of another person, to bridge this gap, Smith thinks that we imaginatively change places with this "person principally concerned," and that we imagine what we would feel if we were in his shoes. We then judge whether our imagined sentiments are commensurate with the actual sentiments of this person. The spectator bases his moral judgment of the actor and the actor's behavior on whether his own sentiments correspond with those of the actor: when a concord or "sympathy" between their sentiments occurs, the spectator renders a favorable judgment; when a discord or "antipathy" occurs, the spectator renders an unfavorable judgment. But the judgments of spectators are often partial and biased as a result of their limited knowledge of the agents' situations, their lack of first-hand knowledge of the agents' actual sentiments, and perhaps also to their reluctance, for whatever reason, to consider the agent's situation in its full detail. Since we are all at various times both spectators and actors, however, each of us has known the unpleasantness of not having his sentiments "echoed" in others. Thus the continuing desire for mutual sympathy pressures us to devise a tool that will not only help us to temper our own sentiments so that they correspond with those who are spectators of our conduct but also help us to engage those spectators' sentiments to correspond with our own. This tool, Smith thinks, is the impartial spectator.

Employment of the impartial spectator as the basis of our judgments of one another leads for Smith to the establishment of an unintended system of moral order reflecting our basic social motivations—the desire for mutual sympathy and the drive to better our condition in life. The desire for mutual sympathy results, by way of what I call the "impartial spectator procedure," in the gradual establishment of the general rules of morality. These rules act as a formal order or structure of the system of moral judging that emerges completely unintentionally, but nevertheless inexorably, as a result of everyone's employing the impartial spectator procedure and modifying his judgments and behavior in terms of it. It turns out that the impartial spectator procedure is itself informed by a continual exchange of information among the people who have contact with one another regarding their sentiments and their judgments of people's sentiments; the established and accepted rules of morality reflect the ever-changing but nevertheless orderly general consensus among these people as to what behavior is proper and what is improper. The other basic motivation, the drive to better our condition in life, leads people to coordinate their respective pursuits by means of economic markets. In this case, it is these marketplaces of exchange that constitute an unintentional yet orderly structure for interactions. By buying and selling certain products at certain prices, people communicate to each other their interests and desires, and the markets that emerge are merely the result of individuals bartering and trucking for their own mutual advantage.

Smith's central idea, which I think is also his most important, is that an unintended, or "spontaneous,"[3] order emerges from people acting on these two basic, natural drives, an order that they did not consciously intend to create but that nevertheless unfolds on its own and serves both to strengthen the interpersonal bonds and increase the wealth of the community. The tool that enables the unintended order to emerge is the impartial spectator, and my contention is that, for Smith, the general rules of morality and the general rules and regulations of economic markets are analogous in the sense that they develop, change, and are sustained by the interactions and mutual exchanges of information among the people of the relevant communities as they strive to satisfy their interests in cooperation with one another. Smith thinks that the rules and protocols that flow from these exchanges then become gradually internalized in each individual. Thus the unintended orders of morality and of economic markets

---

[3] I prefer the term "unintended order" to the more familiar "spontaneous order" because the former conveys that the system of order was not anyone's intentional design without suggesting, as "spontaneous" might, that there is no way to account for the creation of the system.

are self-regulating because each individual disciplines his own actions according to this internalized impartial spectator, which he consults when judging his own behavior. This personal internal spectator is then what we refer to as our "conscience." On this interpretation of Smith, the various motives and behaviors of people in all areas of life result from their using the impartial spectator procedure to guide them, modulated by their familiarity with the people with whom they interact in various situations. Thus the people Smith describes in TMS and WN, far from operating on the basis of fundamentally inconsistent natures, turn out on examination to have a single and constant nature that reflects their natural desires for mutual sympathy and a better condition in life. In TMS, Smith focuses his attention on the desire for mutual sympathy and the unintended order to which it leads, namely, the general rules of morality; in WN, he concentrates on the desire for better conditions in life and the unintended order to which it leads, namely, economic markets.

But I shall argue that Smith's general notion of a market forms the background for the conceptions of human interactions he describes in both TMS and WN. Indeed, I think the concept of a market explains the development of all human social customs and institutions for Smith. The overarching unintended order is that set out in TMS, but it manifests itself in various areas of community life in terms of unintended suborders. The exchange of goods of production—the marketplace—is one such suborder, a particularly important one because it covers perhaps the greatest range of human interactions among all the suborders (second only to the overall order of morality). Other suborders might be, for example, the accepted and commonly endorsed rules of behavior that govern academic professors in their interactions with one another, professional athletes in their interactions with one another, subscribers to particular religious faiths in their interactions with one another, and so on. In all the various cases, the proper codes of motivation and behavior are determined by the impartial spectator procedure, but only as it is informed by the actual spectator's knowledge of the particular situation and the people involved, and as it is prompted by the two basic human desires. The particular suborder in which one is interacting with others sets the parameters for the impartial spectator procedure, and the result of the procedure will be heavily influenced by how well one knows the people with whom one is interacting. The codes of behavior obtaining in the various suborders can then be understood, I argue, in terms of Smith's conception of a market—unintended orders that naturally emerge from the free, everyday interactions of people with one another as they strive to satisfy their interests.

## Plan of the Work

My study begins with an explication of the central elements of Smith's moral theory. Each of the first two chapters is divided into two sections, representing what I take to be the four central parts of Smith's moral theory. In the first section of Chapter 1, I examine Smith's notion of sympathy and the technical way in which he uses that term. I lay out the role sympathy plays in Smith's theory, including the role he thinks it plays in passing moral judgments. Smith's conception of human sympathy is not the same as that of Hume, although the two are sometimes conflated; I take some time in this section to specify in what ways Smith's conception is unique. In the second section, I lay out what I call Smith's "impartial spectator procedure," that is, the process by which we arrive at moral judgments. In this section, I discuss in detail the nature of Smith's "impartial spectator," including the controversial issue of whether the impartial spectator represents a perfect ideal or whether he represents any informed, but impartial, person. I argue that he represents the latter. I also discuss the role considerations of utility play in the passing of Smithian moral judgments, again taking care to distinguish Smith's view from that of Hume—in part because Smith takes pride in the belief that his view corrects and is superior to Hume's on this count. In the first section of Chapter 2, I look at Smith's explanation of the human conscience, or the inner voice we all have that seems somehow to know right from wrong. In this connection, I have occasion to discuss how Smith thinks that the "general rules of morality" come to be formed and whence they derive their authority over us. I show how on Smith's analysis the conscience is an internalization of the impartial spectator and of the general rules by which the impartial spectator procedure functions. Chapter 2 concludes with a discussion of Smith's general conception of human nature and, in particular, those fundamental characteristics that Smith believes not only enable us to form and maintain civil society but also drive us to develop and maintain moral standards.

In Chapter 3, I introduce what I call the "marketplace of morality," or the mechanism that, according to my reading of Smith, regulates and forms the basis of our moral judgments. I argue that a principal goal Smith had in TMS is to explain how during their lifetimes human beings go from a state of utter amorality as infants to adults with a sophisticated—if often largely unconscious—system of moral principles that both enables them to pass judgment on an impressive array of situations and behaviors and provides extensive common ground between them and the other members of their communities. In this chapter, I trace Smith's discussion of this natural development of moral standards and moral judgments, as well as his discussion of the development and internalization of the impartial spectator's viewpoint, and I draw out the underlying conceptual structure of Smith's account, which I identify as a market model. I then look at some passages in Hume that suggest something like the notion of unintended order that Smith develops later to see what debt, if any, Smith owes to Hume on this count and what differences there are between them. I close the chapter by identifying and briefly addressing some potential problems with the market model.

In Chapters 4 and 5, I address the Adam Smith Problem. I first argue that the problem is not so easily dismissed as some twentieth-century scholars have supposed. To support my position, I look closely at several passages from TMS and WN. I lay out in detail the conception of moral virtue that Smith develops in TMS, including in particular his conception of the motives that are at work in the morally virtuous person. Smith's conclusion is that moral propriety resides in balancing four principal virtues in one's life: justice, benevolence, prudence, and self-command. I also call attention to the criticisms Smith offers in TMS of Bernard Mandeville and his "licentious system" of morality, where Smith argues that a moral system is licentious if it holds that all human action is, or—worse yet—ought to be, governed solely by self-interest. I then examine the picture of human motivation that Smith gives in WN, which seems decidedly different from the picture he gave in TMS. My conclusion is that the nineteenth-century critics were on to something, at least as regards the apparent tension between Smith's two accounts of human motivation. I then look at some important treatments of Smith's moral philosophy that defend Smith's consistency, and I show why the reasons for their dismissal of the problem are unsatisfactory. In Chapter 5, I turn to explore the extent to which I believe the problem can indeed be resolved, given the examination and interpretation of Smith's moral theory offered in Chapters 1–4. I argue that on my interpretation of Smith all important questions about the consistency of the two books are answered: the books are fundamentally consistent insofar as they both develop and utilize Smith's market model for understanding human social institutions, and insofar as the familiarity principle laid out in TMS explains why people acting in economic markets would and should behave the way WN describes.

Chapter 6 addresses the question of whether Smith's theory of moral sentiments is purely descriptive, or whether it is normative as well. The concern here is whether standards of moral judgments, if they are formed in the manner Smith describes, allow for any measure of objectivity. Can they be called transcendently right—or are they relative to the time or place in which they "unintentionally" developed? Are they inherently or intrinsically right—or are they merely (contingently) efficient? I ask whether Smith sees his theory generally as merely descriptive, or whether he sees our natural moral sentiments as having an ultimate justification beyond the mere fact of their existence. That Smith's theory is descriptive seems indisputable. It is an extended depiction of the process by which mankind make moral judgments—what we would today perhaps consider an exercise in moral psychology. Indeed, in one place Smith explicitly states that he is not concerned with matters of right, but rather with matters of fact.[4] This has led some commentators to argue that Smith is not a moral philosopher at all, but rather what we might call a social scientist. On the other hand, there is a significant amount of discussion in TMS that sounds suspiciously like Smith telling us how people ought to act and how people ought to judge others, not just how they actually and in fact do these things. On the basis of such passages, other scholars have argued that Smith's theory of moral sentiments is normative as well as descriptive. I agree with the latter scholars.

In Chapter 6, I show how the normativity arises as a result of Smith's belief that our moral sentiments, when properly ordered, are natural, and that as such they are part of God's grand benevolent design, which ultimately aims at promoting human happiness. On examination, it turns out that the impartial spectator, the tool that regulates our

---

4 TMS, 77, §10.

interactions with one another, tends, as it operates in the marketplace of morality, to produce an equilibrium that is reflective of the natural and tranquil state of mind that Smith thinks constitutes true human happiness, the state in which God intends us to be. Building on the discussion in Chapter 2, I here lay out the full complement of desires, instincts, and inclinations Smith thinks human beings naturally have. It turns out that the happiness Smith thinks we are thus naturally designed to achieve, combined with the natural limitations of the human intellect he thinks we have, enable us to understand Smith's intriguing discussion in TMS of the "man of system," which otherwise seems out of place. The conclusion I draw is that the normativity of Smith's theory is in the form of a hypothetical imperative: given the way you are constructed, if you want to be truly happy, here is what you should do. In this connection I again have occasion to make recourse to Hume, and to look at the way in which he thinks moral judgments are ultimately legitimated. I look at his use of utility and compare it to Smith's treatment, resuming a discussion that was left incomplete in Chapter 1. It will be seen that Smithian utility operates in a way far different from the way in which Humean utility operates: for Smith, unlike for Hume, considerations of utility are not what immediately prompt moral judgments, though utility does play a role—if an unconscious one—in the unintentional process of evolutionary selection of moral standards. I show how Smith's theory in this way conforms to a structure that allows utility to be the ultimate foundation for moral judgments and can thus provide the means to bridge a gap that Hume seems to leave unbridged, namely, that between the individual's private utility and the development of general rules of conduct necessary for the survival and flourishing of communities or society at large. Smith gives us a way to understand how individuals could come to endorse rules that conduce to the overall utility of their communities but that on occasion are adverse to their own individual utility. I then conclude this chapter by showing that for Smith what is in our nature was put there intentionally by God, from which emerges in TMS another level of normativity, beyond the hypothetical imperative: you should obey the long-standing moral rules of your community because in the last analysis they manifest the will of God.

In Chapter 7, I strengthen the case for my "marketplace" interpretation of Smith's moral theory by showing that the same model is present both in his early essay on the origin of languages and in his other principal work, *The Wealth of Nations*. I also find evidence of this model elsewhere in Smith's corpus, leading me to suggest the larger claim that on Smith's view the market model he developed in TMS correctly describes the creation, growth, development, and maintenance of human institutions generally. I here make explicit the formal elements of this model as they are found in TMS, WN, and the essay on languages.

Finally, after a brief summation of the central parts of my interpretation of TMS and my account of Smith's central goals in it, I close my study by making several reflections on Smith's theory. I first make two general observations about the theory. The first relates to an aspect of the Adam Smith Problem: I suggest that the way markets work according to the argument of WN could be shown to enable the growth and extension of natural benevolence out of actions that are initially prompted only by self-interest. Hence, contrary to what one might have expected, according to Smith's account, allowing the extension of self-interested behavior (within, as always, the bounds of justice) in economic markets can actually lead to an extension of natural affection for and benevolence toward others—indeed, perhaps more so than in other types of economic arrangements. The second observation is connected with what I think is an important failing of Smith's theory as he presents it, namely, its handling of the phenomenon of moral deviancy. Smith has no explicit discussion of this phenomenon, which is a serious omission; nevertheless, there is some material in Smith on which, I argue, a plausible "Smithian" explanation of them can be constructed. I next cite and discuss some intriguing and suggestive recent sociological evidence that tends to support parts of Smith's conception of human nature—and hence, perhaps, his market model for understanding morality and other human social institutions. Finally, I close the book by arguing that Smith's moral theory puts him in the first tier of Scottish Enlightenment thinkers, and I indicate what I think still remain as the most promising parts of Smith's theory.

# Adam Smith's Moral Theory, Part One

## *Sympathy and the Impartial Spectator Procedure*

Virtually all features of Adam Smith's moral theory can be found in elementary form in the first three chapters of *The Theory of Moral Sentiments*. One finds there discussions of natural human sympathy, of what I shall call the "impartial spectator procedure," and of central aspects of Smith's conception of human nature; one finds references to the general rules of morality that guide the human conscience; and one finds hints of Smith's account of human passions that become clear only after one has read the rest of the book. In both TMS and his other central work, *An Inquiry into the Nature and Causes of the Wealth of Nations*, Smith begins with what he thinks is the central idea of the book: the first chapter of TMS is "Of Sympathy"; the first chapter of WN is "Of the Division of Labor." The remainders of both of Smith's books are in large part elaborations and extensions of the ideas brought out in rudimentary form in those first short chapters.

*The Theory of Moral Sentiments* went through six editions during Smith's lifetime, the second and sixth receiving significant revision. The sixth edition, which was published only months before Smith's death in 1790, represents his most mature thought on the subject. He had had thirty-one years to reconsider his original examination since its first publication in 1759, and fifteen years since the publication of WN in 1776. The sixth edition also includes Smith's response to objections that had been raised to earlier editions of TMS, including some raised by one of Smith's closest and most respected friends, David Hume. The sixth edition contains, moreover, numerous editorial revisions and extensive additions,[1] all of which suggest that Smith had in fact done some rethinking in the years after the first publication of TMS and that the sixth edition represents his final word on the matter. Despite the differences between the sixth and the other editions of TMS, Smith's overall argument suffered no changes: the additions and revisions mainly concern less important details and cosmetic aspects of the presentation. Smith had been concerned throughout his scholarly career with rhetoric and the art of good writing,[2] and in my judgment the majority of the changes he made were in an effort to make his argument clearer and more persuasive to his reader, not to change the argument itself. We shall therefore focus our attention on the sixth edition, and we shall consult earlier editions only when that seems necessary for reasons of textual clarity.

*The Theory of Moral Sentiments* has seven parts. The first three parts contain the core of Smith's theory; the latter four parts, supplements to the theory. It takes its cue from other areas of natural science that had seen great success in recent times and aims to describe the way in which people make moral judgments. Smith proposes to investigate moral philosophy empirically, the way astronomy had been investigated, and in so doing to examine the two questions he thinks ought to be examined in a theory of moral sentiments: "First, wherein does virtue consist?" and "Secondly, by what power or faculty in the mind is it, that this character, whatever it be, is recommended to us?" (TMS, 265). Smith's answer to the first question is "propriety," or an action's suitableness to the object that excites it. Smith's answer to the second question is "by . . . a modification of sympathy" (TMS, 266), or the degree to which we can sympathize with the motives and actions of the person principally concerned (as Smith often calls the agent). Part I of TMS, "Of the Propriety of Action," includes Smith's examination of the answers he gives to these two questions. It turns out that our natural sympathy can be modified in two ways. The first is when we consider an action's relation to the cause that excites it—what Smith calls the

---

[1] For example, part six, "Of the Character of Virtue," is entirely new to the sixth edition. See Raphael and Macfie's introduction to TMS, 43–52, for a detailed account of the differences between the sixth and previous editions.

[2] From the 1750s to the mid-1760s, Smith delivered a series of lectures at the University of Glasgow on this topic, students' notes of which are now collected in *Lectures on Rhetoric and Belles Lettres* (1983; hereafter LRBL).

propriety (or impropriety) of an action. The second is when we consider an action's "relation to the end which it proposes, or to the effect which it tends to produce" (TMS, 67); this Smith calls the merit (or demerit) of an action. Part II of TMS consists of Smith's discussion of merit and demerit. Finally, the third part of TMS deals with the last central issue that a theory of moral sentiments should address, namely, how we judge ourselves and how we regulate our own behavior—two processes commonly comprehended by the term "conscience." Part III discusses how one's conscience is formed and how it is able to give one what Smith calls a sense of duty.

Parts IV through VII are, as I said, supplementary. Part IV considers the role utility plays in passing moral judgments, and it can fruitfully be seen as a critique and refutation of the position Hume had adopted on this head. Hume had argued that moral judgments ultimately rest on considerations of utility, but Smith argues that such considerations come into play only *after* the moral judgment has been passed and hence cannot be the foundation of the judgment itself. In Part V, Smith looks at the influence that custom and fashion have on our moral judgments. One might have hoped that in this part Smith would explicitly address the issue of whether our moral judgments are objectively true in some sense of the word "objective," but this hope goes largely frustrated. Smith's position on this point must instead be pieced together from what he says in this discussion and from other discussions throughout TMS. Part VI, new to the sixth edition, is something of a catalogue of virtues, reminiscent of (and perhaps occasioned by) the similar discussion in the latter parts of Hume's *Enquiry Concerning the Principles of Morals.* Here Smith discusses four principal virtues—justice, benevolence, prudence, and self-command—and the place each of them occupies in a virtuous person. This part also contains the intriguing discussion of "the man of system," a passage in TMS that has received remarkably little scholarly attention, but that turns out to play an important role in Smith's general conception of human nature. Finally, Part VII contains Smith's critical examination of other important moral systems, including those of Plato, Aristotle, the Stoics, Hobbes, Mandeville, Locke, Hutcheson, and Hume. Smith shows what those authors got right and what they got wrong; all the things that those systems got right, Smith argues, are encompassed in his own system, while his system contains none of the errors of those other systems. Smith considers this to be an important confirmation of his own theory.

The four central features of Smith's moral theory are his conception of natural human sympathy, his conception of the process by which moral judgments are made, his conception of the human conscience, and his general conception of human nature. To arrive at an understanding of Smith's theory, we must come to an understanding of each of these elements. In this chapter, I look at Smith's conceptions of sympathy and the impartial spectator; in the next, I look at his conceptions of conscience and human nature.

## I. Sympathy

Smith begins TMS with the assertion that no matter how selfish some individuals, or mankind in general, may be, "there are evidently some principles in [man's] nature, which interest him in the fortune of others, and render their happiness necessary to him, though he derives nothing from it except the pleasure of seeing it" (TMS, 9). This statement is striking for several reasons, each of which will turn out to be the germ of an important aspect of Smith's moral theory. First is the claim that there is a distinctive human nature, which drives human beings into associations with others. Societies, for Smith, are not in the first instance rational arrangements or compacts entered into on the basis of a self-interested calculation. Nor is Smith making a moral exhortation that we *should* care about people other than ourselves. He thinks it is simply a fact that we do. This concern for our fellows is not, according to Smith, the sole basis of political association; self-interest plays an important role as well. Nevertheless, it is one of the two central features of human nature that explain human associations, perhaps, even, the prepollent feature.

Smith thinks that human beings are naturally interested in the fortunes of others, by which he means two things: one, wherever there are human beings there will be society or social unions;[3] and two, no one, however hard-hearted or self-interested, is wholly indifferent to the interests of others. Our natural interest in the fortunes of others forms the basis of the second important element of the previously cited passage, namely, that the happiness of others is "necessary" to human beings.

[3] See Otteson (October 2000).

Smith makes liberal use of the term "necessary," and what he means by it—he seems in fact to mean more than one thing—will be discussed in more detail later. For now we can say that here Smith means that, for whatever reason, we find ourselves interested in whether others are happy or not and compelled to consider their happiness when contemplating our own actions. Finally, we act out of consideration of the happiness of others merely from the pleasure we take in seeing their happiness, not from any consideration of a good that might come about for us as a result of our action—in other words, not from any consideration of utility. These three claims are the pillars on which Smith bases his argument concerning our motivation to be moral, that is, our propensity to strive to adhere to general rules of morality. Our natural sociability and our natural, nonutilitarian interest in the fortunes of others result in everyone's striving to bring home to himself what those around him are thinking and feeling: this is what Smith calls natural human sympathy.

Smith uses the word "sympathy" in three ways, and he introduces the three uses one at a time in the first few chapters of TMS. Roughly, Smith's three meanings of sympathy, in order, are: natural fellow-feeling for others, pity for others, and correspondence of sentiments between two or more people. The first meaning Smith attaches to sympathy is the "natural fellow-feeling" he said we all have, which manifests itself in the general interest we take in the fortunes of others. In the first few paragraphs of the chapter entitled "Of Sympathy" (TMS, 9–10), Smith writes as if this fellow-feeling were confined only to those cases in which we pity others—I shall call this his second meaning for sympathy. He quickly expands his understanding of sympathy, however: "Neither is it those circumstances only, which create pain or sorrow that call forth our fellow-feeling. Whatever is the passion which arises from any object in the person principally concerned, an analogous emotion springs up, at the thought of his situation, in the breast of every attentive spectator" (TMS, 10). Thus sympathy, understood in the first sense as a fellow-feeling we have for others, is an emotion we have that is similar to whatever emotion the person principally concerned has. In using the word "sympathy" this way, Smith is following the etymology of the word; the roots of "sympathy" mean "feeling with" or "like feeling." This usage would hence comprehend the second way in which Smith uses the word, namely, as a synonym for compassion or pity. This second, more specific, meaning has today nearly crowded out the larger first meaning, and it had already begun to do so in Smith's time. Perhaps it is for this reason that Smith on occasion uses "sympathy" when he might just as well have written "pity."[4] Strictly speaking, sympathy used in this way refers to the fellow-feeling one has specifically with the unpleasant sentiments another is having. It does not refer to a fellow-feeling with pleasant sentiments, which, perhaps for lack of a felicitous English term, Smith also simply calls "sympathy." The third and final way Smith uses the word is the usage on which he bases the real work of his moral theory: it means a correspondence or harmony between the sentiments of the person principally concerned and the spectator. This usage is technical. It is in this kind of sympathy that we experience a certain pleasure, and it is this sympathy that ultimately grounds Smithian moral judgments.

Contrary to what some early commentators thought, Smith thus does not use "sympathy" exclusively to mean pity or compassion, and for Smith acting on the basis of sympathy does not necessarily mean acting from benevolent motives.[5] Indeed, when developing his formal account of the psychological foundations of moral judgments, he almost invariably uses sympathy in the technical sense of a correspondence between sentiments, not in the common sense of pity. He generally uses sympathy in the common sense only when relating anecdotes to support his theory. In his philosophical analysis, however, he says that the word "sympathy" may "be made use of to denote our fellow-feeling with any passion whatever" (TMS, 10). We sympathize with another when we have the same passion, to the same degree, that he does. Thus we can sympathize with anger, happiness, sadness, or any other passion. Sympathy in this technical sense, however, is not itself a passion: it is the "concord" or "correspondence"[6] that exists between one's sentiments and those of another.

---

[4] Smith writes, "The word sympathy, in its most proper and primitive signification, denotes our fellow-feeling with the sufferings, not that with the enjoyments, of others" (TMS, 43).

[5] The fact that Smith uses the word "sympathy" in more than one way led to early scholarly confusion about Smith's moral theory. For a discussion, see Raphael (1985), 29–33.

[6] Smith uses these terms throughout TMS. See, for early examples, TMS, 16 and 17, respectively. When Smith uses "sympathy" to denote either fellow-feeling generally or pity in particular, the sympathy in those cases *will* represent passions. It is only when Smith uses "sympathy" in his technical sense that it does not denote a passion.

What happens is this. We see the misery or happiness of another, we imagine ourselves in the same situation, and a real or imagined feeling wells up in us as a result of this imaginative changing of place. We then compare what our own feelings would be if we were in the other's situation with what his actual feelings are in his situation. If our respective feelings are commensurate, Smith says that we sympathize with that other; if they are not, we do not. Thus sympathy is correspondence between the imagined feelings of the spectator and the actual sentiments of the person principally concerned. Now the feelings that we as spectators have, which we compare to those the agent has, must not necessarily have the same potency as the agent's. Feelings of lesser intensity—which are the result of our only *imagining* another's situation, not of our actually being in it—can nonetheless be sufficient grounds on which to judge whether we sympathize or not as long as these feelings are "somewhat analogous" to the agent's (TMS, 22). "Though they will never be unisons," Smith writes of the sentiments of the spectator and of the agent, "they may be concords, and this is all that is wanted or required" (ibid.). When we view the misery of another at, say, the death of his father, we do not actually have to feel the same level of misery to know that we sympathize. It is sufficient for us to imagine what we would feel and how we would act in such a situation to know whether we sympathize because, by imaginatively changing places with the person principally concerned, we will have triggered, or not triggered, an analogous (imagined) feeling in ourselves.

What does Smith mean when he says that we imaginatively change places with the person principally concerned? He describes it in this way:

By the imagination we place ourselves in his [the agent's] situation, we conceive ourselves enduring all the same torments, we enter, as it were into his body, and become in some measure the same person with him, and thence form some idea of his sensations, and even feel something which, though weaker in degree, is not altogether unlike them. (TMS, 9)

We must separate the elements of this passage. When we see the suffering of another (the example Smith uses here is seeing our brother on the rack), we imagine—contrary to what one might have thought—not what our brother feels, but rather what we would feel in his situation;

we then assume our brother is feeling what we would feel. This, Smith thinks, can be no other way because "we have no immediate experience of what other men feel, [and hence] we can form no idea of the manner in which they are affected, but by conceiving what we ourselves should feel in the like situation" (ibid.). Smith argues that because experience is essentially private, the only means we have of understanding another's reaction to a situation is by imagining our own reaction to the same situation. And because our senses cannot "carry us beyond our own person" (ibid.), Smith concludes that whatever feeling we have on viewing the suffering of the person on the rack must have resulted from this imaginative changing of places and a consideration of what we would feel were we in his situation. In our position as spectators, we do not feel the same pain and misery that our brother on the rack feels; we do not even feel pain and misery to the same degree. Whatever sympathy might exist between his feelings and ours is instead entirely predicated in terms of our own past experiences and our own sensibilities. We imagine what we would feel were we in his situation, and we imagine how we would behave given what we would feel. If our brother's behavior is similar to what we imagine ours would be, we conclude that his feelings are similar to what ours would be, and a sympathy thus exists between our imagined feelings and his actual feelings.

When Smith writes that, on viewing our brother's misery, "we enter as it were into his body, and become in some measure the same person with him," we must hence not misunderstand his meaning: we enter his body and become the same person with him in the sense that we imagine ourselves occupying the same physical position as he, in the same circumstances as those in which he actually is. Smith's insistence on the privacy of personal experience entails that once we have imaginatively adopted our brother's position, it is still we who are reacting to the situation. We remain ourselves: we have not become the person principally concerned; the precise nature of his experience—we might say the *qualia* of his experience—remains known by and private to him alone. There hence remains an ineluctable gap between his actual experience and our imagined experience.[7] Smith thinks that

---

[7] This gap will be of great importance when we consider, in the next section, Smith's conception of the process by which we make moral judgments.

this gap nevertheless does not preclude a sympathy of sentiments: "These two sentiments [i.e., those of the spectator and those of the agent], however, may, it is evident, have such a correspondence with one another, as is sufficient for the harmony of society" (TMS, 22). We are able to overcome this gap as a matter of fact, so, for the most part, Smith is content to leave the matter at that. He does not inquire into the nature of phenomenological qualia, and he does not explain how two independent sets of private experience can generate a sympathy. In fact, Smith develops no significant theory of mind at all—a lack we shall have occasion to remark more than once. But Smith thus sees a close connection between feelings and actions: we judge what another's sentiments are on the basis of his actions. Now, one might object that there is no logical connection between the two; one's actions do not necessarily reveal one's feelings. True enough. Smith's response is twofold. First, the actions of others are the sole evidence we have regarding the inner feelings of others; we simply have nothing else to go on. On the other hand, there seems to be good reason to think that there is an intimate connection between the two—perhaps we should say generally or over the long run—because it turns out that we are able to communicate and associate with one another effectively (i.e., as if there were this connection). But I think Smith is willing to rely on the personal experience of his reader to prove that this gap is routinely bridged, and, if that is not enough, the fact that a community of people can generate a consensus about moral standards should be decisive.

Because our knowledge is limited to what we have experienced, sympathy can only be the result of an operation of the imagination, and not, as we might say, the result of an operation of the understanding that leads to knowledge. In fact, the imaginative changing of place is often an entirely unconscious process. "The passions," Smith writes, "upon some occasions, may seem to be transfused from one man to another, instantaneously, and antecedent to any knowledge of what excited them in the person principally concerned" (TMS, 11). This transfusion of passions is a result of the naturalness of sympathy. The happiness of others is (for an as yet unexplained reason[8]) necessary to us, so we naturally seek to share their sentiments. Depending on how well we know the person we are viewing, the process of imaginatively

---

[8] See the second section of Chapter 2.

changing places with another eventually becomes so habitual and quick that we no longer notice when it takes place.[9] All we notice is that we either have or do not have sentiments similar to those of the agent; perhaps we do not even notice that: it often happens that all we are aware of is the vague sense of correspondence or lack of correspondence, which manifests itself as a judgment about the agent's actions. The better we know the person we are judging—that is, the better we know his passions, interests, and inclinations—the more readily will we be able to understand why he acts the way he does, which, in turn, makes it easier to judge whether we would have the same sentiments as he if we were in his shoes. The judgment we make, whether we realize it at the time or not, ultimately reflects the result of the imaginative changing of place and the consideration of whether a sympathy or correspondence exists between our own and the agent's sentiments. A favorable judgment signifies that a sympathy has been reached and an unfavorable judgment signifies a lack of sympathy. It is this judgment that, Smith argues, we call "moral," and thus the moral judgment represents in the first instance the presence or absence of sympathy.

Before turning to Smith's conception of the moral judgment, we must look more carefully at what Smith thinks is involved in cases of sympathy. Smith uses the terms "sentiments," "feelings," and "passions" largely interchangeably to refer to what involuntarily wells up inside us as reactions to various situations we witness or find ourselves in—for instance, grief, joy, gratitude, resentment, horror, and anger, to take examples from the first chapter of TMS. We have sympathy for another when the sentiments, feelings, or passions we have are, or we imagine they would be, similar to those of the person principally concerned. But whether or not we sympathize with another, and, if so, to what degree, depends on our knowledge of his situation:

> General lamentations, which express nothing but the anguish of the sufferer, create rather a curiosity to inquire into his situation, along with some disposition to sympathize with him, than any actual sympathy that is very sensible. The first question which we ask is, What has befallen you? Till this be answered, though we are uneasy both from the vague idea of his misfortune, and still more from torturing ourselves with conjectures about what it may be, yet our fellow-feeling is not very considerable. (TMS, 11–12)

---

[9] TMS, 135–36.

The fact that our sympathy is often withheld until we know the cause of our fellow's passion leads Smith to conclude that sympathy arises more from the knowledge of the situation that excites our fellow's passion than from the sight of the behavior the passion caused—a conclusion that supports Smith's contention that the natural fellow-feeling we have for others comes about only through consideration of the imaginative changing of place. To make the point, Smith offers two examples. First, he says that we "sometimes feel for another, a passion of which he seems to be altogether incapable" (TMS, 12). We blush from embarrassment at the rudeness of another who seems to be insensible to his own improper behavior. In such a case, we do not respond to his actual sentiments; instead, we are moved by what would be our embarrassment if we were to act in that way. When we realize that our respective sentiments do not correspond, we judge the person principally concerned unfavorably, that is, we say his behavior is improper or wrong. Second, Smith points out that we can sympathize even with the dead. We are obviously not able to pity the dead out of recognition that we have the same feelings they do; nor do we pity them out of any consideration of what their actual situation is—they might be in eternal bliss, after all. Aside from whatever sadness we might feel because they are no longer living among us, our pity for them is a result of what we, as living people, would feel if we were in the physical position they are now. *We* certainly would not like to be in a small, dark box, deep in the cold earth, without any air to breathe. It is this realization, Smith thinks, that gives us the cold shudder we feel when we attend a funeral.[10] But, again, this common experience can only be explained by assuming that an imaginative change of place occurred in us, whether we realized it or not.

So far I have been focusing on Smith's psychological description of sympathy, but that is only a part of Smith's project. He is also concerned with the end that natural human sympathy ultimately serves: it becomes the foundation of our moral judgments. Smith thinks that sympathy understood in his terms explains the two kinds of moral judgments we make. First, it explains why we judge a person's actions to be what Smith calls proper or improper. In such cases, the propriety refers to whether the agent's actions are suitable to the situation in which the agent finds

---

[10] See TMS, 12–13 and 71.

himself. We judge this by employing the imaginative-changing-of-place procedure and deciding whether we would have acted similarly in the same situation, that is, whether we would have been moved by his situation to act in the same way the agent was. If the answer is yes, then we judge the agent's action to be proper and the agent himself to have acted with propriety; if the answer is no, then we judge his action improper and the agent to have acted with impropriety. The judgment of propriety or impropriety we commonly refer to as signifying right or wrong behavior, and it results from the realization of a sympathy or lack of sympathy between our imagined and the agent's actual motive. The propriety of an agent's motive is what in the first place, Smith thinks, gives rise to our moral approbation or disapprobation. Suppose, for example, I see a Boy Scout help an old lady across the street.[11] I imagine what I might have wanted to do had I been in the Boy Scout's position, which is to have helped the old lady. The correspondence between my imagined motive to act and the Boy Scout's apparently similar actual motive to act constitutes a sympathy in me that brings me to approve of the Boy Scout's act. His act seems proper to me, and I call it the right thing to do. Conversely, suppose I see a child who has been severely beaten by his father because the child broke a glass. In this case, I imagine what would have been my sentiments had I been this child's father: I see that I might have been angry but that my anger would not have been so great as to occasion such a beating, and so I perceive a discord between the father's motive and what I imagine mine would be. I thus disapprove of the father's action as having been improper, and I say that what he did was wrong.

There is, however, a second kind of moral judgment we make, which concerns "the end which [an action] proposes, or . . . the effect which it tends to produce" (TMS, 67). This judgment depends on whether the act tends to promote beneficial or harmful ends, and hence whether it deserves to be praised or blamed, rewarded or punished. This judgment signifies what Smith calls the merit or demerit of an action, and it is generally a secondary consideration to the propriety of the action. Smith thinks this judgment rests primarily on the sympathy or lack of sympathy one has for either the gratitude or the resentment that the

---

[11] Raphael gives a somewhat similar example to illustrate this point. See Raphael (1985), 30.

person affected by another's action has for the actor. Let me use the preceding example. When I approve of the Boy Scout helping the old lady cross the street it is because I sympathize with the Boy Scout's motives—I would like to have done the same thing had I been in his place. But a second judgment I might make is that the Boy Scout's action deserves praise or even reward. According to Smith, this is an "indirect" judgment I make because I sympathize with the gratitude that I imagine the old lady feels for the Boy Scout. I once again employ the imaginative-changing-of-place procedure, and I realize that if I had been in the old lady's place, I should have appreciated what the Boy Scout did. When I see that my imagined gratitude corresponds with her apparent gratitude, I am "prompted" to think that the Boy Scout's action is "the proper and approved object of that sentiment, which most immediately and directly prompts us to reward, or to do good to another" (TMS, 67). The sentiment Smith has in mind here is "gratitude"; on the other hand, "resentment" is the sentiment that immediately and directly prompts us to punish or "to inflict evil upon another" (TMS, 68). When I judge that the Boy Scout's action is the proper object of gratitude—which just means that I would have felt gratitude toward it had I been in the shoes of the old lady—I say that his action has "merit." The sentiment of merit is thus "compounded," that is, it is "made up of two distinct emotions; a direct sympathy with the sentiments of the agent, and an indirect sympathy with the gratitude of those who receive benefit of his actions" (TMS, 74). The case of demerit is, then, the converse of the case of merit: when I view the situation of the child who has been beaten by his father, not only do I *not* sympathize with the father's motive for what he has done, but I *do* sympathize with the resentment the child feels for his father's action. The child's resentment seems to me appropriate and I judge the cause that has given rise to it unfavorably. The feeling of proper resentment combines with the lack of correspondence between my imagined motives and the father's actual motives to produce the compound sentiment that the father's action deserves blame or punishment.

Judgments in which our sentiments are "compounded" in this way involve what Smith calls the "social passions," like "Generosity, humanity, kindness, compassion, mutual friendship and esteem" (TMS, 38). These passions, Smith thinks, are "agreeable," and hence we willingly enter into them when we see them in another. Thus we frequently find cause to make favorable judgments when we view people acting out of or in response to these motives. Smith thinks it is possible, however, for our sentiments to be divided, when the case we are viewing has to do with what he calls "the unsocial passions" of hatred and resentment (TMS, 34). These emotions are disagreeable, and hence we are generally less willing to enter into them when we see them in another. In fact, Smith thinks that we are more often inclined to sympathize with the object of these passions than we are with the person displaying them. For example, we might be in sympathy with the anger a man feels toward the man who has wronged him. Given the circumstances, we might think that the former is acting properly when he lashes out at the latter. On the other hand, we might at the same time be in sympathy with the fear or resentment that the latter feels as he bears the former's anger. Smith says that in attentively observing a situation such as this, we separately judge the propriety of the one's action and the propriety of the other's response, and our judgment of each moderates the sentiments we have with regard to the other. Hence I may be less inclined to "go along with" the angry man if I realize that the resentment the other man feels is proper (meaning I would feel it, too).[12]

Smith thinks that in the case of conflicting sentiments—that is, where a conflict exists between the sentiments of the agent and those of the person acted upon—we adopt or go along with the principle of action of the person with whose action we sympathize. If the actor's anger is closer to what we would have felt in his shoes than the resentment of the person acted upon is to what we would have felt in his shoes, then we will tend to think that the actor is justified in what he does despite the resentment of the object of his anger. Or vice-versa: if the resentment of the recipient is closer to the resentment we would have felt than is the anger of the actor, we will tend to think that the actor is unjustified in what he does. Because in cases such as these our sympathies are divided, they are among the hardest cases to judge and, depending on the degree to which they engage our sentiments, the hardest or most unpleasant to watch. It is very difficult, for example, to take sides when our mother and father are engaged in a bitter fight. We tend to sympathize with the anger and resentment of each of them.

---

[12] TMS, 34–38; see also 73–74.

Smith would argue that the reason such a case is so difficult for us is that we imaginatively change places with both of them and discover that our sentiments would correspond with those of both of them—we thus have a correspondence with inconsistent, even antithetical sentiments, making the case difficult (and likely unpleasant) to judge.

In the second section of part one of TMS, Smith examines, as he puts it, the degrees of the different passions that are consistent with propriety, among which are the social and unsocial passions that we just discussed. The other passions he looks at in the same place are the "selfish" passions, like grief and joy; "passions which take their origin from the body," like hunger and sexual attraction; and "passions which take their origin from a particular turn or habit of the imagination," like a philosopher's interest in reading philosophy books.[13] It is not necessary to look separately at each of these discussions,[14] for they all illustrate the same central point Smith wants to make: in each case we judge the propriety or impropriety of others' actions and motives by using the imaginative-change-of-place procedure and looking for a sympathy or correspondence with our own imagined sentiments. In his discussions of the various passions, Smith shows how the judgments we make in various situations correspond to and are explained by our imagining that we occupied the place of the person principally concerned. The way we decide that someone laughed too long at a joke, that someone did not show his superior enough respect, that someone treated another impolitely, that someone overreacted to the news of his promotion: these as well as any number of other everyday judgments we make are founded on the basis of what we would have thought, felt, or done in the other's place.

*Two Brief Criticisms*

I have two criticisms to register about Smith's discussion of sympathy and the passions. The first is that Smith does not clarify whether the sentiments the spectator has that are candidates for sympathy or antipathy with the sentiments of the person principally concerned are

---

[13] TMS, 40, 27, and 31, respectively.
[14] For a careful discussion of Smith's treatment of these passions, see Campbell (1971), 98–103.

only imaginary, or can also be actual—and if the latter, under what conditions the imagined sentiments can become real. Smith describes the apprehension of sympathy as an act of moral imagination: we imagine what our sentiments would be were we in the agent's place. Given Smith's claim that experience is private, he writes, "As we have no immediate experience of what other men feel, we can form no idea of the manner in which they are affected, but by conceiving what we ourselves should feel in the like situation" (TMS, 9). This sounds like a purely imaginary process. Yet there are obviously cases in which a spectator can actually *have* emotions similar to those of the agent—as Smith recognizes:

> The passions, upon some occasions, may seem to be transfused from one man to another, instantaneously, and antecedent to any knowledge of what excited them in the person principally concerned. Grief and joy, for example, strongly expressed in the look and gestures of any one, at once affect the spectator with some degree of a like painful or agreeable emotion. A smiling face is, to every body that sees it, a cheerful object; as a sorrowful countenance, on the other hand, is a melancholy one. (TMS, 11)

I think Smith's view is that it is indeed possible for a spectator to have actual sentiments aroused in him on viewing another's situation, but that that possibility is dependent on several factors: how well the spectator is familiar with the other person, how fully the spectator brings home to himself the details of the other's situation, how strong the agent's sentiments are, and, finally, to what extent the spectator is willing to let the other's situation affect him. The word "attentive" in the following passage encompasses several of these elements: "Whatever is the passion which arises from any object in the person principally concerned, an analogous emotion springs up, at the thought of his situation, in the breast of every attentive spectator" (TMS, 10). In most cases the spectator will judge the agent's sentiments and behavior on the basis of the spectator's imagined sentiments, but there will be cases in which all these factors combine in the right way to precipitate the arousal of actual sentiments in the spectator—though, as Smith notes, they will rarely be as strong or lively or vivid as those of the agent:

> What [spectators] feel, will, indeed, always be, in some respects, different from what [the agent] feels...; because the secret consciousness that the change of situations, from which the sympathetic sentiment arises, is but imaginary, not

only lowers it in degree, but, in some measure, varies it in kind, and gives it a quite different modification. These two sentiments, however, may, it is evident, have such a correspondence with one another, as is sufficient for the harmony of society. Though they will never be unisons, they may be concords, and this is all that is wanted or required. (TMS, 22)

When one adopts the position of an impartial spectator to another's conduct, the relevant sentiments for judging will be those that the impartial spectator has, not (necessarily) those the actual spectator has; this means that a resultant sympathy would be between the agent's actual sentiments and the sentiments the actual spectator imagines the impartial spectator would have. Thus any real sentiments the actual spectator experiences would not be the focus of the impartial moral judgment, though they might well be the focus of the spectator's initial, partial judgment, to which Smith alludes in the preceding passage.

It seems clear that Smith believed that sympathy could only be created by an imaginative switching of places and an imaginative investigation into what would be one's sentiments in the place of another; and it also seems clear that Smith realized that this exercise of moral imagination would often produce real sentiments in a spectator. But a complete account of how this sympathy operates must include an account of exactly what it is between which the sympathy can obtain— that is, whether imagined or real sentiments—as well as an account of precisely under what conditions sympathy can obtain. It may be that Smith thought that this was more detail than what was required for his project. As I shall argue in Chapter 3, one of Smith's principal goals in TMS was to explain the development over time of common moral standards; the desire for mutual sympathy of sentiments is, for Smith, the key to understanding this development. It may be that Smith thought that to explain *this* phenomenon, it did not matter whether sympathy was with imagined or actual sentiments—sympathy of either kind (or both) was what mattered—and hence he did not need to analyze sympathy more finely than he did. Nevertheless, his account of sympathy is incomplete without this specification, and statements to the effect that the spectator's "secret consciousness" that the sympathy arises only from an imaginary switching of places "varies [the spectator's sentiments] in kind" from those of the agent (TMS, 22) cry out for further elaboration. We shall again have occasion later on to discuss this lacuna in Smith's account. When speaking of Smithian sympathy in what follows, however, I shall, unless I state otherwise, mean the sympathy between an agent's actual sentiments, on the one hand, and, on the other, either the (i) imagined or (ii) imagined and then real sentiments of the spectator. For reasons that will become clearer, I think that construal of Smithian sympathy is closest to Smith's conception.

My second criticism pertains to a point Smith makes in his discussion of the degree to which various passions are consistent with propriety. Smith argues that the "passions which take their origin from the body"—Smith's examples: hunger and sexual attraction—are more difficult for others to enter into because one's "body can be but little affected by the alterations which are brought about upon that of [one's] companion" (TMS, 29). By contrast, those passions that arise from the imagination—Smith's examples: love and ambition—are more easily entered into because the "imagination is more ductile" than the body (ibid.). It may be true that we are less moved by another's hunger than by his love, but the reason Smith here gives for that is unpersuasive. On Smith's account, all the sympathies into which we might enter are, at least initially, imagined: we imagine what we ourselves would feel if we were in that other person's circumstances, and then look to see whether our imagined sentiments match what we infer, on the basis of his behavior, the other person's actual sentiments to be. Hence the relative ductility of a person's imagination would affect his ability to enter into *any* sympathy, whether with things like hunger or with things like love. There are further complications attendant on the claim that the one set of passions relates exclusively to the body, whereas the other set is exclusively mental, but, putting those aside, if there is a difference in our ability to sympathize with one kind as opposed to the other, then there must be some other factor responsible.

*Smith and Hume on the Role of Sympathy in Moral Judgments*
Smith's conception of natural human sympathy is different from Hume's, although in discussions about the history of ethical philosophy they are sometimes treated as if they were the same. Hume's use of the term "sympathy" is often in line with the more usual contemporary usage, that is, as a synonym for compassion or pity—as in this case: "A parent flies to the relief of his child; transported by that natural sympathy, which actuates him, and which affords no leisure

to reflect on the sentiments or conduct of the rest of mankind in like circumstances."[15] Like Smith, however, Hume also makes a philosophical point with his notion of natural human sympathy, a point that is connected with his larger treatment of moral sentiments as resulting from considerations of utility. He writes that although it is understandable why some moralists, Bernard Mandeville for example, have thought that "self-love" is the principal or even sole motivation for human action, given its obviously enormous influence on much of what people do, it is nevertheless a mistake to conclude from this that no other principles are ever at work in human beings.[16] For it is frequently the case that we undertake to do things that are independent of any good we ourselves might receive from our actions. There is no way to explain such actions on the hypothesis that people are solely self-interested. Hence Hume concludes that another principle must also be part of the human fabric, a principle Hume alternately calls benevolence or sympathy. Now benevolence and sympathy do not mean the same thing, even on Hume's usage of "sympathy," but the fact that Hume so closely allies them in his discussions indicates what his argument means to show: we are naturally moved by pity when we see others suffer, and this emotion ultimately results from a consideration of the disutility that the sufferer's situation creates for him and the benefit our help could provide. The notion of others' utility is captured by the word "benevolence," the notion of pity by "sympathy."

Hume thinks that we praise benevolence in each other ultimately because it conduces to the general utility of mankind by encouraging motives that lead to generally beneficial actions; it thus in addition flatters and encourages the natural sympathy or compassion we generally feel for all mankind.[17] For Hume, what triggers or engages our natural sympathy, and what thus underlies our moral judgments, is in the end considerations of utility—whether our own, that of others, or that of mankind in general. Hume's argument is that we can make sense of the protocols of behavior and rules of etiquette that are endorsed in a community if we consider them as the result of something

---

[15] Hume, *Enquiry Concerning the Principles of Morals* (1983 [1751]; hereafter 2E), 93.

[16] Hume's discussion of sympathy can be found in ibid., 42–51. Compare the similar but not identical treatment Hume gives sympathy in *A Treatise of Human Nature* (1978 [1739–40]; hereafter T), 574–91.

[17] 2E, 39.

like a self-selection along utilitarian lines. Those protocols and rules that prescribe behavior that is conducive to the utility of individuals and ultimately of communities are accepted and endorsed because it is utility that underlies moral approbation; those that are not conducive to utility are hence not endorsed. With regard to the general rules of justice, Hume sketches something of an evolutionary account of their development.[18] Hume thinks that these rules in particular have survived and become fixed in our minds because they conduce to general utility; his so-called rule utilitarianism is based on his claim that even if the rules of justice seem unjust in isolated cases, nevertheless the overall system of justice conduces to aggregate utility—or else we would have no such system.[19] Hence for Hume considerations of general utility inform the general rules of justice, which then take precedence over whatever behaviors might conduce to the more narrowly restricted utility of a particular individual. Thus utility in the end founds our moral standards, as well as the moral judgments we make in terms of them.

Hume argues that utility is what gives rise to our moral approbation, but an obvious problem concerns those cases, to which Hume himself refers when addressing thinkers like Mandeville, in which we approve of actions that have no effect on our own utility, that of anyone we know, or even that of anyone now living. Why do we approve of heroes from generations gone by? Since it is utility that engages our approbation, Hume thinks, it must mean that we approve of these past heroes because they are useful—they serve someone's interest. But whose? Hume's answer: "It must, therefore, be the interest of those, who are served by the character or action approved of; and these we may conclude, however remote, are not totally indifferent to us" (2E, 42). Hume argues that when we read about the virtuous actions of some long-ago hero, we conjure up an idea of the utility his actions had for those he served. The idea of utility we thus imagine engages our moral approbation because, as Hume says, we are naturally inclined to

---

[18] The notion that these rules could have resulted from a natural selection along utilitarian lines is limited in Hume to the origin of the rules of justice. Though Hume thinks that considerations of utility ultimately underlie all moral judgments, I do not think he uses an evolutionary explanation to account for the rules of morality other than those of justice. I shall return to this issue.

[19] T, 497.

sympathize with the happiness or sorrow of our fellow human beings, despite the distance in time or space that separates us. Hume then gives a number of concrete instances that are meant to demonstrate the following principle: "In general, it is certain, that, wherever we go, whatever we reflect on or converse about, every thing still presents us with the view of human happiness or misery, and excites in our breast a sympathetic movement of pleasure or uneasiness" (2E, 44). The kind of sympathy Hume has in mind here is this: we have Humean sympathy for another if we have (roughly) the same sentiment of happiness or sorrow he does. The sentiment we develop comes as a result of imagining the causes of the relevant sentiment in the other person, which then, by means of the mind's natural principles of association,[20] causes us to have an analogous sentiment ourselves. Hume's sympathy is thus closer to what we today might call empathy (which is the first, and nontechnical, definition of "sympathy" that Smith uses): it is taking part in or sharing the sentiments of another. In Hume's moral theory, this natural sympathy or empathy is what explains why moral approbation can be aroused by viewing actions that lead to utility for people other than ourselves. We are not strictly self-interested; we are also actuated by a principle of benevolence, a natural empathy for the sentiments of others. It is still a consideration of utility that excites our moral approbation or disapprobation, but because we are naturally sympathetic with others, considerations of their utility can suffice.

I think Hume's settled view of sympathy is that natural human sympathy is empathy—the propensity to have the same, or roughly the same, sentiments as another. But one finds many places, particularly in the *Treatise*, where Hume seems to use "sympathy" to refer to something else. Some have suggested that by "sympathy" Hume actually means the mechanism by which an idea is turned into an impression.[21] Thus on viewing, say, the sorrow of another, one gets an idea of that sorrow, which the mechanism of sympathy turns into an impression of roughly similar proportions. One would then have a "sympathetic impression," meaning that the similar impression was created by means

---

[20] See Hume's *Enquiry Concerning Human Understanding* (1748 [1977]; hereafter 1E), 14–15.

[21] See, for example, T, 317. For commentary, see Árdal (1966), Chapters 3 and 6; see also Haakonssen (1981), 45–49.

of the mechanism of sympathy. The sympathy itself, however, would not be a passion, sentiment, or impression at all, but rather something like a mental operation. Several passages in Hume fit this interpretation. For example, Hume introduces his discussion of sympathy in the *Treatise* this way: "No quality of human nature is more remarkable, both in itself and in its consequences, than that propensity we have to sympathize with others, and to receive by communication their inclinations and sentiments, however different from, or even contrary to our own" (T, 316). The notions of conversion and communication recur many times in Hume's discussion. Here is one instance:

> 'Tis indeed evident, that when we sympathize with the passions and sentiments of others, these movements appear at first in *our* mind as mere ideas, and are conceiv'd to belong to another person, as we conceive any other matter of fact. 'Tis also evident, that the ideas of the affections of others are converted into the very impressions they represent, and that the passions arise in conformity to the images we form of them. (T, 319; Hume's italics)

Hume goes on to argue that the sympathetic impression one receives from one's idea of another's passion can convey the entire vivacity of the original impression and "lose nothing of it in the transition" (T, 320). Later Hume writes that "sympathy, as I have already observ'd, is nothing but the conversion of an idea into an impression by the force of the imagination" (T, 427).

This interpretation is not without difficulties, however, especially when one compares Hume's use of "sympathy" in the *Treatise* to his use of it in the second *Enquiry*. In that *Enquiry*, Hume again and again suggests that sympathy is itself a passion. For example, when describing the "*poetical* fiction of the *golden age,*" Hume writes that it was supposedly the case that "Cordial affection, compassion, sympathy, were the only movements with which the mind was yet acquainted"—implying that sympathy is another sentiment like affection and compassion.[22] In another discussion, Hume writes that when we contemplate a great and virtuous person, "The ideas of happiness, joy, triumph, prosperity, are connected with every circumstance of his character and diffuse over our minds a pleasing sentiment of sympathy and humanity" (2E, 52). Does sympathy here refer to a mechanism of communication?—

---

[22] 2E, 24. All italics are Hume's.

or does it represent a passion roughly analogous to humanity or benevolence? Hume has a footnote to the passage just cited:

One may venture to affirm, that there is no human creature, to whom the appearance of happiness…does not give pleasure, that of misery, uneasiness.…But they are only the more generous minds, that are thence prompted to seek zealously the good of others, and to have a real passion for their welfare. With men of narrow and ungenerous spirits, this sympathy goes not beyond a slight feeling of the imagination, which serves only to excite sentiments of complacency or censure, and makes them apply to the object either honourable or dishonourable appellations. (2E, 52, n. 26)

Again, "sympathy" in this passage seems not to indicate the principle of communication Hume said sympathy was in the *Treatise;* rather, it seems to indicate an empathy for the sentiments of others. Let me cite two other passages. When he views a "good-humoured, humane landlord," along with the people who have the good fortune to live under his care, Hume says, "I have a pleasing sympathy in the prospect of so much joy" (1E, 44). When we read Tacitus, and contemplate the depravity of Nero and the miserable circumstances of Nero's people, Hume writes, "What sympathy then touches every human heart!" (1E, 45). In these passages sympathy appears to be synonymous with empathy or fellow-feeling on the one hand, and pity or compassion on the other. In any case it seems not to be a mechanical principle but rather a passion itself.

Now this raises the problem of determining the precise relation of the *Treatise* to the *Enquiries* that followed it. In some matters the differences among the three are substantial, raising the question of which account is definitive, which account is the one Hume "really" meant. I cannot resolve this issue here, and in any case I think it can only be fruitfully addressed on a case-by-case basis. Yet as I said, I think that Hume more often than not conceives of sympathy as the resultant impression one has after viewing the character or behavior of another. Perhaps we can say that by "sympathy" Hume variously means parts of or the whole process of receiving an idea of another's sentiment or of converting that idea into an analogous impression, or the resultant impression itself; but when he says that we sympathize with another, he usually means that we have an impression that is analogous to that of the other. The important consideration for us, however, is the connection Humean sympathy makes between the utility or disutility a certain character or behavior has for another person and our moral approval or disapproval of that character or behavior. Our approval or disapproval results immediately from the sympathetic sentiment we have, which will itself result from a consideration of utility. The only way Hume can claim that something conducing to another person's utility could receive moral approbation from us is by claiming that all people are naturally inclined to share in the passions or sentiments of others. Hume's sympathy plays this role—whether that sympathy is conceived of as a mechanism of transforming an idea into an impression, as the resultant impression itself, or as the entire process that comprises both of them.

Let us now return to Smith. Smith criticizes Hume's contention that moral sentiments are ultimately the result of considerations of utility, a contention Smith thinks is false.[23] Most of the moral approbation we give, Smith argues, is antecedent to any consideration of utility; hence utility cannot be the foundation of moral judgment. We shall develop Smith's general argument on this issue in more detail later, but a narrower point in this connection applies here. Utility cannot be the foundation of moral judgments, according to Smith, because an action's utility is irrelevant to what first recommends an action to our moral approbation. Smith argues that it is an action's *propriety* that does this, which is, as we have seen, determined by whether the spectator's sentiments are in sympathy with those of the agent. Smith argues that the correspondence or lack of correspondence between the sentiments of the spectator and agent—which is what I called Smith's technical meaning of "sympathy"—is the foundation of our moral judgment insofar as it is what, as a matter of fact, not speculation, initially prompts us to approve or disapprove of the agent's action. Our first inclination is to judge whether the agent's action is appropriate to the circumstances that excited it, which we determine by imagining ourselves in the same situation and discovering what our action would have been; thus we judge whether the agent's action was right or wrong independently of whether it leads to beneficial consequences. That is not to say that Smith thinks that utility plays no role whatever in a moral theory, but only to say that it plays a secondary role—and is hence not a principal, let alone the sole, foundation for moral judgment.

---

[23] See TMS, 179–93 and 300–306.

Smith accordingly thinks that Hume has misused the term "sympathy."[24] Smith agrees that there are cases, like those Hume enumerates, in which the transfusion of a sentiment from an agent to a spectator takes place so quickly that it is difficult to believe that any conscious process took place at all. That is, there seem to be many cases when it seems not to be an awareness of a correspondence but rather an empathy itself that directly rouses our approbation or disapprobation at the sight of another's joy or misery. Smith nonetheless maintains that a process, however quick and unnoticeable, takes place, and it is only by means of this process that we are able to approve or disapprove of others' motives or actions. This process includes an awareness, however vague, of a correspondence or lack of correspondence between the respective sentiments; there is simply no other way to make a moral judgment, Smith thinks. Although Smith and Hume agree that people are naturally interested in the fortunes of others, for Hume this fact becomes the basis of our moral judgments of others, because it is what makes us concerned to discover the utility or disutility a person's character or behavior has for him. Hume thinks that moral standards and judgments reflect considerations of utility, and we apply these standards and judgments to others because of the natural sympathy we feel for them. For Smith, however, the fact that we are interested in the fortune of others only triggers a more complex process in which we judge people by comparing our sentiments to theirs.

The relation between individual utility and general utility is hard to make out in Hume. Why, for example, should it be the case that rules of justice conducing to general utility would ever develop, given that on Hume's account they follow on the heels of rules that conduce to individual utility? Smith's argument instead is that in the long run individuals acting on their own individual interest in fact conduce to overall utility—that is a central claim of both TMS and the *Wealth of Nations*.[25] But Hume has made no such argument. Hence it is unclear

---

[24] See TMS, 187–93.

[25] In TMS, Smith writes that the rich "are led by an invisible hand to make nearly the same distribution of the necessaries of life, which would have been made, had the earth been divided into equal portions among all its inhabitants, and thus without intending it, without knowing it, advance the interests of the society, and afford means to the multiplication of the species" (184–85). In WN, Smith writes: "As every individual, therefore, endeavours as much as he can both to employ his capital in the support of domestick industry, and so to direct that industry that its produce may be of the greatest value; every individual necessarily labours to render the annual

how Hume's notion of the self-selection of rules of justice can make sense. Who is doing the selecting? If it is individuals, as one would presume it is, then Hume needs to explain how they would come to accept and endorse general rules that at times do not conduce to their own utility. If one takes an expansive view of self-interest, as Smith does when he suggests that it includes the interests of family and friends, one might plausibly maintain that people would adopt rules that conduce to the utility of their families or friends. But the general utility of all society? This is a large step to take, and Hume needs to justify how he gets from the one to the other. Hume attempts to build this bridge by relying on sympathy and a common human nature. That is, because we all have basically the same nature, each of us is capable of sympathizing with any other person. Our natural sympathy for others is what compels us to give their utility serious consideration. But can this sympathy provide the necessary conditions for the development of general rules of justice? How? At first blush it seems as though one's sympathy for others might move one in some circumstances to help others, but accepting the legitimacy of general rules of justice that might be antithetical to one's own utility is another matter. Unless Hume wishes to argue that sympathy for others is the dominant motive in human beings, which apparently he does not, then it seems that this sympathy is just another passion among the many that motivate us. In that case, Humean sympathy—that is, sympathy understood either as a fellow-feeling with others, or as compassion or pity—is by itself unable to bridge the gap Hume hoped it would.

What I think Smith saw, but Hume did not, is that there is no necessary connection between thinking that human beings feel sympathy and thinking that sympathy has something to do with moral judgments. An argument, or at least an explanation, must be given that shows how and why the two are connected. Just this is what Smith has done in his investigation into and development of the role of the impartial spectator in making moral judgments. Smith relies on a

revenue of the society as great as he can. He generally, indeed, neither intends to promote the publick interest, nor knows how much he is promoting it. By preferring the support of domestick to that of foreign industry, he intends only his own security; and by directing that industry in such a manner as its produce may be of the greatest value, he intends only his own gain, and he is in this, as in many other cases, led by an invisible hand to promote an end which was no part of his intention" (456).

correspondence of sentiments between actors and spectators to bind the interests of individuals together in such a way that Smithian sympathy becomes the basis of moral judgments. On his examination, sympathy becomes the foundational motivation for the impartial spectator procedure, and the judgments of the impartial spectator, Smith will argue, can only be understood as issuing from sympathy in Smith's technical sense. Smith's impartial spectator and the function of the impartial spectator procedure need yet to be explained—they are the topics of the final part of this chapter—but it will turn out that they provide the link between individuals and their communities that is necessary to explain the development of commonly shared standards of moral judgment, based on Smithian, not Humean, sympathy.

*Innate Human Sympathy?*

The final issue to be addressed before we look at Smith's "impartial spectator" is the question of whether indeed there is such a thing as natural human sympathy. Whether sympathy understood in Smith's technical sense is the true foundation of moral judgments is a separate question; here I am concerned to ask whether there is anything like the natural compassion or fellow-feeling that Smith—in agreement with Hutcheson and Hume, among others—ascribes to human nature. Alasdair MacIntyre, for example, has written that this notion of sympathy "as used by Hume and Smith is the name of a philosophical fiction."[26] MacIntyre argues that the concept of sympathy was invoked by them to "bridge the gap between any set of reasons which could support unconditional adherence to general and unconditional rules and any set of reasons for action or judgment which could derive from our particular, fluctuating, circumstance-governed desires, emotions and interests" (ibid.). He argues further that this gap is "logically unbridgeable" and that Smith and Hume were trying to hide this fact with their invention of a fictional "sympathy." The true father of this "fiction" is probably Hutcheson, however, who called it the principle of benevolence;[27] in opposition to thinkers like Hobbes and Mandeville, Hume and Smith followed Hutcheson in thinking that inherent in

---

[26] MacIntyre (1984), 49. Note that MacIntyre seems to conflate Hume's and Smith's notions of sympathy.

[27] See Hutcheson (1991 [1725]), 261–299.

mankind was what Hume variously called the principle of humanity, sympathy, or benevolence and what Smith called natural sympathy. It is not clear whether in saying that such a principle is a philosophical fiction MacIntyre commits himself to accepting Mandeville's argument that all our actions are motivated by nothing but self-interest, however they may appear to a spectator.[28] But were Hutcheson, Hume, and Smith speaking about a mere fiction?

We must first reiterate the distinction between Smith's use of sympathy-as-pity or sympathy-as-general-fellow-feeling, on the one hand, and his use of sympathy-as-correspondence, on the other. The latter is not, I think, addressed by MacIntyre's objection—which underscores the importance of distinguishing Humean sympathy from Smithian sympathy. MacIntyre seems to be concerned, rather, with the question of whether we are in fact naturally or inherently disposed to be moved by the fortunes of others. Although some recent evidence suggests that sympathy might in fact be a part of human nature,[29] I am afraid that here this question will have to go largely unanswered. But let me bring out for review some of the examples Smith adduces to support his claim that such a principle is innate in human nature. Here is one:

When we see a stroke aimed and just ready to fall upon the leg or arm of another person, we naturally shrink and draw back our own leg or our own arm; and when it does fall, we feel it in some measure, and are hurt by it as well as the sufferer. (TMS, 10)

Here are two others:

The mob, when they are gazing at a dancer on the slack rope, naturally writhe and twist and balance their own bodies, as they see him do, and as they feel that they themselves must do if in his situation. Persons of delicate fibres and a weak constitution of body complain, that in looking on the sores and ulcers which are exposed by beggars in the streets, they are apt to feel an itching or uneasy sensation in the correspondent part of their own bodies. (Ibid.)[30]

---

[28] Of course, for Mandeville, the alleged fact that all our activities are at bottom motivated by self-interest is nothing evil; in fact, he thinks it leads to good consequences. See Mandeville (1924 [1714]).

[29] I cite and discuss some of this evidence in the Conclusion.

[30] See also the short chapter in TMS entitled "Of universal Benevolence," 235–37.

What could explain these phenomena? Why is it that we tremble and shudder when we watch the torture of another person? Why are we sometimes moved to tears at a dramatic portrayal of human tragedy? In each of these cases, we are presumably entirely secure in our own person and unthreatened by any harm. The causes of the actions and sufferings of others do not obtain in our case, yet we often behave and feel as if they did. And this phenomenon is not restricted to the unpleasant passions: we are often overjoyed at the success of a loved one or filled with gratitude at a good turn done for another. Smith argues that these common human experiences cannot be explained in terms of utility because in each case there are instances when the actions are irrelevant to our own utility. Moreover, they cannot be explained in terms of pure self-interest because in each case there seem to be instances when people's actions are indifferent or even contrary to their self-interest. Whether a stroke falls on a stranger's leg might bear no relevance whatever to my utility; or I might approve of the courage and fortitude of an enemy whose greater skill is about to vanquish me.[31]

Despite what people like Mandeville (and perhaps MacIntyre) think, Smith seems to think that it is all but self-evident that human beings have a certain fellow-feeling for each other, and he thinks that there are so many instances in our lives demonstrating this that it hardly bears discussing:

That we often derive sorrow from the sorrow of others, is a matter of fact too obvious to require any instances to prove it; for this sentiment, like all the other original passions of human nature, is by no means confined to the virtuous and humane, though they perhaps may feel it with the most exquisite sensibility. The greatest ruffian, the most hardened violator of the laws of society, is not altogether without it. (TMS, 9)

Smith provides a number of other similar examples,[32] but they need not be rehearsed. It might be more accurate to say that Smith thinks we naturally take an interest in the fortune of others, which leads us to bring their passions "home to ourselves" (TMS, 9) and imagine how we would feel and behave were we in their place. I think that Smith is right. A certain fellow-feeling with others seems to be a plausible explanation

---

[31] See Smith's discussion of a soldier's virtue in wartime, TMS, 191–93.
[32] See TMS, 10, §§1 and 3.

of many of the interactions people have, particularly those in which people act toward one another in ways that do not affect their respective utility. Moreover, I tend to agree with Smith that it is a distortion to portray all human behavior as the result of self-interest.[33] The sacrifices a parent makes for his child, for example, cannot plausibly be ascribed to the parent's self-interest—or so it seems to this parent, at least. Although no conclusive case has been made, let us be satisfied for now if it seems at least possible that human beings tend to have a natural fellow-feeling for one another; we shall revisit this issue in more detail later.

## II. The Impartial Spectator Procedure

Sympathy, as we have seen, is the ultimate source of moral approbation and disapprobation, according to Smith. Yet a true sympathy occurs between the sentiments of the spectator and those of the agent only infrequently, due in large part to the fact that the imagined sentiments of the spectator are almost always "weaker in degree" than the sentiments of the agent they simulate.[34] As we have already seen, when judging an agent, the spectator does not in any sense become the agent; he remains himself and his judgment therefore is founded on his own experiences and sentiments. The fact that we are each restricted to our own experiences when judging the actions or characters of other people indicates the existence of an unavoidable gap between the agent's actual sentiments and the spectator's imagined sentiments. Smith writes that this gap is often first brought home to us when we go to school as children (TMS, 145). It is here that we first realize that we are not the most important person in the world to everyone—only to ourselves. This realization impresses upon us the need to moderate the expression of our own interests if we want to get along with and understand the sentiments of others. Throughout our lives, we exchange subtle and not-so-subtle cues with each other regarding how we should balance the interest we take in ourselves against the interest we take in others, an exchange that forms the foundation of the general rules

[33] Smith makes this claim during his criticism of Mandeville's "licentious system" of morality, TMS, 306–14.
[34] See TMS, 19–23.

that we and the rest of our society come to endorse as the transcendent rules of morality (TMS, 23).

But first things first. What becomes clear to us in our earliest dealings with other people is that they do not always share the sentiments we do to the extent we do, and that they judge us in the same way we judge them—namely, by the degree to which *our* apparent motives and behaviors correspond with what *their* motives and behaviors would be if they were in our place. Smith thinks that this is an unsettling realization. It suggests to us the possibility that we are alone in judging things the way we do, which, Smith writes, is a horrible thought that leads us to do two things: first, to temper our concern for ourselves so that our sentiments, actions, and self-judgments more closely resemble what others would approve of; and second, to modulate our judgment of others in terms of how a disinterested third party would judge them (TMS, 82–85). Smith thinks that both of these actions are effected by the operation of an imagined impartial spectator, and the mental process that each of us executes to arrive at a moral judgment is what I shall call the "impartial spectator procedure." I shall devote the remainder of this chapter to elaborating Smith's account of the impartial spectator and the impartial spectator procedure.

Each of us has his own unique set of experiences, which at once limits and enables his capacity to understand the sentiments of others. It limits us by failing to include the one group of experiences that would allow us to have a perfect understanding of others, namely, the actual experiences of those others. Experience is essentially private, and we have no first-hand knowledge of the thoughts or sentiments of others. On the other hand, our set of experiences enables us to come to an understanding, albeit imperfect, of others because in many and perhaps most cases we share similar experiences with others. When it comes to things like human passions, we have all had remarkably similar experiences. Who has not experienced joy or grief or anger? Who has not felt embarrassment or pride or shame? Smith goes further than just this: not only have we all had such experiences, but the fact that we live in similar communities—perhaps the same community— means that we even share many of the particularities of time, place, and circumstances of those experiences. We have read many of the same books, seen the same plays, heard the same music; we have engaged in the same religious rituals, held the same offices, shared the same responsibilities, and taken part in the same kinds of familial, friendly, and social relations. All this means that there is considerable overlap in the circumstances of our respective unique sets of experiences, which in turn means that, despite the privacy of experience, we are able to come to some understanding of each other. I can in a sense know how you feel, and you can in a sense know how I feel. We are able to do this, Smith thinks, by a process of the imagination: I imagine how I would feel if I were in your shoes, and, given the considerable overlap of our respective experiences, the more vividly I conceive of your situation, the closer are my imagined sentiments to your actual sentiments.

Our ability to imagine how others feel depends on two main factors. The first is our knowledge of the agent's situation. Included in this are not only the so-called external facts about the situation—time and place, for example—but also the internal facts about the agent, including his sensibilities, his interests, and his habits. The more I know about you, Smith thinks, the better able am I to place myself in your shoes and to understand how your situation brought you to have the sentiments you do. The other variable in the process is the spectator's own sensibility. How completely can the spectator bring home to himself the situation of another? To what extent is he willing to do so? Some are of course better than others at imagining the sentiments of other people, and some people are more willing to do so than others. But Smith thinks that we are all prompted to engage in this imaginative change of place to the best of our ability by the realization that it is only when others do this for us that we can be understood and thus enjoy a sympathy of sentiments. We therefore learn to place ourselves in others' shoes when we judge them so that we can reach an accurate judgment. And the person being judged accordingly does the same:

As [the spectators] are continually placing themselves in [the agent's] situation, and thence conceiving emotions similar to what he feels; so he is as constantly placing himself in theirs, and thence conceiving some degree of that coolness about his own fortune, with which he is sensible that they will view it. (TMS, 22)

Each party learns to view the situation with the eyes of the other in an effort to reach a mutual sympathy of sentiments, which Smith thinks is intrinsically pleasurable and desirable to all (TMS, 13–16).[35] Moral approval then comes as a result of the awareness of this mutual sympathy: "Before we approve of the sentiments of any person as proper and suitable to their objects, we must not only be affected in the same manner as he is, but we must perceive this harmony and correspondence of sentiments between him and ourselves" (TMS, 78).[36]

As we have more interactions with others over the course of our lives, two things become clear to us. First, the interests people have in various situations in which they act are often partial, and their judgments often reflect this partiality. We are almost universally partial to our own interests, but our judgments are also influenced where they concern other interests of ours, like our friends or family members. On the other hand, we realize early on that we cannot please everyone. Many things we do in an effort to please or help one person offend or are displeasing to someone else—frequently because of the latter's partiality. Smith writes:

In order to defend ourselves from such partial judgments, we soon learn to set up in our own minds a judge between ourselves and those we live with. We conceive ourselves as acting in the presence of a person quite candid and equitable, of one who has no particular relation either to ourselves, or to those whose interests are affected by our conduct, who is neither father, nor brother, nor friend either to them or to us, but is merely a man in general, an impartial spectator who considers our conduct with the same indifference with which we regard that of other people. (TMS, 129)[37]

We now have the introduction of one of the most important contributions Adam Smith made to ethics: the impartial spectator. Bias and partiality color other people's judgments of us, something we find quite vexing because it often leads to unfavorable judgments of us that might well have been favorable if the judgment had been formed impartially. Because we all have felt this vexation, we can easily sympathize with others when they tell us they have been misrepresented or misunderstood, and we are susceptible to pleas that we put aside

---

[35] I discuss the desire for mutual sympathy in detail in Chapter 2.
[36] For a somewhat differing account of what he calls Smith's notion of "spectatorial imagination," see Griswold (1999), Chapter 2, especially 83–96.
[37] This passage was present in editions two through five of TMS as it appears here. In edition six, Smith revised and condensed the passage.

our personal interests and biases when we judge their situation. The result, Smith thinks, is that over time we develop the habit of adopting the point of view of a disinterested third party when judging others, and we expect others to do the same for us. Thus the initial basis for our moral judgments of others—how we would feel if we were in their shoes—gets transformed into something slightly different: we learn to judge people on the basis of what an impartial spectator would think of their motives and their actions.

Smith's impartial spectator is a metaphor: it is a philosophical construction for explaining how people in practice make moral judgments, just as Newton's three laws of motion are a natural philosopher's construction for explaining the way things move. There is a crucial difference, however, between the two cases. Inanimate objects in the universe obey the laws of motion without consciously intending to do so. The same also holds true for the majority of people who consult the impartial spectator. "They have seldom," Smith writes of most people, "enquired after [the impartial spectator's] decisions, and are altogether unacquainted with the rules and forms of its procedure" (TMS, 130). Smith thinks that the fact that even such people almost universally endorse objectivity in judgment is indicative of a process of moral judging that is best described in terms of an impartial spectator. When one observes the judgments people make, how they revise their own judgments, and how they correct the judgments of others, one sees the invisible hand, as it were, of the impartial spectator.[38] I shall examine how Smith reaches this conclusion shortly, but let me first make another point about the status of the impartial spectator. I said that a majority of people are unaware they employ any such device, not that all people are unaware. Smith thinks that a minority has some idea of the rules of the impartial spectator and the structure of his procedure. A measure of reflection "and even of philosophy" are required (TMS, 136), but for those few who engage in them and turn the focus of their deliberations to the nature of moral judgment—as would a moral

---

[38] The metaphor of the invisible hand makes its first appearance in TMS, at 184. In addition to its famous appearance in WN, the metaphor also appears in Smith's posthumously published "History of Astronomy," and collected in *Essays on Philosophical Subjects* (1980; hereafter EPS), 49. The date of this essay's writing is uncertain, however. Emma Rothschild thinks that it was written in the early to mid 1750s, which would predate TMS. See Rothschild (1994).

philosopher like Smith—the role of the impartial spectator reveals itself. In their case, the impartial spectator becomes a metaphor of a special kind, namely, one that also refers to a real thing. In their case, that is, the impartial spectator is not just a philosophical construct by which the moral judgments of others can be understood; it becomes in addition a device consciously employed to render accurate judgments.

Smith thinks that the true standard of morality is the judgment of the impartial spectator, whom Smith calls the "inmate of the breast, this abstract man, the representative of mankind, and substitute of the deity" (TMS, 130). The moral approval and disapproval of the impartial spectator is still based on a sympathy or lack of sympathy, but now the relevant sentiments for comparison are those of the impartial spectator and the agent. It is true, of course, that when we compare the sentiments of the impartial spectator with those of the agent, we are in actuality still comparing our own sentiments to those of the agent because, as we have said, Smith thinks our own sentiments are the only basis we have on which to judge.[39] But Smith thinks that it is possible for us to detach ourselves in our imagination from all the peculiarities about us that would make us interested or partial in some respect. In effect, Smith says, we divide ourselves into two persons, the one we really are and the disinterested version of ourselves: "The compassion of the spectator must arise altogether from the consideration of what he himself would feel if he was reduced to the same unhappy situation [as that of the agent he is judging], and, what perhaps is impossible, was at the same time able to regard it with his present reason and judgment" (TMS, 12).[40] More emphatically, Smith says this:

When I endeavour to examine my own conduct, when I endeavour to pass sentence upon it, and either approve or condemn it, it is evident that, in all such cases, I divide myself, as it were, into two persons; and that I, the examiner and judge, represent a different character from that other I, the person whose conduct is examined into and judged of. (TMS, 113)

---

[39] See especially TMS, 19, §10.

[40] To avoid misinterpretation, I should point out that the qualifier "what perhaps is impossible" refers to a special case in which a sane person attempts to understand the sentiments of an old man gone senile. The spectator thus tries to imagine being devoid of reason while at the same time using his reason to judge the situation— this situation is what Smith says is perhaps impossible. Smith is not saying that the impartial spectator procedure itself is perhaps impossible. See TMS, 12, §11.

In this passage Smith is talking about judging oneself, but he has the same process in mind when he speaks of judging others.

D. D. Raphael argues that Smith's use of the impartial spectator is principally, perhaps solely, restricted to self-judgment,[41] but that cannot be correct. Smith uses the language of impartiality from the very beginning of TMS, when he argues that our desire to understand others prompts us to enter into their situations as completely as possible:

> In all such cases, that there may be some correspondence of sentiments between the spectator and the person principally concerned, the spectator must, first of all, endeavour, as much as he can, to put himself in the situation of the other, and to bring home to himself every little circumstance of distress which can possibly occur to the sufferer. He must adopt the whole case of his companion with all its minutest incidents; and strive to render as perfect as possible, that imaginary change of situation upon which his sympathy is founded. (TMS, 21)

His insistence on the importance of a complete understanding of the agent's situation suggests his belief that we must release ourselves from our own partiality when judging others. The impartial spectator is also present when Smith speaks of our ability to have "conditional sympathy" for another's actions, that is, when we for some reason do not in fact share another's sentiments but nevertheless realize that his sentiments are proper. If we see a stranger weeping, for example, and we are told that his father has just died, we consider the stranger's behavior to be proper even though we do not actually share his sentiments (TMS, 17–18). In this case, we approve of his behavior because we have learned from our own experience what sort of behavior is proper in such circumstances, and we have formed general rules regarding such cases: "the general rules derived from our preceding experience of what our sentiments would commonly correspond with, correct upon this, as upon many other occasions, the impropriety of our present emotions" (ibid.).[42] Smith's notion of "general rules" that "correct" our present sentiments reveals his contention, even at this early stage of TMS, that all moral judgments rest on the approval or

[41] Raphael (1975), 83–99.
[42] Our development of general rules of morality is discussed in Chapters 2 and 3.

disapproval of an impartial spectator. At the very least, this notion suggests that moral judgments rest on the approval or disapproval of a person other than oneself, for one's own sentiments cannot correct themselves: they can only be corrected from a perspective other than one's own, a perspective that would be contained in or reflected by the "general rules" to which Smith refers. The impartial spectator does not make an explicit entrance in these early passages, but a strong devotion to impartiality does—an impartiality that Smith will formally develop into the impartial spectator later in TMS.

In another passage, where Smith is discussing how we must balance our own interests against those of others, he writes: "We must view them, neither from our own place nor yet from his, neither with our own eyes nor yet with his, but from the place and with the eyes of a third person, who has no particular connexion with either, and who judges with impartiality between us" (TMS, 135). And when Smith is introducing his discussion of the "foundation of our judgments concerning our own sentiments and conduct," he says, "[t]he principle by which we naturally either approve or disapprove of our own conduct, seems to be altogether the same with that by which we exercise the like judgments concerning the conduct of other people" (TMS, 109). There is no doubt that the impartial spectator procedure plays a particularly important role in Smith's theory of moral conscience and self-judging, a role that we examine more fully in the next chapter. But we should not ignore the importance Smith places on the perspective of an impartial third party for judging others as well: it is, indeed, the centerpiece of Smith's theory of moral judgment.

We now have the basic framework for Smith's impartial spectator procedure.[43] When we view the motives and actions of another, the first thing we do is imaginatively change places with him to see what our sentiments would be if we were in his shoes. Because experience has shown us the importance of a full and unbiased understanding of the agent's situation before we judge him, we try as far as we are able to view him as if we were an impartial third party who has as complete and sensitive a knowledge of the agent's situation as possible. The second

---

[43] For a similar account of this procedure, see Haakonssen (1981), 51; for differing accounts, see Griswold (1999), Chapter 3, and Raphael (1975).

step in the procedure is the arousal in us of actual or imagined sentiments from this imagined changing of place. If we are executing the
procedure correctly, these sentiments are those a well-informed impartial spectator would have. The third step is the comparison of the two
sentiments—those of the imagined spectator and those of the actual
agent. The fourth step is the judgment we, the actual spectator, pass
in recognition of whether a sympathy exists between the sentiments of
the imagined impartial spectator and those of the agent. Awareness of
a lack of sympathy at this step causes displeasure in us and leads us to
disapprove of the agent's motive or action; the presence of sympathy
causes a pleasure that leads us to approve.[44]

Now, this may seem like a long and cumbersome mental process,
perhaps too much so to be a plausible model for the actual steps we take
in passing moral judgments. But remember that Smith thinks that as
we grow from infancy to childhood and from childhood to adulthood
we get more and more practice at executing this procedure. As we get
more practice, we get better at it, and it stands to reason that it would
take less and less time and would become more and more unnoticeable
to us,[45] like any other complicated task we do often (like typing, playing
the piano, or driving a car in city traffic). Think for a moment of the
everyday judgments we make about other people. We see someone get
angry with his waitress because the food he received was not exactly
as he had ordered it. On hearing him complaining, we might think,
"I know just how he feels!" or, perhaps, "He is overreacting." These
judgments come quickly and easily, yet they can be best understood and
accounted for, Smith thinks, as results of the procedure he describes.

### Smith and Hume on Utility

Smith thinks that the sentiments of the impartial spectator form the
basis of all properly formed moral judgments, and in so thinking
he sides with Hutcheson and Hume in maintaining that reason alone
cannot make moral judgments. Smith allows that a certain process of

---

[44] A third possibility that Smith does not entertain would seem to arise in those cases in
which a determination cannot be made whether one's sentiments correspond with
those of another, or with the imagined sentiments of another. In this case, there
would be neither sympathy nor antipathy, perhaps only neutrality. But Smith seems
to think that only sympathy or antipathy is possible: see TMS, 75, 312, and 327.

[45] See TMS, 135–36.

reason—induction[46]—plays a role in developing the general rules of morality, but, he argues,

> it is altogether absurd and unintelligible to suppose that the first perceptions of right and wrong can be derived from reason, even in those particular cases upon the experience of which the general rules are formed. These first perceptions, as well as all other experiments upon which any general rules are founded, cannot be the object of reason, but of immediate sense and feeling. (TMS, 320)

In fact, however, Smith does not argue for this claim much at all; the entire argument against the claim that reason discerns right and wrong is given only a little more than three pages in TMS.[47] He seems to have taken it for granted that Hutcheson and Hume had already made the case decisively, and so he presumes it in his discussion. Here is what he does say:

> Reason may show that this object is the means of obtaining some other which is naturally either pleasing or displeasing, and in this manner may render it either agreeable or disagreeable for the sake of something else. But nothing can be agreeable or disagreeable for its own sake, which is not rendered such by immediate sense and feeling. (TMS, 320)[48]

This passage is strongly reminiscent of the passages in Hume where Hume makes a similar argument.[49] Smith is in further agreement with Hume on what role reason does play in passing moral judgments, namely, the role of discovering the remote consequences of a proposed course of action. Hume had argued that although reason could not determine right and wrong, it could, based on its experience with the perceived relation of cause and effect, make predictions about what ultimate effects present causes would have. It was then up to our natural sentiment—which for Hume reflected utility—to determine which ends of the proposed actions were virtuous or worth seeking.

---

[46] I discuss Smith's conception of the role of induction in making moral judgments in Chapters 2 and 3.

[47] TMS, 318–321, where Smith is criticizing the view of Ralph Cudworth in particular. For Cudworth's argument, see his *Treatise Concerning Eternal and Immutable Morality* (1991 [1731]), 105–119.

[48] See also TMS, 145, §21.

[49] See, for example, 2E, 82–88.

Although Smith agrees with Hume on this point,[50] he nevertheless disagrees with Hume on another crucial issue, namely, the role that considerations of utility play in making moral judgments. As I have already indicated, Smith thinks that utility plays a secondary role in forming moral judgments, which is clear from his impartial spectator procedure. The only place in this procedure where utility plays a role is when we consider whether the sentiments that the acted-upon person has in reaction to the agent's actions are proper. Here we ask ourselves whether the gratitude or resentment this person feels is appropriate to the situation, and in this connection we consider the consequences of the agent's action and whether they are beneficial or harmful. But Smith has argued that the judgment we reach in this regard is "indirect"—meaning that it is a judgment about the agent's action in terms of the propriety of the sentiments the acted-upon person has in reaction to the agent's action—and in any case is secondary in time and importance to the consideration of whether the agent's motives are appropriate to the causes that excited them. Smith is certainly aware of Hume's contention that utility ultimately underlies all moral judgments; in fact, Smith devotes one of the seven parts of his book to this issue.[51] Moreover, Smith concedes that Hume's view contains a certain speculative attraction. Nonetheless, Smith argues that the view does not stand up to empirical examination; the facts, Smith thinks, demonstrate that utility is not the ultimate foundation of moral judgments. After considering Hume's arguments, he writes:

But I still affirm, that it is not the view of this utility or hurtfulness which is either the first or principal source of our approbation and disapprobation. These sentiments are no doubt enhanced and enlivened by the perception of the beauty or deformity which results from this utility or hurtfulness. But still, I say, they are originally and essentially different from this perception. (TMS, 188)

Smith gives several arguments to support his claim. His first argument is based on the observation that "it seems impossible that the approbation of virtue should be a sentiment of the same kind with that by which we approve of a convenient and well-contrived building;

---

[50] See TMS, 194–95, and also Smith's "History of Astronomy" (EPS, 33–105); see especially Section II, 37–47.

[51] Part 4 of TMS, 179–93. Smith refers to Hume on page 188.

or that we should have no other reason for praising a man than that for which we commend a chest of drawers" (ibid.).[52] Smith thinks that this is impossible on the basis of an introspective observation he has made of the judgments he passes concerning good human beings on the one hand and good buildings on the other. The sentiment each arouses in us is different, from which Smith concludes that the bases of the respective judgments are different. But since the basis of the judgment concerning artifacts like buildings and chests of drawers is utility or convenience, that must mean that the basis of our judgments about people is not utility. There seems no other plausible reason why we would judge a particular chest of drawers to be good besides its usefulness,[53] but the actual sentiment that gives rise to this judgment, Smith thinks, is phenomenologically different from the sentiment that gives rise to a judgment about human beings. Smith thinks that it is obvious to anyone who considers the case that the sources of approbation in the two cases are different. The logical conclusion, then, is that a consideration of utility does not excite our approbation or disapprobation of persons.

Hume's response to this argument is to suggest that although utility does indeed recommend to us the convenient building as well as the virtuous person, the sentiments aroused in us in each case nevertheless feel different because the latter but not the former is "mixed with affection, esteem, approbation, *&c.*" (2E, 39). But Smith's argument is more plausible. The argument that sentiments like affection, esteem, and approbation (and whatever might be included in "*&c.*"), despite the fact that they feel different from sentiments of utility proper, are nevertheless species of such sentiments seems simply to assume that all sentiments regarding moral judgments are products of considerations of utility. For why otherwise would we think that esteem, for example, rests on utility? Smith argues that the esteem we feel for people like Brutus[54]—that is, people who are now long dead—is only implausibly construed as the effect of considerations for utility; the

---

[52] Hume considers this objection; see 2E, 39. Hume had laid the groundwork for a reply to this problem already in the *Treatise,* however (see T, 471–72). I address Hume's reply to this objection shortly.

[53] One might also judge it as good for its beauty, but this, for Smith, would be only a secondary consideration—as it is in the case of judgments of people. See later in text.

[54] Smith takes this example from Hume. See T, 582.

more plausible explanation is that we think that Brutus's actions were right and proper, that is, that they reflected what we think an impartial spectator would have approved of. Smith concedes that the utility that Brutus's actions had for his contemporaries adds a certain beauty to our consideration of them, but "[t]his beauty, however, is chiefly perceived by men of reflection and speculation, and is by no means the quality which first recommends such actions to the natural sentiments of the bulk of mankind" (TMS, 192). Any ordinary person, Smith thinks, who reads about the actions of Brutus will feel esteem for him, but in most cases he will be unaware of the utilitarian consequences of those actions. Only the philosopher is able to perceive such remote consequences, which perhaps explains why only philosophers (he clearly has Hume in mind here) have thought that utility could be the sole or principal foundation for moral approbation.[55]

The second argument Smith makes to support his claim that utility plays only a secondary role in moral judgments is that if we look at what is actually taken into consideration when we pass moral judgments, we will find that utility "is seldom the first ground of our approbation; and that the sentiment of approbation always involves in it a sense of propriety quite distinct from the perception of utility" (TMS, 188). This is true, Smith thinks, "with regard to all the qualities which are approved of as virtuous" (ibid.), including those that Hume characterizes as useful to ourselves and those useful to others. For example, concerning the qualities useful to ourselves—chief among which are, as Smith says, "superior reason and understanding" (TMS, 189)[56]— Smith suggests that it is not the utility of such qualities that originally recommends them to our approbation but rather the realization that they are "just and right and accurate" (ibid.). He thinks that "we approve of another man's judgment, not as something useful, but as right, as accurate, and as agreeable to truth and reality" (TMS, 20). In addition, Smith says that it is in the "abstruser sciences," like physics and mathematics, where the "greatest and most admired exertions of

---

[55] See TMS, 18, §8, where Smith distinguishes between philosophers' speculative explanations of human behavior (the context of this discussion suggests that he once again has Hume in mind) and those of people familiar with "common life," that is, with the actual behavior of real men. Smith thinks that the latter are generally more reliable.

[56] Smith is again addressing Hume, who said that "profound genius" and "sure judgment" are of paramount utility to their possessors (2E, 55–56).

human reason have been displayed" (TMS, 189), and these displays have been widely admired, even by common men who have no special training in physics or mathematics. But the utility of these sciences "is not very obvious, and to prove it, requires a discussion which is not always very easily comprehended" (ibid.), showing, Smith argues, that a consideration of utility could not be the basis of the public approval of such intellectual exertions.

Smith similarly argues that the virtues of self-command, humanity, justice, generosity, and public spirit are all in practice approved of not on the basis of utility but rather on the basis of their propriety to the situation or causes that excite them. We praise a generous person, for example, simply because he has done the right thing, irrespective of whether his generosity actually leads to good consequences—a fact that explains why we tend to forgive an excessively indulgent parent or an indiscriminate almsgiver, each of whose actions might well lead to undesirable consequences in the long run.[57]

Smith calls the ability to control one's passions and consciously direct one's actions "self-command"; he thinks that the possession of self-command is what makes possession of other virtues possible. But even when considering the approval we give to self-command in its relation to prudence, which is a virtue that one might think seems particularly susceptible to explanation in terms of our own utility because it is mainly a self-regarding virtue,[58] Smith argues that this approval arises at least as much because of the propriety of self-command and prudence as from their utility. Smith says that the person possessing self-command is able to temper his present, perhaps more vivid desires out of deference to his long-term, perhaps cooler (though perhaps more important) interests. But the impartial spectator is by definition equally concerned with our long-term interests as with our short-term interests, because they are, after all, only so many interests to him.[59] When we abstain from an immediate interest out of consideration for a remote but greater interest, the impartial spectator therefore "cannot fail to approve of our behaviour" as being appropriate in consideration of all the causes that influence and excite it (TMS, 189). Self-command and prudence, then, are approved of principally in

[57] See TMS, 40.
[58] See TMS, 298–99.
[59] See TMS, 189 and 215.

light of their propriety, not whatever utility they might provide for their possessor. Thus Smith concludes that although a consideration of utility adds a special luster to one's actions, it is nevertheless always a secondary consideration when passing judgment on those actions, and it is frequently altogether absent from our approbation of them.

One final note about the relation between Smith and Hume on this issue. It seems possible that Hume analyzed Smith's notion of sympathy one step further than Smith himself did. If so, perhaps we can understand Hume's theory to hold that the ultimate reason we approve of a motive or action is because this motive or action has proved useful in the past, and that the pleasure Smith thinks we take in mutual sympathy of sentiments is ultimately a result of utility. Hume's claim would be that although we do not know or realize it, utility might nevertheless underlie and be responsible for our moral judgments. Hume's response to Smith would then be to concede that the sentiment of approval for a virtuous person is phenomenologically different from the sentiment of approval for a piece of furniture and to concede that the basis of the latter is obviously utility whereas the basis of the former seems not to be. Hume might argue, however, that Smith's notion of propriety and impropriety are themselves ultimately informed by the utility of the motives and actions under question. So Hume might accept Smith's distinction between three senses of "sympathy"—pity, general fellow-feeling, and correspondence between sentiments—and he might accept Smith's claim that sympathy in the third sense is what immediately prompts us to approve or disapprove of men. But Hume could argue that the sentiments themselves that are generated when we view or reflect on another's action are the result of a natural pleasure we take in characters and actions that lead to utilitarian consequences or the natural displeasure we take in characters and actions that lead to disutilitarian consequences. Hence Hume could concede virtually the whole of Smith's argument and then nevertheless maintain that Smith simply has not explained everything that needs explaining.[60]

Does this argument refute Smith? Before Hume's argument could be accepted, we would need some account of how considerations of

---

[60] Hume's response would still be subject to the problem, discussed earlier, of reconciling individual utility with overall or aggregate utility, but let us put this to one side for the moment. For a defense of Hume's view against Smith's criticisms, see Martin (1990).

utility can be internalized in such a way as to allow them to form the basis of moral judgments without the knowledge or awareness of the person making the judgment. Smith's principal objection to Hume's contention that utility underlies moral judgments is that people making moral judgments do not, in fact, reflect on the relative utilitarian consequences of the case under question. And Smith's claim seems plausible. The act of considering an action's possible utility, however, would seem to require active mental participation. Hence if Hume wanted to maintain that such considerations are at bottom responsible for moral judgments, despite the fact that people are not aware of it, he would have to explain how this can escape the notice of the person passing judgment. A particularly difficult set of cases would be those in which we approve of the actions of people long dead: how can we be said to base our approval on the utility of their actions when not only are we unaware of the utility but we could probably not even say what it is after reflection? As far as I know, Hume gives no such account—which means, I believe, that, although one might raise the "Humean" objection to Smith that despite appearances utility still underlies moral judgments, Hume himself could not legitimately raise it because he does not provide an account that would be sufficient to fill out the objection.

Surprisingly, however, Smith *does* give such an account. Smith's conception of the foundation of moral judgments can allow for a kind of evolution of moral standards on the basis of a criterion like utility. One might be able to argue, then, that Smith's analysis provides the framework necessary for supposing that the moral standards of a society have evolved to the status they enjoy—that is, being regarded as transcendently true—because they had proved to be conducive to various ends the people in that society desired. In other words, one could argue that Smithian moral standards are ultimately reflections of utility while nonetheless accepting Smith's claim that considerations of utility do not immediately prompt moral judgments. I must postpone further discussion of this issue until Chapter 6, however, after I have discussed the framework of Smith's analysis that could allow for the evolution of moral standards along utilitarian lines. There we shall see that utility does ultimately play an important role in the development of moral standards according to Smith's account, but its role is considerably complicated by Smith's belief that this development, if allowed to proceed unfettered, proceeds according to God's plan for the universe and the human beings in it.

### An Ideal Observer?

The final issue to be discussed in this chapter is the thorny and controversial one of whether or not Smith's impartial spectator is in any sense ideal, or whether he represents any informed but impartial person. Some, like Roderick Firth and Kurt Norlin,[61] have argued that Smith's impartial spectator is an "ideal observer," complete with certain idealized and perhaps humanly unattainable characteristics. Others, like T. D. Campbell and D. D. Raphael, have disagreed, arguing that the impartial spectator is a perfectly average fellow who is simply familiar with the situation under question. I agree with the latter group, despite several remarks Smith makes that seem to support the former. This issue bears directly on the plausibility of Smith's impartial spectator procedure. If the impartial spectator is in fact ideal, it will be much more difficult for Smith to claim that such a person's perspective is the one that real people actually adopt when passing moral judgments; on the other hand, if it turns out that the role of his impartial spectator could be filled by any ordinary person, the impartial spectator procedure will have at least greater prima facie plausibility.

Let us look at the passages that seem to suggest that Smith thinks that the impartial spectator is ideal. The first passage is one I already cited when I argued that Smith's impartial spectator procedure applies both to self-judgments and to judgments of others:

In all such cases, that there may be some correspondence of sentiments between the spectator and the person principally concerned, the spectator must, first of all, endeavour, as much as he can, to put himself in the situation of the other, and to bring home to himself *every little circumstance of distress which can possibly occur to the sufferer.* He must adopt *the whole case of his companion with all its minutest incidents*; and strive to render as perfect as possible, that imaginary change of situation upon which his sympathy is founded. (TMS, 21; my italics)

This sounds like a high standard for an ordinary person to meet; indeed, the person principally concerned may himself well not have all the knowledge of his own situation that Smith describes here. It makes

---

[61] Firth (1952) and Norlin ( January 1995).

Smith's spectator sound like the spectator that the leading twentieth-century proponent of the "ideal observer" theory of ethics, Roderick Firth, has in mind. Firth has argued that the meaning of moral statements can be analyzed in terms of the "dispositional reactions" of an ideal observer; to say that an act is right is to say that an omniscient, omnipercipient, disinterested, dispassionate, consistent, and otherwise normal observer would approve of the act (Firth, 1952, 333–45). Moreover, Firth claims that his theory is directly descended from Smith's in that Smith's impartial spectator is simply a less-carefully articulated version of Firth's ideal observer (ibid., 318). And it appears that we can see elements of Firth's ideal observer in the preceding citation from Smith.

Other passages give a similar impression. For example, Smith argues that when the "man without"—that is, an actual person, other than ourselves, who is judging us—falsely reproaches us, we can take solace in the impartial spectator, who has complete knowledge and can thus "immediately correct this false judgment, and assure us, that we are by no means the proper objects of that censure which has so unjustly been bestowed upon us" (TMS, 131). Smith seems to suggest that the impartial spectator knows more about us and our situation than any other person, besides perhaps ourselves and God, ever could. Smith goes on in the same passage to call the impartial spectator "divine," a "demigod within the breast" who is "partly of immortal . . . extraction" (ibid.). Indeed, God himself gave man the capacity to consult the impartial spectator, whom God made "his vicegerent upon earth, to superintend the behaviour of his brethren"; he is the "substitute of the Deity, whom nature has constituted the supreme judge of all [men's] actions" (TMS, 130).[62] Later in TMS, Smith describes impartial spectators as being "cool and candid and consistent with themselves" (TMS, 311), qualities—especially the last—that do not often obtain among most actual spectators. On the basis of these passages, one might reasonably conclude that Smith does not have any mere mortal in mind when he speaks of the impartial spectator. What real person, after all, knows all the minutest details of another's situation? Whose judgment could

---

[62] It is not implausible to suggest that this passage represents Smith's interpretation of Genesis 1:27, "So God created man in his own image." I return to this issue in Chapter 6.

we actually think of as having an immortal extraction, even partly so? Moreover, if we wish to speak of our judgments of right and wrong as if they were absolute—as Smith often does—and if we in addition wish to claim that the basis of these judgments is an impartial spectator, then it seems one must conclude that our impartial spectator has access to absolute truths of morality. And if that is the case, it seems that we are quite a way down the road to saying that our impartial spectator represents an ideal, not an actual, person.

I think this is an inaccurate conception of Smith. Though he is inclined to use phrases like "demigod" and God's "vicegerent on earth" to describe the impartial spectator, I think we can safely attribute most such statements to rhetorical flourish. Here is a description Smith gives of this spectator that I believe exhibits Smith's true conception of him:

We conceive ourselves acting in the presence of a person quite candid and equitable, of one who has no particular relation either to ourselves, or to those whose interests are affected by our conduct, who is neither father, nor brother, nor friend either to them or to us, but is merely a man in general, an impartial spectator who considers our conduct with the same indifference with which we regard that of other people. (TMS, 129)

It takes no extraordinary or ideal person to fill this role. We should not be misled by phrases like "man in general" because for Smith this is equivalent to saying "any man at all." It means any person who has no particular interest in the case he is judging, which would ordinarily rule out a father, brother, or friend, as Smith says. Smith does not mean, however, that the spectator can be no father, brother, or friend at all, but rather that he cannot be the father, brother, or friend of the parties involved in the case in question. Smith concludes this passage not with a claim that the impartial spectator is omniscient, omnipercipient, and all the other things Firth's ideal observer is; tellingly, he concludes it instead by saying that the impartial spectator judges "our conduct with the same indifference with which we regard that of other people." Smith's impartial spectator is any one of us when we are calm and cool, when the judgment we pass is deliberate and not impetuous.

Other passages support my interpretation of Smith. When, for example, we hear someone tell a joke at a party, it sometimes happens that we are not in the mood for laughing, even though we approve of the laughter of others as proper in this case. How are we able to approve of those others' sentiments when we do not share them? We may at the time be in a sour mood; "We have learned, however, from experience, what sort of pleasantry is upon most occasions capable of making us laugh, and we observe that this is one of that kind" (TMS, 17). For Smith, this approval is based on what we know would be our sentiments were we not in our present mood—that is, what would be our sentiments if we were *impartial* spectators of our friend's joke-telling. Such a perfectly common experience as this would not be possible if everyday people in everyday situations could not adopt the perspective of Smith's impartial spectator, a fact that indicates, I think, that Smith saw the impartial spectator as a perspective attainable by anyone.

In a passage cited earlier, Smith says that in balancing our own interests against those of another, we must view our respective interests "neither from our own place nor yet from his, neither with our own eyes nor yet with his, but from the place and with the eyes of a third person" (TMS, 135). Now if we read no farther, we might well think this expresses a humanly unattainable goal: no real person, it might be argued, could adopt such a position from which to view people's behavior.[63] But Smith continues in this way: "Here, too, habit and experience have taught us to do this so easily and so readily, that we are scarce sensible that we do it" (TMS, 135–36). It is we who execute this procedure, not an ideal observer. Later, Smith describes a person who has the virtue of temperance. The essence of a temperate person is that he "has never dared to forget for one moment the judgment which the impartial spectator would pass upon his sentiments and conduct. . . . This habit has become perfectly familiar to him. . . . He does not merely affect the sentiments of the impartial spectator. He really adopts them" (TMS, 146–47). Perhaps the most striking passage is this: "There exists in the mind of every man, an idea of [exact propriety and perfection], gradually formed from his observations upon the character and conduct both of himself and other people" (TMS, 247). A number of other passages[64] indicate the same thing: Smith's impartial spectator is a

---

[63] Of course, not everyone would make this argument. Thomas Nagel, for example, thinks that we can adopt such a perspective. See his *The View From Nowhere* (1986), where he argues for a kind of objectivity that is not altogether unlike that of Smith's impartial spectator, although Nagel acknowledges no debt to Smith.

[64] For example, TMS, 163 and 319–20; see also TMS, 131 and 141, where Smith implies that the impartial spectator is fallible.

well-informed (but not omniscient or omnipercipient), disinterested human being; Smith envisions the impartial spectator procedure as the work of men, not angels.

Perhaps what has led some to think that Smith's impartial spectator is a humanly unattainable ideal is a confusion based on the distinction Smith draws between the actual spectator and his imagined impartial spectator. Recall that when we execute the impartial spectator procedure, we divide ourselves, "as it were," into two persons—one who represents what we imagine our sentiments would be if we were impartial third-party spectators and the other who represents us as we actually are (TMS, 113). It is true that the former is ideal insofar as it represents an unactualized, imagined perspective, but that does not mean that an actual, real person cannot imaginatively put himself in the imaginary person's place. T. D. Campbell was right when he said that Smith's conception of the impartial spectator is an "empirical ideal": empirical in the sense that it represents any real person, ideal in the sense that it represents this same random real person once he is abstracted from the particular interests and biases he has (Campbell, 1971, 127). In actual cases, it will turn out that some people are better than others at detaching themselves from their interests and biases, which, according to Smith, will mean that some are better able to hear the voice of the impartial spectator than are others; their respective judgments will then reflect accuracy or inaccuracy to the extent that they were able to hear the impartial voice. In all cases, we, the actual, real, interested, and biased persons, imagine an impartial spectator and then make the moral judgment; hence, in many cases, the accuracy of our judgment will be limited by our nature. Nevertheless Smith maintains that the perspective of the impartial spectator is attainable—though perhaps only with great difficulty and many years of practice. The Smithian impartial spectator procedure is therefore two things: first, it is the actual foundation of the everyday moral judgments people make; second, it is a tool that allows people to judge themselves and others disinterestedly and sensitively, as each of us would have others judge him.

A final question, related to whether Smith's impartial spectator is ideal, is how many Smithian impartial spectators there are. Smith usually refers to the impartial spectator in the singular: does that mean there is just one, and that all people are supposed to consult this same, single impartial spectator? If so, then we would seem to have another reason to hold Smith's impartial spectator to be a (perhaps) unrealizable ideal. Or are there several impartial spectators, each perhaps indexed to a particular situation or family of situations and consulted only by those who have experience with the relevant situations? If so, then we would seem to run the risk of multiplying the number of impartial spectators almost indefinitely to correspond to the indefinitely large number of kinds of experiences people might have. I suggest that the answer to this is both. There is one idealized concept of what an impartial spectator would be—a person who is disinterested in but informed about the matter at hand—and hence a true impartial spectator consulted in any particular situation will fit this mold. On the other hand, the exact parameters within which the impartial spectator would employ the impartial spectator procedure are determined by the facts of the case in question. By "parameters" I mean the protocols of behavior, speech, and so on, peculiar to this case; part of what is meant by the criterion "informed" is that the impartial spectator knows how this particular game, as it were, is played.

This way of framing it suggests an analogy that I think can illuminate Smith's meaning. The impartial spectator is like an umpire or referee for a sports game. In principle, any ideal umpire will have the same general qualities: knowledge both of the rules of the game and of the situation of the game at hand, an ability to notice the relevant details of the game, and an interest in applying the rules of the game fairly, that is, disinterestedly. Regardless of the sport, any good umpire will meet these general criteria. Nevertheless, additional qualifications are necessary to be a good umpire in, say, ice hockey, as against baseball, as against college basketball, as against professional basketball, and so on. To be a good umpire in any of these sports requires special knowledge of the sport in question. And the umpire's job is to monitor the game in this informed yet disinterested way, informing the players whenever anyone steps out of line and assessing rewards, penalties, retribution, and so on, where appropriate. In the same way, although the Smithian impartial spectator should always meet the general criteria of being informed and disinterested, his judgment in any given case will reflect the protocols of behavior, speech, and so on, proper to the kind of situation at hand. In both cases—that of the sports umpire and Smith's impartial spectator—experience with the relevant kinds of situations, and the habits that have been developed on the basis of that experience, go on to form rules by which the umpire or impartial spectator judges particular cases. Hence again we find, consistent with what I have argued, that Smith's impartial spectator is no metaphysical or other-worldly being with more knowledge than any human can have. Instead he is like the sports umpire who conforms as nearly as possible to the ideal umpire and at the same time draws on his actual knowledge and experience to judge the case at hand fairly.[65]

[65] The suggestion that the impartial spectator will employ different (though overlapping) sets of rules depending on the kind of situation he is judging, anticipates my argument in Chapter 6 and in the Conclusion that Smith's conception of systems of unintended social order also predicts the appearance of distinct suborders.

# Adam Smith's Moral Theory, Part Two

## *Conscience and Human Nature*

Sympathy and the impartial spectator are, for Smith, perhaps the two most important notions to understand if one wishes to understand what gives rise to our moral judgments. Sympathy, or a correspondence between the sentiments of an actor and a spectator, is what one senses or is aware of that prompts a favorable judgment. It is the impartial spectator, however, whose sentiments and judgments correct those of the interested actor and spectator. Indeed, the judgments of the impartial spectator in time assume the role of the ultimate standards of moral judgment, not only for the individual but also for the community at large. The other two main elements of Smith's theory are his explanation of the human phenomenon known as conscience and his conception of human nature. In explaining what the human conscience is and how it develops, Smith puts the rest of his theory to work. Sympathy and the impartial spectator work in concert to create our conscience, and the process of conscience-formation, as well as the natural attraction to sympathy and the impetus to employ the impartial spectator procedure, are all motivated by principles and desires innate in human nature.

In this chapter, I begin by looking at Smith's conception of the human conscience, detailing what it is, how it develops, how it functions, and what role it plays in Smith's moral theory. Then I examine the principal elements of Smith's conception of human nature, which undergirds his entire moral theory. Here we shall have our first introduction to the Adam Smith Problem, an issue that will be examined in detail in Chapters 4 and 5.

## I. The Human Conscience

*What Is the Conscience?*

People have long referred to a phenomenon that is popularly known as "conscience." On some accounts, the conscience is something like an inner voice that tells us what to do; on other accounts, it is a feeling of remorse or guilt for having done something wrong and a feeling of gladness or pride for having done something right; still others believe it is God giving us subtle hints to help us guide our lives. Smith thinks that the human conscience is all three of these. The inner voice we hear is that of the impartial spectator telling us whether or not our motives and actions accord with what would be his motives and actions in the same situation, that is, whether we have proper motives and whether our actions have merit. The voice of the impartial spectator is also accompanied with a feeling of either guilt or joy, which proceeds from our realization that our motives and actions either do or do not accord with those of the impartial spectator. Finally, Smith thinks that the voice of this spectator, when it is prompted by a correct execution of the impartial spectator procedure, ultimately reflects the voice of God: it represents God's grand, benevolent design of nature, which is intended to conduce to the greater happiness of all mankind. The last of these we explore in Chapter 6. Let us here look at how Smith explains the first two, including how he thinks this voice of the conscience develops and whence it derives its authority over us.

Smith employs the impartial spectator procedure to explain the judgments we make of other people, but he employs it perhaps more ingeniously in his explanation of the human conscience. The phenomenon Smith sets out to explain is the familiar one, namely, the inner judgment or sentiment we make or have concerning our own motives and actions. We think something bad about someone, and we silently reproach ourselves for it; we behave badly, and we feel guilty for what we have done. These are certainly common human experiences, but Smith thinks that no adequate explanation has yet been given to account for them, particularly when one considers that believers in God and nonbelievers alike seem to have pangs of conscience. Smith believes that the judgments made as a result of the impartial spectator procedure constitute our conscience and that we condemn or praise our motives and behavior in accordance with the sentiments of this spectator:

we either approve or disapprove of our own conduct, according as we feel that, when we place ourselves in the situation of another man, and view it, as it were, with his eyes and from his station, we either can or cannot entirely enter into and sympathize with the sentiments and motives which influenced it. (TMS, 109–10)

Notice that Smith does not specify the person with whose eyes and from whose station we must view our own conduct. He says only "another man," meaning potentially any person at all—by which he signifies the impartiality that is paramount on his theory. Because our self-judgment is a *critical* judgment, it involves an awareness of our own motives and actions that is one step removed from the motives and actions themselves. Put differently, the self-judgment requires an introspective look at ourselves from a position other than the one we actually occupy. "We can never survey our own sentiments and motives, we can never form any judgment concerning them; unless we remove ourselves, as it were, from our own natural station, and endeavour to view them as at a distance from us" (ibid.).

We find in Smith's treatment of the process that constitutes conscience a development similar to the one we saw in his treatment of sympathy and the impartial spectator. He begins with the perhaps less controversial claim that conscience is informed by our imaginatively changing places with another, by imagining how we should look if we viewed ourselves from the position of another. Smith thinks this is our first inclination, once we realize that others judge us in the same way we do them. We begin to ask ourselves what they must think of us. But there follows on this realization a second realization that others often judge us unfairly or inaccurately, owing to their incomplete knowledge of our situation, their partiality to some interest involved in the case, or some other bias they might have that affects their judgment. This vexes us because it leads others to disapprove of us when we do not deserve it; in particular cases when we have been unfairly judged, our vexation often leads us to implore the relevant spectators to reconsider the case or to supply them with information they did not have. This second realization we make—at some point, Smith thinks, early on in our lives—then connects with the first realization to produce a second course of action. We realize, that is, that not only are we often judged unfairly, but that it must also be the case that others have similar experiences. The result is that we begin to adopt the perspective of a disinterested third party from which to judge our own actions, and we use this perspective as a standard against which to judge the judgments of actual spectators to our conduct. Thus Smith's original claim transforms into a perhaps more controversial one. He thinks that in time we come to believe that the judgment of the disinterested third party— the "impartial spectator"—is the only true standard of judgment, and it begins to reinforce, temper, or replace altogether the judgments others make of us. Let us flesh this process out.

### The Development of the Conscience

The adoption of the impartial spectator as the supreme standard of judgment for our own conduct is a gradual process. It begins, as I said, with our consideration of what the other actual spectators to our behavior must think of us. "Whatever judgment we can form concerning [our sentiments and motives]," Smith writes, "must always bear some secret reference, either to what are, or to what, upon a certain condition, would be, or to what, we imagine, ought to be the judgment of others" (TMS, 110). The fact that this imaginative switching of place begins with the recognition not only that others judge us but also that they judge us without the great interest we naturally take in ourselves suggests what Smith thinks originally brings us to consider the judgments of others: interactions with other people—in particular, people who are disinterested with respect to us. Smith offers a striking thought experiment.[1] Imagine a person who grew up in a solitary place and who had no interaction whatever with other people. How would he, Smith asks, view his own motives and actions? Would he approve of some and condemn others on account of their propriety or impropriety? Smith says he would not: all that would interest him would be the objects of his passions, and whether they pleased him or not; he would

---

[1] TMS, 110–11. But see also TMS, 192, §12.

never reflect on the passions themselves. Why not? Smith thinks that he would never consider such things because he has never been placed under the necessity of doing so. It would be like asking whether he had formed an opinion of the beauty or ugliness of his own face—without a mirror to view them, how can he be expected to have thought of such things? But imagine now that he is introduced into a community of other people. What happens? "Bring him into society, and he is immediately provided with the mirror which he wanted before" (TMS, 110). He suddenly sees, Smith says, that others judge what he does, and he can see what their judgments are not only by their words but also by the looks on their faces and the way they behave toward him. And this realization affects him deeply.

Bring him into society, and all his own passions will immediately become the causes of new passions. He will observe that mankind approve of some of them, and are disgusted by others. He will be elevated in the one case, and cast down in the other; his desires and aversions, his joys and sorrows, will now often become the causes of new desires and new aversions, new joys and new sorrows: they will now, therefore, interest him deeply, and often call upon his most attentive consideration. (TMS, 111)

Now Smith does not think it is possible for a human being to exist outside of society; such a person, if he could even survive (which is doubtful), would be a beast rather than a human being.[2] Hence the example of a solitary man absent the mirror of society is for Smith a counterfactual thought experiment. Nevertheless, the point of the example is clear. Commerce with other people focuses our attention on our own conduct and that moves us to consider others' judgments of it when choosing our own courses of action.

Smith's explanation of self-judgments thus has two levels. The first level concerns the conscious or purposeful judgments we pass on our own conduct. The second level concerns the sentiments that are often involuntarily aroused in us when we have certain motives or engage in certain activities. The first of these is simply the impartial spectator procedure applied to ourselves. Smith describes this process of self-judging in a notable passage:

---

[2] TMS, 85, §1; 110, §3; and 213, §6. I explore this issue further in the next section.

When I endeavour to examine my own conduct, when I endeavour to pass sentence upon it, and either to approve or condemn it, it is evident that, in all such cases, I divide myself, as it were, into two persons; and that I, the examiner and judge, represent a different character from that other I, the person whose conduct is examined into and judged of. The first is the spectator, whose sentiments with regard to my own conduct I endeavour to enter into, by placing myself in his situation, and by considering how it would appear to me, when seen from that particular point of view. The second is the agent, the person whom I properly call myself, and of whose conduct, under the character of a spectator, I was endeavouring to form some opinion. (TMS, 113)

In the first chapter of TMS, Smith had written that maintaining such a dual perspective was quite difficult, given that the spectator's own passions continually intrude upon him (TMS, 12, §11); here we see that this perspective, however difficult, is the very foundation of the judgments we make of ourselves. It is to the impartial spectator's voice that we listen when judging our own conduct, and it is his opinion, Smith thinks, that we take to heart. But several questions need to be answered. First, what actually informs the judgment of the impartial spectator when we judge ourselves? That is, how do we in practice distinguish between the two viewpoints Smith describes in the preceding passage? Second, why do we listen to the impartial spectator's voice? What does it matter to us what this imagined person should think, and why should it move us to praise or condemn our actions? Third, what is the source of the sentiments we feel when we reflect on our own conduct without engaging in any conscious judgment-passing? The answers to these questions can be found in Smith's second-level treatment of conscience, the internalization of and the heed paid to general rules of conduct. Once we have detailed Smith's explanation of our internal conscience, we shall be in a position to address these other concerns.

I argued in Chapter 1 that Smith's impartial spectator should not be viewed as an ideal observer. In so doing, I made reference to a number of passages where Smith indicates that the judgment the impartial spectator passes is based on the everyday experiences of normal people, from which I concluded that one did not need to be ideal to be an impartial spectator—instead, like a sports umpire, simply well-informed about and disinterested in the case in question. Some of the passages I adduced to support my claim there apply here as well.

For example, Smith says that we can judge the propriety of a joke told even though we are not in a humorous mood because we have learned "from experience" "what sort of pleasantry is upon most occasions capable of making us laugh" (TMS, 17). We can judge a man's crying at the death of his father to be proper even though we do not actually share his sentiments because, again, we have learned "from experience" "that such a misfortune naturally excites such a degree of sorrow, and we know that if we took time to consider his situation, fully and in all its parts, we should, without doubt, most sincerely sympathize with him" (TMS, 18). Why is it that when we judge our own conduct, we endeavor to do so from the perspective of a disinterested third party? "Here, too, habit and experience have taught us to do this" (TMS, 135–36). Again and again Smith relies on *habit* and *experience* as the source of the judgment the impartial spectator makes. We can thus extend my argument that Smith's impartial spectator is not ideal. Smith thinks that the judgments this spectator passes are not a priori or directly informed by an infallible source. Rather, they are based on the careful observation we make of two things: one, what motives and behaviors we ourselves actually approve of; and two, what motives and behaviors we find that others actually approve of.

The more experience we have with other people in various situations, the more readily able we are to make judgments of both them and ourselves. Smith thinks that this is because we employ a process of induction on the basis of the individual experiences we have had, and we thereby generate general rules of conduct. For most people this process proceeds unconsciously, but it takes place nonetheless.[3] We see what sorts of behavior we approve of in others, and we gradually form general rules about what behavior is proper and what, improper. This development of general rules first takes place on the individual level: each of us forms for himself general rules of conduct on the basis of what he approves of or disapproves of in other people.[4] But these rules, like the other moral judgments we pass, get influenced and revised on the basis of the judgments we see others passing. Moreover, their judgments are influenced by their observations of the judgments we make. This mutual observation of judgment-making among the people in a community is a continuous process of information exchange

---

[3] See TMS, 130 and 135–36.
[4] The source of these initial preferences is explored in the next chapter.

that shapes and molds the way each member of the community judges himself and others.

> In order to produce this concord [of sentiments], as nature teaches the spectators to assume the circumstances of the person principally concerned, so she teaches this last in some measure to assume those of the spectators. As they are continually placing themselves in his situation, and thence conceiving emotions similar to what he feels; so he is as constantly placing himself in theirs, and thence conceiving some degree of that coolness about his own fortune, with which he is sensible that they will view it. As they are constantly considering what they themselves would feel, if they actually were the sufferers, so he is as constantly led to imagine in what manner he would be affected if he was only one of the spectators of his own situation. As their sympathy makes them look at it, in some measure, with his eyes, so his sympathy makes him look at it, in some measure, with theirs, especially when in their presence and acting under their observation: and as the reflected passion, which he thus conceives, is much weaker than the original one, it necessarily abates the violence of what he felt before he came into their presence, before he began to recollect in what manner they would be affected by it, and to view his situation in this candid and impartial light. (TMS, 22)

The result is that certain judgments about right and wrong develop a general consensus among the people in a community, each member considering them not only the general rules of morality that he has formed for himself but also the general rules that enjoy the support of the other members. The rules that survive this ongoing process of accepting and rejecting, amplifying and moderating the moral judgments that various individuals propose under various circumstances, come to enjoy the status of commonly accepted general rules of conduct. The process that gives rise to them is what I call in the next chapter the "marketplace of morals." To return to the individual level, however, once these rules become internalized by each person, they become the source of the judgments he passes when executing the impartial spectator procedure. The impartial spectator's opinions, then, reflect the general rules that the actual spectator has formed on the basis of his countless particular experiences with his own approval and disapproval, as well as the approval and disapproval of others.

Smith argues that although our own interests are the most important to us, we nevertheless do not always act with regard solely to them. We often act on the basis of our "humanity," which prompts us to benevolence. But how is it that the "soft power" of humanity is able on so many occasions to overpower the "strongest impulses of self-love"? Smith answers that it is not benevolence itself; rather, it is something stronger: "It is reason, principle, conscience, the inhabitant of the breast, the man within, the great judge and arbiter of our conduct" (TMS, 137). I think Smith has in mind three separate levels of explanation in this passage. The first level represents the first answer we give when someone questions our actions or asks us why we judged the way we did: we justify ourselves on the basis of "reason" or "principle," which for Smith reflects the general rules of morality that we have formed and adopted on the basis of our experience. When pressed about the justification of these general rules, we fall back on "conscience," or what we presume all people will know in their hearts to be right or wrong. If we are then concerned to know how our conscience can know right from wrong, Smith's answer to us is his third and final level of explanation: the conscience is informed by the impartial spectator or "the man within"—it is his opinion that constitutes the promptings of our conscience and hence establishes the standards of moral behavior and judgment.[5]

Thus Smith thinks that moral judgments are not in the first instance founded on general rules. Rather, the general rules themselves are founded on the individual experiences each of us has and the information regarding those experiences we have shared with each other (TMS, 159, §8). The general rules that we form on the basis of this experience become the rules of thumb by which our conscience—that is, our impartial spectator—judges. "Our continual observations upon the conduct of others, insensibly lead us to form to ourselves certain general rules concerning what is fit and proper either to be done or to be avoided" (TMS, 159). We should note that Smith says this happens "insensibly." Although the resulting general rules are rules to be sure, we have not deliberately or a priori worked out a system of ethics that then becomes the basis on which we judge. They are rules bound up in our judgment as the word "judgment" is used in another, perhaps more everyday, sense. Think for a moment of any complicated task you have mastered—say, driving in traffic. How do you know whether you have enough time to pull out into traffic right now? How do you know if you will have to move into the left-hand lane to avoid merging traffic? How do you know if you are driving too fast for the present

---

[5] See Haakonssen (1996), 151.

conditions? The decisions we make in these and numberless other similar cases we usually relegate to the vague category of "judgment," thinking that one has good judgment if one makes no or few mistakes, bad judgment otherwise. How is it that we are able to judge these cases? A plausible explanation is that we have formed general rules on the basis of the many relevant experiences we have had in the past. When we made mistakes in the past, we amended or rejected previous rules, and when our rules served us well, we retained and fixed them in our minds. All this happens largely unconsciously—or, as Smith would say, "insensibly"—but it nevertheless happens, and the habits we develop from previous experience operate as much like rules as any that would have been deliberately constructed.[6]

Because the rules are based on past experience and the lessons we have drawn from it, our ability to interpret the situations in which we find ourselves and our ability to select and apply the relevant rules properly—what together constitute our moral judgment—is a skill that admits of degrees of better or worse. Like driving in traffic, this skill is honed by practice, and some people are better than others at employing it. In this case, "better" refers to how well a person can execute the impartial spectator procedure, a process that, as we saw in Chapter 1, encompasses the ability to adopt imaginatively the position of another person and flesh out as completely as possible that person's perspective from which to judge. To a somewhat lesser extent, this moral judgment will also be susceptible to instruction from others, but the help others can give one is limited—in the way that, say, a person can learn only so much about sailing from a book or an instructor; most of what goes into being a sailor one learns by sailing. I think Smith has something like this in mind when he speaks of the general moral rules we take to heart on the basis of our experience.[7] Mistakes and successes—which are determined on the basis of the approbation or disapprobation of other spectators or, eventually, of the impartial

---

[6] For a thorough discussion of judgment in general and of Smith's conception of it in particular, see Fleischacker (1999), Chapter 3; see also Otteson (forthcoming).

[7] This is one reason I resist Charles Griswold's claim that Smith is implicitly "protreptic" in TMS, meaning that he subtly intends to encourage virtue in his readers by covertly teaching them the benefits of acting virtuously. See Griswold (1999), 49 and passim. Compare TMS, 307, §5. See also my review of Griswold's book (Otteson, November 2000).

spectator—lead us insensibly to form habits of judgment in terms of which we judge our behavior in particular cases. This, for Smith, is the human conscience: the silent judgment of the man within the breast, a judgment that is passed on the basis of the observations made in the past about what he has found to be praiseworthy or blameworthy motives and behaviors. The sentiment of guilt we have when we have behaved badly is a result of our awareness, however dim, that this man disapproves; the sentiment of joy, from the awareness that he approves.[8]

*Self-Examination and the Authority of Conscience*
When asked why they obey these general rules they have unconsciously developed on the basis of past experience, people will tend to think that it is because these rules reflect transcendent rules of morality. If we wish to inquire further why they think that, most people will be unable to answer: they will often think that the rules are simply self-evident. But Smith has given us an explanation. They think those rules are transcendently right because they embody what an impartial spectator would approve of. People have become so used to recognizing and accepting some rules of conduct that they no longer are aware (if they ever were) that they are approved by the impartial spectator procedure. That does not mean, however, that they regard them as questionable or as lacking justification. In fact, they frequently regard obedience to the rules as their duty. Smith thinks that what we call a sense of duty is simply our regard for these rules.

Now the question remains why we obey these rules. Whence do they derive their authority over us—such authority, in fact, that we can come to regard it our duty to obey them? Smith's answer has three components, or, rather, he thinks there are three reasons that conspire to strengthen the authority, or what people commonly take to be the authority, these rules have over us. First, they are compelling to us because we ourselves played a crucial role in developing them: they are a result of induction we performed on our own experiences. These are not rules that were given to us by another person or by a legislative body. In a real sense, they are our own rules, which hence, as Smith

---

[8] See Smith's striking and vivid description of the "pangs of an affrighted conscience" that "haunt the guilty" (TMS, 118–19). See also TMS, 65, 84–5, and 333.

says, "carry along with them the most evident badges of this authority" (TMS, 165). The authority he has in mind here is our own. We find these rules sensible and obligatory because we regard them as rules we gave ourselves. Second, these rules are reflected and enforced by others. Each of us has developed these rules on his own, not only on the basis of his own natural attractions and aversions, which result from the impartial spectator procedure, but also on the basis of the sentiments of others he has observed engaging in the same procedure. In our casual conversations and interactions with others—through our "free communication of sentiments and opinions" (TMS, 337)— we exchange information about the way we are inclined to judge all manner of people and events, and each exchange becomes a datum of experience that influences the shape of our general rules of morality. The general rules, then, can be seen on the one hand as the result of each individual's contribution to his own code of behavior and on the other hand as the joint product of all members of the community. The latter aspect, the communal endorsement of the general rules, gives them further authority over us and inclines us to see them as transcendent obligations on us.

Third and finally, Smith thinks at least a few of these rules are obeyed because people come to view them as what Smith thinks they truly are: manifestations of God's will. Smith thinks that the central rules of morality, as they are internalized in each of us as his conscience and as they are endorsed by those around us, enjoy the status of duties for us. The more often we have obeyed them and the longer we have believed them, the stronger is our sense that we are duty-bound to follow them, and the more easily can they exercise control over our actions in practice. As they are habitually consulted, referred to, and obeyed, and as they are passed on from one community member to the next, from one generation to the next, we start to regard them as sacred rules of morality. Indeed, we come to think that no one who flouts or disobeys these sacred rules can have integrity or be trusted. "Without this sacred regard to general rules, there is no man whose conduct can be much depended upon. It is this which constitutes the most essential difference between a man of principle and honour and a worthless fellow" (TMS, 163). What makes a person virtuous is his ability to obey these sacred rules of morality unfailingly.

So what allows the virtuous man to follow these rules even when, say, he is in a sour or contrary mood? Why does he not greet his friend with rudeness when in such a state? "What renders you incapable of such a rudeness, is nothing but a regard to the general rules of civility and hospitality, which prohibit it" (TMS, 163). Smith explains why these rules direct us as they do:

That habitual reverence which your former experience has taught you for these, enables you to act, upon all such occasions, with nearly equal propriety, and hinders those inequalities of temper, to which all men are subject, from influencing your conduct in any very sensible degree. (Ibid.)

Thus the truly virtuous person is the one who has so thoroughly adopted the opinions of the impartial spectator as the general rules of morality by which he leads his life that he regards them as sacred and inviolable. We are pushed to this point, Smith thinks, simply by nature, that is, by our natural commerce with others. But Smith thinks there is another step to take.

This reverence is still further enhanced by an opinion which is first impressed by nature, and afterwards confirmed by reasoning and philosophy, that those important rules of morality are the commands and laws of the Deity, who will finally reward the obedient, and punish the transgressors of their duty. (Ibid.)

Smith considers it a matter of historical fact that "religion, even in its rudest form, gave a sanction to the rules of morality, long before the age of artificial reasoning and philosophy" (TMS, 164). The sacredness of the general rules of morality was considered as issuing from the gods, so that transgression of them was regarded as a punishable sin. Fear of the wrath of the gods thus gave these rules an almost absolute authority over the lives of men. But even in Smith's enlightened, philosophical age, one can see that the reverence these people paid to the general rules was not unfounded. These rules can be seen—by Smith, that is— as the result of various forces of nature intermingling with the free exchanges of human beings, which means that they must indeed be manifestations of God's will. Smith's calling them "natural" implies a connection to or extension from God.[9]

---

[9] Smith's theory of the way a society's moral standards are gradually internalized in each of that society's members, becoming a personal conscience embodied in the voice of the impartial spectator, could provide one plausible explanation for where our so-called moral intuitions might come from and why people take them to be authoritative.

In Chapter 6, we explore in more detail how Smith thinks the general rules of morality not only are regarded as transcendent, but why they should be so regarded. Here it is sufficient to see that the fact that people regard these rules as manifestations of God's will gives them substantial authority over and above the already significant authority that they enjoy by being considered rules generated by each individual and reflected by the members of his society.[10]

We must still address Smith's notion that we divide ourselves into two persons when judging our own conduct: one representing the impartial spectator, the other representing ourselves as we actually are. This for Smith is no metaphysical question of the relation between mind and body; there is no mysterious body-switching or mind-splitting going on. Instead, he is referring to what he takes to be the perfectly pedestrian phenomenon of self-examination. It hinges on his claim that there are two points at which we can judge our own actions: first, when we are about to act; second, after we have acted. The distinction between these two opportunities to judge, and the separate, often opposing, judgments we are inclined to make at the two opportunities, is the basis on which Smith claims that we divide ourselves into two. "When we are about to act," Smith writes, "the eagerness of passion will seldom allow us to consider what we are doing, with the candour of an indifferent

[10] Objectivity is standardly considered an important virtue of moral, legal, political, and what we might call interpersonal reasoning: moral judgments must be disinterested; judges and juries are supposed to weigh the evidence without bias; politicians are to consider all interests equally; people should deal with one another fairly and justly. In each of these cases, some kind of objectivity is and has long been necessary before one's dealings with and judgments of others could enjoy approval from others. Although recently some have begun to question the value, or even possibility, of objectivity—Richard Rorty comes to mind—most people in most cases still, I think, would agree that they expect to be treated and judged by others objectively (though people might have different notions about what precisely constitutes objectivity). An interesting question is why people prize objectivity so highly. As we saw in Chapter 1, Smith's discussion of the development of conscience can afford us what I think is an intriguing theory about the source of our attachment to objectivity. In the process of developing rules of behavior, our desire for mutual sympathy of sentiments impels us to judge our own behavior from the perspective of a disinterested third party; Smith argues that the marketplace of morals encourages each of us to habituate himself to judging from this impartial perspective and to internalize the judgments formed when he adopts this perspective. This habituation and internalization become for us, Smith thinks, the voice of an impartial spectator who occupies the position of the voice of our personal consciences—and could be the source of our general insistence on objectivity.

person" (TMS, 157). The sentiments that have reached a sufficient pitch to move us to action are often violent, and they prevent us from employing the impartial spectator procedure effectively. Smith cites Malebranche as an authority who held that the passions "all justify themselves, and seem reasonable and proportioned to their objects, as long as we continue to feel them" (ibid.).[11] We sometimes know, Smith thinks, even at the moment we begin to act, what the impartial spectator thinks of what we do, but the din of the present passions drown out his calm, reasonable voice.

After we have acted, however, the passions that drove us subside, and we can once again assume the perspective of the impartial spectator with equanimity and poise. It is then frequently the case that the "man of to-day" can see the actions of the "man of yesterday" for what they were—and the man of today is frequently embarrassed or ashamed at the way the man of yesterday behaved. Smith thinks this can result in a kind of self-deception. We do not take pleasure in viewing our previous actions for what they were, and so we may decide not to do so. We pretend not to know what an impartial spectator thinks of our behavior, rather "than see our own behaviour under so disagreeable an aspect" (TMS, 158). We thus carry on with two separate levels of knowledge: the one, which is conscious, is what we want to believe about ourselves; the other, subconscious but always lurking just below and readily accessed, is the steadfast voice of the impartial spectator. These are the two selves Smith has in mind when he says we divide ourselves into two, and the case of self-deceit shows how he envisions doing it. It is as if we have two streams of consciousness vying for our attention, and we must choose one. Yet even as we choose one, we are never completely unaware of or unaffected by the other.

Now some readers, and I am one of them, might be disappointed that Smith does not delve further into the theory of mind that must underlie such an account. Smith does not explain how it is possible to have two streams of consciousness between which one must choose— or, indeed, who or what it is that chooses between them. He does not, for example, say that the soul has three parts, one always trying to tame

---

[11] The passage from Malebranche that Smith has in mind is in *De la recherche de la vérité* (1992 [1674–75]), Volume 11.

and guide the other two.[12] In fact, he offers no metaphysical conception of the soul at all. But we must remind ourselves that Smith is specifically trying to avoid metaphysical speculation. His goal here is only
to explain what happens when we judge ourselves, not to explain how
that is possible. Smith is willing to let his theory stand or fall on the basis
of people's actual experience. The reader can judge for himself: Does
it ever happen to you that you choose to act in a way that you somehow know is wrong? Do you have the ability to step out of yourself in
your imagination and reflect on your own motives and actions, even in
the midst of having certain motives and acting in certain ways? Smith
thinks that everyone will answer "yes" to these questions—however it
is metaphysically possible to do so—and it is on the foundation of
that fact that he builds his theory of conscience.[13] The conscience is,
then, an empirical fact: it is developed over time as a result of social and
psychological factors in each of us, and it culminates in the internalization of a common—perhaps universal[14]—standard of judgment, the
impartial spectator.

## Hume, Smith, and Cause and Effect

Hume had argued earlier that reason was unable to discern a connection between cause and effect, which means, strictly speaking, that
reason is unable to discover the remote consequences of any proposed
courses of action.[15] We could speculate on the remote consequences,
but this speculation would be based on inferences we make from our
past experience—a process that Hume argued was nonrational. This
raises a difficulty with Hume's account of moral judgments, which
comes to the fore when Hume argues that rational considerations of
utility are the basis of moral approbation or disapprobation. If reason

---

[12] I have Plato's metaphor of the charioteer with the black and white horses in mind.
T. D. Campbell and D. D. Raphael have both argued that Smith's analysis lends itself
quite readily to Freud's analysis of the mind into ego, superego, and id. See Campbell
(1971), 149–51 and Raphael (1985), 41–43.

[13] See Griswold (1999), 104–109.

[14] One is right to see here foreshadowings of Kant: Smith's impartial spectator gets transformed in Kant into the universal voice of the rationally autonomous self-legislator.
And the similarity is not coincidental. Kant was an interested reader of Smith, apparently even referring to him in correspondence as his "*Liebling.*" For discussion, see
Haakonssen (1996), 148–53.

[15] In 1E, especially Sections IV and V, 15–37.

cannot determine the remote consequences of actions, then any considerations of utility that would give rise to moral judgments must be based on nonrational inferences made from past experience. This conclusion presents a problem for Hume not only because it contradicts what he says about reason's role in passing moral judgments,[16] but also because it is difficult to see how considerations of *future* utility could determine present moral judgments if such considerations are nonrational. Hume argues emphatically that it is by reflecting on what one by reason determines will be the future consequences of proposed actions that one arrives at a consideration of utility that can prompt a moral judgment:

One principal foundation of moral praise being supposed to lie in the usefulness of any quality or action: it is evident, that *reason* must enter for a considerable share in all decisions of this kind; since nothing but that faculty can instruct us in the tendency of qualities and actions, and point out their beneficial consequences to society and to their possessor. (2E, 82; Hume's italics)

His argument here thus appears inconsistent with the argument in the first *Enquiry* concerning our knowledge of cause and effect. There he thought that our expectations about future effects from present causes were based on past experience of causes and their effects, and he made no claims—indeed, his argument was to show it is not possible to make such claims—about reason's ability to discern the future. We only know the past:

In a word, then, every effect is a distinct event from its cause. It could not, therefore, be discovered in the cause, and the first invention or conception of it, *a priori*, must be entirely arbitrary. . . . These ultimate springs and principles are totally shut up from human curiosity and enquiry. (1E, 19; Hume's italics)

In the second *Enquiry*, however, not only does he argue that reason can discern future utilitarian or disutilitarian effects from present causes, but he also grounds the moral judgment on precisely such discernments. In the first *Enquiry*, Hume thought that our expectations about the future were sufficient guides despite their nonrationality; yet in the

---

[16] See 1E, 82–88.

second *Enquiry* he relies on no such instincts. When it comes to considerations of utility, apparently, a more rigorous process of discovery is required.[17]

Although Smith seems to accept Hume's analysis of our knowledge of cause and effect,[18] I think Smith's understanding of moral judgment can nevertheless avoid this tension that Hume faces. Hume runs into the problem because he thinks that utility is ultimately what gives rise to our moral approbation and disapprobation. We need to discover the remote consequences of actions before we are able to approve or disapprove of them because in so doing we are discovering their utility or disutility. But Smith sees himself as correcting this problem in Hume's account by arguing that considerations of utility do not underlie our moral judgments. Such judgments are made, rather, on the basis of their propriety, which is determined by the approval of the impartial spectator:

> The same ingenious and agreeable author [i.e., Hume] who first explained why utility pleases, has been so struck with this view of things, as to resolve our whole approbation of virtue into a perception of this species of beauty which results from the appearance of utility. . . . But I still affirm, that it is not the view of this utility or hurtfulness which is either the first or principal source of our approbation and disapprobation. These sentiments are no doubt enhanced and enlivened by the perception of the beauty or deformity which results from this utility or hurtfulness. But still, I say, they are originally and essentially different from this perception. (TMS, 188)[19]

The general rules that Smith thinks regulate our conduct are not products of considerations of future utility; they are instead solely inferences based on past experience. It is true that in public debates about moral issues, "we frequently appeal to [the general rules of morality] as to the standards of judgment"; they are "upon these occasions commonly cited as the ultimate foundations of what is just and unjust in human conduct" (TMS, 160).[20] Smith argues, however, that this circumstance has led "several very eminent authors"—he no doubt means

---

[17] For an interpretation of Hume that claims to resolve this tension, see Livingston (1984), especially Chapter 7.

[18] See TMS, 194 and Smith's "History of Astronomy," EPS, 40–41.

[19] See also TMS, 160 and 179–93 passim.

[20] But see also TMS, 89, §8.

Hume—to the mistaken conclusion that moral reasoning begins with a universal rule or principle and then proceeds to judge particular acts or traits in terms of it. This of course was Hume's strategy: general utility is the universal principle or standard of morality, and we judge characters and actions in terms of it.

But this gets the cart before the horse, Smith thinks. "The general rules which determine what actions are, and what are not, the objects of each of those sentiments, can be formed no other way than by observing what actions actually and in fact excite them" (TMS, 160). Because, then, no future considerations of utility constitute the foundation of moral judgments according to Smith, Smith can avoid the problem Hume faces in explaining how such considerations can be the basis of judgments we make when these same considerations involve principles that are, on Hume's own analysis, impossible for human reason to discern. Unlike Hume, Smith thinks that the rules we form on the basis of past experience are sufficient to allow us to make accurate moral judgments about present cases. On Smith's conception of the process of making moral judgments, one does not need the precise knowledge of the cause-and-effect relation that Hume had demonstrated to be so elusive. The result of a Smithian moral judgment is instead a pronouncement on the *propriety* of an act or trait, that is, a pronouncement on whether the act or trait in question is suitable to the situation that excites it. The object of the Smithian judgment is thus the situation itself—which includes not only the character or trait in question but also the other internal facts of the person principally concerned and the external circumstances in which he acted. In this way, Smithian judgments are "backward-looking":[21] they are judgments about the suitability of an agent's action to the past situation that excited it. They are not, as Hume conceives them, forward-looking, which for Hume means that they must take into consideration a hypothetical or imagined future state of affairs. It is precisely this implication of Hume's theory—namely, that the moral judgment entails an estimate of future utility or disutility—that runs him afoul of his earlier analysis, and it is precisely the "backward-looking" nature of Smith's theory that steers him clear of this difficulty. Smith is right to trumpet his discovery:

---

[21] This phrase is Knud Haakonssen's. See Haakonssen (1981), 47.

But that this fitness, this happy contrivance of any production of art, should often be more valued, than the very end for which it was intended; and that the exact adjustment of the means for attaining any conveniency or pleasure, should frequently be more regarded, than that very conveniency or pleasure, in the attainment of which their whole merit would seem to consist, has not, so far as I know, been yet taken notice of by any body. That this however is very frequently the case, may be observed in a thousand instances, both in the most frivolous and in the most important concerns of human life. (TMS, 179–80) [22]

## II. Smith's Picture of Human Nature

We have already discussed the fact that Smith thinks human beings have a natural fellow-feeling for one another, that, in fact, the happiness of others is "necessary" to them (TMS, 9). We have not discussed, however, what "necessary" means in this context. Once we have understood this, we shall understand why it is that Smith thinks we engage in the impartial spectator procedure at all. In other words, we shall see what Smith thinks drives people to be moral. Smith believes that a few fundamental, innate principles in human nature operate in connection with various environmental circumstances—particularly intercourse with other people—to produce people who are susceptible to making moral judgments and amenable to altering their behavior due to moral exhortation from others. Two things about these principles of human nature are crucial on Smith's account. First, they are part of human nature in the sense that all human beings have them to some extent. Second, they manifest themselves as inclinations or sensibilities, not necessarily as specific rules or behaviors.

### *Sympathy, Self-Partiality, and Sociability*

The first and most important of the principles of human nature that Smith discusses is what he calls the desire for mutual sympathy. We take great pleasure, Smith thinks, in knowing that our sentiments either reflect or are reflected by the sentiments of other people: "nothing pleases us more than to observe in other men a fellow-feeling with all the emotions of our own breast; nor are we ever so much shocked as

[22] See also TMS, 20, §4 and 35, §4.

by the appearance of the contrary" (TMS, 13). For Smith, this is an irreducible pleasure; it cannot be explained in terms of anything else, although it in turn explains many of the behaviors in which we engage. Perhaps the most important social phenomenon it explains is the impartial spectator procedure. We saw in Chapter 1 that we are inclined for the first time to engage in this procedure when we realize that others judge us, often with partiality and without the great concern we take in ourselves. But that is only part of the story, for this realization by itself is not sufficient to get us to do anything. There must be a desire we attach or value we hold relevant to this realization that provokes us to act. Smith argues that the relevant desire is for mutual sympathy. We naturally find it disagreeable and unpleasant when our sentiments are not reflected by anyone else. It makes us feel alone, which, for a reason we shall shortly address, is a horrible and intolerable feeling.[23] The desire to avoid this intolerable feeling leads us to strive imaginatively to enter into the sentiments of others. In fact, this desire leads us to do two things. On the one hand, it leads us to temper our own sentiments so that they more closely resemble those of a disinterested spectator; on the other hand, it leads us to make an effort to have a complete and sensitive understanding of the situation of others, so as to make our judgment of them as accurate as possible. Both of these actions are comprehended in the impartial spectator procedure.

Smith merely presumes a few characteristics of human nature without argument. Paramount among these is that we naturally take a greater interest in our own situation than in that of anyone else. The interest we take in others varies directly with their closeness to us, or, what amounts to the same, our concern for others is naturally engaged only to the degree to which we know them. In addition to considering this characteristic natural to all human beings, Smith thinks it is as it should be, for several reasons. The first reason is this:

Every man is, no doubt, by nature first and principally recommended to his own care; and as he is fitter to take care of himself than of any other person, it is fit and right that it should be so. Every man, therefore, is much more deeply interested in whatever immediately concerns himself, than in what concerns any other man. (TMS, 82–83)

[23] See TMS, 84.

We are better fitted to take care of ourselves than we are of anyone else because we know more about ourselves than we do about anyone else. We are more likely to know our interests, passions, inclinations, and abilities than is anyone else; after ourselves, we are most familiar with our family members, then with our friends, our acquaintances, and finally strangers. Thus the descending degree of concern we naturally feel matches our familiarity with others and suits our ability to take care of them. There have been those "whining and melancholy moralists," Smith writes, who have endeavored to discourage us from considering ourselves first and foremost above everyone else and who have tried to encourage us to consider the remotest souls with the same intensity as that with which we consider ourselves.[24] But Smith thinks it is both fruitless and pointless to entreat people to this end. It is fruitless because whatever behavior we could muster that would display concern for others equal to what we have for ourselves would be artificial and affected: our nature prevents us from truly considering ourselves just one of the many, with no special significance. Experience with other people shows us that other people do not consider us to be as significant as we consider ourselves, a realization that triggers the impartial spectator procedure. Nevertheless, we are and always will be the most important person to ourselves. Moreover, Smith argues that it would be pointless to encourage people to be so concerned with the interests of people with whom they have no connection because they are not in a position to help such people. It would produce only anxiety in them; it would help those others not at all.[25]

Smith argues that it seems "wisely ordered by Nature" (TMS, 140) that we should consider our own interests first, then those of our family, then friends, and so on, with a descending degree of intensity. This is wise, Smith thinks, because it is necessary both for the preservation of the species and the maintenance of society. If it should turn out that we valued everyone's interests equally, then we should take no particular interest in, for example, caring for our children, any more than for any other person. But it takes no keen intellect to see that this would be disastrous for the preservation of our species, given

---

[24] TMS, 139–40.
[25] For a discussion of the connection between our familiarity with others and our duties to help them that relies in part on Smith, see Otteson (July 2000).

the enormous care and concern human infants and children require before they are able to fend for themselves. We all have limited abilities, and our resources—including not only our money but also our time and energy—are scarce. If our abilities and resources were equally divided among everyone whom we could help, the effect would be simply to dissipate our efforts, not to actually help anyone.[26] Because communities likewise require considerable attention and maintenance, an equal concern for everyone, including those of other communities, would lead to the dissolution of such communities, which could then lead us into something resembling a Hobbesian state of nature (TMS, 86). Thankfully, then, nature has made it so that our natural concern for others diminishes as its object recedes from us, and, Smith thinks, it is a good thing too.

Yet our desire for mutual sympathy always beckons us to establish and maintain amicable relations with those around us. Thus despite the fact that the interest we take in others is limited by our familiarity with them, we strive to interact with them on terms that are congenial to both of us. The tool that allows us to do this is, as we have said, mutual employment of the impartial spectator procedure. Now another feature of human nature according to Smith is that we naturally desire to be praiseworthy rather than just praised, and that we fear being blameworthy more than we fear merely being blamed. This is a controversial claim, and Smith offers disappointingly little argument for it. He for the most part speaks as if it is another irreducible fact about human nature: though some people may seem to seek praise and avoid blame, their real desires are to merit the praise and to avoid deserving blame, and insofar as these people seek the former goals at the expense of the latter, they will be restive, dissatisfied, and unhappy.[27] Smith writes that there is also a natural desire for receiving praise and a natural aversion to receiving blame, but he thinks that if those were the only things motivating us, we simply would not be fit for society. Smith does not elaborate on why such a motivation would make men unfit for society. Instead, he proceeds to explain why a

---

[26] Economist David H. Miller argues that the most important scarce resource that must be "economized" (i.e., conserved) is love. See his "To Economize on Love: An Alternative Approach to Social Philosophy and Economy," available at http://www.foresight.org/essays/econlove.html.

[27] TMS, 113–134.

challenge like the one offered in Plato's story of the ring of Gyges[28] is not a real problem for human beings constituted as they actually are:

> The man who has broke through all those measures of conduct, which can alone render him agreeable to mankind, though he should have the most perfect assurance that what he had done was forever to be concealed from every human eye, it is all to no purpose. When he looks back upon it, he finds that he can enter into none of the motives which influenced it. He is abashed and confounded at the thoughts of it, and necessarily feels a very high degree of that shame which he would be exposed to, if his actions should ever come to be generally known. (TMS, 118)[29]

Smith's response does not seem to constitute much of an argument. It seems, rather, to stipulate a certain characteristic of human nature— namely, that we desire praiseworthiness and wish to avoid blameworthiness, not just praise and blame—and then simply to circumvent the ring of Gyges problem altogether.[30]

I think we can piece together an argument, however, that, once fleshed out, will illuminate another important aspect of what Smith thinks is the natural motivation to engage in and guide one's behavior by the impartial spectator procedure. When discussing man's desire to be worthy of praise and not blame, Smith writes, "Nature, accordingly, has endowed him, not only with a desire of being approved of, but with a desire of being what ought to be approved of; *or of being what he himself approves of in other men*" (TMS, 117; my italics). I think the italicized phrase is the kernel of Smith's argument. If we think for a moment of what it is that we praise in others, it is certainly not the appearance of virtue masking a reality of vice. We do not praise others, or we do not wish to praise others, for their ability to deceive us into thinking that they are virtuous when they are not. On the contrary, when we are aware of it we usually condemn such dissembling as immoral. Thus when we form the general rules of morality, one of the principles by which we do so is that we approve of praiseworthiness and disapprove of blameworthiness, not the mere appearance of either.

---

[28] *Republic*, 359b–361d.

[29] See also TMS, 137.

[30] Charles Griswold thinks that this is a deep problem for Smith. See Griswold (1999), 129. I address Griswold's concerns in Chapter 3.

After stating that a person who broke the general rules of morality would feel guilty even if never discovered, Smith writes that this person "anticipates the contempt and derision from which nothing saves him but the ignorance of those he lives with. He still feels that he is the natural object of these sentiments, and still trembles at the thought of what he would suffer, if they were ever actually exerted against him" (TMS, 118). This is a telling passage. What might he suffer if he were discovered? Perhaps physical punishment, but what is more important for Smith is the contempt and derision others would have for him. They would judge him unfavorably, and he would know that he deserves the unfavorable judgment: the result would be that he would know that no one would sympathize with the sentiments he had when he did what he did. Thus, I think, the desire for praiseworthiness reduces to the desire for mutual sympathy of sentiments. To be precise, in this case it is the desire for an *imagined* sympathy of sentiments that drives us—a testament, I think, to the power Smith believes this desire holds over us. A corrupt person knows that if others knew him for what he is, they would judge him unfavorably because they would not sympathize with his motives. Because it is unpleasant and disagreeable to know that others do not sympathize with one—that is, because it is unpleasant even to imagine an antipathy of sentiments—one would therefore strive not only to avoid blame but also to avoid blameworthiness. Indeed, Smith argues that the ability to achieve mutual sympathy of sentiments is one of the main things about poverty that makes it so disagreeable:

The poor man, on the contrary, is ashamed of his poverty. He feels that it either places him out of the sight of mankind, or, that if they take any notice of him, they have, however, scarce any fellow-feeling with the misery and distress which he suffers. He is mortified upon both accounts; for though to be overlooked, and to be disapproved of, are things entirely different, yet as obscurity covers us from the daylight of honour and approbation, to feel that we are taken no notice of, necessarily damps the most agreeable hope, and disappoints the most ardent desire, of human nature. The poor man goes out and comes in unheeded, and when in the midst of a crowd is in the same obscurity as if shut up in his own hovel. (TMS, 51)[31]

In scenarios like that supposed in Plato's story of the ring of Gyges, there would in fact be no mutual sympathy of sentiments at all because

---

[31] See also TMS, 84–5, 117–19, and 333.

the spectator's imagined sentiments would not match the actor's actual sentiments. Because we seek actual sympathy of sentiments, however, we hence have a strong incentive to strive to be praiseworthy, not just praised.

It turns out, then, that the desires to be worthy of praise and not to deserve blame are not irreducible facts of human nature; they can instead be explained in terms of a desire that is irreducible in Smithian human nature, the desire for mutual sympathy. Now Smith has already argued that in practice the way we determine what motives and actions deserve praise or blame are those that are approved of or disapproved of, respectively, by the impartial spectator. Thus Smith can argue that we are "by nature" (TMS, 128) impelled to adopt the perspective of the impartial spectator when judging because it is only in this way that we can regulate our behavior so that we deserve praise and not blame— which in turn satisfies our desire to enjoy the pleasure we receive from the knowledge that others sympathize or would sympathize with our sentiments.

The other characteristic Smith thinks is innate in human nature that is crucial for Smith's moral theory is sociability. Human beings can exist nowhere but in society (TMS, 85). Smith writes that we "can subsist only in society" because "[a]ll the members of human society stand in need of each others assistance" (ibid.). Smith thinks that two of the most primitive drives in us are for self-preservation and security, and given our generally weak constitution and the limited scope of our intellect—not to mention our complete defenselessness for several years after birth—we stand under a practical necessity of living with others if we are to survive. As far as Smith is concerned, however, our physical survival is less important than the psychological necessity we have to be members of a community. This necessity is manifested in our overarching desire for mutual sympathy. The person whose sentiments never correspond with those of anyone else leads a wretched and undesirable life. The loneliness to which such a person's unique sentiments confine him places him in an unending, dreadful dilemma. He can either remain in society, in which case he must face daily reminders that no one shares his sentiments; or he can remain in solitude, never enjoying the pleasure that only interactions with other people can provide. Smith describes this lonely state quite vividly:

But solitude is still more dreadful than society. His own thoughts can present him with nothing but what is black, unfortunate, and disastrous, the melancholy forebodings of incomprehensible misery and ruin. The horror of solitude drives him back into society, and he comes again into the presence of mankind, astonished to appear before them, loaded with shame and distracted with fear, in order to supplicate some little protection from the countenance of those very judges, who he knows have already all unanimously condemned him. (TMS, 84–85)

This, I think, indicates what Smith means when he says that the fortunes and happiness of others are necessary to each person. Without the help of and associations with other people, we cannot physically survive or psychologically flourish, and we cannot engage the help or associations of others without taking a sincere interest in their situations. Nature, again thankfully, has constituted us so that before any philosophy or deliberation we are inclined to be interested in others. This inclination makes possible the mutual concern that ultimately, Smith thinks, forms the basis of civil society.

## Summary

We can now tie some of these strands together to get a more complete understanding of Smith's conception of human nature. First, we stand under a practical and psychological necessity of living with other people, of living in society. Barring extraordinary circumstances, we cannot meet all our physical needs for survival on our own, and hence we find ourselves dependent on others to meet at least some of our needs. This requirement, which leads us into communities with others, is a result of two principles that nature has implanted in the breast of all animals, human beings included, namely, self-preservation and security.[32] In addition, the psychological well-being that is peculiar to human beings requires that they have frequent intercourse with others and that they at least on some occasions achieve a sympathy between their own sentiments and that of others.[33] This requirement is a

---

[32] TMS, 77, 87, and 212–13.
[33] Smith even argues that the psychological bonds created between people who share mutual sympathy of sentiments can be stronger than the bonds of biological relation: children love a caring stepfather better than they do their absent biological father (TMS, 220–21, 223).

result of the pleasure we naturally find in knowing that our sentiments enjoy a mutual sympathy and the displeasure we find when no sympathy is achieved. These two fundamental needs of human beings— intercourse with others and mutual sympathy—combine in various ways to create other goals that we find we are thus naturally constituted to seek. For example, Smith writes of an "original desire to please, and an original aversion to offend his brethren" (TMS, 116) with which nature has endowed man. This functions as a corollary of our desire for mutual sympathy: one cannot achieve sympathy with the sentiments of others if one is indifferent to their interests or if one offends them. Similarly, Smith speaks of a strong desire we have "to feel how each other is affected, to penetrate into each other's bosoms, and to observe the sentiments and affections which really subsist there" (TMS, 337). This "passion to discover the real sentiments of others" (ibid.) is a necessary first step to achieving mutual sympathy and is the reverse side of another natural desire we have, namely, "The desire of being believed"—which Smith suggests might even be "the instinct upon which is founded the faculty of speech" (TMS, 336).[34] All these native drives lead us not only to form societies but also to create the means necessary to maintain society, and they culminate in the tool that forms the centerpiece of Smith's moral theory, the impartial spectator procedure.

Smith mentions in TMS several other characteristics that he thinks are innate in human nature but that are of less importance for our discussion. They are things that Smith takes to be objects of universal human attraction, like being loved, and objects of universal human aversion, like being hated.[35] He also describes various passions that he thinks everyone has from time to time and to varying degrees, like resentment, envy, malice, and vanity.[36] Smith does not use his claim that these are natural human traits to extend or develop his theory

---

[34] In WN, Smith speculates that our natural "propensity to truck, barter, and exchange one thing for another" might "be the necessary consequence of the faculties of reason and speech" (WN, 25). If so, then, by the argument given here, even our propensity to truck, barter, and exchange might ultimately bear some deep connection to our desire for mutual sympathy of sentiments.

[35] See TMS, 113.

[36] See TMS, 34, 244, 42, and 255, respectively. On several occasions Smith indicates that the presence of envy in a spectator can distort the spectator's judgment, though he does not explain exactly why or how. See TMS, 44, 45, 46, 51, 140, 226, 246, and 250.

of moral judgment; rather, he uses them as confirmations of his theory that we judge moral propriety and impropriety by consulting the impartial spectator. That is, he discusses these and other human passions with an eye towards showing that the degrees of the passions that we approve of in various circumstances are strictly in accordance with what the impartial spectator endorses—and hence that the judgment of the impartial spectator is *the* standard against which we come to judge all expressions of human emotion.[37] In fact, much of the bulk of TMS is taken up with Smith demonstrating that his theory can account for many disparate phenomena of human social life. These discussions are of less importance for us here since they do not develop Smith's theory, but they are important for other reasons: first, an examination of them would be necessary for determining whether Smith's theory is overall an adequate explanation of our moral judgments; second, they play a crucial role in developing the teleological and normative character of Smith's conception of the human system of morality. This second issue constitutes the theme of Chapter 6: it is not just coincidence that we have the innate features we do; we have been purposely designed this way by a benevolent god (which is why we should be "thankful"). One point bears mentioning here, however: these discussions show that Smith believes that the various characteristics one finds in human nature do not automatically lead to specific behaviors or specific rules of conduct. They are interests, inclinations, proclivities; but at every turn they are, Smith argues, regulated by the impartial spectator's judgment of what are proper or improper motives or behaviors under the circumstances. This indeterminacy will play a crucial role in our discussion of Smith's notion of unintended orders and suborders later on.

## The "Adam Smith Problem": A Prelude

We must address a final issue in this section. There is one principle that Smith ascribes to human nature that is something of a maverick: the continual desire for a better station in life. Smith makes extensive use of this principle in *The Wealth of Nations*. For example:

[37] See TMS, 262.

But the principle which prompts to save, is the desire for bettering our condition, a desire which, though generally calm and dispassionate, comes with us from the womb, and never leaves us till we go into the grave. In the whole interval which separates those two moments, there is scarce perhaps a single instant in which any man is so perfectly and completely satisfied with his situation as to be without any wish of alteration or improvement, of any kind. An augmentation of fortune is the means by which the greater part of men propose and wish to better their condition. (WN, 341)

Here is another:

The uniform, constant, and uninterrupted effort of every man to better his condition, the principle from which publick and national, as well as private opulence is originally derived, is frequently powerful enough to maintain the natural progress of things toward improvement, in spite both of the extravagance of government, and the greatest errors of administration. (WN, 343)

Let me cite a few others. "In the midst of all the exactions of government, this capital has been silently and gradually accumulated by the private frugality and good conduct of individuals, by their universal, continual, and uninterrupted effort to better their own condition" (WN, 345). Elsewhere Smith speaks of the "natural effort of every individual to better his own condition," a principle that is "capable of carrying on the society to wealth and prosperity" and "of surmounting a hundred impertinent obstructions with which the folly of human laws too often incumbers its operations" (WN, 540). Finally, when Smith is criticizing the economic theory of François Quesnay, he writes that Quesnay

seems not to have considered that in the political body, the natural effort which every man is continually making to better his own condition, is a principle of preservation capable of preventing and correcting, in many respects, the bad effects of a political œconomy, in some degree, both partial and oppressive. (WN, 674)[38]

This characteristic of human nature, Smith thinks, is responsible for, among other things, the fact that if people are left to their own

---

[38] See also WN, 405, where Smith suggests that people begin to act on the natural desire of bettering their condition only after they feel secure in their property and possessions.

devices—that is, if they are free from government interference—they will, in Smith's famous phrase, "truck, barter, and exchange one thing for another" for their mutual advantage (WN, 25). On the basis of this claim, Smith proceeds to argue that markets, the general name for the opportunity to exchange privately owned goods, are not only the most efficient means of increasing the wealth of nations, but also reflect and are the result of natural human liberty—the result, that is, of allowing "the obvious and simple system of natural liberty [to establish] itself of its own accord" (WN, 687). If we had no universal desire to better our condition, then Smith could not argue that markets are natural. Smith thinks that government policies and systems of political economies are artificial, that is, deliberately created as systems; markets, on the other hand, are natural in the sense that they simply emerge from the associations and exchanges people freely make if they are left to their own devices.

The reason I called this principle of human nature a maverick is that Smith uses it to a substantially lesser degree in TMS than he does in WN, and this difference constitutes a central piece of evidence that the Adam Smith Problem is a real problem. Nowhere in TMS does one find such sweeping and general claims about it like those one finds in WN; and where it does make an appearance, it seems to be put to a somewhat different use. In TMS, Smith speaks of this characteristic of human nature precisely once: he refers to "that great purpose of human life which we call bettering our condition" (TMS, 50). Whereas in WN reference to this characteristic is made repeatedly and forms the foundation of Smith's analysis of our propensity to employ our stock to our own advantage, in TMS it is explained in terms of class distinction and vanity. Raphael and Macfie do not think there is any tension in the two accounts. Though they concede that there is a difference in tone, they maintain that "both books treat the desire to better our condition as natural and proper."[39] Two things seem at first glance to suggest that they have underestimated the difference in Smith's two accounts of this desire. The first is that there is a tremendous difference in the degree to which Smith uses this desire in the two books: in WN,

---

[39] Raphael and Macfie, Introduction to TMS, 9. See also Macfie's extended defense of the unity of Smith's two books in Macfie (1967), Chapters 3–4.

it is treated as if it were the sole motivation people feel, but in TMS it receives at best secondary attention. Perhaps the more important indication, however, is, as I have said, that the desire seems to play a somewhat different role in the two books. Let us look for a moment at the way in which Smith treats this desire in TMS. That will put us in a better position to decide whether there is a tension of any moment and will prepare the way for the more detailed discussion in Chapter 4.

The sole reference in TMS to our desire to better our condition comes in a chapter entitled "Of the origin of Ambition, and of the distinction of Ranks" (TMS, 50–61). As I said in my treatment of Smithian sympathy in Chapter 1, Smith thinks that we are more apt to sympathize with some sentiments we see in others, like joy, than with others, like grief, because the former are agreeable and the latter are not. In Smith's chapter on ambition, he draws out the consequences of this natural aptness to explain the common human social phenomena of ambition and the often related desire to maintain distinctions between ranks or classes of people. Smith argues that, contrary to what one might have thought, people do not pursue riches and wealth because these things supply the necessities of nature—that is, because they serve utilitarian ends. Indeed, "the wages of the meanest labourer can supply [these necessities]" (TMS, 50). Rather, it is at bottom the desire for mutual sympathy that drives us to better our condition. We realize on some level that people prefer and hence are more likely to sympathize with the "social passions" than with the "unsocial passions," so we strive to put ourselves in positions to engage the social passions as much as we can. We find that success in life engages the social passions (and failure, the unsocial passions), so we therefore strive to succeed—and to display our successes publicly. "To be observed, to be attended to, to be taken notice of with sympathy, complacency, and approbation, are all the advantages which we can propose to derive from" the "great purpose of human life which we call bettering our condition" (ibid.).

This is an unusual explanation of why men seek riches, but perhaps a plausible case can be made for it. It seems reasonable to think that at least part of the reason we want wealth is because we enjoy the attention it brings us. It moreover seems reasonable enough to maintain that the attention we give to wealthy people—particularly the fashionably and ostentatiously wealthy[40]—results at least in part from the fact that we admire them because we know that if we were in their shoes we too would enjoy all the attention and adoration they receive. We thus receive a certain vicarious pleasure from observing and pursuing them. If it is true that the food the wealthy eat makes their bellies no fuller than the food the peasants eat (TMS, 50), then it would be implausible to suggest that it is primarily for things like better food that people seek wealth. Elsewhere Smith argues, against Hume, that people do not seek baubles, gewgaws, and trinkets because having them brings their possessors greater utility (TMS, 179–87). On the contrary, Smith argues, all the pains that are required to obtain such things frequently outweigh whatever modest increase in utility they provide. Golden toothpicks, ear-pickers, and machines for cutting the nails are examples of things that require money, and hence labor, to obtain, things that wealthy men in fact spend their money on, but that provide little or no real increase in convenience (TMS, 182).

> In what constitutes the real happiness of human life, they [poor people] are in no respect inferior to those who would seem so much above them. In ease of body and peace of mind, all the different ranks of life are nearly upon a level, and the beggar, who suns himself by the side of the highway, possesses that security which kings are fighting for. (TMS, 185)[41]

Thus it cannot be real considerations of utility that motivate the common man's adoration of the rich man and the rich man's possessions. Smith thinks there is only one remaining explanation for the inordinate attention that every aspect of rich people's lives receives: "Every body is eager to look at [the man of rank], and to conceive, at least by sympathy, that joy and exultation with which his circumstances naturally inspire him" (TMS, 51). Smith goes on to argue that all ambition, along with its concomitant distinction of ranks, is the result of our imaginatively changing places with the successful—however we define

---

[40] In Smith's time, such people were primarily royalty (see TMS, 52); in our day, such people are primarily athletes and entertainers.

[41] See also the passage in which Smith discusses an ambitious but poor young man who yearns to have the accommodations that a rich man enjoys. "To obtain the conveniencies which [wealth and greatness] afford, he submits in the first year, nay in the first month of his application, to more fatigue of body and more uneasiness of mind than he could have suffered through the whole of his life from the want of them" (TMS, 181).

success—and realizing that we too would enjoy having the status and occupying the position that they actually enjoy.

A corollary of Smith's argument is that he thinks that we are particularly interested in and admire the fortunes of the rich and powerful not because of "any private expectations of benefit from their good-will"—that is, not out of any consideration of utility, since those benefits "can extend but to a few"—but rather simply because of our "admiration for the advantages of their situation" (TMS, 52). Thus our desire not only for sympathetic harmony of sentiments, but harmony particularly with the agreeable sentiments, leads us first to admire the rich and then to want to be rich ourselves. Thereafter it then does not take much, Smith thinks, for ambition to become one of the strongest passions we have:

> That passion [i.e., ambition], when once it has got entire possession of the breast, will admit neither a rival nor a successor. To those who have been accustomed to the possession, or even to the hope of public admiration, all other pleasures sicken and decay....
>
> Of such mighty importance does it appear to be, in the imaginations of men, to stand in that situation which sets them most in the view of general situation and attention. And thus, place, that great object which divides the wives of aldermen, is the end of half the labours of human life. (TMS, 57)

Although Smith writes that ambition is responsible for half, and not all, the labors of human life, it is clear how important Smith thinks ambition is for accounting for many of the behaviors in which human beings engage. By explaining ambition and our search for wealth as an effect of our desire for mutual sympathy of sentiments, it is possible that Smith is laying the groundwork for a link between ethics and economics, that he is opening the door for a unifying interpretation of both of his books. I shall consider this possibility in Chapter 4.

We have now seen what place the desire to better one's condition occupies in Smith's moral theory: he thinks it is an inevitable fact of human nature insofar as it is the result of intercourse with others, the desire for mutual sympathy, and the fact that success in life engages the social passions with which people are more likely to sympathize. But can this explanation of our drive to achieve "place" be reconciled with the treatment this drive receives in WN? The final word on this issue will have to wait until we have looked at Smith's discussion of the development of markets, which comes in Chapters 3 and 5. At this point, however, it would appear that the two *can* be reconciled. If we understand the desire to better one's condition as it is explained in TMS, then perhaps the same understanding can explain its use in WN. In TMS, Smith traces the origin of ambition back to the desire for mutual sympathy. Despite appearances, Smith maintains, the desire for wealth and power is not a foundational principle of human nature. The desire for mutual sympathy is, and, combined with certain environmental accidents—in particular, communities of people living and working together—it in time leads us to strive for success. Thus in market-based, or what we would today perhaps call capitalistic, economies, our desire to better our condition will manifest itself as our trying to have more property, and success will in large measure be evaluated in terms of one's possession of property.

An objection that has been raised by many critics of capitalistic economies is germane here. Perhaps the incessant and universal desire to better one's condition, on which WN is predicated, is actually produced by the capitalistic order itself and hence is not innate in human nature at all. William Booth, for example, argues that the market, "through its extensive presence and its capacity to structure choices, creates a situation in which *pleonexia*, the ancient malaise of the acquisitive soul, becomes a systemic property driving out goods other than its own."[42] In communities that are not formally capitalistic— such as, perhaps, some seventeenth-century hunting communities of the American Indians[43]—it has been argued that no universal desire to better their condition is present. Smith's answer to this objection, at least on the basis of what can be gleaned from his discussion in TMS, would be to argue that the desire to better one's condition should still manifest itself even in Indian communities, but not necessarily in the

---

[42] Booth (September 1994), 658.
[43] A Gaspesian (now Micmac) Indian chief wrote this in 1676 to a group of French captains in Nova Scotia: "I beg thee now to believe that, all miserable as we seem in thy eyes, we consider ourselves nevertheless much happier than thou, in this that we are very content with the little that we have.... As to us, we find all our riches and all our conveniences among ourselves, without trouble, without exposing our lives to the dangers in which you find yourselves constantly through your long voyages.... Learn now, my brother once for all, because I must open to thee my heart: there is no Indian who does not consider himself infinitely more happy and more powerful than the French." Cited in McLuhan (1971), 48–49.

way that it manifests itself in explicitly market-based communities. That is, Smith would suspect that although the Indians were perhaps not as interested in acquisition of property as were some Europeans in the seventeenth century, they probably were nevertheless still concerned with making a better life for themselves or their families— a prediction based on the effects of the universal desire for mutual sympathy of sentiments, as its operation is described earlier. It must be stressed, however, that this objection is not trivial, and if it turned out that the Indians were not interested in bettering their conditions, Smith would have to consider this fact a significant anomaly that a true theory of moral sentiments would need to explain.[44] I raise this objection because it underscores the remarkably different treatments the desire to better one's condition receives in TMS and WN—too different, perhaps, to be ascribed merely to tone, as Raphael and Macfie suggest. I raise it moreover to lay the groundwork for the argument I make in Chapter 4 that the Adam Smith Problem is not easily dismissed. It is a long way indeed to go from TMS's "how selfish soever man may be supposed, there are evidently some principles in his nature, which interest him in the fortune of others, and render their happiness necessary to him" (TMS, 9) to WN's "uniform, constant, and uninterrupted effort of every man to better his condition" (WN, 343). The coherence of the two accounts of human motivation, then, for now remains in question.

[44] The view that American Indians were not market-oriented has now come under sustained criticism. For an example, see Birzer (Spring 1999).

# 3

# The Marketplace of Morality

A central aim of Smith's *The Theory of Moral Sentiments* is to give an account of the process of making moral judgments that is grounded in empirical evidence. He wanted to make a study of human relations in the same way Newton made a study of heavenly bodies—by observing the phenomena and attempting to generate rules that describe their regular behavior. In this chapter I shall argue that an examination of Smith's analysis of human morality in TMS reveals that the rules he has found that describe our moral behavior conform to a determinate model, a model that Smith develops throughout the course of his book. This model is of a market in which free exchanges among participating people give rise, over time, to an unintended system of order. Specifically, Smith understands the nature of moral judgments, including their concomitant features of the impartial spectator procedure and the human conscience, to be the codified results, both at the social and the individual levels, of a coherent and orderly system of morality that is effected by individuals who did not intend to effect it. Put differently, this human institution has developed and is maintained by what I propose to call a "marketplace of morality."

Now the mention of a market will conjure up in the contemporary mind only one thing—economics. In Smith's day, too, the term was primarily used to refer to arenas in which merchants exchanged their goods or in which consumers bought the goods of producers. In Chapter 7, I connect the model of a market that underlies Smith's moral theory with Smith's treatment of economic markets in *The Wealth of Nations*. Here I wish to argue that Smith's understanding of the development of standards of moral judgment, along with his conception of the impartial spectator procedure and the human conscience, can be seen as an example of a large-scale market at work. Now, that some seminal thinkers of the Scottish Enlightenment were working on "spontaneous order" explanations of human social institutions has become a commonplace among scholars,[1] and that Adam Smith in particular attempted to explain human moral judgment by employing some version of this model has been suggested by several.[2] Yet the details of Smith's account remain to be assembled into a coherent and plausible model,[3] and Smith's conception has yet to be seen as an instance of the general model of a market. I think such a version of Smith's account can be assembled, however, and my principal goal in this chapter is to reconstruct this account.

## I. The Development of Moral Standards

### Reason and Sentiment

As we saw in Chapter 2, Smith claims in TMS that an irreducible feature of human nature is the desire for mutual sympathy of sentiments. It gives us great pleasure to know that our own "sentiments"—which, for Smith, can be feelings, beliefs, judgments, or all of these—are echoed in others, and the desire to achieve this sympathy is perhaps the most fundamental overall social desire man has (TMS, 13).[4] Smith thinks that investigation shows that these sentiments are a crucial element in the passing of moral judgments—indeed, that such judgments are ultimately founded on them.[5] Smith writes that the alternative view, that

---

[1] See, for example, Berry (1997) and Hamowy (1987).

[2] See, for example, Berry (1997), 44–47 and passim; Campbell (1971), especially Chapter 4; Fleischacker (1991); Muller (1993), Chapter 3 and passim; and Teichgraeber (1986), 133–39 and passim.

[3] Eugene Heath (July 1995) has recently argued that Smith's account *cannot* be assembled into a coherent model. For a rebuttal to part of Heath's argument, see Otteson (October 2000). I return to Heath's argument at the end of this chapter.

[4] Remember that for Smith "sympathy" means concord or harmony, not pity. See TMS, 10; but see also TMS, 43.

[5] As will become clear, Smith's use of the word "judgment" is perhaps more justified here than the use of the same word by some other sentimentalist theorists of the period, whom Reid in particular was later to take to task for calling something a "judgment" that was really a "feeling." See Reid (1788), 305 and passim.

"the first principles of right and wrong can be derived from reason," is "altogether absurd and unintelligible" (TMS, 320); he thinks Francis Hutcheson and David Hume have already made the convincing case for this claim. But there is an indispensable role for reason in the Smithian moral judgment: Smith also writes that "reason is undoubtedly the source of the general rules of morality, and of all the moral judgments which we form by means of them" (ibid.). How are these claims to be squared, and what exactly did he take reason's role to be?

What Smith has in mind when he speaks of the role of "reason" in making moral judgments is induction. "The general maxims of morality," he writes, "are formed, like all other general maxims, from experience and induction" (TMS, 319). This sentence is found in a chapter of TMS in which Smith is concerned with refuting the notion that reason is the "principle of [moral] approbation," that is, the notion that reason is the final adjudicator in moral matters. Smith's position is that although reason undoubtedly plays a role in moral judgments, it is not their *source*—and hence it is not the "principle" of moral approbation. According to Smith, we use reason to "discover those general rules of justice by which we ought to regulate our actions" (ibid.). That we discover, as opposed to create, these rules is crucial for Smith, but not in the way it was for Ralph Cudworth (whom Smith has in mind here). Cudworth had argued that reason discovers good and evil by something like a logical proof: certain actions, like lying, were self-contradictory; whereas others, like fulfilling a promise, "the intellectual nature obligeth to of itself, and directly, absolutely and perpetually."[6] Thus, for Cudworth, reason discovers right and wrong by judging actions to be consistent or inconsistent with fundamental, self-evidently true moral rules. But Smith argues that reason cannot alone be the source of all judgments of right and wrong. He accepts the Humean claim that reason can determine whether this or that course of action will lead to this or that end,[7] but he maintains that the rightness or wrongness of an end cannot be given by reason. For this, Smith thinks, a prior sentiment is necessary, what Smith calls an action's being "agreeable or disagreeable for its own sake"—which is determined, Smith argues, by "immediate sense and feeling" (TMS, 320).

---

[6] Cudworth (1991[1731]), 109.

[7] I put to one side for the moment the problems that, as I argued in Chapter 2, this position poses for the consistency of Hume's two *Enquiries*.

Thus the source of moral approbation and disapprobation is in immediate sense and feeling. We can connect this claim with Smith's position on the role of reason in making moral judgments in the following way. As we gain experience with persons and actions that we find agreeable or disagreeable, we form, by (unconscious) induction, first habits and then general rules of agreeableness and disagreeableness. Once these rules have been formed, we judge future cases against them and base judgments of approbation or disapprobation on them. Smith writes that judging all acts and actors on a case-by-case basis according to the immediate feeling we have as we view them is an "uncertain and precarious" process because our feelings are so easily colored by "the different states of health and humour" we have from day to day (TMS, 319). For this reason, the formation of general rules requires a great deal of time and regulative assistance from friends and family. It is also indispensable for creating a stable, orderly system of judging, that is, one that can render consistent judgments over time. The rules must also come early on. Smith thinks that our first formulations of these general rules come at the earliest stages of childhood, after which the rules go through endless multiplying, deleting, and revising throughout our years of life.

In his rejection of Cudworth's position, then, Smith's real criticism seems to be that Cudworth failed to analyze the matter far enough. There is a role for reason in moral judging, and there are general rules by which we judge particular acts or actors. And indeed a certain deductive process may take place when we judge a particular instance against the general rule. For example, I determine that this person is taking the news of a distant acquaintance's death too gravely by thinking of what a person in his position should feel, seeing that his behavior reveals that his sentiments are excessive, and thence deducing the judgment. Nevertheless, Smith thinks the general rules themselves could not have arisen from this deductive reason, for there is nothing from which to deduce them. We must, then, look into the source of the general rules—which, for Smith, is ultimately our sentiments.

After one has formed by induction on past experience habits and then rules of judging, one begins, Smith thinks, to form a conscience. As we saw in Chapter 2, Smith thinks that the conscience is actually an internalized impartial spectator. It is the subtle but nagging reminder that we ought to judge persons and their actions, ourselves included, from a disinterested but sensitive viewpoint. In practice, we do this by asking ourselves what an impartial spectator would think. Thus the next step in capturing Smith's view that the principles underlying our moral judgments can be ascertained empirically is to link them to his conception of the impartial spectator. Now Smith's impartial spectator is a metaphor, but unlike his other famous metaphor, the invisible hand, the impartial spectator is not wholly imaginary. Smith thought that observation of the way people make moral judgments, and the way they correct their own and others' sentiments and behaviors, reveals that the process of moral judging takes at some level the form of referring to what an impartial spectator would think. The qualifier "at some level" is important. For most people, the impartial spectator procedure is wholly unconscious; they may be aware that they are judging or correcting, but they are unaware of what underlies their judgments, that is, what principles give rise to their judgments.[8] In such cases, only an outside observer, like a moral philosopher, can infer a principle or standard to account for the judgments people make.

For a minority of people, however, the impartial spectator procedure might not be entirely unconscious. These people might understand that they consult something like a "demigod within the breast," and this knowledge might then help them to focus their moral judging, as well as provide them with a reasonable justification for the judgments they make. To this group would belong people who make a conscious effort to be virtuous or "moral," and who thus (on Smith's account) more actively consult the impartial spectator—even if they do not think of their judgments as resulting from a consultation of an impartial spectator. Then there is an even smaller, final category of people who are aware not only of the role the impartial spectator procedure plays in passing everyday moral judgments but also of the origin of the impartial spectator viewpoint and the nature of the process that leads to the principles that the impartial spectator uses to judge.[9] Now these three categories of people are not discrete; they form a continuum, with people falling at all points along it. The common thread that constitutes the continuum, Smith argues, is the standard

---

[8] Smith says that most people "have seldom enquired after its [the impartial spectator's] decisions, and are altogether unacquainted with the rules and forms of its procedure" (TMS, 130).

[9] This group might include only philosophers: Smith says that "some degree of reflection, and even of philosophy" is required to see the role the impartial spectator plays in making moral judgments (TMS, 136).

of the impartial spectator, which people consult with varying degrees of awareness.

On Smith's view, the impartial spectator procedure is what produces our moral judgments in practice. But how does this fit with Smith's contention that the source of our moral judgments is in "immediate sense and feeling"? For Smith, this procedure comprehends both the "immediate sense and feeling" as well as his conception of reason. Smith thinks that we have no innate moral sense and that we have no natural attraction or aversion to specific behaviors. In contrast to Hutcheson, who held that we have a moral sense that gives rise to moral judgments in the way that our sense of smell gives rise to judgments about the pleasantness or unpleasantness of odors,[10] Smith argues that our moral approbation comes as a result of our perception of a sympathy between our imagined sentiments and those of the person we are judging (TMS, 321–27). The imagined sentiments are in turn determined by imagining what sentiments an impartial spectator would have, a process that itself operates on the basis of the general rules of morality we have formed. And these general rules, in their turn, were formed on the basis of our experience with what we approved and disapproved of both in ourselves and others (TMS, 152 and 319). But now we have come full circle: Smith rejected the notion of innate moral attractions and aversions, but we now seem left without an explanation of why we approve or disapprove of various acts and motivations. It was at just this point that Hutcheson saw no alternative but to conclude that we have a special moral sense—how else to explain our attractions and aversions? I suggest that Smith's answer is that when he speaks of the approval and disapproval we feel on the sight of various acts and motives, the "we" he means is adults—meaning people who have already gone through the gradual, largely unconscious process of rule-formation. They have already developed habits of approval and disapproval based on long experience, and these habits are what have become the rules that guide the impartial spectator procedure.[11]

---

[10] For Hutcheson's account, see his *Inquiry Concerning Moral Good and Evil* (1991[1725]), 261–99, and *Illustrations upon the Moral Sense* (1991[1728]), 305–21.

[11] I should perhaps emphasize that I am discussing Smith's descriptive conception of how we come to have moral principles that inform our moral judgments, not whatever normative justification principles arrived at in this way would have. For a passage in which Smith explicitly addresses this topic, see TMS, 77, §10.

*The Development of Moral Standards*

The case with infants and children is thus entirely different, and it is the transition to this 'moralized' adulthood that Smith is at pains to explain. Infants and young children have no notion of right or wrong, Smith thinks. They simply have wants, which they express violently and expect to be satisfied forthwith. "A very young child has no self-command," Smith writes, "but, whatever are its emotions, . . . it endeavours always, by the violence of its outcries, to alarm, as much as it can, the attention of its nurse, or of its parents" (TMS, 145). The child has no capacity to regulate or moderate its behavior, for the simple reason that it has never had to. Consider again the passage in TMS when Smith speaks of a solitary man who had grown up alone on a desert island (TMS, 110–11). Smith argues that this man "could no more think of his own character, of the propriety or demerit of his own sentiments and conduct, of the beauty or deformity of his own mind, than of the beauty or deformity of his own face" (TMS, 110). Why? The solitary man had no occasion to see that others judge him; in Smith's words, he lacked the mirror that society provides for viewing one's own behavior. Bring this man into society and suddenly he discovers that others judge him; his natural desire for mutual sympathy rouses to life for the first time, and he begins the ongoing process, to which the rest of us (adults) are already habituated, of adjusting his behavior to achieve this sympathy. It is thus the reproach of others that first alerts one to one's own motives and behavior and that first introduces one to the necessity of what Smith calls self-command.

Now relate this argument to the case of children. The infant has no capacity to approve or disapprove of his own behavior (or that of others) because, like the solitary islander, he has had no mirror held up to him. But this situation soon changes as the infant grows into a child. The child finds himself frequently corrected and reprimanded by those who care for him. At first the reprimands must seem arbitrary because the child has no conception of the general rules that underlie the particular reprimands. In time, however, the child comes to have an appreciation of the rules, even if he could not formulate them. He has learned by habit what behavior, under what circumstances, is approved and what not, and he develops the ability to predict with increasing accuracy what reactions those around him will have to his behavior. These are the first stages of what will eventually coalesce into the rules of behavior by which the child, when grown to an adult, will execute the impartial spectator procedure.[12]

Throughout our lifetimes, Smith says, we harbor a natural partiality for ourselves, a partiality that is checked only by intercourse in society. As young children, however, this partiality is not always checked; indeed, it is often alimented by forbearing parents or other caregivers. The child is then in for a rude awakening. "When it [the child] is old enough to go to school, or to mix with its equals, it soon finds that they have no such indulgent partiality" (TMS, 145). Yet the child "naturally wishes to gain their favour, and to avoid their hatred or contempt" (ibid.). Smith continues that the child

> soon finds that it can do so in no other way than by moderating, not only its anger, but all its other passions, to the degree which its play-fellows and companions are likely to be pleased with. It thus enters into the great school of self-command, it studies to be more and more master of itself, and begins to exercise over its own feelings a discipline which the practice of the longest life is very seldom sufficient to bring to complete perfection. (Ibid.)

We find in this passage two distinct elements that should be emphasized. First, the introduction to the school of self-command that takes place is necessitated by the child's natural desire for mutual sympathy of sentiments, the feature of human nature that is the sine qua non of Smith's theory. Second, we see that people first see the need to discipline themselves when they have contact with others. Here we can tie this passage in with the discussion of the solitary islander. It is intercourse with others that not only triggers the desire for mutual sympathy but also begins the process of disciplining oneself in accordance with others' judgments of one. One develops habits of behavior as one has experiences with others' judgments; the habits of behavior eventually become the principles or standards by which one in turn judges others.

---

[12] One should use caution in speaking of Smithian "rules" informing moral judgments. Smith thinks there are hard and fast rules only regarding the virtue of justice; the other virtues, he thinks, are judged rather by having a general picture of virtue against which the judge compares the case at hand. (Smith says that the rules of justice are like the rules of grammar, whereas the rules of the other virtues are like the rules of style [TMS, 175–76].) Although there is this distinction between the relative precision of these moral rules or principles, it is still the case that rules inform our judgments. The vaguer or looser rules are more like habits, as my argument in the text suggests.

Let me now repeat from Chapter 1 the steps of Smith's impartial spectator procedure for making moral judgments. It has four steps, though, as noted earlier, any or all of these steps may, according to Smith, proceed subconsciously.[13] Experience has shown us the importance of a full and unbiased understanding of a person's situation before we judge him. Hence, if we are to judge a person's action as an impartial third party, we should strive for complete and sensitive knowledge of his situation. So the first thing we do is imaginatively change places with him to see what our sentiments would be if we were in his shoes. To illustrate with the example from before, we imagine our situation if a similarly placed distant acquaintance of ours died. The second step in the procedure is the arousal in us of actual or imagined sentiments from this imagined changing of place: what would my acquaintance's death make me feel? If we are executing the procedure correctly, these imagined sentiments are those a well-informed but impartial spectator would have. The third step is the comparison of the two sentiments, those of the imagined spectator and those of the actual agent: are my imagined sentiments the same as those revealed by the behavior of the "person principally concerned"? The fourth step is the judgment we, the actual spectator, pass in recognition of whether a sympathy exists between the sentiments of the imagined impartial spectator and those of the agent. Awareness at this step of a lack of sympathy—that is, an "antipathy" (TMS, 75, 312, and 327)—causes displeasure in us and leads us to disapprove of the agent's motive or action; the presence of sympathy causes a pleasure that leads us to approve.[14]

Smith's picture, then, is this. Babies know only their own desires, and they have no tincture of remorse, shame, or guilt at desiring something improper. As they grow into children they have the first experience of discipline, which teaches them that others judge them and expect them to behave in particular ways. Their desire for mutual sympathy encourages them to strive to enter into situations in which such sympathy

---

[13] In addition to the discussion in Chapter 1, see TMS, 21, §6; 22, §§8; 78, §11; and 129–30.

[14] On TMS, 326, Smith lists the considerations that lead us to "approve of any character or action"; this list should not be confused with the procedure described here. In that place, Smith is giving the four possible sources of moral approval—propriety, merit, adherence to general moral principles, and utility, respectively; he is not listing the steps of the impartial spectator procedure.

can be obtained, which encourages them to learn what others expect of them and to strive to achieve it.[15] The more experience they have, the better they become at anticipating others' expectations and hence of behaving in ways that lead to mutual sympathy. The children then develop habits of behavior that reflect what they have learned; what were once rules handed down from on high become internalized principles by which the children routinely order their lives. As adults, larger and larger experience has led to more, and more complicated, internalized principles. The principles now cover a large range of actions and motivations, and they have been revised, corrected, and fine-tuned as further experience proved necessary. These principles now inform Smith's impartial spectator procedure: they are the standard against which people judge themselves and others; they are what, in practice, render the moral judgment. A moral judgment, then, is the result of a deduction by which one determines whether a given act or motivation accords with these principles.

## II. Assembling the Model

There are many passages in TMS where Smith addresses the process of forming moral standards that I have sketched. Let me now bring several of them together to show how they combine into a single, coherent account.

In an early passage, when Smith is first introducing his contention that we judge "the affections of other men, by their concord or dissonance with our own" (TMS, 16), Smith cites a common experience:

We may often approve of a jest, and think the laughter of the company quite just and proper, though we ourselves do not laugh, because, perhaps, we are in a grave humour, or happen to have our attention engaged with other objects. (TMS, 17)

How can we approve of others' laughter despite our own grave humor?

We have learned, however, from experience, what sort of pleasantry is upon most occasions capable of making us laugh, and we observe that this is one of that kind. We approve, therefore, of the laughter of the company, and feel that it is natural and suitable to its object; because, though in our present mood we

[15] See Raphael, 1985, 93.

cannot easily enter into it, we are sensible that upon most occasions we should very heartily join in it. (Ibid.) [16]

Here we have a single example that comprehends several elements of Smith's theory. Once again, the "we" Smith has in mind are adults. We adults have, on the basis of long experience with similar situations, developed habits or rules of judging that reflect what we have learned to be the objects of approval or disapproval. In the situation before us now, we find that the jest falls within the scope of the objects that normally meet with approval, and hence we approve of the laughter the jest caused. The dual role of reason is present in this case: we employed induction on our past experience to form the rules of judgment; and (if we had reflected on our judgment, we would have seen that) we employed deduction to find that this case fits with a general rule, which thereby rendered the judgment.

Following the passage about jesting and proper laughter there is an analogous passage concerning the sentiment of grief.

A stranger passes by us in the street with all the marks of the deepest affliction; and we are immediately told that he has just received the news of the death of his father. It is impossible that, in this case, we should not approve of his grief. Yet it may often happen, without any defect of humanity on our part, that, so far from entering into the violence of his sorrow, we should scarce conceive the first movements of concern upon his account. Both he and his father, perhaps, are entirely unknown to us, or we happen to be employed about other things.... We have learned, however, from experience, that such a misfortune naturally excites such a degree of sorrow, and we know that if we took the time to consider his situation, fully and in all its parts, we should, without doubt, most sincerely sympathize with him.... [T]he general rules derived from our preceding experience of what our sentiments would commonly correspond with, correct upon this, as upon many other occasions, the impropriety of our present emotions. (TMS, 17–18)

We see in this passage a hint of what will later get developed into the impartial spectator procedure. We approve of the grieving son's behavior because we realize that if we only took the time to consider the situation fully we would have the same feelings in his place. The general rules we form reflect our "common" sentiments—by which Smith means the sentiments we have when we are in possession of full knowledge of the case and are not biased in any way relevant to the case—which squares with Smith's claim that the procedure we employ to pass judgment on any particular instance is that of an *impartial* spectator. Smith has argued that we could not rely simply on sentiment to adjudicate each and every case that comes before us because the inconstant nature of our sentiments would give rise to inconstant judgments. As a remedy, we generate, with the help and insistence of those around us,[17] general rules by which we adjudicate individual cases, rules that apply regardless of the sentiment we might have at the moment. In the preceding citation, Smith gives a concrete instance when the general rules override the present emotion—they "correct" it—so that the spectator's judgment is not affected by the bias, interest, or prepossession he might currently have.

Elsewhere Smith discusses the nature of self-deceit, which arises, he argues, when we seek to avoid the impartial spectator procedure—that is, when we do not want to view ourselves the way a disinterested third party would. When we have done something that we know such an observer would disapprove of, our natural self-love sometimes leads us to pretend not to know what the impartial spectator would think, or perhaps even to pretend that the impartial spectator would approve of our behavior. We nevertheless somehow know[18] that if we faced the impartial spectator's judgment squarely, "a reformation would generally be unavoidable. We could not otherwise endure the sight [of ourselves]" (TMS, 159). Happily, however, we have a natural remedy for the weakness of self-deceit, and we are not helpless in the face of our own self-love.

Our continual observations upon the conduct of others, insensibly lead us to form to ourselves certain general rules concerning what is fit and proper either to be done or to be avoided. Some of their actions shock all our natural

---

[17] This "help" of others is crucial, as will be come clearer, as the analogue to the "negotiation" that takes place in economic marketplaces. I return to this issue momentarily.

[18] Smith's phrase is that this fact is "secretly conscious" to us (TMS, 161). See also TMS, 22, 113, 148, and 158. As I discussed in Chapter 2, Smith does not develop a theory of mind that would explain how a secret consciousness is possible—an omission that, as I said then, might disappoint some readers (myself included). The gravity of the omission is mitigated, however, when it is realized that Smith's task is not to develop any such theory. Rather, he merely wants to describe what in fact happens. On this count, I am inclined to think Smith is right about one's secret consciousness, however it turns out that such is possible.

sentiments. We hear every body about us express the like detestation against them. This still further confirms, and even exasperates our natural sense of their deformity. It satisfies us that we view them in the proper light, when we see other people view them in the same light. We resolve never to be guilty of the like, nor ever, upon any account, to render ourselves in this manner the objects of universal disapprobation. We thus naturally lay down to ourselves a general rule, that all such actions are to be avoided, as tending to render us odious, contemptible, or punishable, the objects of all those sentiments for which we have the greatest dread and aversion. (TMS, 159)

This process not only leads to the development of general rules concerning behavior we disapprove of but also to rules concerning behavior that we approve of.

Other actions, on the contrary, call forth our approbation, and we hear every body around us express the same favourable opinion concerning them. Every body is eager to honour and reward them. They excite all those sentiments for which we have by nature the strongest desire; the love, the gratitude, the admiration of mankind. We become ambitious of performing the like; and thus naturally lay down to ourselves a rule of another kind, that every opportunity of acting in this manner is carefully to be sought after.

It is thus that the general rules of morality are formed. They are ultimately founded upon experiences of what, in particular instances, our moral faculties, our natural sense of merit and propriety, approve, or disapprove of. We do not originally approve or condemn particular actions; because, upon examination, they appear to be agreeable or inconsistent with a certain general rule. The general rule, on the contrary, is formed, by finding from experience, that all actions of a certain kind, or circumstanced in a certain manner, are approved or disapproved of. (Ibid.)

This passage reiterates, first, the process of induction that leads to the formation of general rules, second, how these rules become the principles by which we judge others and ourselves, and, third, how our natural desire for mutual sympathy of sentiments impels us to act on those principles we develop—and hence why those principles are aptly called "natural." Additionally, however, this passage discloses another element that is crucial to Smith's account: the role that other people play in the development of our own standards of moral judgment.[19]

---

[19] Smith also discusses this element in the passage about the solitary man with no societal mirror, TMS, 110–11. See also the discussion of the child first going to school, TMS, 145–46.

Although our judgments are based on the sentiments we have, the judgments are not rendered in a vacuum. When they are right, they are confirmed by the judgments of others; when they are wrong, they are not. Since the desire for mutual sympathy is common to all of us, it follows that our judgments likewise affect the judgments of others. An exchange of information thus takes place—you inform me of your judgments, I inform you of mine—an exchange that resembles the negotiations in economic marketplaces; and, because we both want sympathy, this "free communication of sentiments" (TMS, 337) tends toward a general consensus of judgment in the way in economic marketplaces it tends toward agreement on a price.[20] The established and settled rules of morality that a community comes to endorse are then at the same time a reflection of and an instantiation of the general rules of judgment each of us forms on the basis of these countless common experiences.

In another early passage, Smith is laying out how he thinks the universal desire for mutual sympathy modulates the sentiments both of the spectators and the person principally concerned. He writes: "that there may be some correspondence of sentiments between the spectator and the person principally concerned, the spectator must, first of all, endeavour, as much as he can, to put himself in the situation of the other" (TMS, 21). By bringing home to himself the situation of the person principally concerned, the spectator puts himself in a position to understand and appreciate this person's actions, thereby enabling a sympathy of sentiments. Inevitably, the spectator must enliven his sentiments so that they may correspond with those of the person

---

[20] Smith also writes, "The most vulgar education teaches us to act, upon all important occasions, with some sort of impartiality between ourselves and others, and even the ordinary commerce of the world is capable of adjusting our active principles to some degree of propriety" (TMS, 139). In WN, he writes, "In [the man of small fortune's] own conduct, therefore, he is obliged to follow that system of morals which the common people respect the most. He gains their esteem and affection by that plan of life which his own interest and situation would lead him to follow. The common people look upon him with that kindness with which we naturally regard one who approaches somewhat to our own condition, but who, we think, ought to be in a higher. Their kindness naturally provokes his kindness. He becomes careful to instruct them, and attentive to assist and relieve them. He does not even despise the prejudices of people who are disposed to be so favourable to him, and never treats them with those contemptuous and arrogant airs which we so often meet with in the proud dignitaries of opulent and well-endowed churches" (WN, 810).

principally concerned. Despite his efforts, however, "the emotions of the spectator will still be very apt to fall short of the violence of what is felt by the sufferer" (ibid.).

> Mankind, though naturally sympathetic, never conceive, for what has befallen another, that degree of passion which naturally animates the person principally concerned. That imaginary change of situation, upon which their sympathy is founded, is but momentary. The thought of their own safety, the thought that they themselves are not really the sufferers, continually intrudes itself upon them; and though it does not hinder them from conceiving a passion somewhat analogous to what is felt by the sufferer, hinders them from conceiving any thing that approaches to the same degree of violence. (TMS, 21–22)

The sufferer, for his part, is aware of this because he has been a spectator as well, and hence he strives to moderate his own sentiments so that they may correspond to what he estimates a spectator's would be. Although there no doubt will remain a difference between the "violence" of the respective sentiments of the spectator and the person principally concerned, "These two sentiments, however, may, it is evident, have such a correspondence with one another, as is sufficient for the harmony of society" (TMS, 22).

> In order to produce this concord, as nature teaches the spectators to assume the circumstances of the person principally concerned, so she teaches this last in some measure to assume those of the spectators. As they are continually placing themselves in his situation, and thence conceiving emotions similar to what he feels; so he is as constantly placing himself in theirs, and thence conceiving some degree of that coolness about his own fortune, with which he is sensible that they will view it. . . .
>
> Society and conversation, therefore, are the most powerful remedies for restoring the mind to its tranquillity, if, at any time, it has unfortunately lost it; as well as the best preservatives of that equal and happy temper, which is so necessary to self-satisfaction and enjoyment. (TMS, 22–23)

The desire for mutual sympathy motivates spectators and actors alike to place themselves continually in each other's position. The ultimate end of this bilateral attempt to achieve a concord of sentiments is tranquillity of mind and happy temper,[21] and the principles of action

---

[21] These seem to comprise Smith's notion of human happiness: "In what constitutes the real happiness of human life, [the poor] are in no respect inferior to those who would seem so much above them. In ease of body and peace of mind, all the different ranks of life are nearly upon a level, and the beggar, who suns himself by the side

that most efficiently tend toward this end are those that will endure long enough to get endorsed aloud, even taught to children, perhaps even—for the select, transcendent few[22]—regarded as the community's publicly established standards of morality for generations.[23]

One more passage makes Smith's picture complete. The principles that get adopted after experience with one's own and others' judgments become internalized in each individual and form the basis of the impartial spectator procedure that he performs when he passes judgment. They constitute, in other words, one's conscience. In a chapter entitled "Of the Influence and Authority of Conscience" (TMS, 134–56), Smith sketches how one's experience together with one's desire for mutual sympathy lead one to adopt the perspective of the impartial spectator when judging oneself and others. Smith begins this chapter by referring to our continuous and largely unconscious practice of correcting our visual perceptions for distance and perspective. When he observes an "immense landscape of lawns, and woods, and distant mountains," Smith writes: "I can form a just comparison between those great objects around me, in no other way, than by transporting myself, at least in fancy, to a different station, from whence I can survey both at nearly equal distances, and thereby form some judgment of their real proportions" (TMS, 135). How is he able to adopt this, as we might say, *disinterested* position?

Habit and experience have taught me to do this so easily and so readily, that I am scarce sensible that I do it; and a man must be, in some measure, acquainted with the philosophy of vision, before he can be thoroughly convinced, how little those distant objects would appear to the eye, if the imagination, from a knowledge of their real magnitudes, did not swell and dilate them. (Ibid.)

The correction of visual perceptions is analogous, Smith thinks, to the correction that both the spectator to an actor's conduct and the actor

---

of the highway, possesses that security which kings are fighting for" (TMS, 185); "Happiness consists in tranquillity and enjoyment. Without tranquillity there can be no enjoyment; and where there is perfect tranquillity there is scarce any thing which is not capable of amusing" (TMS, 149). For other discussions of happiness and tranquility, see TMS, 39, 41, 45, 113, 114, 149–54, 181, 219, 232, and 245.

[22] Smith says that the principles that ultimately survive this winnowing process "are justly regarded as the Laws of the Deity" (TMS, 161–70).

[23] Athol Fitzgibbons rightly thinks of the Smithian development of such standards in evolutionary terms. See Fitzgibbons (1999), 64–65. See also Campbell (1971), 137.

himself must make if a sympathy is to be achieved. They must both correct for perspective.

> In the same manner, to the selfish and original passions of human nature, the loss or gain of a very small interest of our own, appears to be of vastly more importance . . . than the greatest concern of another with whom we have no particular connexion. His interests, as long as they are surveyed from this station, can never be put into the balance with our own, how ruinous soever to him. Before we can make any proper comparison of those opposite interests, we must change our position. We must view them, neither from our own place nor yet from his, neither with our own eyes nor yet with his, but from the place and with the eyes of a third person, who has no particular connexion with either, and who judges with impartiality between us. (Ibid.)

Again the question arises how we are able to do this. Smith continues:

> Here, too, habit and experience have taught us to do this so easily and so readily, that we are scarce sensible that we do it; and it requires, in this case too, some degree of reflection, and even of philosophy, to convince us, how little interest we should take in the greatest concerns of our neighbour, how little we should be affected by whatever relates to him, if the sense of propriety and justice did not correct the otherwise natural inequality of our sentiments. (TMS, 135–36)

Although the desire for mutual sympathy is ever-present, Smith thinks that we are not often conscious, in our everyday dealings with others, that we must alternately enhance or moderate our sentiments, as the present case may require, to achieve this sympathy. As adults who have insensibly developed principles of action and judgment, we simply do so. But when, for example, our self-interest is strongly prescribing one course of action, whereas the impartial spectator would approve of another, what is it that moves us to follow the latter and not the former? "It is not," Smith answers, "the soft power of humanity, it is not that feeble spark of benevolence which Nature has lighted up in the human heart, that is thus capable of counteracting the strongest impulses of self-love" (TMS, 137). Instead, he argues, "It is reason, principle, conscience, the inhabitant of the breast, the man within, the great judge and arbiter of our conduct" (ibid.). Smith continues:

> It is he who, whenever we are about to act so as to affect the happiness of others, calls to us, with a voice capable of astonishing the most presumptuous of our passions, that we are but one of the multitude, in no respect better

than any other in it; and that when we prefer ourselves so shamefully and so blindly to others we become the proper objects of resentment, abhorrence, and execration. (Ibid.)

Here is the impartial spectator procedure at work. To prefer our own small advantage to the greater advantage of others is to call upon ourselves the disapprobation of the impartial spectator, which means that we become the "proper objects" of disapprobation. It is this that our original desire for mutual sympathy encourages us to avoid. But now connect this passage to what was cited in the previous paragraph. There Smith said that it is "habit and experience" that teaches us how to correct our selfish propensities; here he says it is "reason, principle, conscience," which resolve themselves into the impartial spectator. The connection between the two, I think, is this: the habits of behavior and judgment we form on the basis of our experience become, as the habits get more ingrained and fixed over time, what constitute our conscience, and we come to regard the promptings of our conscience as the embodiment of moral principle from which the conscience (by using "reason") derives its judgments. The voice of our conscience then is, we become sure, the voice of a knowledgeable, but disinterested, third party—in other words, the impartial spectator. Hence what began as an uncertain trial-and-error attempt to determine rules that were effective at enabling us to achieve mutual sympathy grew into the mature impartial spectator procedure, complete with a watchful conscience and principles of adjudication.

### Hume and Smith on the Unintended Order of Morality

We can see here some important connections to Hume, and a brief discussion of them will further illuminate Smith. In a chapter entitled "Of the origin of justice and property" (T, 484–501), Hume gives an account that on inspection contains elements quite similar to some found in Smith's notion of unintended order. Hume begins by pointing out that human beings are in a particularly vulnerable station in life because, on the one hand, their desires and needs are so great, and yet, on the other, their ability to satisfy them is so scant. It is for this reason that people form societies—so that they can better satisfy their wants. At first blush, it sounds as if Hume has something like a constitutional convention in mind:

For when men, from their early education in society, have become sensible of the infinite advantages that result from it, and have besides acquir'd a new affection to company and conversation; and when they have observ'd, that the principal disturbance in society arises from those goods, which we call external, and from their looseness and easy transition from one person to another; they must seek for a remedy, by putting these goods, as far as possible, on the same footing with the fix'd and constant advantages of the mind and body. This can be done after no other manner, than by a convention enter'd into by all the members of the society to bestow stability on the possession of those external goods, and leave everyone in the peaceable enjoyment of what he may acquire by his fortune and industry. (T, 489)

By using the word "convention," and by prescribing that all the members of society know what the content of that convention is, Hume might seem to be thinking of a formal gathering where everyone drafts and ratifies a social contract. But the phrase "from their early education in society" recalls something he said only a few pages earlier, which gives this passage a somewhat different meaning. What is the early education in society that makes us aware of the advantages of having a society? Hume wrote: "In a little time, custom and habit operating on the tender minds of the children, makes them sensible of the advantages, which they may reap from society" (T, 486). We are not, in other words, convinced of the advantages of association with others by an argument, and we do not create notions of property and justice ex nihilo on the basis of a debate and a vote.[24] Instead, we learn of these things as habits we have formed from countless interactions with others over the course of their lifetimes. Hume makes clear what he means by "convention" in this passage: "This convention is not the nature of a *promise*. For even promises themselves, as we shall see afterwards, arise from human conventions. It is only a general sense of common interest" (T, 490; Hume's italics). He goes on to give the famous example of two men pulling the oars of a boat: they "do it by an agreement or convention, tho' they have never given promises to each other" (ibid.). This example suggests that for Hume it can be expression either by words or by actions that constitute the sort of convention he has in mind. Something along the lines of a formal written or

---

[24] See also Hume's essays "Of the Original Contract" and "Of the Origin of Government," which are contained in his *Essays, Moral, Political, and Literary* (1987 [1741]), 465–87.

spoken contract or compact between consenting parties is hence not a necessary condition for a Humean convention. Thus a rationalistic interpretation of Hume's notion of convention would be incorrect, if by "rationalistic" is meant an express, deliberate general rule agreed to in advance by all concerned parties.

The same notion of convention applies, Hume argues, to our notions of justice and property.[25] As it was by enjoying the advantages of society that people learned of them; so it is by buying, selling, and trading property have they learned what property is; and by experiencing justice and injustice have they learned what these are. Hume argues that the rules and laws respecting property and justice arise "gradually" and acquire "force by a slow progression, and by our repeated experience of the inconveniences of transgressing" them (T, 490). Haakonssen puts it this way:

The long-term effect of individual men's 'selfish' actions is thus something very far removed indeed from what they did have, and could have, in mind. The idea of justice 'wou'd never have been dream'd of among rude and savage men'. Justice, in the form of institutionalized general rules, is the *effect* of individual human actions, but they are not the *intended* effects. (1981, 19: Haakonssen's italics)[26]

Hume's argument is thus similar to the picture Smith gives in TMS.[27] To be specific, the similarities between their respective accounts are two: first, they both think that formal rules, laws, and protocols came about after and as a reflection of already established habits and customs, not the other way around; second, they both think that people will of their own accord—Hume would say "naturally," Smith would say if allowed their "natural liberty"—establish and enforce an order that will regulate their interactions with one another. Thus they both seem to have a conception of unintended order, and they both seem to see it as the genesis of certain human institutions.

---

[25] Haakonssen uses the word "evolutionary" to describe Hume's "considered view of the origin of justice." See Haakonssen (1981), 18.

[26] Ibid., 19. The cited remark inside this quotation comes from Hume's *Treatise*, 488.

[27] Hume also suggests, in a brief, casual remark, that languages are "gradually establish'd by human conventions without any promise" (T, 490), just as the rules of justice and property are. I address Smith's discussion of the origins of language in Chapter 7.

There is, however, an important difference between their respective accounts. Hume develops his notion of an unintended order only in connection with the moral and legal standards that arise concerning justice and, by extension, property,[28] whereas Smith believes that this notion explains the origin and nature of all human moral judgments. It is possible, I think, to trace the roots of Hume's arguments about the institution of government, the sense of allegiance, and the laws governments pass back to his early claim that the original notions of justice and property arose from people's practice and not people's reason.[29] But this would be a somewhat distant connection to make— Hume himself does not seem to make it—and it would require more argument to demonstrate than the scope of this chapter allows. Judging at least from what he explicitly says, it appears that Hume drops any notion of unintended order after his treatment of the origin of justice in his *Treatise* and does not, as far as I know, return to it, at least insofar as his moral philosophy is concerned.[30] In particular, he does not employ it in his discussion of moral judgment and the virtues, and he makes no mention of it to explain the origin of moral standards. Haakonssen, for example, agrees that Hume had come upon an intriguing and insightful idea that he for some reason did not pursue:

If he [Hume] had worked out what he implies in . . . his whole theory of justice, as an 'unintended consequence' phenomenon, he would have seen that there is a third category between natural and artificial, which shares certain characteristics of both. The things in this category resemble natural phenomena in that they are unintended and to be explained in terms of efficient causes, and they resemble artificial phenomena in that they are the result of human action,

---

[28] Hume sees a very close connection between the rules of justice and the rules regarding property. See in particular T, 501–13. Haakonssen writes that Hume "points out that men in general are not so stupid that they do not see that most of the trouble in the world arises when one man makes free with what is in somebody else's possession" (1981, 15).

[29] See, for example, the chapter in Hume's *Treatise* entitled "Of the source of allegiance," 539–49; see especially 542–43.

[30] There is some indication that Hume is operating with an implicit notion of unintended order in a few other places scattered throughout his extant writings, particularly in his *Dialogues Concerning Natural Religion* (1779) and *History of England* (1754–62). For a discussion of these passages, see Hamowy (1987), 11–13.

including of course rational human action. But it remains a fact that Hume did not work out such a theory, although he virtually stated the idea... and although he gave a superb example of this third category in his idea of justice. (1981, 24)[31]

But Smith takes the notion much more seriously, exploring in detail the many applications it can have in explaining all walks of human life and interaction. In this respect, then, I think that Smith's treatment is superior to Hume's. In Hume we find only a germ of an idea, which gets neglected and withers. Smith, however, finds in this idea a key to understanding a much larger range of human institutions. With him, the notion of unintended order reveals to be a powerful insight that can explain more about human beings than Hume—or even, perhaps initially, Smith himself—might have imagined. To be sure, Hume had the idea, and he had it before Smith; Smith may even have taken the idea from Hume, although we do not know for certain.[32] Moreover, the fact that Hume had discussed the notion, even if only incompletely, indicates that we do not have to assume that Smith generated the notion out of thin air (which might lend further credence to the reading of Smith's moral theory that I have offered in this chapter). Nevertheless the claim that standards of moral judgment arise unintentionally from the moral judgments and actions of individuals, and that the standards that develop in this way constitute a self-regulating order or system of morality, is a claim that Smith can rightly consider to be his and his alone.

### III. A Summary of the Model

With the groundwork now laid, let us trace more explicitly the steps of Smith's treatment that together will constitute the marketplace model on which I think he understands the ongoing development of human

---

[31] Haakonssen later writes: "But although Hume arrived, through his theory of justice, at the basic idea of social order arising spontaneously and without the intervention of deliberate constructions, it is at least doubtful whether and to what extent he carried this into his general social philosophy" (1981, 37).

[32] We know that Smith had read Hume's *Treatise* by 1750, but he might have seen it in 1744. See Ross, 1995, 76 and 106. John Rae's early biography suggests that Smith might have written an abstract of the *Treatise* as early as 1740, when Smith would have been only seventeen years old. See Rae, 1895, 15.

morality. First, Smith argues that moral judgments, along with the rules by which we render them, develop without an overall, antecedent plan. They arise and grow into a public system of morality—by which I mean a general consensus regarding the overall nature of the virtuous life—only on the basis of countless individual judgments made in countless particular situations. Second, Smith argues that as we grow from infants to children to adults we develop increasingly sophisticated principles of action and judgment, which enable us to assess and judge an increasingly diverse range of actions and motivations. Third, what seem when we are children to be isolated and haphazard interactions with others lead as we grow older to habits of behavior; as adults the habits solidify into principles that guide our conscience. Fourth, people's interests, experiences, and environments change slowly enough to allow long-standing associations and institutions to arise, which give a firm foundation to the rules, standards, and protocols that both brought these associations into being and in turn are supported by them.

Smith next argues that the development of personal moral standards, of a conscience and the impartial spectator procedure, and of the accepted moral standards of a community all depend on the regular associations people make with one another. It is in these associations, in the daily intercourse people have with one another, that they encourage each other to discover and adopt rules of behavior and judgment that will lead to mutual sympathy. Without such interactions with others—recall the case of the solitary islander—people would have no occasion to pursue such rules, and hence they would not. In that case moral judgments would not be made at all, and people would not, as the solitary man does not, have thoughts about virtue or vice, propriety or impropriety. Finally, a person's (largely unconscious) adoption of general rules, development of a conscience, and employment of the impartial spectator procedure are motivated by a fundamental, innate desire: the desire for mutual sympathy.[33] I have called this desire the sine qua non for Smith's theory of moral sentiments, and now we see why: without it, there would have been no reason to devise rules that enable people to achieve it, and, on Smith's theory, there would therefore have been no moral standards at all.[34]

---

[33] Other motivations (e.g., self-interest) will routinely complement this one.
[34] See Campbell (1971), 234–5.

The analysis in TMS thus shows human morality to display four central substantive characteristics: it is a system that arises unintentionally from the actions of individuals, it displays an unconscious and slow development from informal to formal as needs and interests change and progress,[35] it depends on regular exchange among freely associating people, and it receives its initial and ongoing impetus from the desires of the people who use it. But this account also adheres to a framework that, I would like to suggest, has the central elements of a system of unintended order modeled on an economic market. These higher-level or formal elements of TMS can be schematized in this way:

1. *Motivating desire:* the "pleasure of mutual sympathy" of sentiments (TMS, 13 and passim).
2. *Rules developed:* rules determining propriety and merit.
3. *Market* (i.e., medium or arena of negotiation or exchange): mutual exchange of personal sentiments and judgments.
4. *Resulting "unintended" system:* commonly shared standards of morality.

As I shall argue in Chapter 7, the same four structural elements can be found in the system of unintended order described in Smith's *Wealth of Nations*—what Smith calls "the obvious and simple system of natural liberty," which, if allowed to unfold without external obstacles, "establishes itself of its own accord" (WN, 687)—and can be schematized similarly. Moreover, the same schematization can apply to Smith's analysis of linguistic development in his 1761 essay, "Considerations Concerning the First Formation of Languages" (LRBL, 203–26). Indeed, in addition to conforming to the same methodological model, TMS, WN, and "Languages" can be even more closely united if one construes the motivating desire in each case as particular instances of the same general desire (viz., the desire of each individual to satisfy his interests). In any case, to limit my claim to the subject of this chapter, we can, I think, accurately view Smith's conception of the system of interactions in which moral standards develop as a marketplace of morals.

---

[35] See Campbell (1971), 79–83.

## IV. Questions

Questions concerning Smith's account present themselves, however. One is this: is there an ultimate sanction of the moral standards that develop in the way Smith describes—or are the rules simply conventional or (contingently) efficient, as the rules of other marketplaces might be? This question can be put in the terms of the schematic given in the previous section: is Smith's claim only that the marketplace mechanism gives rise to some system of order or other, or that it gives rise to *good* orders—that is, systems of order that are preferable to others? Smith seems clearly to believe that these unintentional orders are good and preferable to other, particularly centrally or rationally planned, orders,[36] but there is a question about what criterion of judgment he uses or is entitled to use. This topic will be the focus of Chapter 6.

*Conscious Planning*

A second question arises from Charles L. Griswold, Jr.'s recent study of Smith,[37] and a short discussion of this question will illuminate an important element of my "marketplace" account of Smith's theory. Griswold argues that Smith does not naïvely believe that "some miraculous 'spontaneous harmony' will take care of everything" (329), whether in economic or moral marketplaces; Griswold maintains that Smith deliberately designed TMS to be "protreptic" (49 and passim), as one important part in encouraging virtue and thereby discouraging the dangerous excesses that systems of unintended order—or, as Griswold puts it, spontaneous harmonies—can create. Griswold claims that because Smith knew the dangers of such unfettered marketplaces, he took his role in moral education so seriously: TMS is a result of Smith's views about what a virtuous person of his abilities and circumstances should do—namely, help educate mankind to virtue.

One place in particular Griswold claims that a marketplace model would break down is in distinguishing between real and pretended virtue, and between real praise and flattery. Griswold argues that the desire for mutual sympathy of sentiments, if left to its own devices, would not necessarily be able to encourage the former and discourage

---

[36] See, e.g., TMS, 232–34.
[37] Griswold (1999). In this section, references to Griswold are to this work, on the page given in parentheses.

the latter: sympathy is sympathy, after all, whether with actual or pretended sentiments. Griswold writes: "while our natural desire for sympathy might normally force us to check our most outrageous indulgence in self-delusive egoism, since spectators would not go along with *that*, it would not necessarily force mutual sympathy to rise above mutual flattery" (129, Griswold's italics). More generally, but along the same lines, one might raise the concern that perhaps a problem exists in thinking of Smith's understanding of common morality as a marketplace model because Smith takes care in TMS to point out that there is a difference between seeking mutual sympathy with the sentiments of actual observers, on the one hand, and with seeking sympathy with the sentiments of an imagined impartial observer, on the other. Smith argues that in many cases virtue lies in aligning one's conduct with the latter and not the former. One might argue that this feature of Smith's position is not susceptible to a "marketplace" analysis because it seems to go against the "unintended" nature of such an analysis.

But I think that the marketplace model Smith outlines is more powerful than this objection would portray it. As I argued in Chapter 2, the desire for mutual sympathy of sentiments is sufficient, within the functioning of Smith's marketplace of morals, to encourage not just the appearance of virtue and flattery, but actual virtue and earned praise, because in the former cases there would in fact be no mutual sympathy at all from which to garner pleasure. The notion of mutual flattery is premised on the fact that what are displayed and praised are pretended, not real, virtues—and whatever else is the case, it seems certain that the pleasure Smith thinks accrues on a sympathy of actual sentiments would exceed whatever would accrue on a sympathy of pretended sentiments. Smith is aware of the opposite possibility but argues in response:

But this desire of the approbation, and this aversion to the disapprobation of his brethren, would not alone have rendered [man] fit for that society for which he was made. Nature, accordingly, has endowed him, not only with a desire of being approved of, but with a desire of being what ought to be approved of; or of being what he himself approves of in other men. The first desire could only have made him wish to appear to be fit for society. The second was necessary in order to render him anxious to be really fit. (TMS, 117)

Now this solution may seem like a deus ex machina, about which empirical study will determine whether Smith is right or wrong. But I suggest that Smith need not have recourse to a contrivance because his model already has a way to handle it. When Smith indicates that the second desire is equivalent to "being what he himself approves of in other men," he is reintroducing the mechanism of the marketplace model. For in this way Smith relates this desire to the desire for mutual sympathy of sentiments as moderated by the impartial spectator: once we are adults and have internalized the viewpoint of the impartial spectator, we now desire to have mutual sympathy with this spectator perhaps even more than with actual spectators, creating in practice a desire to be praiseworthy and not blameworthy as these will be what the impartial spectator approves of.[38]

Hence on Smith's view people would be "naturally" more inclined to adopt and praise actual virtue than they would pretended virtue, an inclination that—since on Smith's account it is universal—would tend to encourage virtue and discourage mere flattery on its own. Moreover, the sentiments of the impartial spectator that Smith thinks arises un-intentionally out of this process would, for the same reason, unin-tentionally become commonly adopted as the standard of morality, because doing so would turn out to enable the greatest chance of achieving mutual sympathy of sentiments. This is of course not an in-stantaneous or perfect process—indeed, Smith describes the process as "slow, gradual, and progressive" (TMS, 247)—and it will proceed no doubt in fits and starts. But such is to be expected from a development that proceeds with no overall, centrally directed plan. The strength of Smith's model is that it shows how the workings of an unplanned sys-tem like this can produce anything good at all without such a plan. The claim that it can produce virtue in individuals without their intending such is the "invisible hand" of WN at work in TMS.

I should note that it does not follow from my account that there is no place for moral exhortation. Indeed, moral education and encour-agement would serve the analogous roles in the moral marketplace

---

[38] As I suggested in Chapter 2, I think that Smith sees this process as his answer to the Platonic problem of the ring of Gyges. See TMS, 117–19. Note also the description of the process of internalization given in the same section of the book, TMS, 129. See also TMS, 22.

that *Consumer Reports* and advertising do in the economic marketplace. They would be part and parcel of the active, ongoing negotiations that influence the choices and behaviors of agents interacting with one another. On my interpretation of Smith, however, the role of moral exhortation would not take on any privileged status—at least no more so than any other strong interest people in the marketplace have. Thus Smith, as a "moral philosopher," can have an understanding of the way the marketplace of morals works that exceeds the understanding of the majority of people who constitute the market, and his "synoptic" view, as Griswold calls it (319 and passim), may well inform his "protreptic" manner of writing about ethics. But my interpretation in addition preserves the integrity of the marketplace model Smith has developed, while allowing Smith himself to avoid the mistake he thinks one can easily make in overestimating one's own importance in the functioning of the system.[39]

### The Emergence of Morals

A third and final question has been raised by Eugene Heath. Heath argues that he has located a problem in Smith's moral psychology.[40] The problem is that the moral apparatus with which Smith thinks human beings are equipped is insufficient to explain how an "emergence of morals" can in fact take place. Instead, Heath argues, Smith's "psychology leaves underdetermined the conditions by which such a uniform agreement could emerge" (448). Heath argues that it seems as though Smith's description of the development of moral standards is an account of how an individual comes to adopt moral rules within the context of a community in which a common standard of morality is already in place. But this account then seems to avoid the more difficult—and more interesting—question of how such a system of order can arise in a community from a previous state in which no such system obtained. If Smith's model cannot explain *this* kind of development, it seems lacking in an important respect.

Heath writes that "[t]he emergence of a standard of virtue or a standard of the ideal spectator presupposes that there has already emerged

---

[39] See Smith's notable description of the "man of system" (TMS, 233–34).

[40] Heath (July 1995). In this section, references to Heath are to this work, on the page given in parentheses.

in society some prior consensus as to what is appropriate or required."
Since Smith's account is meant to explain the origin of just this prior
consensus, "[t]he original situation out of which these patterns emerge
must be one in which there operate no moral constraints" (451)—and
Heath thinks that the psychological mechanisms Smith has described
cannot get us from the initial stage without moral constraints to the
stage of a general moral consensus. Heath's first argument is that the
pleasure of mutual sympathy of sentiments does not seem sufficient by
itself to motivate an individual to seek it out with others. Differences
in two people's preferences or in their esteem of one another might, if
large enough, sufficiently dilute the pleasure of a prospective sympathy to disincline them to seek it out (454–56). Moreover, even if their
preferences and mutual esteem are commensurable, their motivation
to seek sympathy of sentiments will still depend on their estimation
that the chances of a sympathy are good, on their not having any over-
riding conflicting preferences, and on the sympathetic passion's not
being unpleasant enough in itself to outweigh the pleasure accruing
upon the sympathy (457–59). Heath argues that these considerations
show that a certain *discrimination* is required among possible objects of
mutual sympathy if the desire for this sympathy is to lead to any shared
system of behaviors and judgments. And this discrimination presupposes that a prior series of constraints must be in place; for if there
were no such constraints, the desire for mutual sympathy would lead
to haphazard and random attempts at satisfaction, merely dissipating
the desire—and not providing the regular motivation necessary for a
shared system to develop.

Heath argues that Smith's account gets the cart before the horse:
Smith had set out to explain how a shared system of moral judgments
could come about, but his analysis simply presupposes the prior existence of just such a system. Indeed, absent this prior system, it seems
that, given Smith's picture of human moral psychology, a moral consensus *could not* emerge. Heath argues that for a system of morality
to be an actual *system*—including, that is, agreed-upon standards of
judgment and behavior—the seeking of mutual sympathy that Smith
argues gives rise to it must itself be regulated and directed. Otherwise,
people's varying preferences, values, and even judgments about which
facts are relevant would incline them to seek mutual sympathy in irregular, unpredictable ways; and this can lead to no shared system of

morality (461–64). The conclusion is that for mutual sympathy to do what Smith thinks it does, it would require guidance from a moral system just like that which Smith seeks to explain. Heath concludes:

> The extent to which one is willing to consider another's point of view determines how the sympathetic imagination will operate. What our discussion has attempted to show is the difficulty of determining how the sympathetic imagination would operate if it were not subject to [prior] moral constraints. (464)

In Chapter 6 and again in the Conclusion, I shall argue that Smith's model allows for, or even perhaps predicts, the appearance of unintended *sub*orders of morality within the single, overall unintended order; those discussions will address Heath's concerns about discriminating among possible sympathies. Here I would like to argue that part of Heath's concerns fall outside the scope of Smith's analysis. Two considerations will illuminate my point. First, recall Smith's discussion of the solitary islander (TMS, 110–11). Smith asks us to imagine a man who has grown up entirely outside the company of other people. What notions of propriety or impropriety, merit or demerit would such a man have? Smith answers: "he would no more think of his own character, of the propriety or demerit of his own sentiments and conduct, of the beauty or deformity of his own mind, than of the beauty or deformity of his own face." The reason he would have no such thoughts is that he has never had occasion to have them. Though the pleasure of mutual sympathy of sentiments is innate in us, a desire for it is only triggered by interaction with others—and it is only this desire that leads us to think about what will become our notions of propriety. Hence if one has never had interactions with others, one will have no such thoughts.[41] But note that the point of this imagined scenario is precisely that this person would *not* develop any kind of moral sensibilities, let alone any moral principles. Smith's argument is that moral sentiments and principles *cannot* begin from nothing: a previously existing claim on one is necessary to trigger their development, presupposing interaction with other people. The same point is made in Smith's discussion of the child first going to school (TMS, 145). The shocking

---

[41] Smith thinks that the solitary islander may nevertheless have favorable or unfavorable notions about some of his character traits insofar as they affect his ability to fend for himself (i.e., insofar as they affect his utility). See TMS, 192.

and unpleasant discovery that others do not enter into one's high estimation of oneself is what first engages the search for mutual sympathy of sentiments, and, hence, ultimately the search for agreeable principles of conduct. Smith would therefore concede the point that if a person did not grow up within a community in which some habits of behavior and judgment already obtained, this person would be unable to develop any such habits on his own. Indeed, this is precisely what his argument is meant to show.

But this leads to my second consideration, which is that all the moral development of which Smith speaks invariably takes place within some kind of community—even if only within a family. I believe this suggests that for Smith the consideration of an amoral state of nature is an impossible counterfactual and is hence irrelevant.[42] The development Smith describes takes place on the level of one or more individuals interacting among other individuals who already have some habits, however rudimentary or unconscious, of behavior and judgment. Heath's argument that Smith's model presupposes a community endowed with a prior, full-blown moral consensus might overstate things, but Smith does think that human beings have *always* been members of some community, starting with a family. There has never been a time when human beings were born unto themselves, only to confront one another later as adults totally devoid of moral sentiments. Note, for example, that Smith's discussion in WN of the four stages of societal development begins at the "lowest and rudest" stage, which is that of nomadic tribes like those found in North America—not amoral communities or isolated amoral adult individuals.[43]

Smith's account of human morality concerns itself first and foremost with explaining how individuals born into even small, primitive communities come to adopt principles of conduct and judgment. The question of how a community as a whole could have gone from a morally devoid state to a morally rich state would thus be for him otiose, and in any case outside the scope of his investigation. Insofar as Heath's objections to Smith depend on this question, then, I think

---

[42] Note the way the discussion of the solitary islander is begun: "Were it possible that a human creature could grow up to manhood in some solitary place, without any communication with his own species…" (TMS, 110). The use of the subjunctive mood indicates, I think, that Smith considers this an impossible scenario.

[43] See WN, 689–708.

they are beside the point of Smith's project. Heath himself indicates that his criticisms center chiefly on the problematic transition from an amoral community to one with shared moral standards: "The above summary focuses on how uniform moral judgments arise within a society (or group of individuals). A separate question, which I do not discuss, concerns how an individual develops morally" (451, n. 14). But to pursue the former question independently of the latter is indeed to get the cart before the horse. Smith's study investigates two aspects of shared morality, namely, its emergence in individuals and its development in communities. Smith's entire examination into the first aspect concerns how the individual goes from not having moral sentiments to having them, but this process, according to Smith's analysis, is only intelligible—and, indeed, given what he takes to be human nature, only possible—within the context of an already existing community of other individuals.[44]

Thus Smith never intended to address the problem Heath charges him with not addressing. Now, this answer may well not satisfy Heath, since it has not yet resolved the problem with which he is concerned. But it may suggest that the problem of explaining community-wide transition from moral non-order to moral order is not peculiar to Smith: it would be an obstacle *any* unintended-order explanation would have to face.[45] It remains true, however, that Smith's examination simply does not address this issue, and this may indicate a genuine limitation in Smith's theory of moral sentiments. The limitation would be analogous to what Smith faced in trying to account for the origin of human language in his "Considerations Concerning the First Formation of Languages." Although in this essay Smith explicitly discusses "savages" in their first speaking situations, an examination of the essay shows, I believe, that its primary value is in the model it employs to explain the *development* of language from early stages to later stages, not its origin ab nihilo.[46] A similar claim can be made about Smith's treatment in

---

[44] One may disagree with Smith's conception of human nature, and perhaps Heath does so disagree. But that is a different kind of objection from those that Heath raises and that I have been considering.

[45] For discussion of what such explanations can actually explain, see Ullmann-Margalit (1978); see also Lal (1998) and Nozick (1974), 18–22.

[46] See Otteson (January 2002).

TMS. My suggestion, then, is that Smith would not view this limitation as a flaw in his account. TMS is meant to be an examination of the unintentional development of a system of shared morality among people as they really are in the situations in which they actually find themselves—not, as I think he would view it, of hypothetical people, or a hypothetical community of people, in a counterfactual situation.

# 4

# The "Adam Smith Problem"

By the time August Oncken published his article in 1897,[1] the scholarly tide was already beginning to turn regarding the so-called Adam Smith Problem. During the previous half-century or so, several commentators had developed and pressed what the German scholars called the *Umschwungstheorie*, which held that Adam Smith the moral philosopher, who had originally thought that human relations were based on a "sympathy" people felt for one another, at some point became Adam Smith the economist, who thought that self-interest was what motivated them. A series of nineteenth-century scholars had argued that there were, after all, two Adam Smiths, not one.[2] The problem was exacerbated by the fact that Smith had produced several editions of *The Theory of Moral Sentiments* during his lifetime, including a final, substantially revised edition only months before he died (and thus some fifteen years after the first publication of *The Wealth of Nations*). How could one take Smith seriously if he not only failed to realize his fundamental conversion in philosophical outlook, but also failed to recognize the two distinct views when he was revising them side by side? The conclusion many nineteenth-century scholars drew was that Smith's two books were simply inconsistent. Smith may have been a great economist, but he was no philosopher.

---

[1] Oncken 1897.
[2] See, for example, Hildebrand (1848), Knies (1853), and Skarzynski (1878).

By the close of the nineteenth century, however, several books had appeared that challenged Smith's alleged inconsistency. Principal among these were John Rae's *Life of Adam Smith* and Edwin Cannan's publication of a student's notes from Smith's lectures on jurisprudence.[3] On the basis of these works and his own study, August Oncken argued that the Adam Smith Problem should be put to rest. The earlier scholars thought that Smith had undergone a radical change of mind while in France in the mid-1760s, specifically when he visited Helvetius and other Physiocrats in Paris in 1766.[4] TMS had first come out in 1759, and we know that Smith had begun work on WN almost immediately after returning from Paris.[5] The nineteenth-century scholars argued that TMS was written by a bright though naïve young man who, still under the influence of his teacher, Francis Hutcheson, thought that benevolence and sympathy were the foundational motivations people felt toward one another. After living with the Physiocrats for a year, however, Smith began to view the world and man differently as he came to believe, as did the Physiocrats, that "self-love," not benevolence, drove human beings. *The Wealth of Nations*, then, is the result of this change in perspective, and, accordingly, self-love is the motivation that drives the argument in WN. This story was in an important respect factually incorrect, and Oncken trumpeted the error. Smith had been lecturing on jurisprudence for several years prior to his trip to Paris, and the content of these lectures, as Rae and Cannan had discovered, revealed that much of the material that was to form the core of WN already occupied a significant place in Smith's thought concerning jurisprudence. Hence whatever else happened in Paris in 1766, Smith's visit did not cause him to change his mind. Smith seemed to have developed the ideas for WN much earlier, and he was doing so about the same time he was preparing the second edition of TMS.[6]

---

[3] Cannan (1896) and Rae (1895).

[4] For a discussion of the Physiocrats and their relation to Smith, see Muller (1993), 77–83.

[5] See Rae (1895), 194–260, and Ross (1995), 220–47.

[6] The second edition of TMS was published with material revisions in 1761. Some manuscript fragments from what was to become WN still exist and are thought to date from the early 1760s. These fragments are reprinted in Smith, *Lectures on Jurisprudence* (1978 [1762–63, 1766]; hereafter LJ), 562–86.

Oncken's article was a turning point in Smithian scholarship because it marked the time when Smith scholars began to take for granted that the French Physiocrats had not changed Smith's mind, and they began to pay increasingly less attention to what had been a celebrated problem.[7] But Oncken's article by itself does not constitute a satisfactory solution to the Adam Smith Problem. Oncken is right that the earlier scholars exaggerated and perhaps even misrepresented the development of Smith's thought during his year in Paris, but precisely where or when Smith changed his mind is not as important as *whether* he changed his mind. Oncken adduces a number of passages from TMS that show Smith's early awareness and consideration of self-interest as a natural human motive,[8] revealing what any careful reader should have seen, namely, that Smith never thought that benevolence was the sole or even predominant motive in human action. Smith knew the power of self-interest already in TMS, so its appearance in WN was not new. But the important question, again, is whether Smith changed his mind. The import of the Adam Smith Problem was the allegation that Smith's books offer conflicting conceptions of human nature. The two books seem to agree that self-love or self-interest[9] is a part of human nature, but do they grant it the same significance in their respective accounts? The claim of the early scholars was that these accounts were inconsistent—and that charge is not answered by responding that Smith had been thinking about the second book for a long time, or that some of the same words appear in both books.[10]

In this chapter I shall argue that, contrary to what many contemporary scholars hold, there is a real Adam Smith Problem that must be addressed. It is not in the end insurmountable, but its most potent formulation is not resolved by standard contemporary responses. I shall begin formulating what I believe is the real Adam Smith Problem by

---

[7] A notable exception to this change in scholarly opinion was Jacob Viner (1928), 116–55.

[8] See Oncken (1897), 447.

[9] Athol Fitzgibbons suggests that Smith used "self-love" to mean something like selfishness or vanity, whereas he used "self-interest" to mean something like a regard for one's own well-being; see Fitzgibbons (1999), 137–45. I shall treat the terms as roughly equivalent, however, because as far as my argument here is concerned they seem to result in the same thing.

[10] See Dickey (September 1986).

first looking at Smith's treatment of self-interest and benevolence in TMS; then I shall look at the seemingly different picture of human virtue and motivation offered in WN. I shall then examine a few attempts to resolve this problem, and I shall argue that they are unsatisfactory. In the next chapter I shall introduce my own resolution, which will draw on and extend the interpretation of Smith's moral theory that I gave in Chapter 3 and developed in Chapters 1 and 2.

## I. Virtue in TMS

As I said in the Chapter 1, the first three parts of TMS contain virtually all of Smith's theory; Parts IV through VII are complementary. Part IV is Smith's response to the claim that utility is the ultimate ground for moral judgments (he is largely addressing Hume), and Part V examines the extent to which "custom and fashion" influence moral judgments. In parts VI and VII we find lengthy discussions that bear on the issue under question here. Part VI is entitled "Of the Character of Virtue" (TMS, 212–64). In it, Smith puts to work what I have called the impartial spectator procedure—the process by which one attempts to determine what an impartial spectator would judge proper in one's situation—laying out the results of this procedure as it concerns several virtues. Here we see Smith spelling out to what degree we ought to have self-interest, benevolence, or other motives in various circumstances. In part seven, "Of Systems of Moral Philosophy," Smith examines what he considers to be the four leading explanations of human moral judgments: those that in turn make virtue consist in propriety, in prudence, in benevolence, and, finally, the "licentious systems"—those that argue that the prevailing motivation human beings feel is self-love. It is principally in these two parts that we find discussion bearing on the Adam Smith Problem.

### Self-Interest in TMS

Smith has argued that we are by nature first recommended to our own care and that the happiness or fortunes of others are necessary to our own happiness.[11] In Part VI, he explains how those two concerns play out when they are regulated by the impartial spectator. "Concern for

---

[11] TMS, 219 and 9, respectively.

our own happiness recommends to us the virtue of prudence: concern for that of other people, the virtues of justice and beneficence" (TMS, 262). Prudence is the virtue that allows us to weigh our present desires against our long-term desires without regard to what at times is the pressing feeling of immediacy connected with the former and the cooler, less immediate feeling connected with the latter. To the impartial spectator, interests are interests, and prudence is the virtue by which we moderate our desires to accord with the impartial spectator's judgments.[12]

> In the steadiness of his industry and frugality, in his steadily sacrificing the ease and enjoyment of the present moment for the probable expectation of the still greater ease and enjoyment of a more distant but more lasting period of time, the prudent man is always both supported and rewarded by the entire approbation of the impartial spectator.... The impartial spectator does not feel himself worn out by the present labour of those whose conduct he surveys; nor does he feel himself solicited by the importunate calls of their present appetites. To him their present, and what is likely to be their future situation, are very nearly the same. (TMS, 215)[13]

Smith arrives at this conclusion about the impartial spectator's concerns in two different ways. First, he hearkens back to the earlier passage in TMS when he described the case of a person judging himself as the person's dividing himself in two—into the impartial spectator and judge of his conduct, on the one hand, and the person whose conduct is being judged, on the other (TMS, 113). A similar division goes on in this case. When one is facing the dilemma of deciding between a current, pressing interest that is of overall lesser importance and a long-term, presently cooler interest that is of greater importance overall, one must again divide oneself, but this time in three: one representing one's current interest, one representing one's long-term interest, and one the impartial spectator. The impartial spectator adjudicates between the other two indifferently—that is, without regard to the relative strength of passion that either connects to his interest—and concludes that a greater interest is more important than a lesser interest. This deference of less important present interests to more important

---

[12] See TMS, 189, §8 and 215, §11.
[13] See also TMS, 189, §8.

future interests is called "prudence," and thus the impartial spectator approves of prudence. The other reason that leads Smith to conclude that the impartial spectator views all interests without regard to their attached feeling of immediacy is a simple one that reminds the reader of the overall project Smith has in TMS: Smith merely observes that this is in fact how the impartial spectator judges (TMS, 213–16). His own experience employing the impartial spectator procedure proves that the impartial spectator views present and future interests "nearly at the same distance, and is affected by them very nearly in the same manner" (TMS, 215).

Justice and benevolence are the virtues connected with our concern for others. According to Smith, justice is the necessary and sufficient condition for a society to survive (TMS, 86), and it is the necessary basis for successful interaction of all individuals; hence the impartial spectator approves of people treating one another with justice in all cases, and he always denounces breaches of the rules of justice. Smith describes justice this way: "A sacred and religious regard not to hurt or disturb in any respect the happiness of our neighbour, even in those cases where no law can properly protect him, constitutes the character of the perfectly innocent and just man" (TMS, 218). In Smith's *Lectures on Jurisprudence*, not disturbing the happiness of one's neighbor is elaborated as preventing "the members of a society from incroaching on one anothers property, or siezing what is not their own"; or again, it is "maintaining men in what are called their perfect rights," which amounts to refraining from doing a person "any injury or hurt without a cause" (LJ, 5–7).[14] Smith considers an observance of the rules of justice to be the minimum level of conduct necessary for a society to survive, because without it no one has security in his person or possessions; and a community, which requires people to work with and among one another, cannot arise or endure in such a state. Smith's "perfect rights" are similar to what today are frequently called the "negative rights" to life, liberty, and private property.[15]

---

[14] The citation is exactly as it appears in the text, spelling errors and all; I shall not pepper citations from LJ with "[*sic*]" to remind the reader that these are students' notes, with all the imperfections that implies. See also TMS, 84.

[15] Isaiah Berlin made this use of the term "negative rights" famous. See the chapter "Two Concepts of Liberty" (Berlin, 1969, 118–72).

Although justice is required for the existence of a society (which for Smith means that government's first and most important duty is establishing justice[16]), a society with nothing but justice is not a particularly inviting one. Benevolence in addition to justice is what makes a society inviting and enjoyable. Whereas justice, Smith says, is the foundation that supports the building of society, benevolence is the ornament that embellishes the building (TMS, 86). But how much benevolence does the impartial spectator approve of, and in which situations?

Because justice is necessary for society, the impartial spectator approves of its strict observance at all times. But it turns out that the impartial spectator approves of an increasing level of benevolence toward others in direct proportion to our familiarity with them. Thus toward a stranger, conduct that displays only justice, with little or no benevolence, is approved of; toward immediate family members, justice along with a benevolence approaching, equal to, or even exceeding our concern for ourselves is approved of. The reason for this, Smith thinks, is that we are "recommended by nature" to care for and pay attention to others with a descending degree of intensity beginning with ourselves, then our family members, then friends, then acquaintances, and, finally, strangers (TMS, 219–27). It is a happy coincidence that nature has so constructed us,[17] given that our own happiness and success in life is dependent on others in the same descending-degree fashion: the most important person on earth for securing one's happiness and success in life is oneself; after that it is one's family members, then one's friends, and so on. It is thus a good thing that our natural care and attention—which, since we all have it, is mutual—runs the same way.

This descending degree of our natural concern and benevolence is also, Smith thinks, conducive to our psychological well-being because, as we saw in Chapter 2, it matches our ability to help others. The less familiar we are with other individuals, the less are we in a position to help them when they need it; thus nature has thankfully spared us the psychological anguish we would experience if our natural benevolence and concern extended beyond our ability to help (TMS, 139–40). In a different sense, however, Smith thinks that our native benevolence

[16] See LJ, 5.
[17] In Chapter 6, I argue that for Smith this is no sheer coincidence after all.

is "universal," but by this he means that it can be invoked for any "sensible being" (TMS, 235), not that it should extend equally to all human beings.[18] Although, as it turns out in the course of our everyday lives, our "effectual good offices can very seldom be extended to any wider society than that of our own country" (TMS, 235), our common nature makes it possible for us to imagine ourselves in the shoes of any other person, and hence we can in principle achieve sympathy with anyone whose situation becomes known to us.

The virtuous person as determined by the impartial spectator, then, is one who acts out of respect to a balance of virtues: "The man who acts according to the rules of perfect prudence, of strict justice, and proper benevolence, may be said to be perfectly virtuous" (TMS, 237).[19] The precise mixture of motivations that the virtuous person would allow to move him will depend on the circumstances of the situation and the relation he bears to the other people involved; the proper action to take is then prescribed by the impartial spectator procedure, and exact accordance with this spectator's dictates constitutes what Smith considers to be perfect virtue.

What is important for our purposes is the part self-interest plays in the behavior of the person of perfect virtue. We can see that Smith does not consider self-interest, or actions that are motivated by self-interest, to be always and everywhere immoral, as Francis Hutcheson did. Hutcheson argued that moral virtue consisted in pure benevolence, and that any admixture of self-interest tended only to take away whatever merit an action might have had.[20] On the contrary, Smith thinks that self-interest has its place, indeed an important place:

Regard to our own private happiness and interest, too, appear upon many occasions very laudable principles of action. The habits of oeconomy, industry, discretion, attention, and application of thought, are generally supposed to be

---

[18] This is an important departure Smith takes from the Stoicism that he otherwise finds quite attractive. Smith writes: "The plan and system which Nature has sketched out for our conduct, seems to be altogether different from that of the Stoical philosophy. [¶] By Nature the events which immediately affect that little department in which we ourselves have some little management and direction, which immediately affect ourselves, our friends, our country, are the events which interest us the most, and which chiefly excite our desires and aversions, our hopes and fears, our joys and sorrows" (TMS, 292).

[19] See also TMS, 152 and 161–63.

[20] See Hutcheson (1991 [1725]), 261–99.

cultivated from self-interested motives, and at the same time are apprehended to be very praise-worthy qualities, which deserve the esteem and approbation of every body. (TMS, 304; see also 189–90 and 212–17)

The central criticism Smith levels against Hutcheson is that his former teacher fails to recognize the virtuous actions to which self-interest can prompt one and the important place self-interest occupies in the overall scheme of a virtuous person's life.[21] Hence it is clear that any critic who claimed that there was no accounting of self-interest in TMS, or that the notion that self-interest is a strong, at times dominant, motivation to act is new to WN cannot have read all of TMS.

Self-interest underlies the general virtue of prudence, which comprises or leads to the virtues listed in the preceding citation—economy, industry, discretion, and so on. It is out of concern for our own long-term well-being, or what Smith calls our happiness, that we develop the self-command necessary to cultivate and exercise these qualities. Now the extent to which self-interest and benevolence should properly motivate our actions is, for Smith, determined by the impartial spectator, but generally speaking they stand in inverse relation to one another, benevolence being the factor that determines the appropriate level of self-interest.[22] The impartial spectator approves of acting out of nearly pure benevolence when the case involves our own children, for example, and this determination leads to the conclusion that self-interest should play (virtually) no role at all. Conversely, the impartial spectator approves of behavior regarding strangers that displays no or virtually no benevolence—assuming, as always, that the behavior is in accord with the rules of justice—and this determination leads to the conclusion that self-interest may properly inform the agent's actions in such cases. Smith's discussion of the prime importance of what he calls self-command[23] underscores the necessity of reining in our natural self-interest so that it accords with the proper measures of benevolence and self-interest that the impartial spectator approves of.

Thus we see the relative importance of the four principal virtues that Smith thinks the impartial spectator approves of, namely, justice, beneficence, prudence, and self-command. Because justice is

---

[21] See TMS, 300–306.
[22] See TMS, 218.
[23] See TMS, 237–62.

necessary for any social association at all, the impartial spectator gives it pride of place as the first virtue with which a person's actions must accord. Beneficence takes second place in importance because its proper presence or absence is the secondary concern of the impartial spectator and is in turn what determines the proper level of prudence. Prudence comes in third for two reasons: one, since we have a natural inclination to be concerned first and foremost with ourselves, it is the least difficult virtue to cultivate; and two, self-interest, which motivates prudence, is approved of only after the proper level of benevolence has been determined. Finally, although Smith considers self-command a virtue along with the other three, it is best understood as the necessary quality a person must have in order to act on the other three virtues. Smith thinks of self-command as the ability to discipline oneself to act in accordance with the impartial spectator's judgments. It thus enables virtuous behavior more than it is a virtue itself, giving, as Smith says, the other virtues "their principal lustre" (TMS, 241)—by which he means that without it one could not be virtuous at all, except perhaps in rather vapid ways.[24]

### The Licentious Systems

What Smith calls the "licentious systems" of morality are those that suggest that virtue consists in self-interest or self-love (TMS, 306–14). His discussion comes in section two of the final part of TMS, in which he is concerned with examining the leading "systems of moral philosophy"; in the other chapters of this section he looks at the systems that made virtue consist in propriety, in prudence, and in benevolence (TMS, 267–306). The fourth chapter of this section is entitled simply "Of licentious Systems." According to Smith, the philosophers who argued that virtue consists in propriety were the ancients Plato, Aristotle, and Zeno, though each in a distinctive way, and the moderns Clarke, Wollaston, and Shaftesbury; the principal philosopher holding that virtue consists in prudence was Epicurus, though Smith also mentions Aristippus; and the principal philosopher holding that virtue consists in benevolence was Hutcheson, though Smith also mentions

---

[24] As candidates for behavior expressing what I call vapid virtue, Smith suggests cases in which one acts in accord with the dictates of justice, benevolence, and prudence when there is no temptation to do otherwise. See TMS, 240–41.

Cudworth, Henry More, and John Smith. In his examination of each of these men's systems, Smith lays out both what he thinks they got right and what they got wrong. In each case, he finds that at least some part of their respective systems was true, though in no case did any of them get the whole truth (Zeno probably came closest, however[25]). Perhaps unsurprisingly all the points on which those other philosophers were right are comprehended within Smith's own theory, which Smith takes pains to demonstrate and which he takes to be an important confirmation of his theory, and Smith's theory suffers from none of the problems that beset the other theories. Smith's examinations in these sections contain interesting interpretations of the moral systems of the other philosophers, but they contain little that is new regarding Smith's own theory. For this reason, we need not examine them in detail here. What does interest us here, however, is that Smith was unable to find any significant redeeming value in only one system: the licentious system that holds that virtue consists in self-interest.

The principal problem with the licentious system, according to Smith, is that it collapses the distinction between virtue and vice: all action is seen to issue from self-interest, so there can be no judgment of proper motivation and improper motivation.[26] Smith is speaking principally of Mandeville, though he later takes Hobbes and Pufendorf, as well as Mandeville, to task for maintaining, in Smith's words, that the principle of moral approbation derives from self-love.[27] Mandeville argued that all human beings are naturally more concerned with their own interests than with those of others; so far, Smith agrees. Mandeville

---

[25] Although Smith writes that his own theory is "altogether different" from that of Zeno (TMS, 292), many of the differences he specifies seem to concern only less important details; see TMS, 272–93. It is perhaps suggestive that of the twenty-one pages dedicated in TMS to examining Zeno's position, twenty extol its virtues; only one page is dedicated to criticism. Vivienne Brown argues that Smith's theory of moral sentiments is essentially the same as that of the Stoics, despite what Smith himself has to say (1994, Chapter 4). See also Griswold (1999), 7–21 and 324–30. Nevertheless, I am less inclined to see Smith as one with the Stoics not just because he says that not only are we naturally inclined to care more for those close to us but also it is morally proper to do so, but additionally because he more than once suggests that the Stoical *apatheia* is humanly unattainable. See, for example, TMS, 12, §12 and 293, §47.

[26] Smith's concern is with real distinctions between virtue and vice (as I argue shortly), not with merely verbal distinctions, as Jean-Pierre Dupuy claims. See Dupuy (1993), 45–57.

[27] Smith's discussion of Hobbes and Pufendorf is at TMS, 315–17.

argued further, however, that it was therefore impossible for a person to prefer anyone else's interest to his own, from which he concluded that all of our activities are at bottom driven by self-interest. Even those acts that seem supremely or purely other-regarding, Mandeville argued, only conceal the actor's true motivation, which is to receive some honor for his act—whether that be praise, accolades, or money. Smith thinks, however, that Mandeville has implausibly reduced the various motivations that prompt men to act out of "self-love." While Mandeville argued that all actions were ultimately an attempt to flatter our own vanity, Smith distinguished vain actions from two others: those prompted by "the desire of doing what is honourable and noble" and those prompted by "the love of well-grounded fame and reputation, the desire of acquiring esteem by what is really estimable" (TMS, 309). Neither of these, Smith argues, can be reduced to mere vanity, although he allows that they do bear "a certain remote affinity" to vain actions, "which, exaggerated by the humorous and diverting eloquence of this lively author [i.e., Mandeville], has enabled him to impose on his readers" (TMS, 310).

Smith concedes that morally proper actions can, if misleadingly described, be made out to seem as though they ultimately sprang from self-love since they issue from man's natural desire for mutual sympathy. The desire to achieve mutual sympathy is in a sense self-regarding because the pleasure this sympathy gives, or the displeasure the lack of it gives, prompts us to seek it. But the general rules of morality that individuals form as a consequence of their numberless attempts to achieve sympathy with others throughout their lifetimes become internalized, as Smith has shown, as an impartial spectator in each person's conscience; once these rules have been internalized in this way, our appeal to them in making moral judgments is no longer immediately prompted by the desire for mutual sympathy, but by what we come to see as the requirements of our conscience, our moral duty. The general rules thus begin as habits of self-regarding behavior reflecting how each person can best achieve mutual sympathy; as the habits develop into society's general rules of conduct, however, they take on an objective authority that reflects not self-interest but propriety. Behavior governed by these rules becomes, then, the standard of morality, which manifests a moral duty that transcends the interests of any given individual person:

The man who acts solely from a regard to what is right and fit to be done, from a regard to what is the proper object of esteem and approbation, though these sentiments should never be bestowed upon him, acts from the most sublime and godlike motive which human nature is even capable of conceiving. (TMS, 311; see also 109–78, especially 171–78)

Smith then argues that virtue, as we have said, is constituted by our adherence to the impartial spectator's judgments, even when our own present interests or passions are contrary to them. Indeed, Smith writes that

[t]he happiness of the [truly virtuous man] . . . is altogether secure and independent of fortune, and of the caprice of those he lives with. The contempt and hatred which may be thrown upon him by the ignorance of mankind, he considers as not belonging to him, and is not at all mortified by it. Mankind despise and hate him from a false notion of his character and conduct. If they knew him better, they would esteem and love him. It is not him whom, properly speaking, they hate and despise, but another person whom they mistake him to be. (Ibid.)

Now Smith confesses that it only "seldom happens" that "human nature arrives at this degree of firmness" (ibid.); nevertheless the fact that this is the ideal state of the perfectly virtuous person shows that Mandeville was wrong. Self-love alone cannot account, Smith argues, for the adoption of general rules of morality and the sense of duty that people come to form as they grow into adulthood.

Smith had another line of attack against Mandeville available to him that, I think to Smith's discredit, he did not employ. He could have quite straightforwardly pointed out that Mandeville has ignored the other obvious motivations that prompt human beings to act. Most importantly, Mandeville has ignored benevolence, which, though certainly not the sole motivation we feel, is certainly not altogether absent, either. When Smith was describing how the impartial spectator approves of, and people accordingly act on, a declining level of benevolence as the actor's familiarity with the others involved in the situation declines, he adduced examples from common everyday experience to enforce the point. Perhaps the most striking case is the parent's care for his child. The toil and concern a parent undergoes in rearing a child cannot plausibly be explained by the parent's self-love. Though one might claim that a parent who has reared his child well will feel pride and receive congratulations as the child grows and succeeds in life, that cannot, Smith thinks (and I agree), counterbalance all that rearing a child well requires. Hence self-interest cannot reasonably be considered the parent's sole or even principal motivation for the sacrifices he makes for his child.

Smith calls Mandeville's system "licentious" because Mandeville argues that self-interest *ought* to be the sole motivation for action, not just that it is in fact. Mandeville argued that if people universally extirpated their self-interest and adopted benevolence and altruism as their sole motivations—as many "whining" moralists would have it (TMS, 283)—"it would," in Smith's phrasing of Mandeville's argument, "be pernicious to society, by putting an end to all industry and commerce, and in a manner to the whole business of human life" (TMS, 313).[28] For this reason Smith argues that Mandeville has collapsed the distinction between virtue and vice: for, if all actions are really motivated by self-interest, and if this is a requirement for the beneficial and generally desired progress of society, then on what basis could one impugn a person for his actions? Everything, on Mandeville's account, must ultimately conduce to the good of society, which means that nothing should be morally discouraged or legally banned. Smith does not call Hobbes's philosophy "licentious" because, I suppose, Hobbes does not believe that human beings have much choice in what they do; they are materially constructed to seek their self-interest, and for that reason Hobbes does not advocate seeking

---

[28] Mandeville writes: "To expect, that others should serve us for nothing, is unreasonable; therefore all Commerce, that Men can have together, must be a continual bartering of one thing for another. The Seller, who transfers the Property of a Thing, has his own Interest as much at Heart as the Buyer, who purchases that Property; and, if you want or like a thing, the Owner of it, whatever Stock or Provision he may have of the same, or how greatly soever you may stand in need of it, will never part with it, but for a Consideration, which he likes better, than he does the thing you want" (1924 [1714], 349). Compare this famous, and strikingly similar, passage in WN: "Give me that which I want, and you shall have this which you want, is the meaning of every such offer; and it is in this manner that we obtain from one another the far greater part of those good offices which we stand in need of. It is not from the benevolence of the butcher, the brewer, or the baker, that we expect our dinner, but from their regard to their own interest. We address ourselves, not to their humanity but to their self-love, and never talk to them of our own necessities but of their advantages" (26–27). I shall discuss this passage shortly. Jean-Pierre Dupuy argues (with justification, I think) that there is ultimately no significant difference between Smith and Mandeville on this point. See Dupuy (1993), 45–57.

one's self-interest so much as he tells us that we will all do so anyway. Smith argues, however, that seeking mutual sympathy, as Smith understands sympathy, cannot be construed as a self-interested project because, when one judges another, one places oneself in that other's shoes. One imagines what motivations or actions one would have or undertake were one in his shoes, meaning that one really becomes that other (in imagination at least) and hence one does not view the situation from one's own perspective. This is a process, Smith argues, that can only mendaciously be portrayed as essentially self-regarding.[29]

How does Smith's examination of other moral systems, including in particular Mandeville's licentious system, relate to the Adam Smith Problem? It seems evident from these passages, as well as those we have already scrutinized, that Smith views self-interest as a principal natural motivation—but not the only one. All people act on it to varying degrees depending on the circumstances and the character of the person in question, but self-interest does not exhaust natural human motivation, and it assuredly does not exhaust morally appropriate human motivation. Smith wishes to maintain a "real and essential distinction between vice and virtue," a "real and essential difference between the propriety and impropriety of any affection, between benevolence and any other principle of action, between real prudence and short-sighted folly or precipitate rashness" (TMS, 306), and he believes that any moral system worthy of serious consideration must do the same. Ascribing all human actions to self-love or self-interest not only falsely portrays human nature and offers a truncated view of the wide scope of actual human motivation, but it also, Smith thinks, misunderstands the process that underlies human moral judgments and the nature and genesis of the principles that inform those judgments. Benevolence is a real and undeniable motive to act in human affairs, and the impartial spectator procedure—which Smith has already shown to be the standard of human moral judgment—renders judgments that approve of benevolent motives in a large variety of situations, judgments that therefore disapprove of actions that do not display benevolence in these situations. To be sure, the impartial spectator does not exclusively approve of actions issuing from benevolent motives (which proves Hutcheson to have been mistaken); it approves of

---

[29] See TMS, 14 and 317.

self-interested motives and actions in a significant range of cases as well, namely, all those in which the actor is less than intimate with the other people involved by his actions. But Smith's argument is that one cannot understand human nature, human motivation, or human moral judgments until one understands the substantial role of natural human benevolence.

### Benevolence in TMS

A brief look at a few other passages from TMS will emphasize the necessity of benevolence in the Smithian virtuous person, and hence further indicate the limited role of self-interest.

When discussing what he calls "the sense of justice," or what he thinks informs our seemingly natural inclination to condemn breaches of the rules of justice, Smith argues that one's concern for oneself, however natural, can never be approved of by an impartial spectator as a reason for a violation of justice. He writes:

Though it may be true, therefore, that every individual, in his own breast, naturally prefers himself to all mankind, yet he dares not look mankind in the face, and avow that he acts according to this principle. He feels that in this preference they can never go along with him, and that how natural soever it may be to him, it must always appear excessive and extravagant to them. When he views himself in the light in which he is conscious that others will view him, he sees that to them he is but one of the multitude in no respect better than any other in it. If he would act so as that the impartial spectator may enter into the principles of his conduct, which is what of all things he has the greatest desire to do, he must, upon this, as upon all other occasions, humble the arrogance of his self-love, and bring it down to something which other men can go along with. (TMS, 83)

Smith follows this passage with one of the few references to economic pursuits that are to be found in TMS:

In the race for wealth, and honours, and preferments, [a person] may run as hard as he can, and strain every nerve and every muscle, in order to outstrip all his competitors. But if he should justle, or throw down any of them, the indulgence of the spectators is entirely at an end. It is a violation of fair play, which they cannot admit of. (Ibid.)

These passages are consistent with the description Smith gives of the virtuous person. Justice is foundational, and self-command must be exercised to direct one's actions into accord with it. In these passages, however, Smith is addressing those cases when we are acting in the company of strangers, which is generally the case when we seek wealth, honours, and preferments. Our competitors are only infrequently people we know well, much less friends or relatives. Hence mention is not made of benevolence. Self-interest is the proper motivation, though always within the bounds of justice. Yet note how Smith describes the actor's motivation even in such a case: he would dare not look others in the face and tell them that his principle of action is unabashed self-interest; such a principle would appear excessive and extravagant to others. Our conscience—that is, the impartial spectator—reminds us that others view us as just one in the multitude, not as the person of prime importance we view ourselves to be. Smith's suggestion is that one cannot be faulted for a lack of benevolence in one's dealings with strangers, but one can and will be faulted for excessive self-love, especially when it leads to a breach of justice.

In another passage, Smith is discussing "the influence and authority of conscience," once one's conscience has been formed the way Smith has described (TMS, 134–56). He gives several common, concrete cases in which a person's conscience overrules his present interests. In a battle, for example, the lives of a group of soldiers may depend on one soldier's squarely facing a mortal risk—perhaps rushing headlong to fight a number of enemy soldiers so that the rest of his platoon has time to escape. It is of course not in this soldier's own best interest to place himself at risk of near certain death, regardless of what good might or might not come to his fellows. Yet soldiers do such things, and, what is more, observers approve and even expect them to do so. Why? Smith writes: "It is deeply impressed upon every tolerably good soldier, who feels that he would become the scorn of his companions, if he could be supposed capable of shrinking from danger, or of hesitating, either to expose or to throw away his life, when the good of the service required it" (TMS, 138). We can see in this example all the central elements of Smith's theory of moral sentiments: the desire for mutual sympathy, the formation of the general rules of morality, the internalization of these rules as an impartial spectator, the ultimate development of a conscience, and the power of self-command that one's conscience wields over one. Observers expect such heroic acts from soldiers because that is what their own consciences tell them they would have done (or should have done) in the same situation. Moreover, the impartial spectator approves of such behavior. Smith formulates the principle on which the impartial spectator judges such cases in this way:

> One individual must never prefer himself so much even to any other individual, as to hurt or injure that other, in order to benefit himself, though the benefit to the one should be much greater than the hurt or injury to the other. The poor man must neither defraud nor steal from the rich, though the acquisition might be much more beneficial to the one than the loss could be hurtful to the other. The man within immediately calls to him, in this case too, that he is no better than his neighbour, and that by this unjust preference he renders himself the proper object of the contempt and indignation of mankind. (Ibid.)

"The man within" is the impartial spectator, whose (morally proper) judgment in such cases not only contradicts one's self-interest, but also possesses the authority to command us to act against our self-interest.

In his short chapter "Of universal Benevolence" (TMS, 235–37), Smith describes the way in which natural benevolence can be considered universal, namely, because it can be provoked by and directed toward anyone. Smith argues, however, that this universal benevolence would be the source only of frustration and misery, were it not the case that the entire universe is directed by "that great, benevolent, and all-wise Being" (TMS, 235). Because this being directs the universe, we can be sure that any injustice we might witness or experience is necessary for the overall prosperity of the universe. "The wise and virtuous man," Smith concludes, is therefore "at all times willing that his own private interest should be sacrificed to the public interest of his own particular order or society" (ibid.). He continues:

> [The wise and virtuous man] is at all times willing, too, that the interest of this order or society should be sacrificed to the greater interest of the state or sovereignty, of which it is only a subordinate part. He should, therefore, be equally willing that all those inferior interests should be sacrificed to the greater interest of the universe, to the interest of that great society of all sensible and intelligent beings, of which God himself is the immediate administrator and director. (Ibid.)

We saw earlier that Smith believes a person's virtue to be dependent on the degree to which his motivations and actions are in accord with what the impartial spectator approves. If we connect that claim to what Smith writes here, we are led to picture the Smithian virtuous person as even more expansively benevolent than we might have pictured him before. In fact, Smith here describes true virtue in a way that seems to combine strands of both Hutcheson and the Stoics: universal benevolence coupled with a serene acceptance of whatever fortune brings. Self-interest seems to be far off indeed:

> And hence it is, that to feel much for others and little for ourselves, that to restrain our selfish, and to indulge our benevolent affections, constitutes the perfection of human nature; and can alone produce among mankind that harmony of sentiments and passions in which consists their whole grace and propriety. As to love our neighbour as we love ourselves is the great law of Christianity, so it is the great precept of nature to love ourselves only as we love our neighbour, or what comes to the same thing, as our neighbour is capable of loving us. (TMS, 25)

Elsewhere in TMS, after fleshing out Hutcheson's system of morality—a system that Smith thinks is ultimately flawed—Smith is nonetheless moved to write this:

> Such is the account given of the nature of virtue in this amiable system [of Hutcheson's], a system which has a peculiar tendency to nourish and support in the human heart the noblest and most agreeable of all affections, and not only to check the injustice of self-love, but in some measure to discourage that principle altogether, by representing it as what could never reflect any honour upon those who were influenced by it. (TMS, 303–304)

I should note that in this passage Smith is neither explaining Hutcheson's system nor criticizing it; this passage comes after the exposition and before the evaluation. It is a transition paragraph in which, as the context implies, Smith is simply stating some of what he agrees with in Hutcheson's "amiable system." Even as Smith goes on to criticize Hutcheson as having failed to recognize the important role self-interest plays in the life of a virtuous person, Smith concedes at least this much to his former teacher: "The mixture of a selfish motive, it is true, seems often to sully the beauty of those actions which ought to arise from a benevolent action" (TMS, 304). Smith's only disagreement is in the explanation of this feeling of sullied beauty: "The cause of this, however, is not that self-love can never be the motive of a virtuous action, but that the benevolent principle appears in this particular case to want its due degree of strength, and to be altogether unsuitable to its object" (ibid.)—that is, in this case acting out of self-interest violates the impartial spectator's dictates.

Self-interest occupies an important place in the life of the virtuous person, according to Smith. This is shown both by the fact that the failure to recognize its importance is Smith's chief criticism of Hutcheson, and by the central part prudence, which is motivated by self-interest, plays in rounding out the virtuous person's character. Where Smith strays from his conception of virtuous action as issuing from balanced motives of justice, benevolence, and prudence, however, he tends to lean in the direction of expanded benevolence. As the last few passages we looked at showed, Smith was not beyond occasional flourishes of moralism that, perhaps still in him as holdovers from his early years at Glasgow under Hutcheson, tend to see the achievement of a virtuous character as coextensive with the expansion of benevolent motivation. We cannot, I think, conclude that at any point Smith disbelieved his own contention that self-interest is a necessary part of virtue—under that assumption we would be unable to make sense of too much of what Smith writes. I believe we can safely assume, however, that Smith was deeply impressed by the virtue of benevolence. We can also assume that Smith thought benevolence required more attention in moral thinking and teaching than did self-interest, since the latter needed no cultivation, only correction as the impartial spectator judged necessary.

## II. Self-Interest in WN

The virtue that predominates in WN is prudence, which Smith there describes, consistent with what he said in TMS, as flowing from self-love. It is out of concern for our own long-term interests that, for example, we restrain a present impulse toward extravagant spending and instead save our money and invest our capital (WN, 330–49). But there is virtually no mention of benevolence in WN, and no suggestion that it should play a role in a virtuous person's life. Why not? The topic of WN concerns only a subset of human behavior, but it is human behavior nonetheless; hence one would think that it should fall under the same purview of human motivation set out in TMS. Yet the picture of human motivation one gets in WN seems decidedly different from that in TMS.

In what has become one of the most famous passages from WN— and one of the few places in WN where the word "benevolence" appears—Smith writes:

> It is not from the benevolence of the butcher, the brewer, or the baker, that we expect our dinner, but from their regard to their own interest. We address ourselves, not to their humanity but to their self-love, and never talk to them of our own necessities but of their own advantages. (WN, 26–27)[30]

Lest one think Smith is speaking of self-love as the governing principle of only a small part of human relations, as a person concerned with resolving the Adam Smith Problem might think, he continues:

> Nobody but a beggar chuses to depend chiefly upon the benevolence of his fellow-citizens. Even a beggar does not depend upon it entirely. The charity of well-disposed people, indeed, supplies him with the whole fund of his subsistence. But though this principle ultimately provides him with all the necessaries of life which he has occasion for, it neither does nor can provide him with them as he has occasion for them. The greater part of his occasional wants are supplied in the same manner as those of other people, by treaty, by barter, and by purchase. With the money which one man gives him he purchases food. The old cloaths which another bestows upon him he exchanges for other old cloaths which suit him better, or for lodging, or for food, or for money, with which he can buy either food, cloaths, or lodging, as he has occasion. (WN, 27)

The scope of Smith's claim should not go unnoticed. He speaks of "all the necessaries of life" as falling under the governance of self-interest and not benevolence, and he specifically names food, clothing, and lodging as some of those necessities. This claim then would seem broad enough to include behavior that TMS might have considered to fall properly within the purview of, for example, benevolence as well as self-interest. Why is there no mention, then, of beneficence? Of justice or self-command?[31]

---

[30] It is noteworthy that in Smith's "Index" to WN, which he included with the third edition in 1784, neither "benevolence" nor "beneficence" appears. He tellingly includes the following entry, however, which refers to the passage cited here: "*Self-love* the governing principle in the intercourse of human society, 26–7" (WN, 1069).

[31] This might be a good place to point out that there might also exist a nascent David Hume Problem similar to that of his close friend Smith. Hume recognized

Here are three passages from WN that will suggest how uniform Smith's treatment of human motivation there is.

With regard to profusion, the principle, which prompts to expence, is the passion for present enjoyment; which, though sometimes violent and very difficult to be restrained, is in general only momentary and occasional. But the principle which prompts to save, is the desire of bettering our condition, a desire which, though generally calm and dispassionate, comes with us from the womb, and never leaves us till we go into the grave. In the whole interval which separates those two moments, there is scarce perhaps a single instant in which any man is so perfectly and completely satisfied with his situation, as to be without any wish of alteration or improvement, of any kind. (WN, 341)

The uniform, constant, and uninterrupted effort of every man to better his condition, the principle from which publick and national, as well as private opulence is originally derived, is frequently powerful enough to maintain the natural progress of things toward improvement, in spite both of the extravagance of government, and of the greatest errors of administration. (WN, 343)

The natural effort of every individual to better his own condition, when suffered to exert itself with freedom and security, is so powerful a principle, that it is alone, and without any assistance, not only capable of carrying on the society to wealth and prosperity, but of surmounting a hundred impertinent obstructions with which the folly of human laws too often incumbers its operations. (WN, 540)

These passages are some of the more conspicuous places in WN in which Smith addresses the desires human beings have that underlie their pursuit of wealth and that inform their interactions with one another.[32] Whether he means that these desires inform all our interactions with one another or only those dealing with economics is a question to which I shall return. But we should not forget that in TMS the impartial spectator sets the standard for proper behavior in all realms, which would include the economic.

---

benevolence as a virtue, yet he also had some understanding that self-interest was what moved markets. For the former, see for example Section II of 2E; for the latter, see for example his essays "Of Commerce" and "Of Taxes," both reprinted in his *Essays: Moral, Political, and Literary* (1987). For discussion of this issue in Hume, as well as some of the connections to Smith, see Danford (1990), especially Chapter 8.

[32] They are not the only passages. See also WN, 99, 285, 374, 405, 454, and 674.

Smith's overall argument in WN, however, seems to presume that human beings are essentially self-interested. The argument seems to be that we act only out of self-interest, but, as far as economic growth and progress are concerned, we should be happy about that because by pursuing our individual interests in bettering our own conditions we act in ways that unintentionally—as if "led by an invisible hand" (WN, 456)—conduce to the greater standard of living and economic growth of our entire community. People will look to increase their personal output of whatever they produce so that they will have more to sell or trade. Because everyone will seek to increase his production this way, the overall production of things will, over time, increase, and the prices of goods will decrease; increases in production coupled with decreases in prices lead to greater overall prosperity. Hence if we want greater prosperity and economic growth, then measures should be adopted that allow individuals greater freedom to pursue their own interests. The analysis in WN, then, is quite utilitarian: respect for life, liberty, and property leads to increasing prosperity and for that reason should be protected. The recommendations Smith makes to abolish or restrict various legal enactments and regulations are principally motivated by their salutary effect on the society's overall prosperity. And, what I hope is clear, they presume no benevolent motives on the part of the people who fall under their jurisdiction; rather, they presume only self-interest.

My conclusion, then, is the negative one that if Smith had thought that any motivation besides self-interest is active in human behavior, he would have appealed to it somewhere in WN, especially given the extremely broad range of human activities he discusses in WN; or, to put it the other way around, he would not have appealed to, and assumed for the coherence of his argument, only self-interest.

### III. The Problem and Attempted Resolutions

Thus we have the Adam Smith Problem. Smith published only two books in his lifetime, and each went through several editions that were supervised and in several instances revised by him. Yet WN seems as though it could have been written by someone other than the person who wrote TMS. Nowhere in WN, for example, is reference made to TMS; nowhere in WN is mention made of the view championed in

TMS that four principal virtues—justice, beneficence, prudence, and self-command—must be balanced in the virtuous person; nowhere is an intimation in WN that benevolence has anything whatever to do with either natural or moral motivation; nowhere in WN can one find discussion of the human conscience, the impartial spectator,[33] or the impartial spectator procedure; and finally, there is in WN no occurrence of Smithian sympathy or the desire for mutual sympathy, which together constitute arguably the central feature of TMS. How is it possible that there could be no connection of substance between Smith's only two books? In both the "Advertisement" to the sixth edition of TMS and in its final paragraphs Smith announced his plan for an overall system of study, of which TMS and WN were to form parts. But this makes the problem more, not less, acute: if he expressly intended a connection between the two books, why did he not make clear what that connection was supposed to be? Worse, how is it possible that the books could be predicated on views about human motivation and virtue that not only seem to take no consideration of each other, but that even seem inconsistent?[34]

Several scholars have offered unsatisfactory solutions to the problem. A. L. Macfie and D. D. Raphael suggest in their Introduction to TMS that the difference between the treatments Smith gives of human virtue and human motivation in TMS and WN differ in tone only, not substance (TMS, Introduction, 20). They continue:

The so-called 'Adam Smith problem' was a pseudo-problem based on ignorance and misunderstanding. Anybody who reads TMS . . . will not have the slightest inclination to be puzzled that the same man wrote this book and WN, or to suppose that he underwent any radical change of view about human conduct. (Ibid.)

---

[33] The phrase "impartial spectators" (note the plural) appears once in WN, in a discussion of England and its American colonies: "The distance of those provinces from the capital, from the principal seat of the great scramble of faction and ambition, makes them enter less into the views of any of the contending parties, and renders them more indifferent and impartial spectators of the conduct of all" (WN, 945). It is interesting that WN's only mention of this phrase couches it in the general terms of the objectivity that distance lends, rather than in the technical terms of Smith's own discussion of the impartial spectator in TMS.

[34] For a detailed, speculative attempt to reconstruct Smith's intended corpus, see Griswold (1999), 29–39.

Given what we have seen in this chapter, however, that position appears implausible. A common argument is that the subject matter in WN is narrower in scope than that in TMS; WN concerns itself only with economics and therefore justifiably concerns itself with that part of human motivation involved in economic affairs, namely, self-interest. So A. L. Macfie, for example, writes:

far from there being any clash between the two books, the later one gives merely a particular development of the broader doctrine in the first. The economic man is the prudent man in the economic sphere. So the economic man also is under the sway of social sympathy and the impartial rulings of the informed spectator. (1967, 75)[35]

The final sentence may be correct, but Macfie does not give us reason to believe it. His argument is that the narrower scope of WN justifies its focus on a narrower range of human motivation (specifically self-interest), but what supports the claim that the "economic man" described in WN is under the sway of the impartial spectator? Smith does not discuss the impartial spectator in WN; neither does he mention "social sympathy" or any other kind of sympathy. When in WN Smith describes the motivations of "economic man," they exclusively relate to and issue from self-interest. Macfie argues that when Smith is criticizing Hutcheson's moral theory in TMS, the character traits Smith lists as virtues that flow from self-interest are primarily economic, and from this Macfie concludes that Smith thinks that human action in the economic realm is governed exclusively, or at least primarily, by self-interest (74–75). But the virtues Smith lists—"oeconomy, industry, discretion, attention, and application of thought"—do not in fact pertain only to economic activities.[36] Moreover, although it is true that in TMS self-interest is incorporated into a larger scheme of human virtue (as we have seen and as Macfie claims), precisely the matter at issue is

---

[35] In this section, all citations from Macfie are from this place, on the page given in parentheses.

[36] Richard F. Teichgraeber III echoes this criticism of Macfie, but he errs, I think, when he writes that the Smithian prudent man "is sociable and capable of friendship, but his particular virtues have no bearing on the 'public business.' His aim is to maintain a polite, comfortable, private life" (1981, 116). Smith certainly does think that prudence bears on one's success in "public business"; it is just that prudence bears on other areas of life as well.

that no such larger scheme of human virtue is mentioned, or, it would seem, assumed in WN.

Now Macfie would probably concede that a larger scheme of human virtue is not presented in WN, but he would no doubt hasten to add that that is as would be expected, since WN's purpose is not to talk about human virtue. He argues that the only important question concerning the consistency of Smith's two books is whether what is said in WN can be subsumed into the overall theoretical structure set out in TMS. Macfie thinks it can. He argues that one of the features about Smith's examination in TMS that sets it apart from other similar examinations of his day is the joint role that both sentiment and reason play in the moral life. Smith's insistence that the standards of morality are set by an informed but impartial spectator, Macfie argues, indicates his reliance on reason: "Feeling alone will not make you 'well informed' or 'impartial'. Only reason can do that—the practical reason" (67). For Macfie, Smith's use of reason is crucial in uniting the projects of his two books, for it is this reason, Macfie claims, that gives rise to the virtue of prudence in TMS and to the behavior of the "economic man" in WN.

When we consider the relevance of the 'prudent' man, who in the *Wealth of Nations* appears as Mill's 'economic man', we shall see that Smith did give the prudent man a *rational* place in his system of the moral sentiments, and we shall realize that only reason could reveal and define this place. (68; Macfie's italics)

Macfie concludes that Smith's conception of self-love, which underlies the general, "balancing" virtue of prudence, is constant throughout Smith's two books. It is, Macfie claims, a rational self-interest that Smith has in mind, and in WN all Smith is doing is working out in great detail how this rational self-interest plays out in the particular realm of behavior in which the impartial spectator endorses its greatest license, namely, economic activity. I find no reason to disagree with much of what Macfie here argues. Reason does play an important role in passing Smithian moral judgments, as I have argued in earlier chapters; it is also true, with some qualifications, that the Smithian virtue of prudence issues from something like reasonable or rational self-interest; finally, the impartial spectator of TMS would indeed endorse this self-interest as the proper motive for most of what goes on in economic behavior. I question, however, whether this is enough to solve the Adam Smith Problem. Macfie's argument would be stronger if the issue under contention were, say, an aberrant chapter of TMS— if, that is, there were a chapter in TMS that talked about how in economic behavior man acts only on self-interest. In that case it would seem reasonable to assume that the aberrant chapter could be rendered entirely consistent with the rest of TMS simply by showing how it can be subsumed into the framework set out in TMS. Then the fact that there was little or no mention of the other central claims of TMS in the single chapter would not, perhaps, be worrisome. But that is not the situation. Rather, we have two independent books, the second of which is over one thousand pages long—certainly long enough, one would think, to allow for a few words about how it fits into the framework of the first book, if that were in fact the author's intention. Indeed, I can find in WN no suggestion that its analysis is meant to be a substantial extension of what was discussed in TMS. If that was Smith's intent, why did he not say so?

I believe that the principle of interpretive charity—striving to give an author the best possible formulation of his argument—is a good rule of exegesis, and I subscribe to it wherever possible and reasonable.[37] In light of this principle, one should perhaps be willing to overlook the fact that Smith makes no explicit connection between his two books, if it could be shown that the two books nevertheless adhere to the same overall structure or are parts of a single overall plan. And this is what Macfie claims. In fact, this will form part of my own argument in the next chapter. But I cannot accept Macfie's argument for Smith's consistency because it does not resolve what I think is a central part of the problem, namely, *why* self-interest should be the sole, or virtually sole, motivation men feel in their economic behavior. Even allowing prudence to be the general, balancing virtue—and the discussion from earlier in this chapter casts doubt on this—Macfie does not offer a reason why the impartial spectator would approve

---

[37] I think Macfie is at times inclined to be too charitable to Smith. He offers this as one argument for Smith's consistency: "Adam Smith was a man of stable integrated character, not subject to deep intellectual doubts or fissures. It is quite unlikely that such a man would write two books over the same period, the one adopting virtue, propriety, rational sympathy as the final human good, the other insisting on the social value of a self-interest which could with any truth be equated to selfishness" (76).

of benevolent motives in some areas of activity but never in economic activity. Macfie would perhaps respond by saying that that is what rational self-interest dictates; rational self-interest dictates benevolent motives in some cases, self-interested motives in other cases, and economic activity falls in among the latter. But that is not enough: we still need an argument explaining why that is the case.

In his discussion of Smith's economic thought, D. D. Raphael writes:

> It will be seen that the whole of this elaborate network of analysis [in WN] depends on the motive force of self-interest, starting from entering into exchange, for easing toil and trouble, and ending with the accumulation of capital, for bettering our condition. The complex system, with its equilibria and its circular or spiral flows, owes nothing to deliberate planning. It exhibits a high and ever-increasing degree of mutual dependence, yet it all comes about naturally from the interplay of self-interest. (1985, 69–70)[38]

I do not need to underscore the conspicuous absence in this citation of benevolence as a natural human motive or of the influence of the impartial spectator in directing human action. Given this understanding of WN, however, one would expect Raphael to take a serious reckoning of the alleged Adam Smith Problem. Raphael discusses the problem, but he offers no way to reconcile his own rendering of Smith's account of human motivation in WN with the account Smith gives in TMS. Raphael writes that those scholars who found a discrepancy between Smith's two books made the mistake of thinking that in TMS "Smith took sympathy to be the most influential of human motives" (88), and they routinely equated sympathy with benevolence (89–90). Raphael is correct to point out that Smithian sympathy is not a motive to action at all; rather, as we have seen, Smith means by "sympathy" a harmony or concordance between the sentiments of an actor and of an observer. It is recognition of this concordance of sentiments that gives one what Smith called the "pleasure of mutual sympathy." And though desire for this mutual sympathy is a motive to action, it cannot be equated with benevolence. So far, so good; but Raphael thinks that is all there is to the problem.[39] As I have suggested, however, the

---

[38] In this section, all citations from Raphael are from this place, on the page given in parentheses.

[39] Griswold gives the same account of the Adam Smith Problem. See Griswold (1999), 260–62. Griswold goes on to argue that, in light of his reconstruction of Smith's

problem concerns not an equation of Smithian sympathy with benevolence, but instead Smith's seeming abandonment in WN of the notion that human virtue comprises a constellation of four virtues, not one, and the notion that motivations other than self-interest are and ought to be present in men. These issues Raphael does not address.[40]

Raphael goes on to argue that the two books display a difference in emphasis, but that it does not follow from this that the two books are mutually incompatible. He writes that one ought to compare the two books "in terms of sociology" (93), by which he seems to mean the way each book treats the development and maintenance of society and social institutions. In TMS, Raphael suggests, Smith describes the "social bond" created by the universal desire for mutual sympathy: "Since pretty well all human beings enjoy esteem and dislike contempt, the effect of approbation and disapprobation is to induce conformity to social norms both in behaviour and in attitude" (93). WN, on the other hand, emphasizes a different kind of social bond, self-interest, which functions in economic realms by inducing participants into appealing to one another's interests—something one can only do if one knows what others' interests are. Hence by desiring to serve only ourselves, we are led to serve others (93–94).[41] Raphael concedes that the social bond discussed in TMS "is quite different from the social bonds" discussed in WN (94), but that does not faze him.

The social bond of sympathy and imagination [discussed in TMS] leads to our code of ethics and to a good part of our code of law. Economic behaviour, on the other hand, has to be explained in terms of self-interest. This does not imply that a person engaged in economic transactions has no regard to what other people will think of him. Apart from anything else, economic exchange depends on contract, and the legal notions about the duties and rights of contract are as much tied up with ethics as they are with economics. But in economic life the thought of social approval and disapproval takes second place to the idea of doing best for oneself. (94)

intended corpus, TMS and WN can be seen as "complementary parts of a larger whole in which moral philosophy, political economy, social science, and history support an unsentimental vision of the decent and productive life of the nonphilosopher" (1999, 265). But he does not resolve what I argue here are the principal conflicts between the books. See also Griswold's Chapters 6 and 7.

40 In fact, Raphael dismisses the issue by calling the notion that there might be a substantial difference between TMS and WN a "fantasy" (89).

41 I think Raphael makes a good point here. I return to this issue in the Conclusion.

The problem with Raphael's account of Smith's two books is that he gives us insufficient reason to think that that is really what Smith intended. It is true that holding that self-interest is the primary human drive in economic matters does not mean that one cannot simultaneously maintain that these same human beings are also concerned with mutual sympathy, which is what Raphael argues earlier. But I do not find Smith saying that, at least not in WN. Smith nowhere in WN argues or even suggests that benevolence or the desire for mutual sympathy are *also* motives that people naturally feel in their economic endeavors in addition to self-interest. On the contrary, as we have seen, he repeatedly writes as if to say that self-interest is their sole and universal motivation. On what basis, then, do we argue that Smith's unstated assumption is that everything he writes in WN is subject to the constraints and arguments set out previously in TMS? I do not argue that this is impossible, only that no evidence has been given to support it. In TMS Smith speaks of virtues relating to self-interest, including virtues that would apply to economic exchanges (virtues such as prudence), but there is no similar discussion of virtue in WN—there is not even an indication in WN that virtue per se is on its author's mind. In light of the prima facie differences between WN and TMS, then, it would seem more plausible to conclude that the books do not accord with the same overall conception of human virtue.

As both Macfie and Raphael remind us,[42] and as we saw in Section I, Smith recognized and discussed in TMS the importance of self-interest in the life of the virtuous person. But that does not settle the matter, since in WN Smith seems to treat self-interest as the *sole* natural motive to act, to the exclusion of benevolence and the desire for mutual sympathy. For three reasons, I think, it will not do to argue that WN is narrower in scope than TMS, and that the narrower, more technical focus in WN makes it understandable that Smith does not discuss benevolence, the impartial spectator, or TMS itself. First, TMS concerned itself with all realms of human behavior, which includes economic. Second, the range of human activity discussed in WN is not, as it turns out, narrow at all; rather, it is strikingly broad, including, besides straightforwardly economic concerns of business, banking, and

[42] Macfie (1967), 74–75, and Raphael (1985), 90. Haakonssen makes a similar argument (1981), 49–52.

commerce, the not obviously economic concerns of education, politics, religion, and many aspects of family relations. Third, LJ is also narrower in scope than TMS, yet here we find Smith mentioning and making use of TMS, the impartial spectator, and the desire for mutual sympathy time and again.[43] Indeed, I think one could aptly characterize his analysis of what constitutes property as an impartial spectator theory of property, and one could aptly characterize his arguments concerning what constitutes proper and improper punishment for crimes as an impartial spectator theory of punishment.[44] Smith delivered his lectures on jurisprudence at the University of Glasgow every year beginning in the early 1750s and continuing until he left for France in 1764, during which time he supervised the publication of the first two editions of TMS and was beginning work on WN. Smith was thus thinking about all of his work during the same periods of time. The fact, then, that the results of Smith's analysis in TMS should find their way into heavy use in LJ, but be entirely absent from WN, would seem to require a deeper explanation than that Smith was just doing (partially) different things in TMS and WN.

Glenn R. Morrow and Richard F. Teichgraeber III have offered attempts to resolve the Adam Smith Problem that I believe do not give enough consideration to all of what Smith wrote. Morrow begins by pointing out how extensive Smith's reliance is in WN on self-interest as the mainspring of human behavior—so extensive, in fact, that it reaches spheres of behavior beyond what we would normally call economic, like the English systems of justice and education.[45] But Morrow

---

43 See, for example, LJ, 17–19, 32, 87, 104–05, 401 (which contains an explicit reference to TMS), 438, 459, 461, and 475. Macfie writes this about WN and LJ: "Both are applied science in relation to the *Moral Sentiments*, the one in Jurisprudence, the other in Economics. Yet no one has suggested that the *Lectures* conflict in principle with the *Moral Sentiments*. Is it not always the case that an author writes on different topics in a different manner and language? Could not a similar situation be found in the different works of John Stuart Mill, or Herbert Spencer, or Henry Sidgwick? Do not both the *Lectures* and the *Wealth of Nations* trace specific lines of development in the social workings of rational sympathy, in the institutions of law and economy? There seems no obvious reason to expect more coherence than appears" (1967, 76). I think the analogy between LJ and WN fails, however, for the reasons given in the text.

44 For the impartial spectator theory of property, see in particular LJ, 17–19 and 459–62 (but see also LJ, 468, where the impartial spectator seems absent); for the impartial spectator theory of punishment, see LJ, 475–76. See also Haakonssen (1981), 135–53.

45 Morrow (1928), 162–66. In this section, all references to Morrow are to this place, on the page given in parentheses.

nevertheless makes the by-now familiar claim that although Smith had expatiated on the importance of benevolence in a virtuous person in TMS, Smith also in TMS spoke of "other, inferior virtues," "such as prudence, frugality, industry, self-reliance" (166). From this, Morrow concludes that

> Adam Smith's employment of self-interest in the *Wealth of Nations,* then, does not mean either that he regarded self-love as the only actuating principle in human nature, or that he recommended only unrestrained selfishness as the best means of promoting public wealth. It merely means that Smith was preaching, in the economic world, the same gospel of individual rights and individual liberty which in one form or another was the burden of eighteenth-century social thought. (167)

Morrow also concludes that the self-interest prevalent in WN can be reconciled with the account of human motivation in TMS after it is realized that even in WN Smith presumes that all behavior is within the bounds of justice and under the watchful eye of the impartial spectator (177–79). But Morrow does not attempt to account for the passages in WN where Smith *does* regard self-love as the only actuating principle in human nature. And why should we think that economic behavior is rightfully subject to the impartial spectator's judgment if there is no mention of any such thing in WN?

Teichgraeber gives in part the same resolution as does Morrow, but Teichgraeber's argument contains the novelty that there is in Smith a radical distinction between public and private spheres of activity.[46] He argues that Smith's use of benevolence in TMS is restricted to the private sphere of activity, that is, to those activities in which one deals with people close to one—principally family and friends. In "Smith's narrowly conceived realm of public 'virtue,'" however, Smith's virtuous person is exclusively a "just, law-abiding individual [who] would not be concerned with joining in efforts of collective self-assertion and self-definition. His primary task was to avoid encroaching on 'the person or the estate or the reputation' of his neighbor" (121). Teichgraeber writes that people engaged in economic pursuits constitute a "society of strangers," in which case Smithian sympathy is "translated into the virtues of self-restraint and self-discipline" (122). His argument is that

---

[46] Teichgraeber (1981), 120–23. In this section, all citations from Teichgraeber are from this place, on the page given in parentheses. See also Teichgraeber (1986, 133–39 and 170–78).

in TMS Smith concentrated on one particular realm of virtue, namely, that concerning "personal moral rules"; whereas in WN, Smith concentrated on another realm of virtue, namely, that concerning "justice" (understood as the rules prescribing the minimum level of conduct necessary for strangers to get along with one another).

As I shall argue in the next chapter, Teichgraeber is on to something important here, but I do not believe it works the way he thinks. Teichgraeber is right to claim that Smith's treatment of human motivation (and moral judgment, which Teichgraeber does not mention) in TMS recognizes a difference between the way family members are treated, for example, as opposed to complete strangers. Nevertheless, the reason for this difference is not, as Teichgraeber suggests, because Smith stakes out a "private" virtue as opposed to a "public" virtue. I find no evidence in TMS that Smith meant to separate out "categorically different kinds" of virtue (122). On the contrary, it seems to me that in TMS Smith argues that all human behavior, private and public alike, is comprehended in one general conception of human virtue by the four cardinal Smithian virtues of justice, benevolence, prudence, and self-command. Moreover, Smith's discussions of justice in WN do not seem to have the moral dimension they did in TMS; rather, they relate almost exclusively to the administration and execution of laws.[47] In any case, all behavior, according to TMS, is judged by the standard of the impartial spectator. Granting that the impartial spectator would approve of activities showing a greater measure of self-interest than benevolence in the "public" sphere of economics does not by itself explain or justify the complete absence of benevolence in WN or WN's reliance on self-interest as the sole motivation for human activity. It is true that the vast majority of the discussion in WN concerns what Teichgraeber would call activity in the "public" realm. Teichgraeber could perhaps argue that this fact supports his claim that Smith had in mind two different realms of virtue, which were separately discussed in Smith's two books. Yet even this would not solve the Adam Smith Problem. We still need an explanation for the fact that in WN Smith explicitly does not speak of a balance of motives, with self-interest predominating over benevolence in economic realms. We also need an explanation of why Smith should write in WN as though self-interest

---

[47] See, for example, WN, 708–22.

were the *only* natural motive people have—why he should not even justify himself by claiming that the impartial spectator endorses self-interest in public economic realms.

Finally, Knud Haakonssen's book concentrates on Smith's theory of jurisprudence, but it also spends a fair amount of time analyzing Smith's moral theory in an attempt to show how LJ in part builds on concepts set out in TMS.[48] In a section entitled "Sympathy and moral approval" (49–52), Haakonssen claims to have made it "futile to take any more rides on that old hobby-horse 'sympathy v. self-interest' in Smith" (197, n. 19). Haakonssen distinguishes the different senses of the word "sympathy" that Smith uses in TMS, deriving the distinctions from Smith's discussion of what Haakonssen calls "sympathetic evaluations" (51)—that is, moral judgments. Haakonssen gives the following schematization of the process of passing a Smithian moral judgment:

First there is the imaginary change of situation by which the spectator tries, as far as possible, to expose himself to the same causal influences as the man originally concerned. We will often find this process alone called sympathy in Smith. Secondly, there is the result of the influence of this cause, namely the reaction of the spectator. This too is called sympathy, or the sympathetic feelings, sentiments, etc. Thirdly, there is the comparison of the original and the sympathetic sentiments. And fourthly, there is the emotion arising from this comparison, which is either a kind of pleasure called approval when the original and the sympathetic sentiments coincide, or a kind of pain called disapproval when they do not coincide. This pleasure is often called sympathy, while the pain ought to be, and occasionally is, called antipathy. (51)

Haakonssen explains that the first two senses of "sympathy" distinguished here are "neutral," meaning that they could ultimately result in either sympathy or antipathy in Haakonssen's last sense listed. He says that the "neutral" usage of sympathy is "technical," while the sympathy/antipathy usage is "closer to the ordinary sense of the word where it implies some kind of positive attitude" (51). He then concludes with this:

What is most confusing of all, however, is that Smith frequently uses sympathy to denote all three of the senses mentioned plus the comparison—that is, he often talks of sympathy as the whole process including its result, which in that case can only be 'positive' (approval). (51)

---

[48] In this section, all citations from Haakonssen (1981) are given in parentheses.

This sentence is then immediately followed by the footnote in which Haakonssen says that he has hereby made future discussion of the Adam Smith Problem futile.

But how does Haakonssen's analysis obviate future discussion of this issue? He does not address the difference in treatments of human motivation one finds in TMS and WN; nor does he address the different conceptions of human virtue each book (TMS explicitly, WN by implication) offers; nor, finally, does he address any scholarly versions of the Adam Smith Problem and show how he has refuted them or solved it. Haakonssen must believe, then, that the resolution to the previously alleged problem in Smith is given simply by virtue of the three senses of sympathy he distinguished. His argument seems to be that the sympathy that underlies a Smithian moral judgment is indifferent as to what motive the person being judged had. That is, the moral judgment will be based on a presence or absence of sympathy, but this sympathy can in principle be had with any sentiment or motive whatever. Haakonssen would then be suggesting that since TMS does not preclude the possibility of self-interested actions receiving sympathetic approval, there is hence no problem to begin with: TMS never argued that sympathy with benevolence was the only basis for moral approval. Even if WN speaks predominantly or exclusively to an innate self-interest in human beings, there is no reason why that should be inconsistent with the theory of moral judgment laid out in TMS.

If this is Haakonssen's resolution, then his dismissal of all future discussion is premature. As we have seen, it is true that TMS does not condone only benevolent actions, and that TMS's conception of sympathy makes it possible to sympathize with various motivations, including self-interest. But in the end, Haakonssen's argument takes a similar tack as did the arguments given by Raphael, Macfie, and Morrow: since in TMS Smith allows room for—even at points extols—virtuous behavior that springs from self-interest, combined with the fact of WN's allegedly almost exclusive focus on the narrow realm of economic activity (in which self-interest is properly the predominant motive), Smith is justified in his complete reliance on self-interest for his analysis in WN. But this argument is subject to the objection that it fails to address two important facts that together constitute the core, as I see it, of the real Adam Smith Problem. First, in TMS Smith presents a picture of human virtue that is composed of a balance of four separate virtues, a picture that is absent from WN; second, in WN Smith on more than one occasion explicitly states that human beings are driven by the universal desire to better their own condition, a desire that apparently issues from self-interest, and Smith treats this universal desire as if it were the sole motive to act that men naturally have. Haakonssen's examination, like Raphael's, Macfie's, and Morrow's, neither addresses nor resolves these concerns. Until these issues are faced, however, I do not believe a satisfactory resolution to the problem will be found.

# 5

# The Market Model and the Familiarity Principle

## *Solving the "Adam Smith Problem"*

The Adam Smith Problem is not of merely historical significance. It is a problem also for us today because it highlights the tension between moral injunctions to beneficence and other virtues, on the one hand, and the seeming amorality of economic markets on the other. If a large portion of the relations people have with other people take place within the context of the market's extended economic order, and if the Smith of WN is right that people's actions in such contexts are informed by their self-interested pursuits, then it is no small matter of concern how moral virtues that are approved in other contexts apply here. If the Smith of TMS is right, one does not—or should not—check one's morality at the marketplace door. Thus the matter of how morality mixes with markets must still be addressed.

Before one can consider that larger problem, however, we must first contend with Adam Smith's version. The core of this problem, as I argued in Chapter 4, is not just the fact that the two books seem to have little obvious connection between them, but also the apparently conflicting pictures of proper human motivation Smith gives in TMS, on the one hand, and in WN, on the other. In TMS, Smith argues that a person should properly be motivated by a balance of self-interest and benevolence, as determined by the judgment of the impartial spectator. In WN, however, Smith's argument seems to presuppose that people are motivated only by self-interest, and his argument there makes no mention of or room for benevolence.

This is a more serious problem than many recent commentators have thought.[1]

Nevertheless, there are ways to mitigate the Adam Smith Problem—two ways in particular. First, a single conceptual model for understanding the growth and maintenance of human institutions underlies both books, a model that at once unifies the philosophical methods Smith employs in each, and gives a single, constant understanding of human nature and the associations and institutions that people naturally form. Simply stated, this model is that of a market in which free exchanges among people pursuing their own interests give rise over time to an unintended system of order. I think Smith sees this model at work in all large-scale human institutions, including in particular common standards of morality (as in TMS) and economic marketplaces (as in WN). If this model proves coherent and capable of actually explaining the institutions it is meant to explain, it might also provide a first step toward solving the general problem of mixing morality and markets.

The second factor is something I shall call the "familiarity principle," which substantially unifies the apparently conflicting pictures of human motivation in TMS and WN. Smith develops the familiarity principle in TMS, arguing that people's natural benevolence toward others varies directly with their familiarity with them—the more familiar a person is to one, the greater the tendency to feel benevolent toward him; the less familiar, the less benevolent. Smith argues in TMS that the familiarity principle is, moreover, justified by the judgment of the impartial spectator. When this principle is applied to people qua actors in economic marketplaces, we shall find that their proper motivations should be quite similar to what it turns out Smith presupposes as the motivations of economic actors in WN. I shall then argue that taking together these two factors—the market model and the familiarity principle—substantially unify Smith's two books, effectively dissolving the Adam Smith Problem, even the "potent" version I pressed in Chapter 4.

---

[1] I should point out that other commentators have also pressed versions of the Adam Smith Problem, though for their own reasons. See, for example, Brown (1994), Dickey (September 1986), Dupuy (1993), Lux (1990), Minowitz (1993), and Viner (1928).

## I. The Market Model

The beginning of the solution to the Adam Smith Problem lies in Smith's general concept of a market, and the way the market functions to create, establish, and maintain human institutions. It is on the model of a market that Smith understands the development of moral standards, as we saw in Chapter 3. TMS shows how a system of moral standards develops as an unintended result of the numberless free exchanges people make with one another of their judgments of one another's motives and actions. The standards that develop inform moral judgments that are best understood as the judgments of an impartial spectator, and Smith shows what this spectator is, how his viewpoint develops, and how people come to view following his judgments as their moral duty. The analysis that Smith gives in TMS indicates that these standards apply across the entire spectrum of human behavior; they are not limited to particular activities or to particular motivations. For this analysis to be consistent with that of WN, then, it would have to be the case that the treatment of human motivation given in WN could be subsumed into the framework set out in TMS. This would mean that we should be able to explain, on the basis of what he wrote in TMS, why Smith makes the assumptions about people and their motivations that he does in WN. It means, in the first place, that TMS and WN must conform to the same conception of the creation, establishment, and maintenance of human institutions. In other words, the general concept of a market would have to inform the treatment of human institutions that are found in both books—and just this is what I wish to argue. In addition, however, it means that we would have to be able to explain, again on the basis of the examination in TMS, why an impartial spectator would approve of a seemingly exclusive reliance on self-interested motives for agents in economic activities. As I argued in Chapter 4, no proposed resolution of the Adam Smith Problem should be considered adequate until this problem of motivation is addressed.

We have already seen that the concept of a market underlies the analysis of human institutions in TMS; here I shall argue that a similar concept of a market underlies the analysis in WN. I intend to show why, on Smith's conception of a market and his analysis of proper human motivation in TMS, we should expect the kind of treatment of economic affairs that Smith in fact goes on to give in WN, and thus how WN is fundamentally consistent with TMS. I shall first lay out the nature and function of the market as Smith describes it in WN, and then I shall link this conception of the market with the conception from TMS that I fleshed out in Chapter 3. I shall then try to reconcile the apparently conflicting accounts of human motivation that one finds in the two books.

*The Market in WN*

The single most important factor responsible for the growth of human productivity is, according to Smith in WN, the division of labor.[2] The division of labor makes possible, in fact, what Smith calls "universal opulence," that is, an opulence that "extends itself to the lowest ranks of the people" (WN, 22). Smith illustrates this claim with an example that would have struck a chord with his contemporaries, but that can be easily extended to situations common today: a factory of pin-makers. He says that if ten pin-makers were working alone—that is, if each were making single pins from start to finish, and then beginning again—they could hope to make twenty pins per man, or a total of two hundred pins in a day. But look at the production of pins from the same ten-man factory as it is carried on at the time of Smith's writing: "One man draws out the wire, another straightens it, a third cuts it, a fourth points it, a fifth grinds it at the top for receiving the head," and so on (WN, 15). With the labor thus divided, the ten men can produce upwards of 48,000 pins in a day; they have increased their production an astonishing 240-fold. Although pin-making might seem a "trifling" example, Smith writes, its lesson applies to "every other art and manufacture" (ibid.), which Smith thinks includes both physical and mental labor. Smith explains that the division of labor accomplishes this enormous increase in productivity in three ways. By focusing the worker's attention on a single task, the division of labor first increases his skill and dexterity, and thus his proficiency; second, it saves "the time which is commonly lost in passing from one species of work to another"—because, after all, "A man commonly saunters a little in turning his hand from one sort of employment to another" (TMS, 19); and third, it leads "to the invention of a great number of

---

[2] See Muller (1993, Chapter 4) for a good summary of Smith's argument in the first parts of WN.

machines which facilitate and abridge labour, and enable one man to do the work of many" (WN, 17).

How does the increase in productivity lead to universal opulence? The division of labor encourages people to specialize in particular tasks, usually according to their peculiar talents or interests.[3] By focusing one's energy in this way, one enables oneself to produce an abundance of whatever one is making or doing, beyond what one needs for oneself. This abundance is necessary for the growth of a community's general wealth. As each person in the community specializes, each person creates a surplus of something, and the increase in supply lowers the cost of each product; as the division of labor and specialization increase, then, more and more products see their availability increase and (hence) their price decrease, which means more and more people are in a position to buy and afford more and more products. The result is increasing "universal opulence." Smith writes:

> It is the great multiplication of the productions of all the different arts, in consequence of the division of labour, which occasions, in a well-governed society, that universal opulence which extends itself to the lowest ranks of people. Every workman has a great quantity of his own work to dispose of beyond what he himself has occasion for; and every other workman being exactly in the same situation, he is enabled to exchange a great quantity of his own goods for a great quantity, or, what comes to the same thing, for the price of a great quantity of theirs. He supplies them abundantly with what they have occasion for, and they accommodate him as amply with what he has occasion for, and a general plenty diffuses itself through all the different ranks of the society. (WN, 22)

Smith argues that it is the division of labor, along with its concomitant increase in productivity and hence wealth, that causes a community to evolve gradually through the four stages of society: first as a community of hunters, then shepherds, then as a community based on agriculture, and finally as a community based on commerce (WN, 708–23). The commerce-based community is the most specialized and therefore sophisticated. In it people focus a great deal of their energies on a small range of skills or tasks, the produce of which they sell to anyone who is interested in buying it and has the wherewithal to do so. Of course, this description not only applies to the Scotland of the late eighteenth century, but also to the market-based economies of today.

[3] See WN, 28.

An important element of Smith's analysis is the role the market plays: Smith argues that the existence of a market is what makes the division of labor possible. If there is no opportunity for workers to exchange their own abundance for that of others, then there is neither incentive nor opportunity for them to specialize and create an abundance of supply. If such opportunity does exist, however, then those who can produce the most at the lowest cost—that is, those who specialize most efficiently—will receive the most in exchange for their work. Thus the availability of widespread opportunities of exchange encourages or "rewards" those things that Smith argued the division of labor effects: greater dexterity and skill, efficient use of time, and the creation of machinery or devices or techniques that decrease labor and increase production. The aggregate of all the opportunities to exchange labor and the products of labor is what Smith in WN collectively calls "the market," although there need not be (and usually is not) any realization on the part of the people who are parties to the market that they in any way constitute, effect, or maintain a larger "system" of exchange. Smith concludes from this—a conclusion Smith rightly considers to be a discovery that is original to him—that the division of labor is dependent on the extent of the market, with a more extensive market enabling more extensive division of labor, a less extensive market, less division of labor.[4] On this basis, Smith argues that a necessary prerequisite for increasing wealth and prosperity is extensive markets, which leads him to recommend that market restrictions such as tariffs, regulations, and taxes be abolished or significantly reduced. It is principally because of these recommendations that Smith has come to be considered the father of laissez-faire economics.[5]

I shall not rehearse Smith's entire argument in WN here (though I shall discuss it in more detail in Chapter 7). But we do have to examine Smith's notion of a market more closely to determine what resemblance it bears to the conceptual model that underlies Smith's analysis

[4] See WN, 31–36. For a more recent examination and defense of this claim of Smith's, see Stigler (June 1951). See also Blaug (1996), 36–37.

[5] I trust that by now the caricature of Smith as a doctrinaire libertarian or anarchist is, however, defunct. He believed a government was necessary, principally for three things: to provide for the defense of national security, to administrate and enforce the rules of justice, and to provide for "public works," such as roads, canals, and public schools. See WN, 689–947.

in TMS. What Smith thinks sets the market in motion is the natural human "propensity to truck, barter, and exchange one thing for another" (WN, 25). Because human beings are so dependent on others for their survival and well-being,[6] producing and exchanging allows them to supply both what each individual needs for himself as well as what others need for themselves. The impetus to produce and the instances of exchange are thus at bottom driven by each person's self-interest. Here is how Smith describes all such exchanges: "Give me that which I want, and you shall have this which you want" (WN, 26). Following this passage comes perhaps the most oft-quoted passage in all of WN: "It is not from the benevolence of the butcher, the brewer, or the baker, that we expect our dinner, but from their regard to their own interest. We address ourselves, not to their humanity but to their self-love, and never talk to them of our own necessities but of their advantages" (WN, 26–27). Our natural desire to satisfy our own interests triggers, then, the natural propensity to exchange things with each other in the hopes of satisfying those interests. It leads, that is, to the creation of a market. The goods that are brought to the market depend principally on two things, various people's peculiar talents and various people's peculiar desires; and the multifarious forms of contracts, bargains, and exchanges will manifest ever more efficient means of satisfying interests, as people continually desire to better their respective conditions in life.

It might appear that the market is a remarkable invention. It can somehow coordinate countless exchanges, allowing an indefinitely large number of people to pursue and satisfy their interests, whatever they are, while satisfying the interests of others. The market thus encourages and even requires a high degree of cooperation among people, although it makes no demands that everyone know or take any real interest in anyone else. And the results of markets have been remarkable indeed. The last two hundred years have seen spectacular growth in the material prosperity and overall well-being of nations allowing market-based economies. This growth is particularly striking when one considers that for thousands of years prior to the existence of large-scale markets, human standards of living had changed relatively little: until the eighteenth century, the majority of mankind

---

[6] WN, 26. Compare the similar passage in T, 484–85.

still had no running water, relied on open flames for heat, had to grow or kill whatever they ate, could travel only short distances at a time, and came in contact with few people outside their own small tribe, clan, or community. But then, in the course of a mere three hundred years, technological and economic progress saw unprecedented growth in the fertile fields of open markets, and the overall level of material prosperity reached levels never before dreamed of.[7] And as Smith correctly predicted, most of the prosperity has been achieved by lower and middle classes: although average standard-of-living levels have gone up across the board, countries where Smithian economic advice has been adopted to the greatest degree have seen particular advances among the economic bottom two-fifths of their citizens.[8] It is self-interest, directed by the market, that encourages and enables the division of labor and the "universal opulence" to which it leads, and it is thus self-interest we have to thank for the material prosperity we have come to enjoy in market-based economies.[9]

Smith writes in WN that an exact administration of justice is necessary for the existence of a market if the market is to yield the beneficial consequences that it can make possible. Though he mentions it only a few times, he nevertheless makes the importance of this requirement clear. Here is perhaps his most pointed statement:

[7] For discussion of this progress, see (1998), Diamond (1997), Landes (1999), Macfarlane (2000), and Rosenberg and Birdzell (1986).

[8] For contemporary evidence, see the annually updated *Economic Freedom of the World* (Gwartney, Lawson, and Samida, 2000); and "Growth *Is* Good for the Poor," David Dollar and Aart Kraay (Washington, DC: World Bank, 2001), available at http://www.worldbank.org/research/growth/pdfiles/growthgoodforpoor.pdf. Also see Fogel (2000).

[9] I do not argue that markets are perfect or that they allow everyone to satisfy all interests. Smith dramatically expresses his own reservations about markets in Book 5 of WN (see especially WN, 781–88). There is by now little debate, however, that market-based economies provide for substantially greater overall material prosperity than other kinds of economy. An interesting recent testimonial to this is Manley (Summer 1992). Manley was the Prime Minister of Jamaica from 1972 to 1980 and again from 1989 to 1992. In this article, he describes the political and philosophical about-face he underwent from the socialist leader of the People's National Party of Jamaica to one of Jamaica's premiere advocates of free markets and laissez-faire government. He says he was forced to change his mind by the hard reality he faced in trying to raise the status of the poor. He reports that he finally and grudgingly came to believe that only "an unfettered market, not the imposition of political control" can be an "effective instrument of opportunity for the poor" (47); he concludes: "One just can't improve on Adam Smith" (48).

> Commerce and manufactures can seldom flourish long in any state which does not enjoy a regular administration of justice, in which the people do not feel themselves secure in the possession of their property, in which the faith of contracts is not supported by law, and in which the authority of the state is not supposed to be regularly employed in enforcing the payment of debts from all those who are able to pay. (WN, 910)

Here Smith states not only the importance of justice but also what he means by the term. As he explains here and elsewhere,[10] Smith thinks the "exact administration of justice" is the first and most important duty of government, comprising chiefly two things—the protection of private property and the sanctity and obligation of voluntary contractual agreements. Unless there is public protection for these two things, Smith thinks, independent producers, merchants, and consumers would not have enough trust in the security of their belongings and goods to risk making more than what their own needs require or to risk making good-faith efforts to exchange their own goods with those of others. Smith writes that when people "are secure of enjoying the fruits of their industry, they naturally exert it to better their condition, and to acquire not only the necessaries, but the conveniencies and elegancies of life" (WN, 405). Indeed, he goes so far as to say that a "man must be perfectly crazy who, where there is tolerable security, does not employ all the stock which he commands, whether it be his own or borrowed of other people, in some one or other of those three ways" (WN, 285).[11]

A general security in one's possessions is thus a necessary prerequisite for the maintenance and growth of the wealth of nations. In fact, Smith thinks that the security Britain provides for the private property of its citizens accounts in large part for its rapid rate of economic growth relative to other countries.[12] For this reason, Smith argues

---

[10] In addition to WN, 708–23 (which has already been cited), see also LJ, 5–37, 398–401, and 422–26.

[11] The three ways are as savings, circulating capital, or fixed capital—all of which, Smith thinks, redound to the benefit of both the individual and his community. See WN, 279–85.

[12] See WN, 345–46, 540, and 610. See Macfarlane (2000), Chapter 8, for discussion. Macfarlane argues that Smith had in Glasgow a city going through the transformation to a commercial society right before his eyes: after the battle of Culloden in 1745, Glasgow rapidly commercialized, substantiating many of Smith's arguments about the nature and causes of this process.

that it is necessary not only for the government to assure a regular enforcement of justice but also for the judicial branch of the government to be separate from and independent of the executive branch (WN, 722).[13] Now Smith of course recognized that these salutary governmental structures have not always been in place. Instead, the realization that they are what is required for the growth of national wealth has only gradually crystallized, and they are still not universally recognized—owing not only to the fact that their connection to the empirical data that undergird them is distant and difficult to see, but also to the frequent occasion that the vested, entrenched interests of both politically protected businesses and bureaucrats have resisted them.[14] Instead, the development of governments that understand their jobs as first and foremost effecting the exact administration of justice has seen a slow and fitful appearance. The "progress of government," Smith writes, "arose, not as some writers imagine from any consent or agreement of a number of persons to submit themselves to such or such regulations, but from the natural progress which men make in society" (LJ, 207). He argues that history shows that

at first there was properly no government at all, that this arose first amongst a nation of shepherds, and that these in certain circumstances would naturally unite themselves and form a city, which at first was under the government of a chief, but afterwards became in the ordinary and naturall progress of things an aristocracy and afterwards a democracy. (LJ, 228).[15]

We are thus slow and undependable learners, but our trial-and-error attempts at creating circumstances that allow for people to flourish nevertheless tend, Smith thinks, in the direction of a government that protects private property and allows markets.

I said earlier that the market, which can and has allowed tremendous growth in prosperity, would appear to be a remarkable invention. But it is not an invention—at least not a consciously or antecedently planned invention. The other crucial feature of the market that Smith

---

[13] See Muller (1993), 146.

[14] For passages discussing the bad faith and deleterious effects of politically protected businesses, see WN, 78–79, 84, 145, 158, and 361–62; for passages discussing the vested and short-sighted interests of political bureaucrats, see WN, 342 and 345–49. For discussion emphasizing the often disorderly and even regressive developments of commercial societies, see Winch (1978), especially Chapter 4, and Viner (1928).

[15] See also LJ, 353, 489, and 521–41.

describes, crucial both for Smith's description of the market and for our purposes here, is, as the passages cited in the previous paragraph suggest, its *unintended* nature. It is a system of unintended order—just like the system of morality and moral judging. The telling passage comes already in the second chapter of WN, entitled "Of the Principle which gives occasion to the Division of Labour" (WN, 25–30). Smith writes:

> This division of labour, from which so many advantages are derived, is not originally the effect of any human wisdom, which foresees and intends that general opulence to which it gives occasion. It is the necessary, though very slow and gradual consequence of a certain propensity in human nature which has in view no such extensive utility; the propensity to truck, barter, and exchange one thing for another. (WN, 26)

Smith writes that only human beings have the requisite capacities to exchange goods and to make contracts, and hence only they are able to benefit from the remarkable variety of goods that get produced and exchanges that get made in open markets. It makes no difference to the dog, Smith observes, that there are many other species of dogs besides its own; it must still support and defend itself without the help of others.

> Among men, on the contrary, the most dissimilar geniuses are of use to one another; the different produces of their respective talents, by the general disposition to truck, barter, and exchange, being brought, as it were, into a common stock, where every man may purchase whatever part of the produce of other men's talents he has occasion for. (WN, 30)

The "common stock" to which Smith refers here is what is coordinated by the market, and, as this passage suggests, the market will be composed of and constituted by as large a range of people's interests as there are people themselves. But the market itself is an unintended result—the "very slow and gradual consequence"—of the actions of individuals. For the most part, the only thing that participants in the market are concerned about is satisfying their interests (which may include, however, the interests of their families and friends, perhaps even their country).[16] As they go about their daily business, most people are

[16] See TMS, 218–34, as well as WN, 455–56.

entirely unaware that they have anything whatever to do with a market; many people moreover are quite unconcerned with anyone's interests other than their own and those of the people close to them. Nevertheless their actions, channeled through the market, conduce, as if led by an invisible hand, to the greater benefit of everyone:

> Every individual is continually exerting himself to find out the most advantageous employment for whatever capital he can command. It is his own advantage, indeed, and not that of the society, which he has in view. But the study of his own advantage naturally, or rather necessarily leads him to prefer that employment which is most advantageous to the society. (WN, 454)

### The Market in WN and in TMS

Let me now summarize what we have seen so far. First, the market is a system that, once an administration of justice is secured, arises unintentionally from the actions of individuals. Though they are unaware of it, individuals' actions collectively constitute a system, the market. Second, the complexity and sophistication of the market increases as the number of people who are party to it and their respective skills increase. A contemporary market—contemporary to Smith or to us— reflects a level of sophistication that is commensurate with the diversity, skills, and interests of its participants; it is highly specialized, it is highly productive, and it encompasses an array of available goods, services, and occupations. Third, the development of the market, from its first inchoate appearances in hunting communities, through shepherding and agricultural communities, up to its full fruition in commercial communities, is a slow and gradual process that is marked by an increasing formalization of rules. What begin as informal habits of exchange grow into increasingly formal ceremonies, practices, and rules, the most important of which eventually get regarded as or written into law. The formal rules of markets are not only what Smith calls the rules of justice, but also various other protocols, most of which center around protection of private property and of contractual obligations. Fourth, the development of markets is slow enough to allow for identifiable rules to form and get enforced, but the exact nature of those rules, as well as other protocols (of address, of apparel, and so on) in force in the market are flexible and reflect the peculiarities of the people, place, and time where the market exists. Fifth, the rules, protocols, and the overall development of the market depend on the continual free exchanges the participants in the market make. It is only when people are allowed to truck, barter, and exchange whatever they see fit and however they see fit that the market will unfold in a way that allows people to satisfy their interests effectively. Finally, the entire system of production and exchange—that is, the market—is driven by an innate desire people have, namely, the desire to better their condition in life. The rules of the market, the goods that get produced, the rates at which various goods are exchanged, and the circumstances under which exchanges are made: all these are determined by the decisions individuals make on the basis of their private judgments about how best to satisfy their interests, how best to better their condition in life.

These features of the marketplace of exchange that Smith describes in WN are the same features he described in the system of moral judgment: a system of order arising unintentionally from individual actions, an increasing complexity of the system over time in relation to the increasing sophistication of individuals, a slow and gradual process leading to the formalization of rules, the conformity of the system's rules to the time and place of its instantiation, the system's dependence on free and continual exchanges between and among individuals, and the natural desires of human beings as the motive force behind the creation and development of the system. The account of the development of moral standards Smith gave in TMS and the account of the development of marketplaces Smith gives in WN thus conform to the same conceptual structure. They are both instances of Smith's marketplace model at work. I shall argue in Chapter 7 that this same model also appears in Smith's early essay on the development of languages—which, together with my argument in this chapter, will allow me to make this larger claim: Smith thinks this market model applies to human institutions *generally*, whether languages, moral standards, or marketplaces. They are all systems of order that result unintentionally from the desires, decisions, and actions of individuals. Moreover, Smith's adherence to this model remained intact and consistent throughout his lifetime. This conception lies at the heart of the analysis in TMS as well as that of WN. It is on this basis I would like to suggest that the Adam Smith Problem begins to be resolved: the two books are fundamentally consistent insofar as they are manifestations of this single conception of human institutions. On at least this Smith cannot be thought to have undergone a radical change of mind.

## II. Human Motivation: The Familiarity Principle

Not all of the difficulties that constituted the Adam Smith Problem are solved, however, once the single conceptual structure that underlies both books is seen. In particular we are still left with the problem of how to reconcile the seemingly conflicting pictures of human motivation given in the two books. These differences can be substantially mitigated, I think, though they cannot all be perfectly reconciled. Let me now briefly lay out how on my interpretation of Smith and his two books the acuteness of these differences is lessened, and then let me indicate what I believe remains nonetheless irreconcilable.

The chief mitigating factor is something that I have already described and that I would now like to call Smith's "familiarity principle."[17] It is this: for Smith, the benevolence one properly feels toward another is a function of the knowledge one has of that other, or of one's familiarity with that other. In TMS, Smith argued that the impartial spectator approves of an ascending degree of benevolence toward others in direct relation to our knowledge of or familiarity with them. Thus the impartial spectator approves of actions motivated more by benevolence than self-interest when the matter concerns one's family or friends, of actions motivated by approximately equal benevolence and self-interest when the matter concerns one's acquaintances, and of actions motivated by more self-interest than benevolence when the matter concerns strangers. Smith argues not only that such motivation is what receives approbation from the impartial spectator, but also that in this case the impartial spectator's judgments are quite in line with what he calls our natural affections. Smith writes that what "is called affection, is in reality nothing but habitual sympathy" (TMS, 220); the more often we have occasion to sympathize with another, the more likely are we to feel a concern for that other's well-being, Smith thinks. Concern for

---

[17] For passages that use or illuminate this notion, see TMS, 17–18, §4; 219, §2; 223, §14; 229, §4; and 237, §6. What I call the familiarity principle should not be confused with what Campbell calls "the familiarity theory," which is something quite different. See Campbell (1971), 34–39.

another's well-being is what Smith generally means by "benevolence." Thus we feel natural affection—that is, genuine, not feigned, concern for others—principally for those who are closest to us, and in these cases benevolence more than narrow self-interest tends to move us. Smith writes of the "cordial satisfaction," the "delicious sympathy," and the "confidential openness and ease" that arise among people "who have lived long and familiarly with one another," all of which enable the "habitual sympathy" that Smith says is "the real principle and foundation of what is properly called family-affection" (TMS, 221). The level of familiarity one enjoys with another is, then, the factor that ultimately determines the extent to which one will be "naturally" disposed to act toward that other on the basis of benevolence.[18]

Smith's argument is that it is not principally the biological connection one has to family members that engenders the affection one has for them. Rather, it is the habitual sympathy one experiences. Thus a father is more apt to have affection for his adopted child than for the biological child with whom he has had little or no contact, and siblings generally have more affection for those of their brothers and sisters who have lived at home than for those who were reared or educated away from the home (TMS, 220–22). But Smith's argument has further implications. Benevolence issues from natural affection, which in turn issues from habitual sympathy; this means that one is also capable of acting from benevolence toward people other than one's family members. Affection and benevolence can thus move one to act in situations involving friends, professional colleagues, or neighbors (TMS, 224)— anyone with whom one has the frequent contact that enables habitual sympathy. In any particular situation, the degree to which benevolence, as opposed to self-interest, is the principal motive to act will be determined by the level of familiarity obtaining among the parties in question. Smith believes, for reasons we explore in the next chapter, that it turns out that the impartial spectator approves of behavior corresponding roughly to our natural affections: he approves of behavior displaying a level of benevolence that varies directly with familiarity. We then have here a correlation between our natural promptings and those motives approved of by the impartial spectator, which, Smith thinks, gives us two reasons to accept the familiarity principle and the

---

[18] See Anspach (1972).

benevolence (or self-interest) to which it leads as proper principles of action.

An implication of the familiarity principle is that people will and should feel relatively little benevolence—even, perhaps, none at all—for distant acquaintances, strangers, and, as Jerry Muller puts it, "the anonymous others" with whom one daily comes into fleeting contact.[19] Because one knows such people so little, and because one has not had the opportunity to form habits of sympathy with them, one feels little or no natural affection for them. In such cases, Smith thinks, the impartial spectator approves of behavior that manifests a minimal level of benevolence (though, as always, his approval is limited to behavior that is within the bounds of justice). And here we can connect this treatment in TMS to the subject under discussion in WN. The people with whom one deals in the marketplace, the people with whom one barters, trucks, and trades, are for the most part strangers: frequently one does not know of them at all, less frequently they are but distant acquaintances, and only rarely are they family members or close friends. On Smith's analysis in TMS, then, we should expect that the proper motivation people would feel as they deal in marketplaces would be chiefly self-interest within the bounds of justice, and only in the appropriate but rare situations would benevolence be required. Thus in one of the only places in TMS where Smith addresses economic concerns, he writes that the impartial spectator would render the following judgment:

In the race for wealth, and honours, and preferments, [a person] may run as hard as he can, and strain every nerve and every muscle, in order to outstrip all his competitors. But if he should justle, or throw down any of them, the indulgence of the spectators is entirely at an end. It is a violation of fair play, which they cannot admit of. (TMS, 83)

The latter two sentences underscore Smith's contention that the rules of justice must always be obeyed and that the impartial spectator never approves of their violation. But what Smith does not say in this passage is, I think, just as important as what he does say. No mention is made of benevolence, and the tone of the passage and the context surrounding it suggest that in such situations the impartial spectator

[19] Muller (1993), 110.

is not concerned with benevolence. Because the people with whom we do commercial business are largely strangers to us, self-interest is the relevant motivation in economic arenas.[20]

### Smith and Hume on Familiarity

To illustrate Smith's familiarity principle more clearly, let me make a brief comparison to Hume. It would seem as though Hume and Smith differ sharply on this count, for in several places Hume is quite adamant that a difference in distance or perspective—which is what underlies Smith's familiarity principle—should not entail a difference in moral judgment. In his *Treatise*, Hume writes this:

> Our situation, with regard both to persons and things, is in continual fluctuation; and a man, that lies at a distance from us, may, in a little time, become a familiar acquaintance. Besides, every particular man has a peculiar position with regard to others; and 'tis impossible we cou'd ever converse together on any reasonable terms, were each of us to consider characters and persons, only as they appear from his peculiar point of view. In order, therefore, to prevent those continual *contradictions*, and arrive at a more *stable* judgment of things, we fix on some *steady* and *general* points of view; and always, in our thoughts, place ourselves in them, whatever may be our present situation. In like manner, external beauty is determin'd merely by pleasure; and 'tis evident, a beautiful countenance cannot give so much pleasure, when seen at the distance of twenty paces, as when it is brought nearer us. We say not, however, that it appears to us less beautiful: Because we know what effect it will have in such a position, and by that reflexion we correct its momentary appearance. (581–82; Hume's italics)

Passages expressing similar notions can be found in Hume's *Enquiry Concerning the Principles of Morals*. Here is one:

---

[20] Another way to see the familiarity principle at work in Smith's analysis is in his discussion of the role local knowledge plays in the efficient functioning of markets. The reason, Smith thinks, that decentralized markets are more efficient at satisfying people's desires, and why centrally planned economies are less efficient, is that in markets people can exploit their knowledge of their own local circumstances—including their own resources, abilities, interests, as well as those of others—to discover new and better ways to get what they want. On this analysis, distant third parties—legislators, for example—do not have the local knowledge necessary to know what policies would benefit individuals. See WN, 28 and 687–88. The advantages of allowing individuals to exploit their local knowledge is evident, for example, in Smith's claim that division of labor allows workers to invent "proper machinery" and other time-saving, production-increasing techniques (WN, 19–21). In TMS, the passage to read is Smith's description of the "man of system" (TMS, 233–34).

A statesman or patriot, who serves our own country, in our own time, has always a more passionate regard paid to him, than one whose beneficial influence operated on distant ages or remote nations; where the good, resulting from his generous humanity, being less connected with us, seems more obscure, and affects us with a less lively sympathy. We may own the merit to be equally great, though our sentiments are not raised to an equal height, in both cases. The judgment here corrects the inequalities of our internal emotions and perceptions; in like manner, as it preserves us from error, in the several variations of images, presented to our external senses. (2E, 48)

I think Hume takes seriously the analogy between moral judgment and sensory judgment.[21] We could not make sense of the world around us, either individually or in intercourse with others, without adopting a steady, fixed perspective from which to judge things; our judgment must, that is, correct for perspective.

In the same manner, Hume thinks our moral judgment must correct for moral perspective. If each of us judged according to how things appeared or related to himself only, no general rules of behavior could be agreed upon and there would be no common standards of morality. Specifically, if the proper way to judge motivation depends on the agent's peculiar familiarity with the person with whom he is presently dealing, then it would seem to follow that each person would judge any given situation differently—because no two people, presumably, would enjoy precisely the same level of familiarity with the persons involved in the case in question. On the reasoning of Hume's argument, then, we should conclude two things about Smith's familiarity principle. First, it would not allow for general rules of morality to develop, because familiarity with another is something that varies from person to person and hence would not lend itself to representation in terms of general rules. Second, what follows from the first conclusion, Smith's familiarity principle must not have been an active factor in the actual historical development of human morality because we do in fact have general rules of morality.

I think a correct understanding of Smith shows, however, that on a more fundamental level he and Hume are in agreement. The point of the preceding citations from Hume is the more general one that peaceful intercourse with others requires a commonly accepted conception of morality, which includes commonly accepted standards of behavior.

[21] Of course, so does Smith. See TMS, 134–36.

His argument is that without these common standards—without these "*steady* and *general* points of view"—there would be no common basis for social interaction, and hence there could be no social interaction. His argument is not, then, aimed at denying the validity of any particular kind of perspective, which may or may not make a particular individual's judgment unique. What our judgment must correct for is any unique perspective that makes one's judgments improperly deviate from the commonly accepted standards. But this is precisely what Smith's impartial spectator does as well. Smith would agree with Hume that if there were no commonly accepted point of view from which to judge actions and motivations, we would have a moral anarchy, and I think Smith would further agree that in that case we would most likely not have any society at all. Hume's argument would distinguish him from Smith only if Smith's familiarity principle relied exclusively on a person's unique familiarity with another as a contributing factor for the proper moral judgment. But that is not the case. Smith's familiarity principle instead draws on both the individuals' unique local knowledge, and the perspective and judgments of the impartial spectator— which, for reasons we shall explore in Chapter 6, match up with our natural sentiments as they are influenced by familiarity. Smith's argument, then, is that one is *properly* motivated by a descending degree of benevolence as one's familiarity with the person involved decreases, not just that this is in fact what happens. The element of propriety is what essentially links the familiarity principle with the judgment of the impartial spectator, and it is Smith's recourse to the perspective of the impartial spectator that, I would argue, rather unites him with Hume on this count than differentiates him.

I wish to argue, then, that the familiarity principle, as it functions to modulate habitual sympathy and thus natural affection and benevolence, is a central link in the conceptual chain that connects TMS and WN. Smith's general conception of a market informs the analysis of human institutions in both books, and the familiarity principle, which was described in TMS, explains why self-interest is the primary (and morally proper) motivation people feel in their economic pursuits, as is presupposed in WN.

We have therefore met the requirements I laid out at the end of Chapter 4 for an interpretation of Smith's two books that demonstrates their consistency satisfactorily: we have identified the single basic conceptual model that underlies both books, which allows us to see how the analysis in WN can be subsumed into the framework laid out in TMS; we have seen how the depiction of natural human motivation set forth in TMS can account for the depiction of people's motivations that is at work in WN; and, crucially, we have seen *why* self-interest is the proper motivation for behavior that takes place in economic affairs. We have, then, only one more issue to address: what to make of the passages in WN where Smith writes as if self-interest were the sole and exclusive motivation men feel, those passages in which Smith seems (especially if read in light of what he wrote in TMS) to go out of his way to avoid discussion of benevolence—not to mention TMS itself, the impartial spectator, and the familiarity principle.

## III. Irreconcilable Differences?

### What Can Be Accommodated

Careful attention to a particularly recalcitrant cluster of passages in WN softens their collective edge. Consider again this famous passage: "It is not from the benevolence of the butcher, the brewer, or the baker, that we expect our dinner, but from their regard to their own interest. We address ourselves, not to their humanity but to their self-love, and never talk to them of our own necessities but of their advantages" (WN, 26–27). Unsympathetic readers sometimes press the Adam Smith Problem virtually on the strength of this passage alone. But two important considerations must be introduced. First, this passage, along with its surrounding context, is descriptive, not normative. Smith is here describing the way things operate in commercial societies without pronouncing on its morality or immorality. The next sentence Smith writes is: "Nobody but a beggar chuses to depend chiefly upon the benevolence of his fellow-citizens" (WN, 27). Now one might be inclined to argue that the tenor of this sentence suggests that Smith is in fact making normative claims—no one, after all, wants to be, or be called, a beggar. But I suggest that Smith's remark pertains more to the ignorance of the beggar than to his undesirable lifestyle. By acting as if everyone had or could have the same affection for him as they would if he were their brother, the beggar misunderstands the nature both of markets and of human sentiments as they have been described here. Smith's argument is thus that the beggar's first vice is ignorance, which is based on a factual claim and serves to illustrate further Smith's depiction of the nature of marketplaces and the operation of commercial societies. In any case, in the pages surrounding these sentences, Smith seems without question to be making only descriptive claims.[22]

Second, note that in this passage Smith speaks of the butcher, the brewer, and the baker. These people are conspicuously not members of one's family and are most likely not one's friends—though, of course, one might be acquainted with them, depending in part on the size of one's community. This point is emphasized when Smith speaks of one not being dependent on the benevolence of one's fellow-*citizens*. Smith does not say that only a beggar chooses to be dependent on the benevolence of his family and close friends. The impartial spectator from TMS would certainly approve of reliance on the benevolence of family under certain circumstances; this passage from WN would not seem to contradict that. "Fellow-citizens" in this context indicates that Smith is thinking of precisely those frequent cases in marketplaces when one deals with people one does not know. They are one's fellow-citizens, but nothing more; thus one must respect the rules of justice toward them, but benevolence is not required.

That Smith is here speaking of people other than those to whom one is close is further suggested by the way he introduces the passage in question. He writes: "In civilized society [man] stands at all times in need of the cooperation and assistance of great multitudes, while his whole life is scarce sufficient to gain the friendship of a few persons" (WN, 26). This statement is of a piece with the rest of Smith's argument in the beginning stages of WN. Material prosperity is dependent on the division of labor, which is in turn dependent on the existence of marketplaces; as the prosperity of society increases, the extent and division of the marketplaces must therefore also increase. Because, however, a person cannot gain the friendship of everyone on whom he depends for the products he needs and enjoys—he can gain the friendship of only a tiny fraction of them in a sophisticated commercial society—he can count on the benevolence, which springs from the natural affection that habitual sympathy effects, of very few people. Thus Smith can conclude that in a commercial society "man has almost

---

[22] Note, in particular, WN, 27, §3.

constant occasion for the help of his brethren, and it is in vain for him to expect it from their benevolence only" (ibid.). Note the "only." Smith's argument is not that it is impossible that others will act on benevolence toward one, or that they never in practice do; rather, it is the more modest claim that when one is dealing with large numbers of strangers, which is the case in large-scale marketplaces, it is foolhardy to think that as a general rule others will act out of benevolence toward one. They do not know you, they have little or no natural affection for you, and therefore they will most likely feel little or no benevolence toward you. The person who nevertheless desires and needs things that others produce must therefore depend on their self-interest, not on their benevolence, if he is to receive what he wants.

Let me address an objection one might wish to raise. I have argued that Smith's examination in WN proceeds on the assumption that the people with whom one deals in the marketplace are strangers to one. But that is not always the case. It might be the case, for instance, that one *does* know one's butcher, brewer, or baker. If one has lived in the same place for some time, it is not at all uncommon that one becomes acquainted, even friendly, with those neighborhood businessmen who provide one with the goods one wants. Indeed, it might even be the case that one is related to some of these businessmen. If one lives in a small town, where perhaps one's family has lived for many years, is it impossible that, say, one's brother-in-law is one's butcher? One might speculate that Smith himself knew his butcher, baker, and brewer in Edinburgh. What could one make of such situations on Smith's argument? One might argue that the fact that Smith did not consider such cases weakens my argument that the examination in WN proceeds by assuming the truth of the familiarity principle set out in TMS.

I do not think this objection has much import, however, because in WN Smith is speaking specifically of business or commercial or economic relations, which places people—even if they know one another—in peculiar relations with respect to one another. When I go to my butcher, I do not expect him to give me a ham solely out of his benevolence for me (he would go out of business if he did so with every-one he knew); rather, even if I know him, even if I am related to him, even if he is motivated out of benevolence toward me, he and I both ex-pect me to pay him for the ham. And the reason for this is a good one. If we assume for a moment that my butcher is, say, my brother-in-law, that does not mean that I bear any relation of familiarity to the people on whom *he* depends qua butcher. That is, almost certainly I will not know the farmers who supply him his pork, the blacksmiths who supply him his cutlery, the masons who built his shop, and so on. Nor am I likely to be familiar with all the other customers my butcher/brother-in-law serves. Expecting him to give me ham out of benevolence, then, is tantamount to expecting the additional forbearance of his suppliers and customers, all of whom would then have to act out of benevolence toward him if he is to stay in business and meet his needs. I do not need to detail the undesirable economic consequences this kind of practice would have if undertaken generally, although an economic Smithian would no doubt trumpet the precipitate decline in overall productivity and material prosperity to which it would lead.

Nevertheless, one might suggest that this practice could be under-taken selectively—say, only with close friends and family—and hence would not necessarily have the detrimental effects it would if under-taken generally. It is not uncommon, after all, for businessmen to present various of their customers gifts, which might indicate that a selective benevolence is indeed practicable in a marketplace environ-ment. Although there might be some controversy about what eco-nomic consequences such a practice would have, I think it is safe to say that it would not be inconsistent with what Smith says here in WN. Recall the wording of the passage under examination: "It is not from the benevolence of the butcher, the brewer, or the baker, that we *expect* our dinner..." (WN, 26–27; my italics). Smith's argument is not that benevolence cannot ever be at work in our business dealings, rather that we do not expect it to be the case. This is a quite different claim, one that contains, I would like to suggest, a hint of TMS's notion of propriety in it. We do not expect benevolence from our butcher because it would not be proper for us to do so; it would be for us to assume a liberty with him and his property, a liberty to which we are not entitled given the nature of the situation in which we are interact-ing with one another. When we engage in economic activity, we deal with one another in our special capacities or roles as businessmen—as producers, consumers, salesmen, servicemen, and the like—not in our capacities or roles as relatives, friends, acquaintances, and so on. When businessmen give gifts of their products to customers, surely it can best be understood as ultimately an act of self-interest, not benevolence, because they are given in the hopes of stimulating future business. On the other hand, when the butcher gives a ham to his brother-in-law as a gift, that, I would suggest, is best understood as an act of benevolence that no longer expresses a business relation; it is a transaction between brothers-in-law, not between a producer and a consumer. In the butcher–brewer–baker passage in WN Smith is working with this understanding of the different roles people occupy in their different areas of life. In this way it then makes sense to speak of specifically economic relations, and the motivations at work in people engaging in them, as opposed to other relations in which other motivations might be at work. I would argue that this passage hence cannot be construed as implying that all interactions between people are driven by self-interest, and it cannot be construed as implying that all interactions between people should be predicated on self-interest. Those renderings are unjust oversimplifications.

### What Trouble Remains

There are other passages in WN, however, that do not admit of ready assimilation into the format laid out in TMS. These include the passages, cited in Chapter 4, in which Smith seems to claim that self-interest is the *sole* motive human beings feel, that the desire for a better condition in life is the *only* desire that animates them. The fact that Smith's overall topic in WN is what is generally called economics, and that the familiarity principle set out in TMS explains—and the impartial spectator justifies—predominantly self-interest in actors in markets, goes a long way toward justifying the descriptions of human motivation in WN. But does it go far enough? On the basis of the analysis in TMS we can see why Smith would ascribe principally self-interested motives to the people he describes in WN. But the descriptions of motive in WN are not just principally self-interested: they are exclusively so, with no hint of benevolence or any other motive that might move people—nor, for that matter, do they contain any suggestion that a balance of four virtues is required for an overall virtuous character. When Smith writes of the "uniform, constant, and uninterrupted effort of every man to better his condition," or writes that the "principle that prompts [us] to save, is the desire of bettering our condition, a desire which, though generally calm and dispassionate, comes with us from the womb, and never leaves us till we go into the grave,"[23] it is difficult to dismiss him as merely indulging in rhetorical flourish. One of the criticisms that I raised against other Smith scholars was that they routinely ignored such passages or proceeded as if they were unimportant or inconsequential; I argued then that these were omissions that gave rise to selective or distorted readings of Smith, and we should not lose sight of that point now.

There is another consideration that might justify the tone and sense of these passages in WN. In Chapter 2, I looked at the unusual explanation of ambition that Smith gives in TMS. Smith had argued that we are more apt to sympathize with "social passions" like joy than with "unsocial passions" like grief because the former are agreeable and the latter are not (TMS, 50–61). This natural aptness, Smith argued, and not considerations of our own utility, fuels ambition. He reasoned that as we come to realize that people, including ourselves, are more likely to sympathize with social passions, the desire for mutual sympathy encourages us to discover and implement ways to foster the social passions. It turns out that success in life, particularly material success in life, engages the social passions more than other activities (like the pursuit of virtue or wisdom).[24] We hence strive to achieve material success in life and to display the fruits of our success publicly. "To be observed, to be attended to, to be taken notice of with sympathy, complacency, and approbation, are all the advantages which we can propose to derive from" the "great purpose of human life which we call bettering our condition" (TMS, 50).[25] People who are extremely wealthy often receive a great deal of attention from other members of society, a fact that Smith thought his account of ambition explains: such people engage sympathy with the social passions to a high degree, and when others view them, they take pleasure in that mutual sympathy; moreover, when others imagine themselves in the position of the wealthy, the prospect of themselves receiving such a degree of sympathy is attractive and appealing enough to flatter and encourage their own ambition. "Everybody is eager to look at [the man of wealth], and to

---

[23] WN, 343 and 341, respectively.
[24] TMS, 62–63.
[25] This is the sole reference in TMS to man's desire for bettering his condition.

conceive, at least by sympathy, that joy and exultation with which his circumstances naturally inspire him" (TMS, 51). Smith's argument was that it is our desire for sympathetic harmony of sentiments—particularly sympathy with the agreeable sentiments—that leads us to admire the wealthy and then to want to be wealthy ourselves. This, he argued, is the true origin of ambition.

As I suggested in Chapter 2, this explanation of ambition provides a possible way of connecting TMS to WN. We could take Smith's assumption in WN that a desire for greater wealth and prosperity is universal to be a consequence of the ambition that wealth in society naturally creates. In commercial societies it is frequently the case that there is a portion of the citizens that possesses great wealth, so we can imagine that in such circumstances ambition understood on Smith's terms would be especially inflamed. We could then argue that WN can be reconciled with TMS in the following way. The repeated references in WN to our desire to better our condition indicate a phenomenon that ultimately reduces to our desire for mutual sympathy of sentiments described in TMS, a desire that gets channeled in certain directions by commercial societies. In particular, this desire is channeled into an ambition for material wealth. Given, then, the rest of Smith's argument in WN, we could conclude that this ambition is good, at least insofar as it provides the necessary impetus to greater overall material wealth and prosperity for society. And this conclusion would square with Smith's claim in TMS that our ambitious exertions to achieve the "pleasures of wealth and greatness" are what "keeps in continual motion the industry of mankind" (TMS, 183).

Although initially promising, there are two problems with this suggestion. The first is that it does not seem plausible to equate the desire to better one's condition with ambition. They are simply not the same thing. Nor does Smith's use of the former in WN seem to jibe with his account of the latter in TMS. I find no reason to believe that the desire to better one's condition, on which much of the analysis in WN is predicated, necessarily bears any significant relation to other people. That is, this desire need not depend on the success of others, it does not seem to be inflamed by covetously viewing the possessions of the wealthy, and it does not seem to be motivated by a desire for mutual sympathy of (agreeable) sentiments. It seems rather to be what it would appear on first glance: a self-interested desire to have things be better for oneself than they currently are. Although one might be ambitious in the pursuit of a better condition for oneself, this sense of ambition seems not to have the negative connotations of the sense in which one seeks wealth in order to have others pay obsequious attention to one.

The second problem with this suggestion is that in WN Smith does not link the desire to better one's condition with any kind of ambition, whether that which he described in TMS or some other kind. Its appearance is always couched in terms that suggest that Smith believes that this desire is innate in us, that we are born with it. There seems, moreover, to be no suggestion that this desire is the result of a process, as would be necessary if it were the result of a desire for mutual sympathy, or that it is excited or encouraged by certain societal economic arrangements. Thus although the passage in TMS opened the door for a unifying interpretation of the desire to better one's condition present in both TMS and WN, I think we must conclude that in the end it provides no such unification. Whatever Smith thought about the true roots of ambition and the desire for wealth in TMS, there is no indication he thought the same thing about the desire for a better condition in life in WN.

One final way one might try to reconcile these passages is to construe Smith's notion in WN of our universal "desire of bettering our condition" (WN, 343 and passim) more broadly than I have done thus far. Perhaps one could understand it to include the desire for mutual sympathy of sentiments as well, on the argument that the attainment of this sympathy gives us pleasure, thereby bettering our (psychological) condition. On this construal, "bettering our condition" would include not only achieving mutual sympathy, but *whatever* a person seeks, monetary or not. Here we might recall the discussion at the end of Chapter 2, in which I broached the claim some have made that there have been some groups of people—notably some tribes of American Indians—who did not continually seek to increase their money or property; the implication was that the existence of such groups might constitute a counterexample to the claims Smith makes in the passages in WN we have been considering. On the interpretation of this universal desire considered here, however, we could argue that even if these groups did not seek betterment understood principally as the accumulation of property, nevertheless they were seeking to better their lives in ways that did matter to them. Hence they would not, in fact, constitute counterexamples to Smith.

I think this consideration is promising and could offer a way to bring even the most wayward passages in WN back, as it were, into the fold. In Chapter 7, I shall again have occasion to consider this possibility further. My only hesitation about it is that it constitutes a rather expansive interpretation of the relevant passages in WN, perhaps too expansive to be supported by the texts. Smith himself does not seem to endorse it: when he makes recourse to our universal desire of bettering our condition, it is to explain particular behaviors within economic marketplaces. And he does not suggest—in these places, or, as shown in Chapter 4, anywhere else in WN—any connection between this desire and the desire for mutual sympathy of sentiments. Still, I think that this might indeed be the final link in the chain connecting Smith's two books.

Thus, to take stock: we have identified the single conceptual framework that underlies both TMS and WN, namely, the notion of human institutions developing along the lines of a market. Moreover, we have shown why, on the basis of Smith's analysis in TMS, a person is justified in acting primarily on self-interest in economic arenas, though other motivations are proper in other situations. Finally, we have seen that one of the most notorious sections in WN turns out not to advocate so severe a selfishness as it might at first blush seem. What we have shown, then, is that TMS and WN are fundamentally consistent. Nevertheless, why Smith does not discuss, and only rarely mentions, benevolence, and why there is no mention of the impartial spectator procedure, of the desire for mutual sympathy of sentiments, or of perfect virtue consisting in justice, benevolence, prudence, and self-command remain unanswered questions. One might speculate that an explicit answer to these questions lay in the volumes of manuscripts he had destroyed upon his death,[26] or perhaps one might, with Glenn R. Morrow,[27] think that when writing WN Smith was simply in the

---

[26] A few days before he died, Smith summoned two friends and asked them to destroy his manuscripts. They complied, burning sixteen volumes of written material. See Rae (1895), 434.

[27] See Morrow (1928), 167.

grips of the eighteenth-century love of individualism that infused so much economic and political writing of the time. But neither of these speculations gets us very far.

I suggest, however, that the absence in WN of mentions of the impartial spectator, of Smith's four cardinal virtues, and of the desire for mutual sympathy constitutes an insurmountable objection to the scholars discussed in Chapter 4 precisely because they did not explain why self-interest is the proper motive in economic activity. They did not explain why the Smith of WN was justified in assuming self-interest as the predominant motive people feel or why he was justified in ignoring the other motives that the Smith of TMS argued were necessary to round out the virtuous person's character. My argument, however, is that the familiarity principle laid out in TMS provides just this explanation: it explains why different motivations in different areas of life are proper, and in particular why self-interest is *properly* the motive people feel in economic activities. The existence of this notion of propriety in the butcher–brewer–baker passage in WN suggests that Smith presumed his familiarity principle from the outset of WN. Once we understand the scope of this principle, then, I think the questions about why Smith did not explicitly speak of benevolence, the other virtues, and the rest lose their punch—especially if we accept the broad construal of "bettering our condition" just suggested. Although it remains true that Smith did not speak of these things in WN, in light of what we have found that unites the two books, those omissions, I submit, no longer warrant the existence of the Adam Smith Problem. We have seen that two books are consistent on the central points, and therefore we can, I believe, at long last, lay the Adam Smith Problem to rest.

# 6

## Justifying Smithian Moral Standards

Adam Smith thinks that human beings are born with a large package of instincts, abilities, desires, and propensities that are channeled or influenced, but not created, by their environment. All of us, for example, have an innate capacity to experience anger, resentment, joy, happiness, sadness, hunger, thirst, and sexual attraction, among many other things. The peculiarities of one's environment determine and limit the range of which particular things will be the objects of one's desires and aversions, as well as under which particular circumstances one will feel or act on various motivations. But the desires, aversions, and motivations themselves are given by our nature. The characteristic of human nature that Smith thinks principally bears on moral standards and moral judgments is, as we have seen, the desire for mutual sympathy, though other characteristics—like one's natural partiality for oneself and the natural interest one has in the fortunes of others—play important roles as well.

Smith argues that these characteristics operate within the context of a community to create a system of morality that includes "objective" moral standards and that forms the foundation of the moral judgments that people in the community make. A person's desire for mutual sympathy of sentiments will lead him to moderate the partiality he has for himself, because he finds that others do not have the same partiality for him, and to try to excite the sentiments of spectators, because he finds that others tend to be partial to themselves. Because the desire for mutual sympathy of sentiments is universal, meaning that all people

have it, this process of alternately moderating and amplifying sentiments tends ultimately toward an equilibrium of sentiment—that is, it
tends to point toward a level of sentiment that is likely somewhere between the agent's initial sentiments and a spectator's initial sentiments,
a level that the agent and the spectator might, if they could judge the
case disinterestedly, agree is proper. This equilibrium comes in time to
represent the sentiments an impartial spectator would have.[1] Smith's
argument is that similar equilibria exist concerning all actions and
motivations, and that as they become widely considered to be the sentiments an imagined impartial spectator would have, they become accepted as the standards against which to judge the sentiments of actual
agents and spectators. The system of morality that develops is, then,
a crystallization of the impartial spectator's judgments into general
rules that function as the standards people use to judge the actions
and motivations of others and of themselves.

In Chapter 3, I called this process by which a system of morality develops a "marketplace of morality" because it shares the same central
characteristics that a marketplace of goods has: a system of order that
unfolds on the basis of the actions of individuals who did not intend
to create the system of order but who, rather, were acting only as their
own interests dictated in response to the particular situations in which
they found themselves. This conception of the nature and development of morals and economics is a leitmotiv in both TMS and WN,
forming the basis of Smith's understanding of all human institutions—
not just those we would call moral and economic. The idea that a
system of order could arise unintentionally from the actions of individuals was not original to Smith, however: as mentioned in Chapter 3,
Bernard Mandeville, for example, had employed a similar notion in
relation to economic markets in his *Fable of the Bees* in 1714, and Hume
had hinted at this kind of explanation for the rules of justice in his

---

[1] The sentiments of the impartial spectator are thus analogous to the "natural price" of
a commodity that Smith describes in WN (see WN, 72–81). Smith writes: "The natural
price, therefore, is, as it were, the central price, to which the prices of all commodities
are continually gravitating. Different accidents may sometimes keep them suspended
a good deal above it, and sometimes force them down even somewhat below it. But
whatever may be the obstacles which hinder them from settling in this center of repose
and continuance, they are constantly tending towards it" (WN, 75).

*Treatise of Human Nature* in 1739–40.[2] Neither Mandeville nor Hume, however, developed the notion as completely, or applied it to as many areas of human action, as did Smith. In Smith, the notion of unintended order resulting from, to use Robert Merton's phrasing, the unanticipated consequences of purposive social action,[3] explained not just this or that isolated phenomenon of human life, but all human institutions and associations inasmuch as these are all governed by the moral system that is itself an unintended result of purposive social action. The system of morality constitutes for Smith the overarching social order, encompassing and applicable to everything else we do.

It is not inconsistent with Smith's analysis, however—even, perhaps, implied by it—that within the framework of the moral system distinct and semi-independent suborders could develop.[4] These suborders would have limited scopes, pertaining only to certain people, places, and circumstances. Although certain rules of conduct, like the rules of justice, must, according to the judgment of the impartial spectator, be observed without exception, nevertheless various protocols and practices of less importance might develop that would characterize particular relations. For example, there might be certain accepted standards of how husbands would treat their wives and vice-versa, how children would behave with their schoolmates, how businessmen would deal with one another, or how professors would conduct themselves with their colleagues—and any of these may or may not overlap with others. The protocols that characterize these suborders are not in lieu of the standards determined by the impartial spectator but are, rather, refinements based on the particular interests served. They arise, moreover, in the same way the general system of morals does, namely, as an unintended result of the actions of individuals who seek only to serve limited interests. Smith's notion of unintended order can, I have suggested, be similarly employed to account for all human institutions and associations.

[2] See Hamowy (1987) for a brief overview.

[3] Merton (1936). In the twentieth century, Friedrich Hayek has perhaps most famously made use of this notion, which pervades and informs much of his writing. See, for example, Hayek (1979), especially Chapters 8–10.

[4] See TMS, 224. See also TMS, Part VI, passim, in which Smith distinguishes different shadings of virtue appropriate for different stations in life.

The Smithian market model of human institutions presents a problem, however, when it is used to explain morality. The problem is that it seems to be an entirely descriptive account and leaves no room for normative moral standards. When this model is used to explain other marketplaces—for example, that of the exchange of goods—there appears to be no problem with saying that things like private property and the sanctity of voluntary contracts are not inherently good; we can, with Smith in WN, simply argue that these things allow communities on the whole to achieve their ends better than they could without them, and that is enough. With moral standards, however, the matter seems different. Do we wish to say that the "proper" levels of self-interest or benevolence and the "proper" actions one undertakes are in themselves entirely indifferent, and that their only worth—that is, the only thing that makes them "proper"—lies in the fact that they arc the codified results of numberless praises and reproaches people have given one another over long periods of time? Although not everyone would balk at this suggestion, it nonetheless brings to a head the problem of justifying moral standards and moral judgments that are arrived at in this way. More generally, it leads to the question of why a system of morality that is understood on the model of unintended order is ultimately legitimate. Why should any individual feel bound by a system of moral standards that arose only because, as a matter of contingent historical fact, it just worked out that way?

This problem is especially acute in Smith for several reasons. First, Smith seems ambivalent in TMS about the ultimate sanction of the moral standards and judgments of the impartial spectator. On a few occasions, he expressly says that his theory does not concern what is right, but rather what is fact.[5] He writes that his goal is merely to examine and explicate the actual origins of our moral standards and the actual process of our moral judging, implying that the issue of whether these standards and judgments are right is the subject of another kind of inquiry and irrelevant to his. On the other hand, there are several passages that seem normative in tone. All of Part VI, for example, entitled "Of the Character of Virtue," is concerned with fleshing out in detail the qualities a virtuous person would have, what motivations he would feel, and what actions he would undertake in various

---

[5] The most explicit passage is TMS, 77, §10.

concrete situations. It seems implausible to interpret this as merely an exercise in descriptive anthropology, however—it seems clear that Smith is making normative claims as well. Second, there is Smith's curious and at times confusing mixture of nature and nurture in his account of morals. His examination mixes a grab bag of natural or innate equipment with various environmental forces to produce the system of morality. Now, one might argue that those elements that constitute our innate equipment are able to anchor a claim for ultimate legitimacy precisely because they are natural, but that argument would have to overcome two obstacles. On the one hand, one would have to explain how the environmental or social component of the moral system, which on Smith's account is integral to it, does not undercut the claim that the moral system is natural and therefore justified. On the other hand, one would be faced with the more general difficulty of explaining how the fact that something is natural implies that it is also good or right—a problem of notorious difficulty especially since Hume's famous distinction of so-called is-statements from ought-statements in the *Treatise.* The issue of justification poses a final problem for Smith in relation to his account of the role utility plays in moral judging. Recall that Smith argued against Hume that utility is not the ultimate spring of our moral judgments. Smith's theory that the system of morality is a system of unintended order, however, would seem to require a criterion of selection. It would seem, that is, to be something of an evolutionary account of the development of morals, but an evolutionary account of the development of anything is not complete until a principle or criterion of selection is identified in accordance with which the evolution proceeds. The obvious criterion would seem to be utility—but how could that be reconciled with Smith's express rejection of utility as the basis of moral judgment?

These issues will have to be sorted out before we can judge whether Smith's theory is normative as well as descriptive, whether the system of morality and the judgments made on the basis of it, if formed in the way Smith describes, are in any way transcendently right or wrong. In this chapter, I propose first to recast and attempt to render coherent the natural and environmental elements that Smith thinks are at work in forming the system of morality. I shall then examine the passages in which Smith discusses whether his theory is normative or descriptive, as well as other passages that bear on the issue, to determine what the nature of his theory is. Then I shall look at a portion of the considerable scholarly discussion that has been dedicated to this topic, reviewing in turn a selection of scholars who argue that TMS is entirely descriptive and others who argue that it is both descriptive and normative. I shall close by presenting my own view of Smith's purpose, which will include an assessment of the role that both God and utility play in his theory.

## I. The Development of Moral Standards

*Natural Elements*

The first sentence of TMS is: "How selfish soever man may be supposed, there are evidently some principles in his nature, which interest him in the fortune of others, and render their happiness necessary to him, though he derives nothing from it except the pleasure of seeing it" (TMS, 9). What are these principles? "Nature, when she formed man for society, endowed him with an original desire to please, and an original aversion to offend his brethren. She taught him to feel pleasure in their favourable, and pain in their unfavourable regard" (TMS, 116).[6] Given Smith's account of the desire for mutual sympathy of sentiments, we can see that the desire to please and not offend others is derivative of it. Acting so as to please others pleases us because we know that if we were in their position, we would like us to behave in the same way. We thus approve of the pleasure others take in our behavior as appropriate, giving rise to a mutual sympathy of sentiments that gives us pleasure. Smith calls the desire to please others "original" because nature endowed us with it at birth; that does not mean, however, that the desire cannot be the derivative or effect of another, more basic psychological feature of human nature—in this case, the desire for mutual sympathy. Elsewhere Smith writes that we are "naturally endowed with a desire of the welfare and preservation of society" (TMS, 77), though he allows that this desire, which is something like an expanded benevolence, is too irregular to be relied upon as a motivation for predictable behavior. To remedy this, nature "has endowed [us] with an immediate and instinctive approbation of that very application which is most proper to attain [the welfare and preservation of society]" (ibid.).

---

[6] See also TMS, 129 and 224, §17.

The result is that mankind naturally approve of punishing "unprovoked malice"—which, if it went unpunished, would precipitate the demise of society. Although in this passage Smith might sound as if our approval of justified punishment is a basic, irreducible element of human nature, it turns out that it is not. It is instead also the effect of the desire for mutual sympathy. It results from an "indirect sympathy" with the sentiments of the person or persons who suffer whatever injustice we now approve of being punished. When a spectator imaginatively places himself in the shoes of the victim of a person's unjust actions, a "sympathetic indignation" "naturally boils up in the breast of the spectator" (TMS, 76); this indignation then results in our condemnation of the initial injustice and in our approval of its punishment. Once again, it is the desire for mutual sympathy of sentiments that ultimately underlies what seems at first by Smith's own description to be an irreducible element of human nature.

Yet the desire for mutual sympathy, which has played a central role in our discussion of Smith's moral theory, is perhaps somewhat misleading when phrased in that way. Smith's argument is that mutual sympathy gives us a great pleasure, perhaps the greatest of all pleasures, and its absence is a great pain. "But whatever may be the cause of sympathy, or however it may be excited, nothing pleases us more than to observe in other men a fellow-feeling with all the emotions of our own breast; nor are we ever so much shocked as by the appearance of the contrary" (TMS, 13).[7] It is therefore at bottom the desire for the pleasure and the aversion to the pain that drive us to seek mutual sympathy of sentiments: we do not have an "original desire" for mutual sympathy of sentiments per se; we have, rather, an original desire for pleasure and an original aversion to pain, and we accordingly seek those things that give us the former and avoid those things that give us the latter. Because, as it turns out, mutual sympathy is the cause of one great pleasure we are capable of experiencing, it is of paramount importance in the ordering and directing of our lives.

Added into this mix of original and derivative desires is, finally, the "natural preference which every man has for his own happiness above that of other people" (TMS, 82). Smith writes that "[e]very man is, no doubt, by nature, first and principally recommended to his own

---

[7] See also TMS, 213.

care" (ibid.). Very young children who have as yet no self-command are unable to check this partiality, but that is only because they have not yet needed to do so. As we saw in Chapter 3, they are often indulged by their parents or other caregivers so that they have free license to express and act on their wants. It is only introduction into society, which entails exposure to people who are not so indulgent, that one's natural desire to please and not to offend others is triggered, putting in motion the complex and life-long process of seeking mutual sympathy of sentiments and developing a moral code centered around an impartial spectator's judgments. The partiality we have for ourselves is not derivative of the desire for mutual sympathy; in fact, the two are frequently in competition, the former encouraging us to temper the latter. Our selfishness, however, is an effect of our desire for pleasure: it gives us pleasure to do things for ourselves and to flatter ourselves. Thus our natural desire for pleasure prompts us toward two competing ends—mutual sympathy and selfish partiality—that compete with one another for the attention of our will, the result of which competition will tend toward an equilibrium that will become a rule of conduct that an impartial spectator would endorse.[8]

According to Smith, then, we are fundamentally pleasure-seeking creatures. It so happens, however, that among the things that give us pleasure are things that inherently concern the good will and welfare of others. Along with the standard package of appetites and biological and psychological necessities, then, the important features from which Smith believes that we naturally derive pleasure and hence desire are experiencing a mutual sympathy of sentiments, pleasing and not offending others, and selfishly serving our own interests. These built-in facts about human nature are what act as the forces behind the development of moral standards by encouraging people to create and maintain close-knit communities and by encouraging individuals to internalize moral standards as their conscience. Close-knit communities are fostered in two complementary ways, roughly corresponding

---

[8] This competition is not unlike that between the producer and the consumer or an employer and an employee as each seeks to satisfy his own interests: they will tend to settle on a fixed point that represents an equilibrium between their respective interests, a point that is reflected in the price of the service or commodity in question. See WN, 72–81, 83–88, and 96–104.

to the division of motivation pointed out respectively by TMS and WN. The pleasures of mutual sympathy of sentiments and of pleasing others can only be had in the presence of others. Smith argues this claim in the passage in which he discusses the solitary man who has grown up outside human society (TMS, 110–11). It is only upon the introduction of the solitary man into society that he is confronted for the first time with others' judgments of him, and it is only then that his desires for mutual sympathy and to please others are engaged. He takes stock of his appearance and of his moral character for the first time, in an effort to gain the approval of those with whom he is now in contact.[9] Smith wants the point of this fictional scenario to be generalized: we all have the capacity to receive pleasure from mutual sympathy and from pleasing others, but the desire for these pleasures, and hence the motivation to seek them, is only activated by intercourse with other people. Because these pleasures are among the greatest of pleasures, we actively seek out companionship and association with others, which leads to the foundation of mankind's community-based life. This is the general description of the creation of human institutions that Smith gives in TMS.

In addition to this, Smith gives another reason why we form communities that speaks to a narrower motivation human beings feel. Smith argues that we come to realize that we cannot satisfy all our interests by ourselves. In WN Smith shows how this realization leads individuals to barter, truck, and trade the surplus of their production with that of other people in an effort to satisfy their wants; Smith calls the opportunities to engage in such activities "markets." As we have already seen, a person cannot satisfy his wants if he is unable to offer something valuable to others in exchange;[10] he cannot offer something valuable to others, however, unless he knows what is valuable to them. To be successful at satisfying one's own interests, then, one is required by the nature and presence of markets to have careful and sensitive knowledge of others and their interests, combined with a willingness and ability to abide by those interests. Thus markets generally, and marketplaces of exchange in particular, provide strong incentives for

---

[9] See TMS, 111–13.
[10] One could steal, of course, but this would breach the rules of justice.

people not just to foster and maintain close ties with others but to take a sincere interest in the interests of others.[11]

The innate features of human nature enumerated earlier also lead, in the context of communities of people, to the development of an "objective" system of morality, with the mature individuals in the community internalizing the shared conception of morality as their consciences. As we saw in Chapter 3, because they have not yet needed it, newborn infants and very young children do not yet have what Smith calls self-command—that is, the discipline to act in accordance with something other than their immediate passions or desires. They express their wants without reservation, and their caregivers generally act to fulfill those wants. As they grow, however, they come into contact with people who are not as indulgent as their parents or nannies, who, in fact, may rebuke their desires or ridicule them for expressing them so freely. According to Smith, these first rebukes constitute a child's first introduction into "the great school of self-command" (TMS, 145). The child finds the rebukes unpleasant and seeks to find ways to prevent experiencing further rebukes. The child discovers that if he tempers his concern for himself he is more likely to achieve a sympathy with others, and this sympathy, he discovers, is pleasurable; he also finds that he can achieve a similarly pleasurable sympathy if he can engage the sentiments of others so as to match his own. He finds moreover that if he occasionally suppresses his selfish partiality and considers the well-being of others when he acts, he receives pleasure from thus pleasing and not displeasing others. Because, as we said earlier, the desire to please others is derivative of the desire for mutual sympathy, the child soon learns that mutual sympathy is what he really desires. What happens, then, as the child grows, is that he develops habits of behavior according to what has proved to be successful means of achieving sympathy. These habits gradually become rules of behavior that in time come to make up the system of morality that the child, now grown to an adult, relies on as the standard of conduct for himself and others. The rules manifest themselves as his conscience—the source of the seemingly instinctive moral judgments that he makes many times a day.

---

[11] I return to this issue in the Conclusion.

*Objectivity and the "Man of System"*

But in what sense is this adult's system of morality objective? On Smith's account, a person cannot develop a conscience in isolation. Other people are required because it is only interaction with others— the "free communication of sentiments and opinions" (TMS, 337)— that can trigger the desire for mutual sympathy and the desire to please and not offend others, thereby beginning the process of tempering one's selfish partiality that ultimately leads to the development of one's conscience. A system of morality thus only develops within the context of a community, and that is one sense in which it can be considered objective. There is another, and more profound, sense, however. Not only does the system develop only in a community, but each member of the community also undergoes the same process of seeking mutual sympathy, desiring to please others, tempering his selfish partiality, and ultimately forming a moral conscience that everyone else undergoes. The occasions that immediately lead to the development or refinement of habits of behavior and then rules of behavior are our daily judgments of ourselves and others, judgments that we frequently share with those concerned. We do not publicly declare every judgment we pass, but we voice a sufficient portion of them to allow others to consider them, to see to what extent they match their own, and to assimilate them accordingly. The system of morality that thus develops in a community is necessarily a product of the joint, collaborative effort of the individuals in the community. It is not—and, on Smith's account, could not be—the product of any one person, even though it is only individuals who give rise to it.[12] This, again, is part of its essence as an unintended system of order: it is caused or produced by the numberless actions, decisions, and judgments of individuals who did not intend to create it.[13] Because each person in the community has knowledge of his own situation that others do not possess,

[12] This fact about morality precludes the possibility, for Smith, that moral judgments could be relative to individuals, though historical or cultural relativity is not necessarily ruled out. I return to this issue later in the chapter.

[13] I include here actions, in addition to decisions and judgments, because Smith thinks that we often learn of others' judgments and decisions not from their words but from what they do. Even a person's facial expression can convey a judgment: the mirror of society "is placed in the countenance and behavior of those [one] lives with, which always mark when they enter into, and when they disapprove of [one's] sentiments" (TMS, 110).

and because each person similarly situated adds to and influences the overall system of morality, the system itself embodies more knowledge than any one person has or could have. It is in this way bigger than any one individual, and in this way it can be considered "objective"—that is, not solely in relation to or dependent on any individual subject. When the system of morality is internalized in each member of the community as the voice of his conscience or of the impartial spectator, that voice then embodies a wisdom—meaning some combination of knowledge and experience—beyond what any individual could have. For Smith, this means that this voice warrants heeding unless there are compelling reasons in a particular case not to do so. Simply not understanding why there is a certain rule of morality, or not seeing any justification for it, would not entitle one to disobey it.

That the unintended system of morality is in this way wiser than any individual could be is crucial for Smith; I think this notion is what underlies the intriguing passage in TMS about the "man of system," a passage that otherwise might seem out of place in TMS. The passage comes in part six of TMS, where Smith discusses "the character of virtue," that is, where he lays out the virtues that the impartial spectator recommends. In a chapter entitled "Of the order in which Societies are by nature recommended to our Beneficence" (TMS, 227–34), Smith argues that nature has so constituted us that we naturally care for our own society or community more than we do for those of other people. The reason is that, as in the case concerning the benevolence we naturally feel toward other people, natural benevolence depends on and extends in direct relation to familiarity. We are most familiar with that society in which "we have been born and educated," and hence that society "is accordingly, by nature, most strongly recommended to us" (TMS, 227). As in the case of our sentiments toward individuals, Smith argues that this is also how it ought to be: since our labor can in most cases help only that community of which we are a part, it is proper that our ability to help should correspond with our naturally prompted benevolence.

About midway through this chapter, however, Smith seems to change the topic, or at least to undertake a substantial digression. He begins to discuss the various actions to which the love of one's own country can lead. He says that this love involves two principles, namely, "a certain respect and reverence for that constitution or form of government which is actually established" and "an earnest desire to render the condition of our fellow-citizens as safe, respectable, and happy as we can" (TMS, 231). In times of peace, Smith writes, these two principles "generally coincide and lead to the same conduct" (ibid.). "But in times of public discontent, faction, and disorder, those two different principles may draw different ways, and even a wise man may be disposed to think some alteration necessary in that constitution or form of government, which, in its actual condition, appears plainly unable to maintain the public tranquillity" (ibid.). He continues: "Amidst the turbulence and disorder of faction, a certain spirit of system is apt to mix itself with that public spirit which is founded upon the love of humanity, upon a real fellow-feeling with the inconveniencies and distresses to which some of our fellow-citizens may be exposed" (TMS, 232).[14] By "spirit of system," Smith means the confluence of two things. On the one hand, he means what he thinks is the natural agreeableness people find in the "utility of any form, its fitness for the useful purposes for which it was intended" (TMS, 199). Smith thinks that the pleasure we feel, which other philosophers (Hume in particular) have ascribed to utility, actually springs more from the "fitness" or "happy contrivance of any production of art" than it does from viewing "the very end for which it was intended" (TMS, 179).[15] The result is that we often take pleasure in viewing or contemplating a well-contrived machine or an orderly artifice, regardless of the actual effect it has on its possessor's utility. On the other hand, by "spirit of system" Smith means the tendency we have to overestimate our own knowledge, and our tendency to exaggerate our ability to construct, direct, or reproduce natural processes by means of purely rational or imaginary schemata. These two principles combine to give people a spirit of system, which, if present in political leaders during times of political turbulence, can lead to undesirable consequences. Of political leaders with this "spirit of system," Smith writes:

They often propose, upon this account, to new-model the constitution, and to alter, in some of its most essential parts, that system of government under which the subjects of a great empire have enjoyed, perhaps, peace, security,

---

[14] Since Part VI of TMS was new to the sixth edition of 1790, it is possible that Smith is here thinking of the recent turmoil in France. See Ross (1995), 385–400.

[15] See TMS, 179–80, 185, and 199–200.

and even glory, during the course of several centuries together. The great body of the party are commonly intoxicated with the imaginary beauty of this ideal system, of which they have no experience, but which has been represented to them in all the most dazzling colours in which the eloquence of their leaders could paint it. Those leaders themselves, though they originally may have meant nothing but their own aggrandisement, become many of them in time the dupes of their own sophistry, and are as eager for this great reformation as the weakest and foolishest of their followers. (TMS, 232–33)

Smith next describes how a wise political leader behaves in times of national turbulence, in opposition to how the man of system behaves. Of the former, he writes:

The man whose public spirit is prompted altogether by humanity and benevolence, will respect the established powers and privileges even of individuals, and still more those of the great orders and societies, into which the state is divided ... [L]ike Solon, when he cannot establish the best system of laws, he will endeavour to establish the best that the people can bear. (TMS, 233) [16]

The man of system handles the situation quite differently:

The man of system, on the contrary, is apt to be very wise in his own conceit; and is often so enamoured with the supposed beauty of his own ideal plan of government, that he cannot suffer the smallest deviation from any part of it. He goes on to establish it completely and in all its parts, without any regard either to the great interests, or to the strong prejudices which may oppose it. He seems to imagine that he can arrange the different members of a great society with as much ease as the hand arranges the different pieces upon a chess-board. He does not consider that the pieces upon the chess-board have no other principle of motion besides that which the hand impresses upon them; but that, in the great chess-board of human society, every single piece has a principle of motion of its own, altogether different from that which the legislature might chuse to impress upon it. If those two principles coincide and act in the same direction, the game of human society will go on easily and harmoniously, and is very likely to be happy and successful. If they are

---

[16] Smith may have Edmund Burke in mind here. Smith and Burke were friends who shared a mutual respect, and they exchanged several letters during Smith's lifetime. See letters 145, 215, 216, 226, 230, 263, and 265 in *Correspondence of Adam Smith* (1987). In addition, the notion of respecting the established or traditional customs and rules is distinctly reminiscent of Burke's thought. See in particular Burke's *Reflections on the Revolution in France* (1987 [1789–90]). Though Smith had contact with Burke many times during his life, he died in 1790, making it unlikely that he ever had a chance to read Burke's *Reflections*.

opposite or different, the game will go on miserably, and the society must be at all times in the highest degree of disorder.

Some general, and even systematical, idea of the perfection of policy and law, may no doubt be necessary for directing the views of the statesman. But to insist upon establishing, and upon establishing all at once, and in spite of all opposition, every thing which that idea may seem to require, must often be the highest degree of arrogance. It is to erect his own judgment into the supreme standard of right and wrong. It is to fancy himself the only wise and worthy man in the commonwealth, and that his fellow-citizens should accommodate themselves to him and not he to them. (TMS, 233–34)

What exactly is the mistake that the man of system makes? No doubt one of his mistakes is his usurpation of the natural liberty of his citizens—each of whom, after all, has a principle of motion all his own, and the man of system cannot legitimately coerce them into abiding by his will. This mistake would be a violation of the rules of justice, which provide that no one may violate another's rights to life, liberty, or property; it would thus be a morally improper act.[17] But Smith's argument in this passage is that the man of system makes another mistake as well: the factual mistake of believing his wisdom to be something that it is not and cannot be. The legislator, sovereign prince, or statesman can neither know nor account for the multifarious interests, desires, goals, dreams, ambitions, needs (i.e., the principles of motion) of every citizen in his society. Whatever comprehensive plan he might fashion for the direction of society, then, must necessarily disregard or reduce to a distorted simplicity a substantial segment of the citizens' interests. What manifests his "highest degree of arrogance" is the mistaken belief that he is intelligent or wise enough to excogitate a sufficiently sophisticated system to take everyone and all of his interests into consideration. Smith's point, I think, is that no single person, and hence no single plan, can take everyone into consideration. Indeed, no group of people smaller than the totality of the individuals in the society itself can gather, let alone store and utilize, all the information that would be needed to execute such a feat.

Smith's discussion of men of system should be seen, I suggest, as an extension and application of a larger argument he has made. Smith's argument is that the inherent limitations of human knowledge play an

[17] See TMS, 84.

integral, if, ironically, often ignored or unnoticed, role in the shaping of human relations, associations, and institutions. Our limited knowledge of others confines the natural affection we feel for them and hence also confines our benevolence as a natural motive to action; it leads to the development of a tool for adjudication of moral disputes, the impartial spectator; and it renders individuals unable to understand the workings of human society except in a schematic way. This last point is germane to Smith's discussion of the man of system. One might be inclined to ascribe this lengthy passage in TMS to Smith's general commitment to the principle of individualism that informed much political, economic, and philosophical thinking in the eighteenth century, but I think that would be to miss Smith's point. Though the "gospel of individual rights and individual liberty"[18] no doubt appealed to Smith, this passage nevertheless ties in to Smith's argument in TMS about the status of moral rules and moral standards. Smith thought that taking an inflated view of one's own knowledge and abilities was a folly that beset political leaders in particular but that was not limited to them. Once it could be seen that no one, however intelligent, could gather or comprehend all the knowledge necessary to guide an entire community to prosperity, the legislator's arrogant foolishness would be revealed as would the nature of human institutions as necessarily the unintentional products of countless individual actions. Society as a whole, then, including its political constitution, is structured and maintained by an unintentional order that not only was not planned but also is beyond the ability of anyone to plan.

Public laws, regulations, protocols, and practices arose, then, spontaneously as the codification of the experience and knowledge of untold numbers of people, many of whom may have no knowledge whatever of each other.[19] These standards that set parameters for decent behavior in society thus embody the collective knowledge of generations of people, knowledge that is otherwise hopelessly scattered in the discrete units of living and dead people's brains. I say "hopelessly" because there is no hope of ever assembling this knowledge in any one

---

[18] This is Glenn R. Morrow's phrase (1928, 167). Morrow suggests that it was not philosophical argument but rather Smith's "faith in the value of the individual and in the importance of freeing the individual man from the fetters of outworn economic institutions" that underlies much of what he says in both TMS and WN (ibid.).

[19] See LJ, 207 and 228.

person, and, perhaps more important, there is no hope of any one person comprehending the origin or ultimate justification of every single rule or protocol of behavior that obtains in his community. Now we can see not only why the man of system is a foolish legislator but also why the system of morality that develops in this way both has a presumptive authority that should be respected and is in an important sense objective. As the product of a kind of collected wisdom that is necessarily greater than that of any one individual, the long-standing and traditional rules of morality should trump individual judgment—except in extraordinary cases. That there are exceptions, it should be noted, is an important implication of Smith's model. Although the moral standards that have withstood the test of time will for that reason "carry along with them the most evident badges of this authority" (TMS, 165), the individual still retains his position as the one who knows his own situation better than anyone else. Thus there will be cases in which an impartial spectator who knew everything the person principally concerned knows would approve of an action that is inconsistent with the standing rules of morality. But these cases will be few. For the most part the impartial spectator will judge that the proper course of action is that prescribed by the rules of morality that have gradually and spontaneously developed in the community and in each individual.

### Environmental Elements

Let me now look for a moment at how Smith thinks some environmental factors will contribute to the shaping and development of moral standards. Smith's thinking here is of a piece with the rest of his general theory. Smith addresses this issue principally in a single chapter, entitled "Of the Influence of Custom and Fashion upon Moral Sentiments" (TMS, 200–11), a chapter that is one of only two in the short part five, "Of the Influence of Custom and Fashion upon the Sentiments of Moral Approbation and Disapprobation" (TMS, 194–211). In the other chapter, "Of the Influence of Custom and Fashion upon our Notions of Beauty and Deformity" (TMS, 194–200), Smith argues that our sense of beauty is closely connected with what we have become used to perceiving. In making this argument, Smith relies on a theory of the psychological foundations of wonder, surprise, and admiration that he later went on to flesh out in his "History of Astronomy" (EPS, 33–105).

He argues there that when we regularly perceive a conjunction of any two objects or events, or when we regularly perceive a series of objects or events, we come to form a habit in the imagination. This habit is such that whenever the conjunction or series is for some reason broken, we are unsettled at the anomaly. This psychological discomfort that we feel spurs us to discover the cause of the anomaly, and Smith thinks that this search is responsible in large part for the birth of philosophy and for the advancement of science down to his own day.[20]

In the chapter in TMS about our sense of beauty, Smith gives an account that draws on the same psychological construction. "When two objects have frequently been seen together," Smith writes, "the imagination acquires a habit of passing easily from the one to the other" (TMS, 194). He continues: "Though, independent of custom, there should be no real beauty in their union, yet when custom has thus connected them together, we feel an impropriety in their separation. The one we think is awkward when it appears without its usual companion" (ibid.). Smith argues that this phenomenon can be seen in virtually all cases where one might find aesthetic beauty—a suit of clothes, the furnishings of a house, the architecture of a building, the rhyme and verse of poetry, and all the other "productions of the arts" (TMS, 195–98). He argues moreover that custom and fashion influence our judgments in this way also "with regard to the beauty of natural objects" (TMS, 198). Given, however, that the "proportions" that are considered beautiful differ greatly from one natural object to the next—witness, for example, the differences among a beautiful flower, mountain, and person—how can our judgments of beauty in these cases be reconciled with psychological accounts of habitual perceptions given in the cases of productions of art? Smith argues that what we consider beautiful is what is most *usual* for each kind of thing; flowers, mountains, and persons being different kinds of things, we should expect that we would look for different characteristics to constitute beauty in each case.

Every class of things has its own peculiar conformation, which is approved of, and has a beauty of its own, distinct from that of every other species. It is upon this account that a learned Jesuit, father Buffier,[21] has determined that the

---

[20] See EPS, 48–53. There are of course strong echoes of Hume here.
[21] Jesuit priest Claude Buffier (1661–1737). The editors of TMS report that Smith's reference is to Buffier's 1717 *Traité des premières vérités et de la source de nos jugements,*

beauty of every object consists in that form and colour, which is most usual among things of that particular sort to which it belongs. (TMS, 198)

All the singular instances we have perceived of a particular kind of thing combine to form something of an average in our imagination; this average is what we come to expect when we view future instances of the kind, and it is the standard of beauty against which we judge those future instances. To take human beauty as an example:

Thus, in the human form, the beauty of each feature lies in a certain middle, equally removed from a variety of other forms that are ugly. A beautiful nose, for example, is one that is neither very long, nor very short, neither very straight, nor very crooked, but a sort of middle among all these extremes, and less different from any one of them, than all of them are from one another. (Ibid.)

Custom and fashion, then, form a considerable part of the basis on which we judge the beauty of things. Smith thinks they do not form the entire basis, however, because we retain a native propensity to take pleasure in an orderly, "connected variety," a propensity that follows from our instinct of taking pleasure in perceiving things the way we have become accustomed to perceiving them; for the same reason, we find "a disjointed and disorderly assemblage of unconnected objects" to be disagreeable and hence ugly (TMS, 199–200). Smith concludes:

But though I cannot admit that custom is the sole principle of beauty, yet I can so far allow the truth of this ingenious system as to grant, that there is scarce any one external form so beautiful as to please, if quite contrary to custom and unlike whatever we have been used to in that particular species of things: or so deformed as not to be agreeable, if custom uniformly supports it, and habituates us to see it in every single individual of the kind. (TMS, 200)

When Smith turns to the consideration of the extent to which custom and fashion influence moral judgments, however, he argues that their influence is not as great as in the case of aesthetic judgments. The reason for this is that the principles of human nature inform moral judgments to a greater degree than they do aesthetic judgments.

Part 1, Chapter 13, though Bonar's *Catalogue of Adam Smith's Library* (1966 [1894]) does not list anything by Buffier.

The principles of the imagination, upon which our sense of beauty depends, are of a very nice and delicate nature, and may easily be altered by habit and education: but the sentiments of moral approbation and disapprobation, are founded on the strongest and most vigorous passions of human nature; and though they may be somewhat warpt, cannot be entirely perverted. (Ibid.)

Smith's argument is that custom and fashion only influence the less important, marginal concerns of the moral judgment, but not the central concerns. So, for example, what is considered appropriate politeness in Scotland would be considered effeminate in Russia, and rude and barbaric in France. Politeness itself, however, is regarded as a virtue everywhere. The same holds true with the degree of frugality that is considered virtuous in different places, as opposed to when frugal behavior is considered to have become "excessive parsimony" (TMS, 204). Smith thinks that the different environmental circumstances in which different nations and different ages find themselves will give rise to different emphases in what is generally considered to be perfect virtue. In "civilized" nations, for example, "the virtues which are founded upon humanity are more cultivated than those which are founded upon self-denial and the command of the passions. Among rude and barbarous nations, it is quite otherwise, the virtues of self-denial are more cultivated than those of humanity" (TMS, 204–205). Because in civilized nations many of the basic necessities of life are met for most people, citizens have time and occasion to devote themselves to more expansive and benevolent concerns—relieving the miseries of the poor, for example, or writing philosophy. In contrast, because among savages and barbarians the paramount concerns center around bare existence, the qualities that most directly relate to survival are cultivated and extolled as virtues. Barbarians therefore praise self-denial, hardiness, and indifference to pain, while they condemn frailty, sensitivity, and indulgence.

Two points are important here about Smith's account. First, despite the differences among various nations and ages, Smith nevertheless believes that there is an underlying core of morality that is common to all—justice, in particular, is universally approved; injustice, universally condemned. Smith argues that the differences concern more what might be called "manners" than what might be called the "general style of character and behavior" (TMS, 209). He thinks that it is a matter of empirical fact that the only real differences among the moral systems obtaining in different places concern matters "of small moment only," like the proper modes of dress and the protocols of comportment that diverse peoples attach to the different "professions and states of life." Although young men and old, clergymen and officers will engage in peculiar practices that are approved of in their situations only, Smith writes that we "expect truth and justice," for example, from each and every one of them (TMS, 209). The second important point is that he seems to think that these minor differences in manners arise unintentionally from the ways individuals act in conjunction with one another to their peculiar environments.

> In general, the style of manners which takes place in any nation, may commonly upon the whole be said to be that which is most suitable to its situation. Hardiness is the character most suitable to the circumstances of a savage; sensibility to those of one who lives in a very civilized society. Even here, therefore, we cannot complain that the moral sentiments of men are very grossly perverted. (TMS, 209)

People must adapt their respective pursuits for better stations in life to the circumstances in which they find themselves, and the environmental differences among various nations and ages may well lead in time to different manners. This process of differentiation thus fits with the general account of the development of moral standards Smith has given. The moral systems—including the minor differences that particular instantiations exhibit—gradually arise as individuals strive to find ways to satisfy their interests. They can only do this by co-operating with others,[22] so rules governing their cooperation develop, which will reflect the external peculiarities of the people in question. Their underlying human nature is the principal determining factor for the moral system that ultimately develops, but outward circumstances necessarily play a role as well.[23]

Given this theoretical account, Smith thinks we should find precisely what we do find: widespread, even universal agreement about the basic virtues that comprise the core of morality, along with regional and temporal colorings reflective of the distinctive region and time

[22] See TMS, 85–86.
[23] See TMS, 209–11.

one examines. Our common, universal human nature explains the universal agreement one finds about the basic virtues of morality, and the environmental differences among the circumstances of various communities explains the minor differences in emphasis placed on these basic virtues, as well as the differences in manners one finds. Smith's explication of the way human nature interacts with the environment to produce an unintended system of morality is not systematic— we get parts of the picture in some places, others in other places— but we can assemble the parts with the profitable result of showing that Smith's diverse discussions fit together to form a coherent whole. Smith was aware of the differences one finds in practices and protocols across cultures, and he took them to be a group of facts that his theory of morality would have to explain. The result is a theory that occupies something of a middle ground between accounts that argue, on the one hand, that moral rules are absolute and admit of no exception whatever, and, on the other hand, those that argue that moral rules are relative to a certain time, place, or even person. Smithian morality is instead the joint product of universal human nature and particular environment, with a larger emphasis on the former than on the latter, striking a balance between these competing theories of morality by accounting for the claims of transcendence and of relativity that each raises against the other.

## II. A Descriptive or a Normative Theory?

We have now a sketch of the main elements of Smith's combination of nature and nurture in his theory of the development of moral standards. The marketplace of morals is an unintended process of evolution in which the elements inherent in human nature— principally the desire for mutual sympathy of sentiments, the desire to please others, and the partiality for one's own interests (although we shall discuss a few other important native instincts shortly)—operate within the circumstances of our peculiar environment to produce a stable yet flexible system of morality. Although this system is entirely unintended by the individuals who give rise to it, they nevertheless continually contribute to it in many ways. Two of these ways that we have already discussed are by each individual's internalizing the standards of morality as his own conscience and by each individual's communicating his own judgments in particular cases to those around him. Another important way is by teaching it to their children. By instilling in their children habits of behavior that reflect their community's settled rules of conduct, they help to make the process through which their children go to develop their own consciences a smoother and easier one. In Chapter 2, I outlined three reasons why Smith thinks that people tend to obey the judgments of the impartial spectator, and why they tend to view their community's general moral standards, which inform the impartial spectator's judgments, as possessing great authority. The first reason was that these moral standards are developed by the individuals themselves: they are an immediate result of induction individuals perform on their own experiences. Second, the rules are enforced and reflected by the other members of one's community: they are developed as the joint, collaborative effect of one's own judgments about attractions and aversions, approbations and disapprobations, as well as the judgments one observes others making in the same situations. Third, people come in time to view the rules of morality as transcendently valid, even as manifestations of God's will. Because the rules are developed and adopted as the standards of an entire community, and because in most instances they have been in place for long periods of time, people come to see obeying the rules as their moral duty. As there is often a close connection between moral duty and religious duty, so too do moral standards often come to be seen as religious standards that are set by God.[24]

Virtually everything we have said, however, about Smith's conception of moral standards up to this point has been descriptive. We have been concerned with understanding how Smith thinks that, as a matter of empirically verifiable fact, moral standards develop in human society. Yet it would appear that Smith also offers a normative justification for the system of morality that develops the way he describes: it conduces to the overall welfare of society and to the general flourishing of individuals.[25] Because we were able to discuss all the essential elements of Smith's theory without reference to any normative claims he may have made, the issue of his theory's normative status immediately

---

[24] See TMS, 161–70.
[25] At TMS, 87, §5, Smith says that nature is "contrived for advancing the two great purposes of nature, the support of the individual, and the propagation of the species."

raises the question of whether Smith intended his theory to be both descriptive and normative. A perhaps more difficult question it raises is how normativity can intelligibly be introduced into a theory of morality that argues that moral standards and moral judgments are chiefly the product of a historical process of development. It might seem that a question of normativity is simply irrelevant to such a system of morality. With our understanding of Smith's conception of the intrinsic and extrinsic elements of the development of moral standards as a background, let us now look at several passages from TMS in which Smith's discussion bears directly on the issue of description and normativity. The goal is to understand what kind of theory Smith thinks his is, as well as to see what difference there is, if any, between what Smith believes and how the theory actually unfolds.

*Descriptive Passages*

Let us begin by looking at the reasons one would think that Smith's examination is solely descriptive. There are, I think, two principal reasons. The first is the passage to which I have already referred, in which Smith explicitly states that he is not concerned with moral exhortation, but, rather, with giving a natural philosopher's—what we might today call a "scientific"—account of the nature of human moral sentiments. The passage comes early in the second part of TMS, where Smith is discussing our sense of merit and demerit. As we saw in Chapter 1, Smith thinks the sense of merit is a "compounded sentiment," made up, on the one hand, of a spectator's "direct" sympathy with the agent's sentiments, and, on the other hand, an "indirect" sympathy with the gratitude of the beneficiary of the agent's action (TMS, 74). When he turns to the analysis of the sense of demerit, he argues that it is again a compounded sentiment composed of a direct antipathy to the sentiments that motivated the actor and an indirect sympathy with the resentment that the victim feels. The chapter in which this discussion appears is quite short, but it is followed by a footnote that is about as long as the main text of the chapter;[26] the passage with which we are concerned is found in the fourth paragraph of the footnote.

---

[26] The chapter, entitled "The analysis of the sense of Merit and Demerit," is found at TMS, 74–78; the footnote begins on the bottom of page 76 and goes to the middle of page 78.

In the footnote Smith intends to address those who believe that resentment is always and everywhere a vice, and who thus might balk at his argument that it is founded on an agreeable sentiment like sympathy. Such people might, Smith thinks, be more willing to accept his analysis of merit, which claims that our sense of merit is founded on sympathy with gratitude, because gratitude and merit are both agreeable sentiments. But even in cases where such people would agree that punishment for an agent's improper actions is deserved, they might still wish to distinguish the "laudable principle" of proper punishment from the "odious passion" of resentment (TMS, 76, §7).

Smith answers this objection in several ways. He first replies that although resentment "in the degrees in which we too often see it" is "the most odious, perhaps, of all the passions," nevertheless it "is not disapproved of [by the impartial spectator] when properly humbled and entirely brought down to the level of the sympathetic indignation of the spectator" (TMS, 76). There are many cases, he argues, when the impartial spectator can go along with the sentiment of resentment a sufferer feels, disproving the sweeping claim some people make that resentment is always a vice. He suggests that those who have pressed that sweeping claim are perhaps moved to make it by the properly disagreeable judgment one forms on seeing a "too violent resentment" (TMS, 77). Because the resentment people feel is often too violent— Smith says it is too violent one hundred times for every one time it is properly moderate (ibid.)—it is understandable that people will come to associate disagreeable sentiments whenever they contemplate resentment; the condemnation of all resentment follows on this association. Nonetheless, there is such a thing as having "too little spirit," Smith claims, which in essence is the absence of proper resentment (ibid.). When someone has wronged one, it is proper that one should resent the wrongdoing—again, as long as it is properly moderated or, what comes to the same thing, accords with the judgments of the impartial spectator. Smith's second reply to this objection is a short one: how could resentment always be wrong if the Bible claims in so many places that God feels it? The "inspired writers" often speak of "the wrath and anger of God" (ibid.); how could a passion that God himself occasionally feels be regarded as universally vicious?

Smith's third response contains the passage for which we have been waiting. He writes:

Let it be considered too, that the present inquiry is not concerning a matter of right, if I may say so, but concerning a matter of fact. We are not at present examining upon what principles a perfect being would approve of the punishment of bad actions; but upon what principles so weak and imperfect a creature as man actually and in fact approves of it. The principles which I have just now mentioned, it is evident, have a very great effect upon his sentiments. (TMS, 77, §10)

The scope of the phrase "the present inquiry" is not clear. Does it mean the discussion of resentment? Does it also mean the discussion of the sense of demerit, or that of both merit and demerit? Does it mean all of TMS? The context of the passage seems to suggest that Smith means to confine his remark to a narrower range than the whole of TMS; it suggests, I would say, that it applies only to the discussion in this chapter. It has nevertheless been taken by some to apply to Smith's theory of moral sentiments generally and hence to indicate that Smith saw himself as a "social scientist" rather than as a "social philosopher."[27] Smith's argument in this passage seems to be that whatever opinion some people have of the relative virtue or vice of resentment is irrelevant to the question of whether a spectator's approval of proper punishment is founded on a sympathy with resentment. In other words, the facts of the matter are unaffected by our feelings or wishes about them. Such an argument would seem to support a claim that Smith sees himself as a scientist and not as a moralist. And even if the words Smith uses seemingly imply that his remark about being concerned with matters of fact and not right applies only to his examination of the sense of demerit, it is easy to imagine how the same remark could also aptly be said at least of his analysis of the sense of merit, if not also of much more in TMS.

There are some problems with interpreting this passage the way scholars like T. D. Campbell do,[28] but I would like to postpone discussing those problems for a moment. Let me now turn to the second

---

[27] These terms and this argument come from Campbell (1971), 46–52.

[28] William C. Swabey adopts a position similar to Campbell's. Swabey writes: "It is possible to interpret Adam Smith as making no ethical statements at all, that is, solely as a moral psychologist engaged in analysing and explaining our acts of approval and disapproval" (1961, 179). Another is D. D. Raphael, who writes that "Smith's theory is primarily an explanation of the origin of moral judgement, something that nowadays would be assigned to psychology rather than philosophy" (1985, 37).

main reason one might think Smith's theory is exclusively descriptive, a reason that, when taken in conjunction with the passage discussed earlier, might seem decisive. This reason is the overall character of Smith's theory—which, as we have seen, is predominantly descriptive. In part seven of TMS, in which Smith examines other leading theories of morality, Smith writes:

> In treating of the principles of morals there are two questions to be considered. First, wherein does virtue consist? Or what is the tone of temper, and tenour of conduct, which constitutes the excellent and praise-worthy character, the character which is the natural object of esteem, honour, and approbation? And, secondly, by what power or faculty in the mind is it, that this character, whatever it be, is recommended to us? Or in other words, how and by what means does it come to pass, that the mind prefers one tenour of conduct to another, denominates the one right and the other wrong; considers the one as the object of approbation, honour, and reward, and the other of blame, censure, and punishment? (TMS, 265)

It seems clear that in his own examination of moral sentiments, Smith treats the second question as a matter of empirical investigation. His answer to it involves a reliance on a psychological explanation that includes all the various elements of human nature that we described in the first section of this chapter (as well as in Chapter 2): a desire for mutual sympathy, a desire to please and not offend others, and a natural tendency to be partial to our own interests, along with a panoply of natural or inborn passions, attractions, and aversions. There seems here little concern for normative claims of morality. Toward the end of part seven, Smith writes, "Before I proceed . . . I must observe, that the determination of this second question, though of the greatest importance in speculation, is of none in practice" (TMS, 315). He continues:

> The question concerning the nature of virtue necessarily has some influence upon our notions of right and wrong in many particular cases. That concerning the principle of approbation can possibly have no such effect. To examine from what contrivance or mechanism within, those different notions or sentiments arise, is a mere matter of philosophical curiosity. (Ibid.)

After reading this, we might expect, as Campbell says, "a secondary and subordinate investigation appended to a vivid description of virtue and vice" (1971, 50). As Campbell correctly points out, however, that is not what we get in TMS. Even sympathy, the centerpiece of Smith's moral theory, receives an empirical, psychological analysis. Moreover, given the way Smith answers the second question, it would seem that the answer to the first question must logically follow suit. That is, if the means of determining virtue and vice is some kind of mechanical psychological process,[29] it appears that the results of this process would also have to be matters of fact unrelated to one's normative moral convictions. One might then argue that virtually the whole of Smith's theory of moral sentiments is an exercise in what we might today consider moral psychology.

In addition to these two main reasons, there are a number of isolated phrases and shorter passages throughout TMS that seem to support this interpretation. Smith's use of the notions of necessity and immediacy, in particular, frequently seem to underscore the idea that moral standards and moral judgments are largely mechanical—and hence factual—affairs. Here are a few short passages to illustrate the point. "When the original passions of the person principally concerned are in perfect concord with the sympathetic emotions of the spectator, they *necessarily* appear to this last just and proper" (TMS, 16).[30] "The man who resents the injuries that have been done to me, and observes that I resent them precisely as he does, *necessarily* approves of my sentiment. The man whose sympathy keeps time to my grief, *cannot but admit* the reasonableness of my sorrow" (ibid.). "If, upon bringing the case home to our own breast, we find that the sentiments which it gives occasion to, coincide and tally with our own, we *necessarily* approve of them as proportioned and suitable to their objects; if otherwise, we *necessarily* disapprove of them" (TMS, 19). "As we entirely enter into the affection from which these returns proceed, they *necessarily* seem every way proper and suitable to their object" (TMS, 70). "When we approve of, and go along with, the affection from which the action proceeds, we *must necessarily* approve of the action" (TMS, 73). When

---

[29] In a few places, Smith uses terminology like this. For example: "In all private misfortunes, in pain, in sickness, in sorrow, the weakest man, when his friend, and still more when a stranger visits him, is immediately impressed with the view in which they are likely to look upon his situation. Their view calls off his attention from his own view; and his breast is, in some measure, becalmed the moment they come into his presence. This effect is produced instantaneously and, as it were, mechanically" (TMS, 145). See also the passage cited in this paragraph from TMS, 315, §3.

[30] The italics here and throughout this paragraph are mine.

a person reflects on an immoral act he has committed, "He is abashed and confounded at the thoughts of it, and *necessarily* feels a very high degree of that shame which he would be exposed to, if his actions should ever come to be generally known" (TMS, 118). Elsewhere Smith says that "natural sympathy" is "*immediate* and instinctive" (TMS, 71). He writes that if we for even a moment serve our own happiness at the expense of that of others, the impartial spectator "*immediately* call to us, that we value ourselves too much and other people too little"; if even a poor man steals from a rich man, "The man within *immediately* calls to him, in this case too, that he is no better than his neighbour" (TMS, 138). One might argue that these passages, and others,[31] suggest that Smith thinks passing moral judgments is a mechanical process, which would seem to call for an empirical investigation rather than normative discussion. In contemporary phrasing, they are facts, not values, and if this sort of investigation forms the bulk of TMS—as it apparently does—then it seems reasonable to conclude that Smith intended TMS to be a descriptive, and not a normative, treatise.

### Normative Passages

It is clear that in TMS Smith nowhere—or, at least, almost nowhere[32]—expressly tells his reader how he ought to act or how he ought to behave. In this limited sense, then, I think there can be no question that TMS is not normative. But it is also true that Smith takes great pains to argue that the judgments of the impartial spectator and the overall system of morality of which it is an integral part are in important respects good. The implication seems to be that they therefore ought to be obeyed. Let us now turn to look at some of the places where Smith expresses this sentiment to determine in what way, if any, these passages show that Smith's theory is correctly regarded as normative as well as descriptive.[33]

---

[31] See also TMS, 72, §3; 77, §8; 112, §5; 259, §47; and 293, §47.

[32] One of the very few places where Smith expresses such sentiments is this: "The violator of the laws of justice ought to be made to feel himself that evil which he has done to another; and since no regard to the suffering of his brethren is capable of restraining him, he ought to be over-awed by the fear of his own" (TMS, 82).

[33] Charles Griswold argues that virtually all of Smith's work, including especially TMS, is "protreptic," meaning that it is written with the subtle and unannounced design of encouraging virtue and discouraging vice in its readers. See Griswold (1999), Chapter 1 and passim. I am not persuaded that Smith had a hidden protreptic design

Smith interlards the whole of TMS with references to God, Nature, the Author of nature, and other similar terms,[34] to whom or to which he in many different ways ascribes mainly one thing: the intelligent and benevolent design of the universe and humanity's place in it. Before turning to look at some of the isolated references, I wish to look at two extended discussions. The first and perhaps most explicit of Smith's discussions is in the chapter entitled "Of the utility of this constitution of Nature" (TMS, 85–91). Smith argues in this chapter that human beings can only subsist in communities because they require the assistance of others to reach their full, flourishing potential as human beings (and not beasts). Communities in which we assist one another require, of course, cooperation, which Smith argues will only obtain once a general security for our persons and their property has been established. For this, the rules of justice must be enforced without exception.[35] Here we find the argument that justice is the necessary and sufficient precondition for the existence of society; whereas "mutual love and affection," "acts of beneficence," as well as mutual "gratitude," "friendship," and "esteem" are the ornaments that embellish and make the edifice of society agreeable, they are not the pillars that form its foundation—justice is (TMS, 85–86). Given this fact, it is quite interesting to observe how Nature[36] has equipped us so as to meet our needs.

(see Otteson, November 2000), but, as I shall argue shortly, I do think TMS is deeply normative as well as descriptive.

34 Whether Smith thought that God and Nature (capital "n") were the same thing and what Smith's general religious beliefs were have been the subjects of considerable scholarly scrutiny. Glenn R. Morrow, for example, wrote that "Nature, spelt with a capital *N*, equals God" (1928, 171). See also Brown (1994), 66–75; Griswold (1999), Chapter 8, especially 314–17; Minowitz (1993), Chapters 8–10; and Rae (1895), 429–30.

35 Recall that for Smith the rules of justice concern principally three things: protection of life, private property, and the sanctity of voluntary contracts: "The most sacred laws of justice, therefore, those whose violation seems to call loudest for vengeance and punishment, are the laws which guard the life and person of our neighbour; the next are those which guard his property and possessions; and last of all come those which guard what are called his personal rights, or what is due to him from the promises of others" (TMS, 84).

36 Note the uppercase "n." Smith uses both an uppercase and a lowercase "n" to begin the word "nature" in TMS. When he writes it as "nature," he generally means the things we find in the universe or the system of things in the universe; when he writes it as "Nature," he generally means the intelligence òr consciousness that is the efficient cause of nature. See Minowitz (1993), 190–207.

In order to enforce the observation of justice, therefore, Nature has implanted in the human breast that consciousness of ill-desert, those terrors of merited punishment which attend upon its violation, as the great safe-guards of the association of mankind, to protect the weak, to curb the violent, and to chastise the guilty. (TMS, 86)

Although we desire mutual sympathy and to please others, Smith continues, these desires frequently pale in comparison to the partiality we have for ourselves. Without, then, an instinct built into us that would make us view breaches of justice with abhorrence, "a man would enter an assembly of men as he enters a den of lions" (ibid.). It is happily the case, however, that nature has endowed us with a natural propensity to abhor and be shocked by injustice—although, curiously but fittingly, nature has not endowed us with a similar propensity concerning the absence or lack of acts of beneficence.[37]

The full story Smith gives to explain this propensity contains several steps. It ultimately relies on the native love Smith thinks we have for order. Because we love (or receive some kind of pleasure from) order,[38] we also love those things that tend to establish and maintain order in society—like acts of beneficence and the strict observance of justice— and we dislike things that tend to disrupt society—like acts of injustice.

The orderly and flourishing state of society is agreeable to him, and he takes delight in contemplating it. Its disorder and confusion, on the contrary, is the object of his aversion, and he is chagrined at whatever tends to produce it ... Upon every account, therefore, he has an abhorrence at whatever can tend to destroy society, and is willing to make use of every means, which can hinder so hated and so dreadful an event. Injustice necessarily tends to destroy it. Every appearance of injustice, therefore, alarms him, and he runs, if I may say so, to stop the progress of what, if allowed to go on, would quickly put an end to every thing that is dear to him. (TMS, 88)

Smith takes this as evidence of two things, namely, that the universe has an intelligent designer, and that this designer as well as his design are benevolent. A society's overall system of morality, along with the judgments of the impartial spectator, are formed unintentionally by individuals as they interact with one another in their peculiar environment. Nevertheless, Smith thinks that "[a]ll men, even the most stupid

---

[37] See Kleer (April 1995), especially 286–88.
[38] See TMS, 179–80. See also Den Uyl and Griswold (March 1996).

and unthinking, abhor fraud, perfidy, and injustice, and delight to see them punished" (TMS, 89). His argument is that this abhorrence is too crucial to our subsistence and flourishing to have been left to the uncertainties and vagaries of human reason: the strength of this abhorrence results from the uniform condemnation of such injustices by the impartial spectator. This abhorrence was instead implanted in each of us from the beginning, thus ensuring that a flourishing society would be possible. But could we reasonably ascribe this innate abhorrence to arbitrary or chance causes? Smith thinks that the reasonable conclusion is rather that an intelligent design is responsible.

When by natural principles we are led to advance those ends, which a refined and enlightened reason would recommend to us, we are very apt to impute to that reason, as to their efficient cause, the sentiments and actions by which we advance those ends, and to imagine that to be the wisdom of man, which in reality is the wisdom of God. (TMS, 87)

Moreover, it is clear that God's wise design was motivated by benevolence because in the case of the natural abhorrence of injustice, as well as in all other cases in which we have natural attractions or aversions,[39] our natural sentiments coincide with and conduce to the overall utility of society. Surely it can only be a benevolent God that would have constructed human nature and the circumstances of the world so that when the two operate spontaneously and freely they lead to an increase in general utility for all of us.

This theme recurs time and again in TMS: the natural exercise of our faculties, including our moral faculties[40]—or, as Smith would put it in WN, people acting under their natural liberty—leads to the development of a system of morality that is ultimately conducive to general utility. It is the underlying theme also of the second of Smith's two extended discussions of this issue, in a chapter entitled "Of the final cause of this Irregularity of Sentiments" (TMS, 104–108). The irregularity Smith has in mind here is our propensity to applaud or decry others' actions or accomplishments, as opposed to their mere intentions. "That the world judges by the event, and not by the design, has been in all ages the complaint, and," Smith concedes, "is the great

---

[39] See, for example, TMS, 87, §5 and 105, §2.
[40] Smith refers to our moral faculties in the plural only a few times. For an example, see TMS, 164–65, §5.

discouragement of virtue" (TMS, 104–105). Yet Smith thinks things are not as bad as they might seem: "Nature, however, when she implanted the seeds of this irregularity in the human breast, seems, as upon all other occasions, to have intended the happiness and perfection of the species" (TMS, 105). Smith supports this claim by the following reasoning. Take the case of malevolent or hateful design, for example. If having such thoughts, sentiments, or intentions were sufficient to warrant punishment—instead, that is, of requiring an *act* of malevolence for punishment—Smith thinks a tyrannous invasion of privacy would ensue. He writes that "every court of judicature would become a real inquisition. There would be no safety for the most innocent and circumspect conduct" (ibid.). It is notoriously difficult to ascertain with any certainty what a person's private intentions are, though it is easy to *imagine* the wildest things to be among another's thoughts. The attempt to determine what a person's intentions are or were, Smith argues, would thus inevitably result in extensive interrogations, confiscations of private papers and effects, and, finally, convictions on little or nothing more than idle suspicions.

On the other hand, take the case of allowing a person's good intentions—again, as opposed to requiring a beneficent *act*—to suffice for praise or reward. The result, Smith thinks, would be the encouragement of inactivity and a lazy indifference to life. Smith writes that a person "must not be satisfied with indolent benevolence, nor fancy himself the friend of mankind, because in his heart he wishes well to the prosperity of the world" (TMS, 106). He continues:

The man who has performed no single action of importance, but whose whole conversation and deportment express the justest, the noblest, and most generous sentiments, can be entitled to demand no very high reward, even though his inutility should be owing to nothing but the want of an opportunity to serve. We can still refuse it him without blame. We can still ask him, What have you done? ... We esteem you, and love you; but we owe you nothing. (Ibid.)

It may seem unjust not to consider one's intentions in addition to, or even in lieu of, one's actions because we know that so much of what one does in life is influenced or determined by factors outside one's control. Smith agrees. Nevertheless, we find ourselves often inclined to consider exclusively or principally actions, not words or intentions. Smith's argument in this chapter is that if we were inclined to praise or blame mere intentions, the preceding disastrous consequences for human society would result. The fact that we are not so inclined, then, that our natural inclinations lead us on the contrary to weigh actions and not intentions, is once again suggestive of intelligent, benevolent design. It was "the wisdom of Nature" (TMS, 107) to see wherein hope for man's long-term prosperity lay, and wherein sure destruction lay. It was moreover the "providential care" and "goodness of God" (TMS, 105–106) that was responsible for implanting in man a tendency toward the one and away from the other. In most instances, then, what is natural is good. We thus have another argument to support Smith's claim that the system of morality that results from communities of individuals freely exercising their natural sentiments conduces to our overall utility and is, therefore, good.

As I have already said, one finds this claim, or suggestions of it, throughout TMS.[41] Smith writes, for instance, that "one of the most important principles in human nature" is "the dread of death, the great poison to the happiness, but the great restraint upon the injustice of mankind, which, while it afflicts and mortifies the individual, guards and protects the society" (TMS, 13). While discussing hatred and anger, Smith writes: "It was, it seems, the intention of Nature, that those rougher and more unamiable emotions, which drive men from one another, should be less easily and more rarely communicated" (TMS, 37). Smith thinks that capital punishment for capital crimes is necessary for the stability of society, though people's judgments in this regard are often clouded by an exaggerated concern for the criminal condemned to death and a depreciated concern for the victim he murdered.[42] Luckily, however, nature has helped us along. "And with regard, at least, to this most dreadful of all crimes [i.e., murder], Nature, antecedent to all reflections upon the utility of punishment, has in this manner stamped upon the human heart, in the strongest and most indelible characters, an immediate and instinctive approbation of the sacred and necessary law of retaliation" (TMS, 71). Smith has argued that we are by nature recommended to our own care before

---

[41] One also finds suggestions of it in Smith's "History of Astronomy." For example: "The benevolent purpose of nature in bestowing upon us the sense of seeing, is evidently to inform us concerning the situation and distance of the tangible objects which surround us" (EPS, 156).

[42] See TMS, 88–89.

that of any others, then to that of our family, then friends, acquaintances, and finally strangers. "That we should be but little interested, therefore, in the fortune of those whom we can neither serve nor hurt, and who are in every respect so very remote from us, seems wisely ordered by Nature" because it relieves us of unnecessary and ultimately fruitless anxiety (TMS, 140). Moreover, "Nature, for the wisest purposes, has rendered, in most men, perhaps in all men, parental tenderness a much stronger affection than filial piety. The continuance and propagation of the species depend altogether upon the former, and not upon the latter" (TMS, 142). The judgments of the impartial spectator also correlate with our utility. "That degree of self-estimation, therefore, which contributes most to the happiness and contentment of the person himself, seems likewise most agreeable to the impartial spectator. The man who esteems himself as he ought, and no more than he ought, seldom fails to obtain from other people all the esteem that he himself thinks due" (TMS, 261).[43]

Closely connected with our utility, Smith thinks, perhaps even identical with it, is our happiness. That is, what is in the long run good for us is also what makes us in the long run happy. By designing the universe and human nature in such a way that actions without larger intentions can lead to greater utility, the author of nature has thus also purposefully designed the universe and human nature to conduce to human happiness. "The happiness of mankind, as well as of all other rational creatures, seems to have been the original purpose intended by the Author of nature, when he brought them into existence" (TMS, 166). Smith argues that this conclusion, "which we are led to by the abstract consideration of his infinite perfections, is still more confirmed by the examination of the works of nature, which seem all intended to promote happiness, and to guard against misery" (ibid.).

If we consider the general rules by which external prosperity and adversity are commonly distributed in this life, we shall find, that notwithstanding the disorder in which all things appear to be in this world, yet even here every virtue naturally meets with its proper reward, with the recompense which is

---

[43] For other important passages in which Smith speaks of the utility of God's or Nature's benevolent design, see TMS, 35, §4; 78, §10; 128, §31n; 168, §9; 188, §3; 218, §3; 226, §20; 229, §4; 253, §30; and 298, §13. See also the "invisible hand" passages in TMS, 184–85 and in WN, 455–56. I shall discuss the "invisible hand" passages shortly.

most fit to encourage and promote it; and this too so surely, that it requires a very extraordinary concurrence of circumstances entirely to disappoint it. (Ibid.)

As this last passage indicates, Smith's suggestion is that virtue—as defined by the judgments of the impartial spectator, whose judgments in turn are a reflection of the unintended system of morality—pays.[44] "By the wise contrivance of the Author of nature, virtue is upon all ordinary occasions, even with regard to this life, real wisdom, and the surest and readiest means of obtaining both safety and advantage" (TMS, 298). "The prudent, the equitable, the active, resolute, and sober character promises prosperity and satisfaction, both to the person himself and to every one connected with him. The rash, the insolent, the slothful, effeminate, and voluptuous, on the contrary, forebodes ruin to the individual, and misfortune to all who have any-thing to do with him" (TMS, 187).[45] Smith thinks that the four central virtues that he has argued form the core of morality—justice, benev-olence, prudence, and self-command—all combine in the life of the virtuous person to make him both happy and prosperous in the long run. Strict observance of the rules of justice enables the cooperation necessary for the existence of a flourishing community; benevolence is always returned to one "with a tenfold increase," filling one's life with friendship and joy; prudence leads to the habits of "oeconomy, indus-try, discretion, attention, and application of thought," which are nec-essary for bettering one's condition in life; and, finally, self-command is the discipline that is necessary to exert oneself in the exercise of the other virtues.[46]

Smith thinks that the connection between the general welfare of society and the happiness of the individual is captured and effected by the smooth running of the machine of the universe, of which human beings with their natural characteristics are the most important part. That humanity's clumsy, fitful attempt to satisfy its interests results in an unintended system of morality comprising virtues that over time ameliorate its condition and conduce to its happiness is thus further evidence, Smith believes, that a benevolent intelligence designed the

---

[44] See Rosenberg (1990), especially page 6.
[45] See also TMS, 163, 166, and 225.
[46] See TMS, 85–86, 224–26, 304, and 241, respectively.

universe. Smith's idea of human happiness is being in a state of what he calls "tranquillity,"[47] by which he seems to mean that one's material needs are met, one's physical condition is good, one has led (or is leading) a life of virtue and wisdom, and one has established and maintained relations with others that are mutually agreeable.

What can be added to the happiness of the man who is in health, who is out of debt, and has a clear conscience? To one in this situation, all accessions of fortune may properly be said to be superfluous; and if he is much elevated upon account of them, it must be the effect of the most frivolous levity. This situation, however, may very well be called the natural and ordinary state of mankind. Notwithstanding the present misery and depravity of the world, so justly lamented, this really is the state of the greater part of men. The greater part of men, therefore, cannot find any great difficulty in elevating themselves to all the joy which any accession to this situation can well excite in their companion. (TMS, 45)

Smith believes that the fact that most people are in this general state of happiness is still further evidence of the universe's intelligent design. What is it, Smith asks in another discussion, that makes us view with such detestation a person who intentionally or spitefully sows discord among his friends?

Is it in depriving them of the frivolous good offices, which, had their friendship continued, they might have expected from one another? It is in depriving them of that friendship itself, in robbing them of each other's affections, from which both derived so much satisfaction; it is in disturbing that harmony of their hearts, and putting an end to that happy commerce which had before subsisted between them. These affections, that harmony, this commerce, are felt, not only by the tender and delicate, but by the rudest vulgar of mankind, to be of more importance to happiness than all the little services which could be expected to flow from them. (TMS, 39)

Smith thinks that it is essential to one's psychological well-being— that is, to one's happiness—that one have friendly and loving relations that are based on sincere mutual affection and sympathy. "What so great happiness as to be beloved, and to know that we deserve to be beloved? What so great misery as to be hated, and to know that we deserve to be hated?" (TMS, 113). In several places in TMS Smith

---

[47] See TMS, 149, §30; 216, §13; and 245, §19.

reiterates his concern for humanity's physical and psychological well-being. I would like to suggest that he believes that the marketplace of exchange, protected by the rules of justice, is the best means of securing physical well-being; that the marketplace of morals, culminating in and governed by the judgments of the impartial spectator, is the best means of securing psychological well-being; and that the combination of physical and psychological well-being is what constitutes the tranquillity that Smith thinks defines true human happiness. With regard particularly to our psychological weal, Smith's larger, or, as we might say, meta-argument[48] in TMS thus takes the form of a hypothetical imperative: if you wish to obtain a tranquil and happy psychological state, then you should abide by the system of morality that has arisen naturally and unintentionally in the way described in TMS. You should, that is, recognize the "natural" moral system as authoritative. With regard to the other constituent of humanity's happiness, Smith's position, which is the meta-argument of WN, is this: if you want to have greater and increasing material prosperity, you must seek to satisfy your interests in the open markets that arise when people are allowed, and allow one another, their natural liberty. You should, that is, protect the sanctity of natural marketplaces, along with the transactions that take place in them.[49]

## What Is Fact, What Is Right

Let us at this time turn our attention once again to the passage in which Smith stated that he is concerned with matters of fact, not right (TMS, 77). We can now perhaps make sense of this passage by fitting it into Smith's larger argument. He said in the passage that his task was to ascertain the facts about the nature of human morality and

---

[48] Swabey argues that there is no meta-argument in TMS because Smith "had in mind no clear distinction between meta-ethics and ethics" (1961, 179). If one means by meta-argument a larger project that emerges from the nature of individual discussions, I believe TMS does have a discernible meta-argument.

[49] We have here, then, another aspect of the link between TMS and WN that extends the argument given in Chapter 5 for the consistency of Smith's two books: not only is the understanding of human institutions as the effects of processes adhering to the market model common to both books, but the hypothetical imperative recommending both kinds of markets—that of morals and that of the exchange of goods—is also structurally the same. See also Campbell (1971), 52.

human moral judgments, not to pronounce on whether they are right or wrong. I think this assertion squares with his discussions of the benevolent, intelligent design of the universe in the following way. That the universe was so designed, that it was designed by such a designer, and that it naturally or of its own accord tends to contribute to the happiness and welfare of mankind are, Smith wants to say, all facts.[50] To the extent that his examination in TMS centers around these issues, Smith is thus sincere in saying that he makes no judgment of value about them. The world is what it is. So far, then, his analysis is descriptive, not normative. On the other hand, it is also a fact (of which Smith is keenly aware[51]) that human beings naturally or instinctively seek happiness, which means, according to Smith's argument, that they seek to achieve material and psychological well-being. The implicit argument is then that the content of TMS is not only a factual examination of the natural process of human moral judging, but that it is also simultaneously a blueprint for achieving the happiness for which all of us strive—a blueprint, that is, that therefore *ought to be* heeded. Just two sentences after Smith writes that he is concerned not with right but with fact, he writes that "it seems wisely ordered that it should be" the case that we are constructed the way we are, for the "very existence of society requires" that we act on precisely the motivations we naturally have (TMS, 77, §10). Given that fact, it follows that we therefore ought to learn, internalize, and encourage others to obey the unintentionally evolving system of morality to which we all jointly give rise—and our allegiance to this system would include securing and protecting the rules of justice that enable the marketplaces of exchange to grow and flourish.

Although I spoke earlier of the "machine of the universe," I think Smith would consider this phrase misleading because human beings are not strictly mechanical. To be sure, they have certain natural capacities and proclivities, which under specific circumstances give them powerful pushes toward certain behaviors. To emphasize the strength these natural pushes can attain, Smith frequently resorts to rhetorical embellishments, speaking in terms of necessity and immediacy. And it

---

[50] See TMS, 87.
[51] See, for example, TMS, 51–52.

is true that Smith seems to think that the process of moral judgment at a certain point becomes somewhat mechanical. If, for example, a sympathy is achieved between the sentiments of the spectator and those of the agent, the spectator "necessarily" or "cannot help but" approve of the agent. But this part of passing moral judgments must be distinguished from, on the one hand, those parts of the process of passing moral judgments that involve conscious direction and hence are not strictly determined; and, on the other hand, the proper and improper motives one allows to move one to act.[52] The development of moral sentiments is, as we have seen, an evolutionary process that begins with a person's native desires and combines with the contingencies of his environment—including especially the experiences he has with others and with their judgments of his behavior and of that of others—to produce over time a scheme of general rules comprising a system of morality. Importantly, these general rules are the result of an induction the person performs on the basis of his experiences with his own and with others' attractions, aversions, and judgments of behavior. I think that for Smith the process of induction to develop general rules of moral judgment and the process of deduction from these general rules that renders judgments in particular cases are not wholly mechanical.[53] Deciding which rule or rules to apply, considering opposing judgments or arguments, and reviewing (and re-reviewing) the specific details of the case under question, are all consciously directed processes that are not, for Smith, susceptible to explanations exclusively in terms of mechanical determination.

It is clear, moreover, that Smith maintains a belief in our fundamental freedom of will, despite the almost overwhelming natural urges we may feel at times. It is this belief that leads Smith to spend so much time stressing the importance of self-command—the importance, that is, of disciplining oneself to act in accordance with the virtuous dictates of the impartial spectator. A virtue of self-command is incompatible with a determined will; it presupposes the notion that one can freely

---

[52] For an interesting discussion of Smith's conception of moral judgment that likens it to the "free play of the faculties" in a Kantian aesthetic judgment, see Fleischacker (1999), especially Chapters 3 and 4. See Otteson (December 2000), as well as an extended discussion of Fleischacker's argument in Otteson (forthcoming).

[53] See Macfie (1967), 89–92.

choose to act in one way or in another way, the decision hanging on the direction one wills to take. If Smith thought we had no free will, he could hardly have extolled the virtue of self-command the way he did. On the contrary, his paeans to the specifically Stoic conception of and laud for self-command, and his insistence that self-command is one of the four cardinal virtues (the one, indeed, from which "all the other virtues seem to derive their principal lustre"[54]), strongly imply, I think, his presumption of human freedom.[55] He thinks that God or Nature has equipped us with the necessary basic capacities that can, when joined with the natural resources of the world, enable a flourishing and happy life. But those capacities do not exercise themselves. We must consciously and freely choose to apply ourselves to become virtuous, and though we may not comprehend the origin or ultimate justification of the system of morality that defines virtue, "even the most stupid and unthinking" of us, even "the rudest vulgar of mankind" will have some vague, intuitive understanding that by following and enforcing this morality, they secure the only possible opportunity for a real, general happiness.

## III. The Role of Final Causes in Smith's Argument

### A Response to Critics
The normative aspect of TMS emerges, then, only once Smith's larger argument is understood. We can see Smith as suggesting to his readers how they ought to behave once we assume that their ultimate goal is authentic human happiness and once we understand that the examination in TMS is a factual description of how one can achieve such happiness given the facts about the human condition. Yet the analysis of Smith's theory that I have given points toward an issue that I have not yet addressed but that has received considerable scholarly

---

[54] TMS, 241.

[55] See Brown (1994), Chapter 4, and Griswold (1999), 202–10 and 217–27. I say "presumption" because Smith does not expressly argue for this belief, though the rest of his position entails it. Note in addition that the impartial spectator procedure could not operate as Smith describes it unless people are able to step back from— that is, free themselves from—their situation and view it from a disinterested—that is, detached or independent or free—position.

attention. This issue is the relation between final causes and efficient causes in the development of Smithian morality, and the relative role each plays in Smith's account. As we have seen, Smith makes numerous references to a benevolent intelligence that designed the universe, calling it God, Nature, the Author of nature, and other names. The question, however, is whether those references do any real work in Smith's theory. Does Smith mean for them to indicate an explanation of anything, or are they, as Ronald H. Coase suggests, "rather a means of evading giving an answer to the question [of the explanation of nature's harmony] than a statement of one"?[56] The relation between the issue of final and efficient causes in Smith, on the one hand, and the ultimate normative status of Smith's theory, on the other, is this: if Smith's references to God are merely rhetorical, and the system of morality that develops the way he describes is in fact a result solely of the dual efficient causes of man and environment, then it seems that the moral rules captured by the system of morality, including the judgments of the impartial spectator, would have no ultimate authority beyond the hypothetical imperative that one should obey them if one wants to be happy. They would be right or good only to the extent that they conduce to human happiness, not because they are right or good intrinsically. In that case, the presumptive authority that established moral rules enjoy would be the full extent of their authority; no rule would be sacred or beyond scrutiny because changing circumstances might well necessitate changing rules or standards.

A number of scholars have addressed this issue, and a review of the literature reveals a considerable consensus: teleological explanations serve no real purpose in Smith. D. D. Raphael, for example, argues that the "association with biblical ideas and phrases does not mean that Smith has abandoned explanation in terms of human nature, what we nowadays call empirical psychology" (1985, 36). He suggests that Smith's references to God and Nature are rhetoric, which can be explained by the fact that "both for Smith himself and for most of his readers an account of natural process was more persuasive, as well as more vivid, if nature were personified or treated as the work of a personal God" (ibid.). Raphael sees TMS as an empirical examination of the process of human moral judging, which Smith discovers to hinge

---

[56] Coase (1976), 538–39.

on the supposed judgments of an imagined impartial spectator. Smith then goes on to give a quasi-historical account of how people come to adopt such a standard of moral judgment, and, as befits an empirical investigation, the account Smith gives is marked by contingent, factual elements. "Smith's account of natural processes," Raphael concludes, "can be read as a would-be scientific enterprise, with no need for an underpinning from theology. In his ethics, as in his economics, scientific explanation was what he was after" (ibid.). Raphael's conclusion seems especially plausible when one considers that Smith was writing at the height of British empiricism's influence, which was developing a strong presupposition against explanations that relied on factors that were not observable. A teleological explanation of moral judgment was heartily eschewed by David Hume, for example, and Smith might have been one with his good friend on this issue.

Knud Haakonssen is also suspicious of Smith's putative teleological explanations of moral standards. Haakonssen agrees with me that Smith's moral theory cannot be rightly understood as exclusively descriptive. He argues that the perspective of the impartial spectator, which Smith contends sets the standard for moral judgment, constitutes a practical principle of moral selection: if the impartial spectator approves of a proposed course of action, it is not immoral; if he disapproves of it, it is immoral (1981, 135–36). Haakonssen goes on to put this claim to a different use from that to which I have put it, however: he argues that it forms the basis for a Smithian theory of critical jurisprudence, a theory that is evident in Smith's *Lectures on Jurisprudence* (ibid., 135–53). It is for this reason, I think, that Haakonssen does not connect his argument about TMS's normative aspect with his own earlier discussion of the role teleological explanations play in Smith's theory. In the earlier discussion, Haakonssen writes:

Nothing hinges on teleological explanations and thus on a guarantor of a teleological order. I think it is safe to say that wherever a piece of teleology turns up in Smith it is fairly clear where we have to look in order to find a 'real' explanation in terms of what we may broadly call efficient causes. (Ibid., 77)

Haakonssen's argument is that Smith's evolutionary view of the development of moral standards is exhaustively explained as the result of actions undertaken by individuals seeking to satisfy their various interests, paramount among which is their desire for mutual sympathy.

The general rules that arise and function both as the objective rules of morality and as the principles that inform the judgment of the impartial spectator are thus the unintended effects of those same individuals. The principles of action that these individuals come to adopt can be seen after the fact as constituting a kind of order that the philosopher recognizes to be the community's system of morality. Haakonssen concludes that there is no aspect of this system of morality left over that needs a supernatural explanation. On Smith's account, natural efficient causes—namely, "men [who] act for their own individual purposes, guided by the ordinary principles of human nature"—explain everything that needs to be explained (ibid., 78). By Ockham's razor, then, we can conclude that final causes in Smith are otiose.

A. L. Macfie argues that Smith's reliance on induction for the generation of the rules of morality makes the teleological component of Smith's presentation in TMS unnecessary. Macfie claims that "the central and fruitful proposition of the *Moral Sentiments* is not the natural theism, but the inductive argument based on the sympathetic feelings of the impartial spectator, with its historical setting of societies developing through the growth of social institutions, education, custom, moral rules and the institutions of justice" (1967, 107). Macfie calls our attention to the famous "invisible hand" passages in TMS and WN. In both places, Macfie argues, the references to an invisible hand leading the activities of individuals so as to ensure that they undertake actions that ultimately conduce to overall welfare do not, contrary to appearances, indicate a belief on Smith's part in actual guidance from a benevolent intelligence. The invisible hand, Macfie suggests, is a metaphor or conceptual construct that a person reflecting on the connection between individual utility and general utility may find useful (ibid., 111–13). Neither in TMS nor in WN, however, does Smith mean to replace the natural efficient (though unintentional) causes of "social harmony" with a supernatural or teleological causation. Macfie argues that the real work in Smith's theory of moral sentiments is found in the induction that individuals perform on the basis of their particular instances of sympathy and antipathy; this induction is what immediately gives rise to the habits of behavior that in time become the generally accepted rules of morality. The connection between the individual's utility and the community's overall utility lies in the fact that in communities efficient usage of resources provides savings in labor and increases in production that everyone enjoys. Moreover, because of the common human nature that members of communities share, the general rules of behavior that allow particular individuals to get along well with others will be the same for everyone—indeed, this is what allows common reference to an impartial spectator as the standard of moral conduct to develop in the first place. Again, then, we find that a reliance on teleological or final causation is simply unnecessary because there is nothing for it to explain. "In its inductive and descriptive arguments," Macfie writes, "the *Theory of Moral Sentiments* did give us a practical principle of moral discrimination, historically and socially as well as individually developed, and backed by the growing traditions of social experience"; but it "is in this system of inductive theory, not in the invisible hand, that [Smith's] most valuable and original contribution was made" (ibid., 125).

T. D. Campbell, finally, also believes that Smith's talk of teleology and of benevolent design are not as central to Smith's theory as one might initially think. Campbell hesitates to ascribe complete irrelevancy to teleology, but he does insist on making a sharp distinction between efficient and final causation in Smith and on placing primary importance on the former. He agrees with Macfie that the "invisible hand" passages do not mean that Smith thinks that God actively intervenes in human affairs to direct the lives and actions of particular human beings. "The 'invisible hand' is no capricious intervener in the natural course of events, but is a figure of speech used to suggest that the total operations of nature betoken the ultimate planning of a benevolent God. It involves no suggestion of a *deus ex machina* brought in to establish the principle of the harmony of interests" (1971, 61; Campbell's italics). Although he thinks Smith means for these passages to suggest an overall design for the universe, Campbell nevertheless believes that

> explanations in terms of the will of God have no place in determining the efficient causes of behavior, but enter at a later stage once the scientific investigation is completed. In fact, it is possible to remove the theological terminology and Smith's reflections about a benevolent Deity and not affect the empirical content of his work. (Ibid.)

He thinks that "the theological idea of God's purpose" is "one of the central organizing principles of Smith's social theory," but he argues that these explanations Smith gives are correctly understood as only "supplementary" to the causal explanations and are not meant to substitute for them (1971, 70–73). Campbell thus tries to strike an intermediate position between arguing that final causes are irrelevant and arguing that they are central to Smith's theory.

I believe Campbell is not entirely successful, however, in working out the details of his position. It seems plausible to argue that either God's benevolent design is responsible for the coincidence of individual and general welfare, or it is not. To argue that it is not *directly* responsible for this coincidence, but that it nevertheless contributes to it in some way, requires an explanation that Campbell does not give. It is difficult to see how it could be the case that God's purpose is "one of the central organizing principles of Smith's social theory" and, at the same time, that nevertheless "it is possible to remove the theological terminology and Smith's reflections about a benevolent Deity and not affect the empirical content of his work." Perhaps Campbell means to posit a radical distinction between explanations dealing with the empirical world and explanations dealing with—how shall we call it?—the immaterial world, efficient causes pertaining to the former and final causes pertaining to the latter. In that case, however, we would require an explanation for how the final causes relate to the efficient causes in such a way as to allow the former to be partly but not entirely responsible for the effects of the latter. I do not think it is impossible to explain how this would work out (as I shall argue shortly), but this is just the explanation that Campbell does not give. In any case, however Campbell might frame such an explanation, and whatever he actually intended,[57] we can, I think, profitably view his interpretation of Smith as arguing that whatever intelligent, benevolent design the universe might have, the process of developing human moral standards is an empirical one and is therefore explained by Smith in terms of efficient, not final, causes.[58]

---

[57] Campbell's entire argument can be found at ibid., 69–78.

[58] Charles Griswold also addresses this issue, but his analysis does not quite fall on either side: he argues that Smith's theology and teleology are indeed important parts of Smith's project, but principally because of the aesthetic role they play in our desire for harmoniously complete understandings of the universe and our place in it. See Griswold (1999), 273–80 and 311–35.

Without attempting to address each of these arguments independently, I think we can address them all at once by arguing that final causes are, in fact, a central part of Smith's argument. If that can be shown, it would follow that anyone who argued otherwise—for whatever reasons—would be in error. And just this is what I wish to argue. I have already argued that on Smith's account a broad range of capacities, proclivities, desires, and aversions that are innate in human nature, in conjunction with the particular environmental circumstances of various communities, combine, as individuals seek to achieve happiness, to create a moral system complete with standards of judgment and protocols of behavior. The innate features of human nature and the actual circumstances in which communities of people live are both necessary to the development of the moral system. Without, for example, the desire for the pleasure of mutual sympathy, or without frequent, close contact with others, morality would not develop. Without the former, Smith thinks there would be no way to answer the challenge posed by Plato's story of the ring of Gyges; with it, however, the answer is clear.

The man who has broke through all those measures of conduct, which can alone render him agreeable to mankind, though he should have the most perfect assurance that what he had done was for ever to be concealed from every human eye, it is all to no purpose. When he looks back upon it, he finds that he can enter into none of the motives which influenced it. He is abashed and confounded at the thoughts of it, and necessarily feels a very high degree of shame which he would be exposed to, if his actions should ever come to be generally known. (TMS, 118)[59]

On the other hand, without interaction with others, notions of propriety and impropriety would never occur to one. One would never begin the process of evaluating one's own or others' conduct because one would not have occasion to do so.

Were it possible that a human creature could grow up to manhood in the same solitary place, without any communication with his own species, he could no more think of his own character, of the propriety or demerit of his own sentiments and conduct, of the beauty or deformity of his own mind, than of

[59] See also TMS, 84, §3.

the beauty or deformity of his own face. All these are objects which he cannot easily see, which naturally he does not look at, and with regard to which he is provided with no mirror which can present them to his view. Bring him into society, and he is immediately provided with the mirror which he wanted before. (TMS, 110)

My argument has been that what for Smith constitutes the system of morality is an unintended result of individuals acting to satisfy their interests. I wish now to underscore the crucial importance on Smith's account of the innate features of human nature that figure in to the interests people seek to satisfy. The desire for mutual sympathy, the desire to please and not to offend others, the partiality each of us feels for himself, are among the built-in qualities of human nature, and they are all necessary elements in the formation of the system of morality.

The question is *why* we have these traits built into us. Smith's answer to this, as we have seen, is that it is part of God's or Nature's grand, benevolent design. These traits tend over time to lead to the development of a system of social cooperation that conduces ultimately both to the utility of individuals and to the utility of society at large: it makes individuals happy, and it increases the wealth and prosperity of society. The system of social cooperation effects the former by providing an unintentional but suitable framework within which we can achieve the tranquillity we seek; the general rules of morality, the four cardinal virtues those rules encapsulate, the internalized standard of the impartial spectator's judgment, and the other elements of the system of morality combine, on Smith's argument, to enable the tranquil psychological state that he believes constitutes true human happiness. This same system of social cooperation also encourages and maintains the practices and behaviors that are necessary for increasing society's material prosperity. It encourages in particular the development and strict observance of rules of justice, which center on protections of people's lives, of private property, and of the sanctity of voluntary exchanges and contractual agreements. Because observation and enforcement of these rules of justice are indispensable for both psychological and material well-being, Smith argued that nature implanted an original abhorrence in all of us to breaches of justice. I think Smith's argument is that there is no plausible alternative explanation for the existence of this or the other inherent features of human nature than to ascribe them to intelligent, benevolent design. If they were accidents of nature, Smith thinks we would find an arbitrary and chaotic array of features in human nature—but that is not what we find. We find instead universal features of human nature that we all have in common; indeed, we find a human nature that is uniquely suited to enabling the happiness and prosperity of mankind. How could that be an accident? How could that *not* be the work of intelligent, benevolent design?

I think this shows that for Smith appeals to final causes or teleology are not superfluous window dressing of his argument. They are rather the final—in the sense of ultimate—explanation for human moral sentiments. Now one might reply that Smith's theory would be complete if one just started with the facts of human nature, without worrying about explaining those facts. One might argue that although the explanation of these facts must necessarily include reference to Smith's teleology, this is a separate issue; Smith's teleology is not required for understanding how the marketplace of life works. But I think that such a view does not take into account the full character of Smith's theory. If my interpretation of Smith is correct, then the issues of explaining human nature and explaining the nature of the marketplace of morals cannot be answered independently from one another—at least not without creating a truncated view of Smith. To stop the analysis when one has understood human nature and the nature of human institutions and associations, even if one has understood them correctly, would be, for Smith, to leave perhaps the most important question unanswered: why is human nature the way it is?[60] Stopping the analysis where Raphael, Haakonssen, and Macfie do would be like explaining a game of chess solely by reference to the moves each player made, without accounting for the existence of the rules of chess that existed before this particular game and in accordance with which this game is played. The rules were created by intelligent design before any game was played; similarly, for Smith, God was the intelligence that designed the rules of the game that leads to the development of moral standards.[61]

---

[60] See Ross (1995), 340; see also Kleer (1995), 295–300.
[61] This analogy can be taken a step farther. Just as it is impossible to predict exactly what the outcome of any future chess game will be (what moves were made, by whom and

The unintended order that constitutes the system of morality and the system of the economic marketplaces, or what one might call generally the system of social cooperation, cannot have developed except as it was driven by interests—this was part of Smith's argument. It is "unintended" because its creation is not part of anyone's plan, not because it appeared out of thin air. If there were no interests guiding it, or if all the interests were subjective and unique to the individuals who had them, no general rules of behavior could develop. The only rules that could develop would be the result of individuals' unique habits of behavior, which would on that account be incompatible with the rules others had developed and would hence be inimical to the stability of a community. One wonders, indeed, whether any community could arise in such circumstances, whether instead mankind would be forever consigned to a Hobbesian state of nature where all are at war with all. But mankind have been able to form communities that have centered around shared conceptions of morality, around shared conceptions of proper and improper behavior. We have been able to do this, Smith argues, because we were originally endowed with a specific collection of precisely those attributes that were necessary for our survival and flourishing.[62] It should be noted, moreover, that these attributes are not the result of our own doing: we did not choose to have them or not to have them; we just do. I think Smith believes that we are hence compelled to conclude that an intelligent, benevolent designer is responsible both for the nature of the universe and for human nature, and that our happiness is the end toward which the design ultimately tends.

when, etc.), so it is impossible to predict in advance exactly what moral judgments will be made, by whom, and so forth; nevertheless in both cases the "play" proceeds in accordance with pre-established rules or mechanisms and can, after the fact, be traced out step by step. Now we today (i.e., after Darwin) might be able to explain even the elements of the world that display design by recourse only to unintelligent processes. But no such explanation was available to Smith. I return to this momentarily.

[62] I intend my account of Smith to fill the gap that I suggested Campbell's account left open. That is, on my interpretation of Smith one can see how it is possible that God could be partly responsible for the development of a system of social cooperation that is conducive to human happiness (namely, by endowing us with the requisite innate characteristics), yet God would not be wholly responsible for this system (our free choice is essentially involved). I suggest, then, that my account of Smith occupies the intermediate position that Campbell sought to occupy.

*Utility and the Development of Moral Standards—Again*

We do not yet have a complete understanding, however, of the nature of the moral system that developed in the way Smith describes. I said earlier that it contains the collected wisdom of the generations of people whose individual actions, decisions, and judgments have influenced and contributed to it over time. But their wisdom about what? What knowledge of theirs is it that becomes embodied in the rules and standards of morality? As we have seen, Smith thinks that the immediate criterion of selection for the general rules of morality is each individual's experience with his own sentiments. That is, as each person gains more and more experience with his own patterns of sentiments as they unfold in particular instances of sympathy or antipathy, he comes to form general rules that represent these patterns. The general rules reflect, then, his own sensibilities. On Smith's account, however, this is not the end of the story. For Smithian sympathy and antipathy are the presence and absence, respectively, of concord between the sentiments of a spectator and a person principally concerned. Hence the relative tendency for certain kinds of sentiments in certain kinds of situations to produce mutual sympathy will be a material factor in the generation of rules of morality. The selection of general rules will then ultimately reflect not only the most efficient ways for an individual to satisfy his own narrowly conceived interests, but also the best way to achieve his interests as they essentially involve others. The real criterion of selection for the Smithian system of morality, then, must be a principle that embodies this larger conception of communal interest; it must be a principle that reflects mankind's collected wisdom about what conduces to the greater harmony, stability, and happiness of all society.[63] I think there is only one principle or criterion of selection that fits this bill: the rules of morality must ultimately be reflections of utility.

We can now complete the discussion begun in Chapter 1 of the differences between Smith and Hume on the role utility plays in the passing of moral judgments. I broached the possibility there that Hume

[63] Thus Smith praises the legislator who understands that the established traditions of morality contain this collected wisdom and therefore ought to enjoy a presumption of authority. Readers familiar with the thought of Edmund Burke will understand why I have suggested that Smith might have had Burke in mind. See TMS, 227–34, especially 233, §16.

might seem to have analyzed the matter further than did Smith. Recall that the central criticism Smith raises against Hume relates to Hume's having thought that utility ultimately underlies all moral judgments. Smith thinks this is just false. Considerations of utility, Smith argues, sometimes add a special beauty to a moral act, but one perceives this sense of beauty only after the moral judgment has been made.[64] While a person is passing a moral judgment, however, he simply does not think of—often he would not know even if he thought of it— what the action's ultimate effect on anyone's utility might be. Instead, Smith thinks that what immediately prompts a favorable or unfavorable moral judgment is the spectator's awareness of a sympathy or lack of sympathy between his own sentiments and those of the person principally concerned. I suggested in Chapter 1 that Hume might accept Smith's claim that it is sympathy, not utility, that immediately prompts the moral judgment, but that Hume might respond in turn that Smith's own analysis leaves us without an explanation for the moral sentiments themselves. Why, Hume might ask, do certain agreeable sentiments well up in us in certain situations, others in other situations? I suggested that Hume's argument might be that it is nevertheless utility that, perhaps quite unbeknownst to us, accounts for our sentiments. He could argue that our sentiments are themselves reflections of utility, that our agreeable sentiments arise from viewing beneficial actions or characters, and that our disagreeable sentiments arise from viewing harmful actions or characters.[65] Thus Hume could conclude that the general rules of morality, which may well form in the way Smith describes, nevertheless manifest considerations of utility, whether or not we are aware of it at the time we are passing a moral judgment.

When assessing this possibility, we must be careful to remember that Smith and Hume wrote long before Darwin (TMS first came out exactly 100 years before Darwin's *Origin of Species*); neither of them, accordingly, had a notion of natural selection for certain biological traits. So the idea that nature could have selected for human beings with certain kinds of traits—in particular, for those with traits that led

[64] See Griswold (1999), 336–44.
[65] See ZE, 39–42.

them to behave in ways that served their own or others' utility—was not available to them. Both Smith and Hume believed that the central features of human nature were universal and fixed. For this reason, even if Hume argues that utility ultimately grounds the general rules of morality, his argument would still be incomplete because he offers no account of how a process of selection along utilitarian lines could have taken place. His argument leaves the connection between moral sentiments and utility inexplicable, as if it were a constant conjunction for which Hume feared to posit a necessary connection. Smith, on the other hand, provides just such an account. As I have argued, Smith's theory of the development of moral standards allows for—indeed, it requires—a principle of selection. By maintaining that the general rules of morality that develop unintentionally are precisely those rules that conduce to the long-term welfare of individuals and of society generally, Smith's theory creates a framework in which utility is both apt and necessary. For the Smithian market model, then, the ultimate criterion of selection that guides the development of moral standards would still be utility; we might say that utility is Smith's meta-principle for the development and justification of moral standards. Smithian utility, however, is a utility of general practices, of general rules, not of individual actions or transactions. Smith can thus still hold that individual moral judgments do not directly appeal to utility, which, he believes, makes his theory square with the observable facts. Nevertheless, the general rules from which individual judgments are deduced are ultimately the result of a spontaneous, unintentional, and unknowing selection along utilitarian lines. And this justifies, I think, Smith's belief that his own theory of morality is superior to Hume's because Smith provides an account for a utilitarian *selection* of moral rules—telling, in other words, just the story Hume needed to tell but did not.

I have claimed that the general rules of morality that form in the way Smith describes comprehend and reflect a wisdom that is greater than what any individual person could obtain. We can better understand the role utility plays in Smith's system if we consider it in light of the wisdom these moral rules contain. I think that, for Smith, to say that these rules contain wisdom is to make not a normative but rather a descriptive claim. Given the nature of these rules and the way in which they form, it is simply a fact that they will manifest a certain kind of wisdom. What kind? Their wisdom will concern the best ways so far discovered for us to achieve true human happiness. They will, that is, embody the experience of generations of people as those people individually strove to achieve this state; the habits of behavior that have proven most efficient are those that have gradually become codified as general rules of morality. I suggest that in Smith's system utility refers to the relative state of Smithian happiness people enjoy, and the relative wisdom that any general rule of behavior manifests just is its utility. Thus utility operates as a de facto principle or criterion of selection for moral rules in the sense that no course of behavior will be repeatedly acted upon—and hence will not form a habit, and then rule, of behavior—unless it enhances one's attainment of this state of happiness. A community's settled standards of morality are then properly considered wise because they tend to represent the fruitful or successful outcomes of earlier attempts to achieve happiness. These standards are, then, the unintentional result of an evolutionary process whose end is to increase utility in an effort to achieve happiness. By arguing that utility does not form a conscious part of anyone's individual moral judgments, but that the general rules that inform these judgments were nevertheless selected for on the basis of their utility, Smith at once captures two important empirical facts: one, that explicit considerations of utility do not seem present when passing everyday moral judgments; and two, that long-standing moral traditions do seem frequently to constitute a reliable guide for leading a happy, flourishing life.[66]

## IV. The Objectivity of Smithian Moral Standards

One final observation. I think we are now in a position to address the question of whether the moral standards that develop in the way Smith describes are in any sense objective. Specifically, does Smith's theory of unintended order imply a historical or temporal relativity for the system of morality? Or can Smith legitimately claim that these moral standards are transcendent or right in themselves? A question

---

[66] Such moral traditions do not always lead to happy, flourishing lives, however. I shall return to this in the Conclusion.

consequent on these is, Why should an individual feel duty-bound to follow the established rules of morality in a case in which they do not conduce to his own benefit?

There is no question that Smith thinks that environmental circumstances, including time and place, play a material role in the development of moral standards. All of part five of TMS (TMS, 194–211), for example, is dedicated to exploring the "influence of custom and fashion upon the sentiments of moral approbation and disapprobation." Put otherwise, it amounts to an examination of the extent to which environmental circumstances peculiar to one or another community affect the moral standards it develops. And we have already seen that a development of Smithian moral standards takes place only on the basis of individuals interacting with other individuals as they are all striving to satisfy their interests. Because the objects of people's interests will be determined in large part by the circumstances in which they live, we can expect that the protocols and rules they develop to regulate their interaction will reflect those circumstances at least to some extent. Moreover, Smith acknowledges in various places in TMS that different people have different dispositions, which may incline them to judge certain things differently from others. For example, Smith devotes a chapter to discussing the difficulty with which others may be expected to enter into sympathy with passions that "take their origin from a particular turn or habit of the imagination" (TMS, 31–34). The ability to achieve sympathy, as we have seen, depends on the spectator's familiarity with the situation of the person principally concerned. Where, then, the spectator has no knowledge whatever of an agent's situation, no sympathy can be achieved. Thus Smith writes that a "philosopher is company to a philosopher only; the member of a club, to his own little knot of companions" (TMS, 34). Similarly, some people are more prone to joviality than others; they will hence tend to sympathize more readily with another's jesting.[67] These dispositions and proclivities can no doubt be inflamed or diminished by the character of the company one keeps, and Smith was not unwilling to make broad assertions about the general character of a race or nationality of people.[68]

---

[67] See TMS, 14, 16, and 17.
[68] See, for example, TMS, 196–97 and 204.

Yet none of this, Smith thinks, detracts from the fact that the central rules of morality enjoy widespread agreement across cultures and times. I have already examined Smith's position on this point, so I do not need to rehearse the argument here. Suffice it to repeat that they are based on his contentions that all of us share a common human nature and that a central part of this common human nature is the group of desires and aversions that prompt human beings to make moral judgments. In "Of the Influence of Custom and Fashion upon Moral Sentiments" (TMS, 200–11), Smith argues that "the sentiments of moral approbation and disapprobation, are founded on the strongest and most vigorous passions of human nature; and though they may be somewhat warpt, cannot be entirely perverted" (TMS, 200). Smith's exposition in this chapter is largely empirical: he thinks that observation reveals that the core rules of morality are universally recognized; the differences one finds from culture to culture concern only the less important niceties of etiquette and manners. Praise of the four cardinal virtues and condemnation of their corresponding vices are, Smith thinks, universal. Hence to the argument that the differences one finds in the deportment and judgments of members of different cultures implies that no single moral standard or system of standards is transcendent, Smith's answer is that these differences have been exaggerated. The core of morality remains intact; there is thus no implication against transcendence.[69]

Besides this somewhat limited argument, which is more a defense of the *possibility* of transcendence, I submit that Smith has two positive arguments that aim to show that the moral system that develops ought to be obeyed by all people. First, it conduces to both individual and general utility. As we have seen, Smith's argument is that the general rules that develop this way tend in the long run to increase individual happiness and the society's overall material prosperity—which are good reasons for everyone to recognize and enforce the authority of the established system of morality, even if in particular situations he sees no reason why. There may well be some occasions on which obeying these

---

[69] Though he could have, Smith did not argue that the fact that people in practice make different judgments does not in any case by itself entail that there is not a transcendently correct judgment or system of judgments.

rules might seem to reduce someone's utility rather than increase it; for example, it might strike one as somehow unfair that a poor man should be punished for stealing a small amount from a wealthy man.[70] Nevertheless, Smith argues, the general rule that all people must be secure in their property is too important for the overall stability and well-being of every person in society to allow any breaches, even in a case that if viewed in isolation might seem to warrant it.[71] Smith's argument does not apply only to the case of justice; he thinks that all the virtues are necessary to the amelioration of individual and, hence, collective weal.

Smith has another argument, however, to show that the unintentionally developed system of morality is transcendent and therefore ought to be obeyed by all of us, an argument that goes beyond the contingent, historical fact that most of us already recognize its authority. This argument is that this system of morality is founded on the unalterable characteristics of human nature that God purposefully implanted in us. The core virtues of morality are not only common to all ages and cultures, but Smith wants to argue that it is no accident that they are such: God planned it that way. The general rules of morality may, therefore, be correctly viewed ultimately as expressions of God's will. The fact that God has designed the world and mankind in the way he has thus anchors the objectivity or transcendent authority of moral standards for Smith. Why else would God have constructed human beings and the universe this way, if it were not that he intended for them to be happy? If it is God's intention that we be happy; if the means he has provided us for the attainment of this state is the complex of natural sentiments he has given to us; and if these natural sentiments, when allowed natural expression in natural associations with others, lead to the development of a system of morality that in the long run conduces to everyone's utility; then the implication would seem to be that all of us ought to obey and enforce this natural system of morality. When Smith writes that the impartial spectator—to which our natural sentiments give rise and which becomes in time the personal conscience of each individual—is God's "vicegerent upon earth," meant

---

[70] See TMS, 138.
[71] See TMS, 86–91.

"to superintend the behaviour of [our] brethren," or when he writes that "this demigod within the breast" is "partly of immortal, yet partly too of mortal extraction" (TMS, 130–31), I think we can now see what he means. The impartial spectator represents the fruition of the system of morality that God wanted us to develop; the impartial spectator is thus the manifestation of God's will in us, the partial manifestation, even, of God himself in us.[72] I think this rescues Smith's theory from the objection that it is essentially relativistic, and it allows him to argue that the natural moral system is intrinsically good and right, not just useful.

I have spoken in this chapter of Smith's larger or meta-argument, and I said that it constituted a hypothetical imperative: if you want to be happy, here is what you should do. The bulk of TMS is taken up with examining the natural historical development of human morality and its conduciveness to human happiness, but we can now see that this examination is conducted within the framework of an understanding that "natural" in this case ultimately traces back to the will of God. Smith thinks that the authority or applicability of the unintended system of morality, which emerges as the result of the efficient causes of individuals seeking to satisfy their interests within the context of their particular environments, is not limited to time or place. It is instead universal and transcendent, receiving its ultimate sanction from God himself. It may be, then, that the normativity of Smith's theory has a second level, beyond the hypothetical imperative—namely, the categorical imperative to obey God's will. This feature of Smith's theory would distinguish it from that of Hume, among other of Smith's contemporaries. Hume's argument that the rules of justice are a system of unintended order does not include or entail—or perhaps even allow— a grand design by God, and his theory that moral virtue reflects utility relies solely on utility as its ultimate sanction. Even though Hume, like Smith, might be called a rule-utilitarian, for Hume the only reason moral rules ought to be obeyed, the only reason they are moral, is that they conduce to overall utility. Hume's argument hence cannot go beyond a hypothetical imperative that simply presumes that

---

[72] This explains my suggestion in Chapter 1 that when Smith writes that the demigod within the breast is partly of immortal and partly of mortal extraction, he might be indicating his interpretation of Genesis 1:27, "So God created man in his own image."

everyone on some level seeks general utility. But Smith's argument emerges as both incorporating the hypothetical imperative and moving beyond it. It is true, his argument maintains, that one can be happy in the long run only if one learns and obeys the community's established system of morality, but that fact is, as it were, the icing on the cake. As the will of God, this system of morality ought to be obeyed quite independently of this consideration.

# 7

## The Unintended Order of Human Social Life

### *Language, Marketplaces, and Morality*

In the last few decades interest in Adam Smith's noneconomic writings has burgeoned.[1] One area of Smith's work that has particularly enjoyed this increased interest is that concerned with language, rhetoric, and belles lettres,[2] though his early essay on the development of languages has seen relatively little attention. This essay deserves attention, however, because upon examination it reveals hints of the same model for understanding the growth and development of human institutions that I have argued Smith employs as the conceptual foundation of his later *The Theory of Moral Sentiments* and in *The Wealth of Nations*. Indeed, it may be the case that Smith thought his market model was the key to understanding the development and maintenance of *all* large-scale human institutions. In the absence of explicit textual evidence of such an intention, however, I will limit my claim to this: the market model is at work in the essay on language, in TMS, and in WN, as well as, to varying extents, in some of Smith's other works, and the model can moreover serve as an organizing principle for understanding his examinations of human institutions generally.

---

[1] For an extensive review of recent work on Smith in these areas, see Brown (1997); see also Copley and Sutherland (1995). The *Cambridge Companion to Adam Smith*, edited by Knud Haakonssen, is slated to appear in 2003, and will contain several essays on Smith's noneconomic work.

[2] The publication of Smith's *Lectures on Rhetoric and Belles Lettres* has perhaps contributed to this increased interest. For a recent general treatment of Smith's work in this area, see Terry (1997).

In this chapter, I would like to examine Smith's short essay on languages, as well as resume the discussion of his argument in WN, and show how Smith's market model is at work in each of them. I shall also take a somewhat briefer look at some indications of this model elsewhere in Smith. I shall argue that the model I have argued is at work in TMS is in its essentials the same as those present in these other places, providing a deep methodological unity for these central elements of Smith's corpus. My conclusion will be that Smith thinks that an enormous part—perhaps even the whole—of human social institutions is created, maintained, and developed according to the marketplace model that he sets out in TMS.

## I. The Market in the Essay on Language

### Background

In 1761 there appeared in *The Philological Miscellany*, a quarterly journal published in Edinburgh, an essay by Adam Smith entitled "Considerations Concerning the First Formation of Languages, and the Different Genius of Original and Compounded Languages."[3] Although the date of this essay's publication is two years after the first publication of TMS in 1759, there are several reasons to think it was in the works before Smith began preparations of what was to become TMS. First, John Millar, who had been a student of Smith's and who went on to become a celebrated professor of law at the University of Glasgow, reported in his notes from Smith's lectures that the first series of lectures Smith delivered at Glasgow in the early 1750s were concerned with "an examination of the several ways of communicating our thoughts by speech."[4] These lectures probably contained some of the thoughts later to appear in "Languages." Second, the story of the savages with which Smith begins "Languages" is also given in the students' notes of his third lecture on rhetoric, which are dated Monday, 22 November 1762 (LRBL, 9–13). Since this was the fifteenth year Smith had delivered these lectures, Smith had likely developed the story well before it appeared in the 1761 article. Another, weaker consideration is that

---

[3] The essay is reprinted in LRBL, 203–26; the essay is hereafter referred to as "Languages."

[4] Cited in Stewart (1966 [1793]), 11.

Smith's first publication was a 1755 essay in the *Edinburgh Review* in which he reviewed Johnson's recently released *Dictionary*, which might indicate that Smith had various topics relating to language on his mind before the first publication of TMS in 1759. Finally, the second edition of TMS, which contained significant revisions, appeared in 1762, the same year that "Languages" came out; if composing TMS required some period of undivided attention on Smith's part, this might suggest that he would have done much of the thinking that went into "Languages" before he composed TMS. Though a decisive case cannot be made, these considerations together make it reasonable to conclude, I think, that the thoughts in "Languages" were in the works before Smith began working on TMS.

The relative chronology of "Languages" and TMS is important because the model revealed by Smith's analysis in "Languages" is also to be found in TMS, and, by the time Smith writes TMS, it has become for him the key to understanding the nature of moral judgment and moral standards, as well as the nature of human association generally. An examination of "Languages" reveals only the rudiments of this model; Smith mentions them periodically, almost in passing, sometimes without elaborating on them or supplying arguments for them. But they are there, and they were to take deep root in Smith: as he matured as a thinker he increasingly drew on these rudiments to construct a model that could explain more and more of human behavior. But before a claim about Smith's later usage of this model can be made, it must first be explicated in his early work. Let us then look at several important passages from "Languages" and see what we can see.

"Languages" is a short essay, only about twenty pages long; it can be divided into roughly three sections.[5] The first section, paragraphs one to thirty-two, may be described as a "conjectural history," in the memorable phrase Dugald Stewart coined to describe some of Smith's writing (Stewart, 1966 [1793], 34).[6] Here Smith speculates on the first formations of words in the earliest human beings. He does not rely on direct evidence, because there is none, but the speculation is not therefore idle. Stewart described Smith's method in the following terms.

---

[5] J. C. Bryce gives a similar breakdown of "Languages" in his "Introduction" to LRBL, 23–27.

[6] The other citations from Stewart in this paragraph are from this place.

It is natural, Stewart thought, that when one looks at the cultivated sophistication of our present-day language and compares it to what prevailed among "rude tribes," one begins to wonder what happened to bring us from there to here. Yet we have no direct evidence.

In the want of this direct evidence, we are under a necessity of supplying the place of fact by conjecture; and when we are unable to ascertain how men have actually conducted themselves upon particular occasions, of considering in what manner they are likely to have proceeded, from the principles of their nature, and the circumstances of their external situation.

Stewart argues that this method of inquiry is not "subservient merely to the gratification of curiosity," however, because it proceeds on the basis of two things: first, those isolated facts that we do possess; second, what we know to be the "natural causes" of the things we see in the world around us, which includes the nature of man and the laws governing the operations of the physical universe. Stewart explains that

although it is impossible to determine with certainty what the steps were by which any particular language was formed, yet if we can shew, from the known principles of human nature, how all its various parts might gradually have arisen, the mind is not only to a certain degree satisfied, but a check is given to that indolent philosophy, which refers to a miracle, whatever appearances, both in the natural and moral worlds, it is unable to explain.

This is a fitting description of the method Smith employs in the first section of "Languages." And precisely because of its conjectural nature, this section yields, on a close look, many of the conceptual assumptions Smith brings to his analysis of linguistic change; it is thus on this section that we shall shortly focus most of our attention.

The second section of "Languages," paragraphs thirty-three to forty, turns to a consideration of actual, as opposed to conjectural, history. Smith discusses the development of inflectional structures as various peoples come into contact with one another. As people needed to learn the languages of their neighbors and fellow merchants, they did so not by systematic instruction but by picking up piecemeal what they heard, creating what a contemporary linguist would call "pidgin." The hardest things to learn by listening to speakers of another language is, Smith says, "the intricacy of its declensions and conjugations" (LRBL, 220); accordingly, these intricacies were among the first things to disappear as older languages, particularly Latin and Greek, evolved. Smith supports his claim with several instances that demonstrate the evolution from more to less complex.

In the third and final section of "Languages," paragraphs forty-one to forty-five, Smith argues that this evolution of language had unfortunate consequences. J. C. Bryce summarizes Smith's position accurately:

> modern analytic languages are, as compared with earlier synthetic ones, more prolix (since a multiplicity of words must replace the old inflections), less agreeable to the ear (lacking the pleasing symmetries and variety of the inflections), and more rigid in their possibilities of word-ordering (differences of case-endings make for flexibility in arrangement without ambiguity).[7]

Smith closes the essay with a consideration that the prolixity, amusicality, and structural rigidity of modern languages makes them unfit for good poetry; the best poetry, Smith thinks, is still written in Latin.

*Basic Elements*

Let us return to the first section of "Languages." Smith begins his conjectural history of the formation of languages with a story asserting that two savages "who had never been taught to speak, but had been bred up remote from the societies of men, would naturally begin to form that language by which they would endeavour to make their mutual wants intelligible to each other" (LRBL, 203).[8] He argues that these hypothetical savages would develop verbs and proper nouns first—the former because they can capture "a complete event" in just one word (LRBL, 215) and the latter because they would refer to those particular objects with which the savages came most into contact; they would only thereafter develop adjectives, adverbs, and prepositions. Although he thinks that verbs and proper nouns were thus "coeval" (ibid.), he discusses nouns first because it is in the case of nouns that one can most easily see his analysis of the process of abstraction that later gives rise to more sophisticated language. In Smith's story, the savages begin by giving names to particular things they find in their

---

[7] Bryce, "Introduction," LRBL, 26.

[8] The story is repeated in the notes from Smith's third lecture on rhetoric, dated "Monday Nov. 22" of 1762, LRBL, 9–13.

immediate surroundings—that is, things with which they become familiar. As they find, however, that the things they have denominated cave, tree, and fountain (Smith's examples) closely resemble objects in the world other than those to which these names were initially given, they "naturally bestow, upon each of these new objects, the same name by which they had been accustomed to express the similar object they were first acquainted with" (ibid.).[9]

According to Smith, this gradual expansion of usage, which comes on the heels of enlarged experience in the world, does not at first presume any metaphysical subtlety on the part of the savages—contrary to what Rousseau had thought. Rousseau had argued that the development of language posed an inescapable dilemma: generalization is possible only if we already possess general words, but it is possible to possess those words only if one already possesses the power to generalize.[10] Smith argues to the contrary that the act of applying what had been proper names to other objects presumes only the ability to detect similarity, an ability that Smith suggests relies on the mind's natural powers of association: "The association of ideas betwixt the caves, trees, etc. and the words they had denoted them by would naturally suggest that those things which were of the same sort might be denoted by the same words" (LRBL, 9). Smith agreed with Hume that one of the mind's foundational natural operations was association of similar impressions,[11] and when Smith speaks of words "naturally suggesting" themselves for new applications, he has this mental process in mind. Extending the usage of "tree" from this particular object to other objects that are similar to it is only an instance of this mental operation. Smith thinks the operation involves no deliberate reflection or mental abstraction, and hence not the conscious metaphysical reflection Rousseau thought it involved and claimed was problematic.[12]

---

9  The view that language developed "naturally" along with mankind itself places Smith in what Christopher J. Berry called the "Organic School" of eighteenth-century linguistic thought. See Berry (1974).

10  Rousseau (1987 [1754]), 44–52. Smith refers to Rousseau's *Discourse* in "Languages" (LRBL, 205), and he quotes from it in his "Letter to the Authors of the *Edinburgh Review*" in April of 1755, which is reprinted in EPS, 242–54.

11  See the first two sections of Smith's "History of Astronomy" (EPS, 33–48). For Hume's treatment, see 1E, 14–15 and passim.

12  It may be that Smith had something like Berkeley's view of general terms in mind, whereby a general term is general only insofar as it is "the sign, not of an abstract

This point is important for understanding Smith's analysis. A crucial element of Smith's approach is the lack of conscious direction it posits for overall linguistic development. Proper nouns get transformed into common nouns on Smith's account by an unconscious process of mental association triggered by the expanding range of experience people had as they evolved from savages to cosmopolitan eighteenth-century Scots. The enlarged corpus of experience brings with it an increasing number of things that require names. Smith adds to this the fact of human nature that our desires expand along with our expanded experience, which gradually led the savages to expand the usage of their proper nouns and create those terms we call general names. This early development of language thus presupposed no conscious direction. The savages did not decide in advance how to make their language more sophisticated; instead, its sophistication arose gradually as their needs required.

Smith does not think, however, that abstraction plays no role whatever in linguistic development. On the contrary, he argues that the development of "nouns adjective" (like "green"), prepositions (like "above"), and abstract nouns (like "greenness") all required a level of what Smith calls "metaphysics" (LRBL, 206–207, 210–11). It is for just this reason that such words were invented only later, however, after other elements of language had been founded "naturally"—that is, nonreflectively. Thus Smith's view of the unintentional nature of language has two parts: in the early stages of development, both the language and its rules, on the one hand, and the words invented and used by individuals, on the other, proceed without conscious direction;

---

general idea, but of several particular ideas, any one of which it indifferently suggests to the mind" ("Introduction" to *The Principles of Human Knowledge* in Berkeley, 1965 [1710], §11, p. 495). For Berkeley, in opposition to what Locke had maintained, there are no "abstract ideas." Though Smith had read other works of Berkeley, however, it is not known whether he read the *Principles*. See Ross (1995), 76–77 and 103–104. On the basis of what can be gleaned from "Languages," it seems as though Smith sides with Berkeley in holding there not to be specific abstract *ideas*, but only general *terms*, which are made general by the way in which they are used. Smith writes, for example: "Afterwards, when the more enlarged experience of these savages had led them to observe, and their necessary occasions obliged them to make mention of other caves, and other trees, and other fountains, they would naturally bestow, upon each of those new objects, the *same name*, by which they had been accustomed to express the similar object they were first acquainted with" (LRBL, 203, my italics). See also LRBL, 205, §2.

in the later stages, individuals begin to consciously invent words by abstraction, though the overall system of language remains no part of their conscious direction or concern.

The unintentional development of language as effected by the expansion of human experience and desires explains, Smith thinks, the eventual appearance of the spectacularly sophisticated languages of Latin and ancient Greek, as well as that of the modern languages. This explanation thus ties in with and fixes the meaning of the wording in the opening of Smith's essay: the two hypothetical savages "would naturally begin to form that language by which they would endeavour to make their mutual wants intelligible to each other" (LRBL, 203). Smith's point is that this natural formation of language happens without conscious deliberation—but that does not mean it happens lawlessly or haphazardly. Indeed, if language developed without rules prescribing proper usage, there could then be no communication, and hence no satisfaction, of wants—which Smith thinks is the final cause of languages. Rules for the use of words are formed even as the words themselves are formed: this word, pronounced precisely in this way, applies to this object; that word, pronounced in that way, to that object. The rules initially constitute informally agreed-upon protocols; in time they become formal rules that get taught to children and sometimes written down as the rules of grammar. The notes from Lecture 3 in LRBL report Smith as having said that the rules form by "mutual consent" (9, §18). Assuming those are the exact words Smith used,[13] they must not be construed to mean that the savages worked out a plan or strategy for the development of language in advance and then all agreed to follow it. To posit this would have been to fall prey to Rousseau's problematic: it would entail presuming a linguistic and conceptual sophistication in order to explain the creation of this same sophistication. The mutual consent would instead be on-the-spot and spontaneous; the newly agreed-to usage would then only gain a wider currency if it proved to be an efficient way to satisfy the savages' wants. The "consent" in that case would come about de facto on the actual employment of the new usage:[14]

---

[13] We must bear in mind that what survives from these lectures is the set of two students' notes. They were carefully compiled, but they are still students' notes.

[14] Smith's usage of "mutual consent" in this case would then be consistent with Hume's discussion of conventions in the *Treatise* (T 488–92).

When there was occasion, therefore, to mention any particular object, it often became necessary to distinguish it from the other objects comprehended under the same general name, either, first, by its peculiar qualities; or, secondly, by the peculiar relation which it stood in to some other things. (LRBL, 205)

The words expressing peculiar qualities are adjectives and adverbs; those expressing relations, prepositions. But note the impersonal way in which Smith puts this: "it often became necessary to. . . ." This phrasing suggests Smith's notion that the linguistic development was not consciously planned in advance. Rather, a desire to communicate some specific new need pressured the savages into creating a peculiarly apt expression. As needs changed, so did language; but changing language as an ordered system was not part of anyone's intention.

### The Invisible Hand of Rule Formation

It is intriguing that all ancient and modern languages have rules. What is particularly intriguing for our discussion is the origin of these rules. Rules might get written down or otherwise codified, revised, and corrected, or taught to new speakers of the language. But whence did they arrive in the first place?[15] Smith thinks that no person or group of persons devised the rules of grammar ex nihilo and handed them down like ukases to the masses; on the contrary, the rules of particular languages are devised and revised on the basis of induction on current and long-standing usage. In other words, the usage comes first; the rules come only later. For example, why is it now considered incorrect by some to pronounce the word "sonorous" with the accent on the second syllable? Why has the preferred pronunciation changed so that the accent is now on the first syllable?[16] It is presumably not because anyone ordered that it be so but rather because some communities of English speakers proved simply to prefer it that way. Examples like these are of course repeated countless times in all languages; they are part and parcel of the living nature of languages. New usages and variations continually change and develop language, "without," as Smith puts it, "any intention or foresight in those who first set the example,

[15] By "rules" here I do not mean the deep Chomskyan-type rules of what is called "universal grammar," rules that (if they exist) underlie all human language. I mean instead rules on the order of "we call things like this 'table'" or "wir nennen das 'Tisch.'"

[16] I take this example from Dear (1986), 247.

and who never meant to establish any general rule" (LRBL, 211). Smith continues: "The general rule would establish itself insensibly, and by slow degrees, in consequence of that love of analogy and similarity of sound, which is the foundation of by far the greater part of the rules of grammar" (ibid.). Let me call specific attention to three features of this passage: first, Smith says that general rules establish themselves "insensibly"; second, this process happens slowly; and third, it is motivated by a desire human beings have.

The description in the preceding citation is reminiscent of the passage in WN in which Smith speaks of the "invisible hand" that ensures that people's self-interested economic pursuits also conduce to the overall welfare of society.[17] There is, of course, no real hand—that is why Smith calls it "invisible." The invisible hand is instead a metaphor standing for no conscious or intentional thing at all: it is a consequence unintended by individuals that their self-interested actions raise the overall standard of living.[18] Although the efficient causes that link individual actions to general welfare can be traced after the fact, the general welfare was no part of the individuals' intention or design; as far as the individuals are concerned, the two are connected by sheer coincidence. A similar point is being made when Smith writes that general rules of grammar establish themselves "insensibly." Smith thinks it is one thing to look for mechanisms in the movement of heavenly bodies, for example, but it is quite another to look for them in human associations and customs; and he thinks it is often difficult for philosophers to accept the possibility that an elaborate, sophisticated institution— like a language—could have developed with no overall rational design because their own preoccupation with rationality leads them to see it at work in any complicated system.[19] But Smith thinks that natural

---

[17] WN, 456. Recall that Smith's first use of the phrase "invisible hand" comes in TMS, 184. The only other mention of the phrase in Smith's extant writings appears in his "History of Astronomy": "Fire burns, and water refreshes; heavy bodies descend, and lighter substances fly upwards, by the necessity of their own nature; nor was the invisible hand of Jupiter ever apprehended to be employed in those matters" (EPS, 49).

[18] Thus Smith's invisible hand is not the same as the "hidden hand" some have argued explains, for example, the progress of science. See Hull (1988) and Way (March 2000).

[19] See Smith's discussion of the "man of system" (TMS, 233–34) and the discussion of this passage in Chapter 6.

human languages are precisely such unplanned systems, and this is his point in saying that the rules of grammar arise "insensibly."[20]

We may not realize that we are creating, revising, or enforcing the rules of our language, but we are, every time we use language. Most of the rules are settled and admit of no variation. There is no question, for example, that English speakers would consider the following construction unacceptable: "She and I *go'd* to the park." Each time, however, that one says, "She and I *went* to the park," one is, knowingly or not, strengthening and enforcing the rule. There are some points of grammar in our language, as in all languages, that are in dispute at the moment: is it correct to write "a historian" or "an historian"? To convey that one is ill, should one say "I don't feel *well*" or "I don't feel *good*"? May one say "to boldly go," or must one say "boldly to go"? Is "dis" an acceptable English word? The interesting question for Smith is not that there are such unresolved questions, but, rather, how they get settled. Are they settled by some few authorities—grammar school teachers?—deciding how things should be and then publicly announcing their decisions? Not usually, the changes in language almost always come about, as Smith says, "insensibly."[21] People spontaneously try out new usages; they might then be corrected, if there is no tolerance for the novelty, or their use might be accepted. If it is accepted, it might catch on, which just means that others, too, will find the new usage to be useful. The new usage may then in time—as Smith says, "by slow degrees"—become the new orthodoxy, and a rule of usage will form that is consistent with actual usage. This happens slowly and insensibly, yet it happens, and without creating a linguistic anarchy.[22]

The other element of this citation from Smith is the fact that the establishment of the rules of grammar results from a desire the speakers have: changes come "in consequence of that love of analogy and

---

[20] For a recent account largely corroborating Smith's claim here, see Pinker (1994), 18–24, 231–61, and passim. I should emphasize that Smith is investigating only natural languages; his analysis thus would not apply to formal or artificial languages that do result from prior rational planning.

[21] The injunction against split infinitives might be a counterexample—that is, it might be a case in which a few authorities are attempting to press a particular usage against commonly held preference.

[22] It is perfectly consistent with Smith's analysis that new words or usages could be accepted by some communities of speakers while being rejected by other communities. So some might think that use of "dis" must be corrected, while others think it is already correct.

similarity of sound." Smith argues in "Languages" that human beings have an innate propensity to take pleasure in the varied associations that words conjure up in them and in series of words that sound alike. He thinks these two facts about us explain many things about language: the former explains, for example, why the new words that are needed to name or describe new experiences are often—perhaps always—the result of combinations of old words or parts of old words; the latter explains why the adjectives and adverbs in inflected languages often end with the same sound as the word they modify—for example, *magnus lupus* or *magnum pratum* (LRBL, 208). A love of similarity of sounds might also explain why alliteration is a common feature of poetry (as well as prose), and why we tend to like rhyming poetry better than nonrhyming poetry.[23] But these two facts of human nature, if they are facts, are not the causes of new usages in language; they would only set the parameters of such changes that were necessary for other reasons. On the contrary, the cause of changes in language is the same as what causes language to come about in the first place, namely, the larger desire to satisfy wants. People have various desires and needs that they want to satisfy. It did not take long to discover that working with others increased one's ability to satisfy one's wants (LRBL, 203, §1), and this discovery, Smith thinks, led to the invention of language, which itself served to increase individuals' ability to satisfy wants. Smith's argument is that the desire to satisfy their interests is what led people to develop the tool of language, and language lives and changes to this day in accordance with its ability to enable people to satisfy their living and changing interests.[24]

## Summary

We see, then, in Smith's early thinking about language several important features. Language is created, changed, and revised by individuals who have no grand scheme in mind. They use it as a means to achieve

---

[23] Karl Brugman makes a similar argument in his classic 1888 paper.

[24] Contemporary linguistics, especially since Chomsky, has tended to move away from quasi-empirical accounts of the origin of language, such as the one Smith gives. On the other hand, Smith's notion that the development of language takes place spontaneously as people seek more efficient ways to satisfy their changing interests is largely within mainstream contemporary linguistic thought. Partly for this reason I am inclined to think that much of the philosophical value of Smith's essay lies more in its account of the *development* of language than of the *origin* of language. I return to this in a moment.

other ends, and they change it as their ends change, without a thought as to what their changes mean for the system of language. As their range of experiences outstrips their limited capacity to know all objects as particulars, the complexity and sophistication of their language grows accordingly.[25] The changes that occur in language take place insensibly, and people's needs change slowly enough to allow general rules of the language to unfold, be formalized, and perhaps get written down. Moreover, the sustaining and changing of the language depends on a continuous, free exchange of words and usage. The history of languages shows that as peoples and nations come into contact with one another and associate in various ways, languages change accordingly to accommodate the new people, ideas, and ways—but not as a result of central, authoritative commands. People using the languages in their everyday associations and interactions change them as the need to do so arises. And all this is brought about by the ever-present, though often in the background, motivation of individuals' various desires and their quest to find means to satisfy those desires. The result is a system of what I have called unintended order: a self-enforcing, orderly institution created unintentionally by the free exchanges of individuals who desire only to satisfy their own individual wants.[26]

## Problems

Smith's model runs into several difficulties on examination. One I will mention but not discuss is the general problem of trying to account for a present state of affairs with a "just-so story"—a story, that is, that postulates a scenario that *might* have given rise to the present state, without providing independent evidence that the postulated scenario is what in fact took place. Even if Smith's story of how the hypothetical savages developed their language is plausible, one can still ask what that proves. There might be any number of conceivable, plausible scenarios: why should we think that Smith's is correct—or, hence, that his story shows anything?

---

[25] See LRBL, 217.

[26] One might think that Smith's belief that modern languages are more prolix, less harmonious, and more rigid than ancient languages is, if anything, an example of unintended *dis*order. But remember that these are faults only, as Smith says, for "versification" (LRBL, 226). On Smith's account, these changes would have come about because of interests people had that outweighed their poetic concerns.

A second difficulty is that it is one thing to talk of the unintended development of the language of savages, but once people and their language reach a certain level of sophistication, it becomes possible for *planned* development of language to take place. Once people attain the ability to talk and think about their language itself, they begin to change it as a result of conscious reflection. An example might be the recent feminist success in greatly reducing the use of the "generic 'he'" in speech and writing. One might argue that this was a change in linguistic usage brought about by a decision an initially relatively small group of English speakers made—in which case the usage succeeded, not preceded, the rule. Smith might respond that, as his model would have predicted, this change in usage gained widespread acceptance only as people came to see it as expressing some interest of their own (perhaps fairness). Novel locutions like "he or she" and "s/he" made little headway until they made this connection to people's personal interests. Nevertheless such changes would not happen unintentionally, and if Smith's argument were that changes in language can take place *only* unintentionally, a case like this would seem a counterexample.

As we saw, however, Smith acknowledges a power of abstraction that shapes later developments in language. But he does not see this power as being directed toward language per se; it is used only to allow further satisfaction of personal interests. Smith's model could, then, comprehend this example insofar as the new locutions satisfied two conditions: one, they took place at a later stage in linguistic development, when the power of abstraction had already appeared; and two, the locutions were introduced because their users wanted to satisfy certain desires and were seeking new ways to do so. In the case of the "generic 'he,'" the first condition is obviously met. With regard to the second, new usages and neologisms, even those planned deliberately, do not by themselves constitute counterexamples to Smith; after all, poets, scientists, and philosophers all create new words and usages. Smith's model provides rather that the novelties come about because they satisfy peculiar, local interests, not because their users are rationally planning language itself. Hence whether the shift away from the "generic 'he'" is a counterexample to Smith will depend on how we understand the motivation behind the change—whether, that is, its users wanted to change language or wanted to better satisfy more immediate wants. If it was the latter, then Smith's model can comprehend it.

If, on the other hand, the call for change arose from a notion about how language ought to function, then it might be a phenomenon Smith's model cannot explain.

A third difficulty stems from Smith's discussion of this process of abstraction he thinks is involved in linguistic change. To avoid Rousseau's dilemma Smith argued that no metaphysical reflection was necessary to develop general or abstract nouns—one needed only the ability to detect similarity. Smith's idea is apparently that one would see one object, then see an object similar but not identical to it, and one would, after naturally recognizing the similarity, categorize the second object with the first and call it by the same name as the first. In this way one would create a general noun from a proper noun. But what characteristics of the objects in question are relevant for one object to be "similar" to another? No two trees are alike, and it is difficult to specify with precision any characteristic they have in common. Would it be color? Shape? Size? Location? None of these would seem to do, so perhaps something more sophisticated is required—perhaps *use* or *function*. But for one to make meaningful use of notions like use or function (however one understands them), it would seem that one would need to be in possession of a fairly high-level capacity to reason or reflect. On Smith's account, that would mean presuming a mental ability at the early stages of linguistic development that can itself only be explained at later stages. And that returns us to Rousseau's dilemma. If Smith's solution is, following Hume, to rely on the mind's "natural" power of association, he may be right but he has not explained anything.[27] For one would then of course ask how the mind is able to do these things. Now we in the twenty-first century may be in a position to explain such a "natural" power of the mind by telling an evolutionary story about natural selection and how an animal that ("naturally") made the right kinds of associations would tend to survive whereas an animal that did not would not. But Smith exploited no such explanation.[28]

On this count, however, perhaps Smith should not be singled out for criticism. The problem of classification is an old one indeed. About a century before Smith, Locke had attempted to describe the process

[27] For more detailed discussion of this problem and Smith's possible answer to it, see Otteson (January 2002).
[28] See Land (1977).

of what he called "abstraction" by arguing that an abstract or general idea is created when we strip away the "circumstances of real Existence" of an individual idea.[29] So, we see this chair, we see that chair, we strip away the things about each of them that make it particular, and we arrive at the abstract idea of chair. But one can object that Locke does not make clear how the mind is able to effect this stripping away and thence creation of generalities. How does it know what to strip away, what to retain? If one answers that the mind simply does it "naturally" (or some equivalent of this), then, it seems, we have only a different way at arriving at Smith's position: the actual mechanism still has yet to be explained. Stephen K. Land writes that it is "an assumption of Smith's theory that objects of the natural world resemble or fail to resemble one another and that this resemblance or nonresemblance is given in perception."[30] This seems right, but a look at Locke (or Hume) shows that this assumption is not peculiar to Smith. Although it remains the case that Smith did not explain how people naturally detect relevant similarities between objects such that it allows them to create general nouns encompassing the appropriate individuals, perhaps, then, the demand to provide such an explanation should perhaps be put to eighteenth-century natural philosophy generally, not to Smith in particular.

*An Implication*

The eighteenth century was replete with theories about how language first developed among human beings; virtually all of such theories— perhaps they are better called "speculations"—have, however, since been discredited.[31] It would similarly be difficult to find much value in Smith's essay if one took it as solely or principally attempting to supply a model for the genesis of language. If, however, one views Smith's essay rather as an attempt to construct a model for the process of linguistic development, the essay gains both philosophical and historical interest. Its philosophical interest would lie in the fact that Smith's model can be seen as an early attempt to explicate elements of

---

[29] Locke, *An Essay Concerning Human Understanding*, Book 2, Chapter 11, §9, page 159.
[30] "Adam Smith's 'Considerations,'" 680.
[31] For a survey of some of these theories and their relations to Smith, see Berry (1974), 131–33 and passim.

this process that still seems plausible today. Indeed, the "unintended order" model of linguistic development that Smith employs is an unelaborated version of the model believed by many contemporary linguists to be at work. One such linguist, Rudi Keller, even put Smith's famous metaphor in the title of his book.[32] This is not to say, of course, that Smith's work has influenced the linguists who maintain versions of this model, but it does suggest that Smith might have been on to something.

The essay's historical interest lies in the fact that it contains the first suggestions of Smith's marketplace model for the development and maintenance of human institutions.

## II. The Market in WN

I think Smith came to see a great deal of power in his model for explaining language development and change, and that he employed it and elaborated on it to a far greater extent in his later works. To substantiate my claim, I would like to show how the interpretation I have given of Smith's conception of the development of language contains the germ of a single, fundamental organizing concept for the central parts of Smith's corpus. Smith's writings on the development of common moral standards in his 1759 TMS—as we saw in Chapters 3 and 5 and as I shall now substantiate—and his writings on the development of economic markets in his 1776 WN reveal that he found both realms of human experience to adhere to the same model he had found earlier in the realm of human language. They are all systems of unintended order: they all develop according to and conform to the model of a *market*.[33]

The notion of economic markets in WN, their nature, and the claim that Smith thought that their relatively unimpeded operation leads to systems of unintended order are more obvious and less controversial than their analogues in TMS and in "Languages." For that reason— and the fact that we have already looked at several parts of Smith's

---

[32] Keller (1994). See also McCawley (1992, 1995).

[33] Knud Haakonssen briefly remarks that there seems to be a connection between morality and language in Smith, but he does not elaborate on the nature of the connection, and he does not extend the connection to Smith's WN. See Haakonssen (1981), 49.

argument in WN—the discussion of WN here will take less space. In any case, an exhaustive case for my claim is beyond our scope here: it is one thing to look closely at Smith's twenty-five-page essay on language; it is something else altogether to examine carefully Smith's 1000-plus-page WN. Let me, then, just elaborate on a few important elements of Smith's analysis in WN that indicate its adherence to the market model.

People find, make, and acquire various things, and if left to their own devices, they will trade some of them with other people for other things. These exchanges are generally mutually advantageous: each party to the transaction trades a possession of his for the possession of someone else, which each person values more than he values what he already has.[34]

But man has almost constant occasion for the help of his brethren, and it is in vain for him to expect it from their benevolence only. He will be more likely to prevail if he can interest their self-love in his favour, and shew them that it is for their own advantage to do for him what he requires of them. Give me that which I want, and you shall have this which you want, is the meaning of every such offer; and it is in this manner that we obtain from one another the far greater part of those good offices which we stand in need of. (WN, 26)

Since we all have interests, desires, and needs, we seek ways to satisfy them through either production or barter. And since most of us cannot satisfy all our own needs, desires, and interests alone, each of us must barter to satisfy at least some of them. As it turns out that we all have particular talents, we tend to seek out our talents and to capitalize on them so as to maximize our advantage in exchanges of goods.

And thus the certainty of being able to exchange all that surplus part of the produce of his own labour, which is over and above his own consumption, for such parts of the produce of other men's labour as he may have occasion for, encourages every man to apply himself to a particular occupation, and to cultivate and bring to perfection whatever talent or genius he may possess for that particular species of business. (WN, 28)

Thus with the freedom to exchange and security in our possessions, we will tend to focus our energies on tasks that we are good at, in the hopes of creating a larger amount of it than we ourselves need. This surplus

---

[34] See WN, 376; see also LJ, 511.

we barter with others for other things that we want or need. Because everyone focuses himself in the same way and for the same reason, the supply of various goods in society gradually rises, which is accompanied by a gradual lowering of prices. The result is that more and more people can afford more and more things. Thus Smith writes:

It is the great multiplication of the productions of all the different arts, in consequence of the division of labour, which occasions, in a well-governed society, that universal opulence which extends itself to the lowest ranks of people. Every workman has a great quantity of his own work to dispose of beyond what he himself has occasion for; and every other workman being exactly in the same situation, he is enabled to exchange a great quantity of his own goods for a great quantity, or, what comes to the same thing, for the price of a great quantity of theirs. He supplies them abundantly with what they have occasion for, and a general plenty diffuses itself through all of the different ranks of society. (WN, 22)

As we saw in Chapter 5, the qualification "in a well-governed society" in the preceding passage is important. Smith shows that under the right conditions human economic systems tend over time to result in marketplaces of ever-widening scope. And he argues that as markets expand, productivity and supply of goods goes up, and hence prices go down. But what are the right conditions that allow the expansion of markets and resulting increase in material prosperity? Smith gives what one might call a natural history of human society, indicating that its four stages of society—communities based on hunting, shepherding, agriculture, and commerce, respectively—are coincident with, and perhaps dependent upon, the gradual development of certain rules of exchange that tend to conduce to greater productivity. These rules generally tend to center around three things: individual liberty to dispose of oneself and one's belongings as one sees fit, protection of one's private property, and the sanctity of voluntary contractual agreements.[35] These rules begin informally, as something like "gentlemen's agreements," but in time they develop into full-fledged codes of behavior that can get written into law, adopted into "common law" judicial codes, or both. In his 1763 *Lectures on Jurisprudence*, Smith writes that government "arose, not as some writers imagine from any consent or agreement of a number of persons to submit themselves to such or

---

[35] See WN, 284–5, 345–46, 405, 412, and 540; see also LJ, 86–102 and 472–75.

such regulations, but from the natural progress which men make in society" (LJ, 207).

Smith's societal history shows that the absence of a controlling authority over people's economic lives does not result in anarchy but rather in the development of relatively orderly systems of exchange—ultimately, that is, in markets. As we have seen, for Smith, a market is an opportunity for people to buy, sell, trade, or otherwise dispose of their belongings with other people however they see fit. Ideally, there are few or no parameters, incentives, or discouragements set by authorities or officials outside the market itself; there are similarly few or no external restrictions on who may conduct business in the market, with whom, where, or under what circumstances.[36] What drives the market and determines what gets produced, at what cost and quantity, and so on is people's private wants and their spontaneous attempts to satisfy those wants by coordinating their efforts with others. This kind of freedom to find ways to satisfy our wants does not, on Smith's view, produce anarchy because in the absence of externally enforced restrictions there nevertheless arise practices, customs, and protocols as results of the ways individual people come to behave in their individual associations with one another.[37] Like the general rules of morality, the laws that get passed to regulate markets, including those defining and restricting private property and contracts, come on the heels of practices already established. We do not a priori define private property and then apply it to our community in the form of laws; rather, the reverse is true. The laws reflect what has already become the commonly accepted understanding, the prepollent (although not, of course, unanimous) consensus. This is the genesis of the unintended order, and it is the historical explanation of those rules and laws that have developed in communities over the centuries.[38]

I should emphasize that for Smith this slow development over time is not uniformly good development. As we saw in Chapter 5, according to Smith, the beneficial progress is often slowed and even temporarily reversed by vested interests, entrenched bureaucracies, or government-business partnerships to plunder some for the sake of

---

[36] See WN, 539.
[37] See LJ, 18–37 and 207–15.
[38] See LJ, 404–41 and 460.

others. In TMS, WN, and LJ Smith recounts several instances in which these problems and others impede society's progress toward greater material prosperity and beneficial laws.[39] Hence Donald Winch is correct that we should not ascribe to Smith a blind "sunny optimism" that markets will always and everywhere produce a beneficial "spontaneous harmony."[40] Moreover, it is of course true that, as commentators like Lionel Robbins, Jacob Viner, and Joseph Cropsey have maintained, Smithian markets require quite a bit of artificial regulative assistance to operate smoothly.[41] Thus Smith was not so naïve that he thought that markets could be perfect, or everything to everyone. His view was, as these commentators remind us, far more skeptical, realistic, and nuanced than that.

But a few things must be said. First, Smith's general skepticism about politics, which Winch rehearses with great care, is in fact a product of his belief that unplanned market-style institutions do a better job of creating practices and protocols that conduce to human benefit than could centrally planned political programs. Hence, contrary to the implication Winch draws, I think the two are quite consistent.[42] Moreover, although the rules defining marketplaces are artificial, that does not mean that they are not still explained by Smith's market model: like language, they still arose on the basis of on-the-spot trial-and-error, without any antecedent, overall plan. To repeat a passage cited a moment ago, Smith writes that government "arose, not as some writers imagine from any consent or agreement of a number of persons who submit themselves to such and such regulations, but from the natural progress which men make in society" (LJ, 207). He continues:

I showed how at first there was properly no government at all, that this arose first amongst a nation of shepherds, and that these in certain circumstances would naturally unite themselves and form a city, which at first was under the government of a chief, but afterwards became in the ordinary and naturall progress of things an aristocracy and afterwards a democracy. (LJ, 228)

Finally, despite his keen awareness of the glitches, backslidings, and disruptions to which the commentators point, Smith nevertheless saw

---

[39] See, for example, in TMS, 86–89, 209–211, 232–34, and 340–41; in WN, 78–79, 84, 145, 158, 342, 345–49, and 361–62; in LJ, 228–40, 521–41, and passim.
[40] Winch (1978), 176.
[41] Cropsey (1957), passim; Robbins (1952), especially 56–57; and Viner (1928), 116–55.
[42] See Winch (1978), Chapters 7 and 8.

the overall market-style development of human social institutions as beneficial, and thus the overall momentum of mankind's progress as being toward good—as shown in particular by his ultimate preference for the "obvious and simple system of natural liberty" (WN, 687). Smith's belief is that these institutions developing according to the market model do in the end progress beneficially, despite the inevitable problems that periodically arise.[43]

Smith argues that the chief motivation people feel in the marketplaces I have been describing is that of bettering their station in life, which includes desires to help their family and friends.[44] Because it is impossible for any one person to assemble all the information regarding the production of all the goods he wants, in such marketplaces a tool develops that encapsulates, as Smith shows, enough of the information a person needs to know in one small, accessible package: a price. Smith thinks that a thing's "natural price" is simply the sum of actual costs to the thing's producer for bringing the thing to the market; but he argues that things also have "market" prices, which reflect a negotiation between what it required to make the thing in question and what others are willing to sacrifice for it.[45] Under a state of "perfect liberty" and "free competition"—which means under the conditions listed earlier—Smith thinks that a thing's market price will be "continually gravitating" toward its natural price, at which point there will be a balance in the marketplace between supply and demand.[46] What pushes the market price toward its natural price is people acting on their natural drives to better their condition. Everyone would like to get more with less. As producers, this means that when the market price of something is higher than the natural price, we will tend to produce more, and we will tend to produce less when the market price is below the natural price. As consumers, this means that when the market price is higher than the natural price, we will tend to buy less, and we will tend to buy more when the market price is lower than the

---

[43] For passages that express what I think is Smith's ultimate optimism about the course of human progress, despite his general skepticism about politics, see WN, 211–33, 344–45, 687, 768, and 810; and LJ, 207–34, 486–87, and 539. For a view of Smith sympathetic to my own, see Macfarlane (2000), especially Chapter 6; for an account that differs, see Rothschild (2001), especially Chapters 3, 5, and 8.

[44] See, for example, WN, 341, 343, and 540.

[45] WN, 72–81; see also WN, 446–47.

[46] WN, 73, 78, and 77, respectively.

natural price. Thus because of the mutual adjustment and negotiation between people qua producers and people qua consumers, over
time prices tend to "gravitate" toward mutual acceptability and relative
stability.

Smith also distinguishes something he calls a "real price," which
underlies a thing's natural price (WN, 47–64). The real price, Smith
thinks, is determined by or reflects the amount of labor that is required
to make something:

> The real price of everything, what every thing really costs to the man who
> wants to acquire it, is the toil and trouble of acquiring it. What every thing
> is really worth to the man who has acquired it, and who wants to dispose of
> it or exchange it for something else, is the toil and trouble which it can save
> to himself, and which it can impose upon other people. What is bought with
> money or with goods is purchased by labour as much as what we acquire by
> the toil of our own body. That money or those goods indeed save this toil.
> (WN, 47)

In this passage begins Smith's famous labor theory of value, for which
several commentators have taken him to task. The claim has been that
Smith tries to measure a thing's value by an objective standard, but that
the criterion he chooses, "labour," fails utterly to do the job.[47] Note
in this passage, however, the subjective nature of the labor Smith discusses: it all relates to the particular individual who wants to acquire a
thing.[48] So although Smith intends labor to be an objective criterion, it
is indexed to—and hence relative to—individuals: it is a *subjective-labor*
theory of value.[49] This point is important because it fits with Smith's
reticence to predict what products will be produced in markets and
what people will be willing to pay for them. Only the individual himself can know how much of his own labor he would save in buying something; hence, only the individual can know whether the price asked
for something is worth it to him. Thus the goods that get produced

---

[47] For discussion, see Blaug (1997), Chapter 2; Hollander (1973), Chapter 4; Otteson
(July 2000) and the references contained therein; and Robertson and Taylor (June
1957).
[48] See also LJ, 495–96.
[49] The typically overlooked element of subjectivity distinguishes Smith's theory of value
from that of, for example, Marx and protects it from the criticisms that have been
rightly leveled against Marx on this count. For an example of the standard—and
I think mistaken—interpretation of Smith's theory of value, see Raphael (1985), 63–64.

in a market are in an important sense unplanned. The entrepreneur produces something at his own cost, and if the value of the good to individual people is greater than what it cost him to produce it—that is, if the market price is greater than the real price—then people will buy it and he will continue to produce it. If it turns out that the reverse is the case, that the good's market price is below its real price to the entrepreneur, then people will not buy it, the entrepreneur will suffer a loss, and he will not continue to produce it. What drives the market, then, is the desires of the people acting in it, and their continuous attempts to satisfy those desires more efficiently.[50]

The price mechanism also allows for mutual exchanges of information between producers and consumers. By buying or not buying, consumers tell producers whether their desire to have the product is worth the effort the producer is expending to make it; likewise, the price that the producer sets for his goods informs the consumers about the relative scarcity of the materials and labor required to bring the product to market. The exchange of information contained in prices thus allows the market to be self-regulating by forcing producers to be sensitive to the preferences that are revealed by people's purchasing habits and patterns, and thus by encouraging the investment of capital in ways that will tend to satisfy consumers' preferences more efficiently. Because we are all both producers and consumers at different times and in different capacities, marketplaces of exchange thus conduce to overall community cohesion by creating arenas in which incentives exist for us to take an interest in each other.

This last point requires elaboration. Because the degree to which one can focus one's productive energies (i.e., specialize) depends upon the chance one has to sell or trade the surplus of what one makes, the division of labor is dependent on the extent of the market: the greater the market, the finer the division of labor.[51] This is reflected in the development of human societies through Smith's four stages. By the time a society reaches the fourth stage of commerce, it is highly specialized: people focus their energies on a relatively narrow range of activities, and they are highly dependent on others for the goods they enjoy. In this way the market order increases exponentially the

---

[50] See WN, 455–56.
[51] See WN, 30–36.

number of people with whom each of us bears a relation, and for the vast majority of such relations the people we depend on are totally unknown to us. "In a civilized society [one] stands at all times in need of the cooperation and assistance of great multitudes, while [one's] whole life is scarce sufficient to gain the friendship of a few persons" (WN, 26). Smith's example of the "woollen coat" vividly illustrates the interdependence of people in a commercial or market economy.

> The woollen coat, for example, which covers the day-labourer, as course and rough as it may appear, is the produce of the joint labour of a great multitude of workmen. The shepherd, the sorter of the wool, the wool-comber or carder, the dyer, the scribbler, the spinner, the weaver, the fuller, the dresser, with many others, must all join their different arts in order to complete even this homely production. How many merchants and carriers, besides, must have been employed in transporting the materials from some of those workmen to others who often live in a very distant part of the country! How much commerce and navigation in particular, how many ship-builders, sailors, sail-makers, rope-makers, must have been employed in order to bring together the different drugs made use of by the dyer, which often come from the remotest corners of the world! What a variety of labour too is necessary in order to produce the tools of the meanest of those workmen! To say nothing of such complicated machines as the ship of the sailor, the mill of the fuller, or even the loom of the weaver, let us consider only what a variety of labour is requisite in order to form that very simple machine, the shears with which the shepherd clips the wool. The miner, the builder of the furnace for smelting the ore, the feller of the timber, the burner of the charcoal to be made use of in the smelting-house, the brick-maker, the brick-layer, the workmen who attend the furnace, the mill-wright, the forger, the smith, must all of them join their different arts to produce them. Were we to examine . . . all these things, and consider what a variety of labour is employed about each of them, we shall be sensible that without the assistance and co-operation of many thousands, the very meanest person in a civilized country could not be provided, even according to, what we very falsely imagine, the easy and simple manner in which he is commonly accommodated. (WN, 22–23)[52]

Because of the Smithian familiarity principle, whereby one's natural affection for another varies directly with one's familiarity with that other,[53] these numberless people on whom each of us depends in a

---

[52] See also WN, 276–78.
[53] See Chapter 5.

commercial society are not the objects of natural affection. But we still behave toward them within the rules of justice, and it is these rules that our society has gradually developed to ease and facilitate just such transactions.

As I have said, Smith thinks that human beings have developed through four stages of society,[54] each marked by increasing formalization of rules protecting "the laws of justice" and, to the extent that they allowed "the obvious and simple system of natural liberty" (WN, 687),[55] by increasing material prosperity as well. Smith's description of the progress of human society through these four stages contains several crucial features. First, the development was effected by individual people acting in conjunction with one another but without their intending to effect any overall development. Here Smith's notion of the "invisible hand" that connects people's attempts to satisfy their narrower, private interests to a better satisfaction of everyone else's similar interests plays an important role: people intentionally enter into various relationships with others in the market, and these relationships taken together constitute a larger system of a generally beneficial marketplace, but they did not intend to constitute the larger system.[56] Second, the development came about gradually and proceeded from informal to formal as people's needs and interests dictated. This feature is evident in Smith's description of the passage of various communities through the four stages, each of which is marked by increasingly complicated and formal rules by which their peculiar governments function. Third, the development depends on regular associations and exchanges among individuals. This indeed is the immediate constituent of markets, the trucking, bartering, and exchanging of one thing for another that Smith thinks inevitably happens when people are left to their own devices. Finally, the development was initially and has continued to be motivated by the desires of the people within those societies. Put generally, this is the ever-present desire each of us has, as Smith

---

[54] Smith's notion of the four stages of human social evolution is a leitmotiv throughout WN. It is first broached in Smith's "Introduction and Plan of the Work" (WN, 10–12), and it is especially apparent in Book v, Chapter 1 (WN, 689–816).

[55] For a discussion of the connection Smith sees between liberty and the rules of justice, see LJ, 275–82.

[56] See WN, 455–56.

puts it in WN, to better his own condition.[57] This single passage from near the beginning of WN contains early hints of all these features:

> This division of labour, from which so many advantages are derived, is not originally the effect of any human wisdom, which foresees and intends that general opulence to which it gives occasion. It is the necessary, though very slow and gradual consequence of a certain propensity in human nature which has in view no such extensive utility; the propensity to truck, barter, and exchange one thing for another. (WN, 25)[58]

Let me make one final point about Smithian economic markets. A distinction should be drawn between the concept of a market on the one hand and actual marketplaces on the other. The concept of a market with which I argue Smith works is the theoretical model of a system of free exchange in which rules of exchange spontaneously develop. Marketplaces are the particular instantiations of this model that one finds virtually everywhere. The universal features of marketplaces for the exchange of goods of production are protections of individual liberty, of private property, and of voluntary contracts, but all the other features one finds in any particular marketplace—which may include forms of address, codes of behavior, protocols of attire, even customs about precisely what counts as property and what counts as a contract[59]—will be heavily influenced by the traditions and practices of the particular peoples who are parties to the exchange. Even within a single community, there will be various orders or suborders of protocols that will display variations on the basic theme of a market. For example, the protocols of exchange at a contemporary suburban shopping mall are not the same as those in an auction at Sotheby's in New York, are not the same as those at a baseball card show, and are not the same as those at a farmer's market in any of a number of American cities. These are all marketplaces that to varying extents fit the general model of a market, but each displays its own concrete accidental features that reflect its place, time, and members. This feature of economic marketplaces parallels Smith's analysis of morality in TMS when he claims there that the "custom and fashion" of a particular place and time affect only the less important matters of,

---

[57] See WN, 285, 341, 343, 345, 374, 454, 580, 674, and 405.
[58] See also WN, 345–47 and LJ, 351.
[59] See LJ, 71–76.

for example, manners, but not the substance of the central moral notions of propriety and merit (TMS, 200–11).

## III. Language, Market, and Morals

My purpose in looking at "Languages" was to show that it revealed a conceptual structure or model that was to become the key to understanding Smith's analysis of moral judgment in TMS. It also appears, however, that this same model is at work in Smith's WN, suggesting that Smith recognized the explanatory power of the model and was sympathetic to it for much of his scholarly life. Let me now show explicitly how the market model of TMS links up with the models present in "Languages" and in WN.

Smith's account of morality in TMS displays a structural similarity to his account of the marketplace of goods and thus also adheres to the general model of a market. Like the economic marketplace, the "marketplace of morals" is driven by a single chief motivation, in this case the desire for mutual sympathy of sentiments (see, e.g., TMS, 13). A moral judgment, Smith thinks, is passed either on the motivations behind a person's action or on the action itself. Yet because we can never have complete knowledge of another person's motivations, and because we do not know all the circumstances surrounding another person's actions, we develop a tool that helps to compensate for our limited knowledge—the impartial spectator. By asking ourselves how an impartial spectator would judge the act or motivation in question, we make it possible for all of us to come to some agreement or consensus of judgment. The consensus we reach is the result of something like a competition of judgments: in our everyday intercourse with others, we offer our own and hear others' judgments, and each of us in turn modifies his judgments in response to the information he receives from others.[60] Some judgments will change or be discarded

---

[60] Haakonssen writes that the "general rules of morality are thus the unintended outcome of a multitude of individual instances of natural moral evaluation" (1981, 61). He also writes that "[t]his is the theory of mutual sympathy as a selection mechanism of behaviour" (1981, 78) and calls Smith's view a "philosophy of unintended consequences" (1981, 78). Haakonssen does not, however, relate Smith's views to the nature of a market, and he does not attempt to connect Smith's analysis in TMS with the analysis in WN.

over time—protocols of dress, for example—and others will survive, becoming codified as transcendent, even sacred rules of morality—for example, that incest or murder of innocents is wrong. This marketplace of morals is thus self-regulating in the same way that the marketplace of goods is, namely, by the continuous exchange of information that is embodied in the tool developed for this purpose (the impartial spectator). In both marketplaces, the rules and regulations that develop do so "naturally," by which Smith means without any central plan or authoritative interference, and are enforced voluntarily by the people who are parties to the marketplaces because it is in their interest—for mutual sympathy and for a better condition in life—to do so.

It should be clear from this sketch that the development of the institutions of economic markets and of the development of language bear striking similarities to the market model that, I have argued, underlies Smith's understanding of the system of morality. Indeed, the central structural elements of this market model can be mapped onto all three of Smith's works in this way:

1. Motivating Desire
   (i) TMS: the "pleasure of mutual sympathy" of sentiments (TMS, 13 and passim);
   (ii) WN: the "natural effort of every individual to better his own condition" (WN, 540; see also WN, 26–27, 341, and 343);
   (iii) "Languages": the desire to make "mutual wants intelligible to each other" (LRBL, 203).

2. Rules Developed
   (i) TMS: standards of moral judgment and rules determining propriety and merit;
   (ii) WN: the "laws of justice" (WN, 687), including in particular protocols protecting private property, contractual agreements, and voluntary exchanges;
   (iii) "Languages": rules of grammar, pronunciation, and so on.

3. Currency (i.e., what gets exchanged)
   (i) TMS: personal sentiments and moral judgments;
   (ii) WN: private goods and services;
   (iii) "Languages": words, ideas, and wants.

4. Resulting "Unintended System of Order"
    (i) TMS: commonly shared standards of morality and moral judgment;
    (ii) WN: economy (i.e., large-scale network of exchanges of goods and services);
    (iii) "Languages": language.

A fifth feature of the market model is a mechanism developed for facilitating relevant judgments: in TMS, this is the impartial spectator, or one's "conscience"; in WN, this is the price system. But there is no clear analogue of this in "Languages." Grammar books, grammar experts (as in contemporary France), or even grammar schools might play this role, but Smith fails to mention any such device in the essay. Nevertheless, the three works can be even more closely united than the preceding schematic suggests if, as I suggested in Chapter 4, one construes the motivating desire in each case as particular instances of precisely the same desire: the desire of each individual to satisfy his interests, whatever they are and in whatever arena they would be satisfied.

I believe that on an examination of Smith's works—not only TMS and WN, but also in particular LJ and "History of Astronomy"—a convincing case can be made that the market model informed Smith's understanding of many other aspects of human life as well, including the development of governmental bodies, the development of notions of crime and proper punishment, the development of the institution of marriage, the development of science and scientific method, and even the development of religious[61] and educational institutions. On this basis, I would like to make the large claim that Smith saw his market model as the key to understanding the creation, development, and maintenance of human social life generally. Although I shall return to this briefly in the Conclusion, I cannot make a complete case for my claim here. Indeed, showing how the market model manifests itself in Smith's accounts of all human social life is the burden of another book. But I do hope that by showing its presence in TMS, as well as in

---

[61] Griswold argues that Smith proposes a "'free market' in religions" to combat the negative effects of superstition and enthusiasm. See Griswold (July 1997).

"Languages" and WN, I have at least lent plausibility to my larger suggestion.[62]

Aside from this structural unity of the works themselves and the fact that Smith apparently continued to appeal to this model for several decades, there is also some additional historical reason to think that Smith intended the unity all along. The Scottish Enlightenment has become famous for developing what I would call "market" explanations of large-scale social institutions—more typically called "spontaneous-order" explanations[63]—and Smith was in the thick of this development. To take an example that greatly influenced Scottish Enlightenment thinkers, in his *Fable of the Bees*, Mandeville argues that activities that are publicly considered to be "vices" are in some cases actually virtues. In particular, self-interested activities that we formally disapprove turn out to conduce to economic progress, and, by a process not unlike Smith's invisible hand, general economic benefits arise from private vices.[64] Hume also employs something like the marketplace model in his explanation of the development of our notions of "justice." Hume argued that the rules and laws respecting property and justice arise "gradually" and acquire "force by a slow progression, and by our repeated experience of the inconveniences of transgressing" them (T, 490). Hume's idea was that what people come to consider "just" and "unjust" with respect to property arises unintentionally, as the result of habits and conventions that people adopt in their dealings with one another. Such sociological explanations were thus very much in the air in eighteenth-century Scottish thought, and so it would not be unlikely that Smith had them in mind while constructing his own studies of major areas of human social life.

One might mention other figures in this context—in particular, Adam Ferguson, Thomas Reid, and Dugald Stewart—but Smith stands out among them because he was the first to fully understand the possible scope of the marketplace model. He saw that it could explain economic institutions (such as economic markets, as in Mandeville) and isolated aspects of morality (such as our sense of justice, as in Hume);

---

[62] Campbell argues that much of Smith's work is united by the operation of sympathy, which I think is plausible, but it does not take into account the entirety of the model that unifies Smith's work. See Campbell (1971), 234–5.

[63] See Hamowy (1987).

[64] Mandeville (1924 [1714]), Volume 2, 349 and passim.

however Smith employs it to understand the development and evolution of human social institutions generally. Ferguson, Reid, and Stewart also see the general applicability of this model, but their work comes after Smith's. In this way Smith looks ahead not just a few decades, but indeed two centuries—in anticipation of twentieth-century "sociobiological" explanations of human institutions, which, building on insights drawn from evolutionary biology, seek to explain human behavior by employing models not unlike Smith's. Some contemporary sociobiologists and ethical theorists have even attempted to explain various aspects of human morality by relying on individual motivations that lead to behaviors that over time gradually create systems of unintended order.[65]

A final remark. The claim that Smith developed a single "marketplace" model to account for the development and maintenance of all human social institutions provides further support for the resolution of the Adam Smith Problem that I gave in Chapter 5. As we saw in Chapter 4, the core of the problem dealt with apparent discrepancies between the accounts that TMS and WN respectively give of human motivation; as I argued in Chapter 5, however, the familiarity principle resolves most of those discrepancies. If, however, as I have suggested here, the same market model that was present in Smith's early essay on languages also informed not only the analyses in both TMS and WN, but perhaps also those in LJ and "History of Astronomy," then there seems even better reason to think that the central parts of Smith's corpus are, on a deep level, united.

---

[65] I discuss some sources of this view in the Conclusion.

# Conclusion

Let me close my study by introducing several brief considerations that were not appropriate to introduce into previous chapters. I begin with a short summary of the main parts of Smith's moral theory, as I see it. I then make two general observations about the theory: one relates to an aspect of the Adam Smith Problem, and the other is connected with what I think is an important omission in Smith's theory as he presents it. In the third section, I look at some recent work that tends to support parts of Smith's conception of human nature—and by extension, perhaps, his explanation of the development of moral standards. Finally, I close with a few words about what I think Smith's most important contribution to moral philosophy is. I say something about Smith's use of this contribution in comparison to others who have used it and a word about this contribution's plausibility in the context of contemporary moral thought.

## I. Summary of Smith's Argument

Adam Smith's *The Theory of Moral Sentiments* is a presentation of the observations he has made about human beings and human moral judging, the regular patterns the latter seem to form, and Smith's explanation of why human moral judgments adhere to those patterns. The result is a theory that provides, perhaps for the first time,[1] a

---

[1] See Morrow (1928), 172 and 177.

careful account of the joint innate and social factors at work in the development of a society's moral standards. The relative extent to which "nature" and "nurture" are responsible for the behavior and established practices of human society is a debate that remains live to this day: Smith's theory occupies something of a middle ground. It posits a collaborative effort of the two factors, arguing that without both no system of morality would have developed at all. Thus Smith sees truth in the general notion that we are independent individuals who to a significant extent shape our own futures. Smith thinks there would be no civilization—no culture, no moral refinement, no arts— were it not that individuals have striven to exert their energies to create it. Free human choice, embodied in Smith's notion of the virtue of self-command, is a necessary and substantial contributing factor to the progress and development of mankind. On the other hand, no man is an island. The material prosperity that we have achieved was only possible because we cooperated with one another in ways that came to constitute markets. And the success of markets depended on a level of cooperation that could obtain only because people freely and sincerely concerned themselves with the interests of others. Moreover, the protocols of behavior that allowed us to interact with one another peacefully, on the one hand, and the mutual sympathy and natural affection that underlay loving relations, on the other—which together constitute one of the two principal ingredients of true human happiness, namely, psychological well-being—developed only in the context of communities of people, where frequent intercourse with others was the norm. Thus moral judgments, and the general moral system that frames them and of which they form a part, are, according to Smith, properly understood as the result of an ongoing development effected by autonomous individuals striving to be happy in their necessarily social environments.

In an effort to facilitate their respective searches for happiness, individuals spontaneously try out, and then discard or adopt various habits of behavior. This trial-and-error process begins very early on in each person's life and is driven by the innate desires Smith thinks all of us have. These desires include those that we might say pertain largely to oneself only, like hunger, sexual attraction, and the second-order desire of wishing to have one's own desires satisfied, as well as those that essentially include others, like the desire for mutual sympathy of sentiments and the desire to please and not offend other people. The latter group of desires are awakened in one when one is first capable of understanding that others might approve or disapprove of one's actions, of one's expressions of wants, or of one's motivations. One then becomes sensitive to the pleasure associated with achieving a sympathy with another's sentiments, and the pain when instead an antipathy is present. Because this sympathy provides one of mankind's most pleasurable experiences, one's first exposures to the approval and disapproval of others strongly encourages one to seek the former and avoid the latter. We have here, then, the beginning of a process that acts as a natural cement for human society: because mutual sympathy is sought by all, each person strives to put himself into situations in which such sympathy can be obtained. In practice, that means that each of us works to establish and maintain relations with others that, because they are based on mutual sympathy, are amicable and loving. Smith thus sees sympathy, and the natural desire to achieve it, as a powerful social bond that enables us to form communities and that provides strong incentives toward social stability.

The development of society is an ongoing process, and the people within the society will occupy something of a bell curve with respect to the society's overall progress. That is, at any given time, there will be a minority of people who are in the beginning stages of learning the society's already long-established practices and knowledge; there will be another minority of people who are at the forefront of the society's progress, devising new practices, discovering new knowledge, or using traditional protocols in new ways; and, finally, the largest number of the society's members will be somewhere between the two other groups, somewhere between learning and innovation. The principal constituent of the remedial learners will be children. They have only recently been introduced into "the great school of self-command," in which they are required to moderate their own sentiments in order to increase their chances of achieving a sympathy with the sentiments of spectators. This process of moderation manifests itself as the children's attempting—fitfully, at first, because this process often conflicts with their immediate desires—to discipline themselves to adopt various behaviors that they find to please others and allow sympathy. These behaviors slowly become habits of behavior, and the children gradually need to pay less and less conscious attention to the rules governing their own behavior. Society's general rules of proper and improper conduct are in this way transmitted to a new generation. The now-older children, like most adults, accept these rules—which they variously follow in nearly every social circle in which they turn in their community—as a given. They do not, that is, spend much or even any time worrying about the ultimate justification of the rules; when their conversations turn to ethical concerns, the discussions will center rather on whether this or that act or this or that person followed the rule in question, not whether the rule itself is a good one or whether it ought to be obeyed. The rebelliousness of teenagers is simply a heightened creativity for discovering and testing new behaviors; even they, however, tend as they grow older to adopt the accepted behavioral protocols of those around them.

For most adults in any community, the established general rules of behavior have become second nature, used and appealed to without a second thought. Indeed, these rules become internalized in each person and personified in the voice of an impartial spectator. In the earlier stages of a person's moral development, he passes judgment on others on the basis of whether he thinks he would have done or felt the same thing had he been in that other's shoes. He imaginatively places himself in the shoes of the person principally concerned, and he imagines what would have been his own sentiments. He then approves of the other's sentiments if they accord with those he imagines he would have had but disapproves if they do not accord with them. It does not take long, however, for each of us to realize that it is difficult to place ourselves completely in another's shoes. One cannot know all the details of another's situation, no matter how well one might know him, because one cannot *be* that other person. Hence there is an unavoidable gap between the agent's perspective of his own situation and the spectator's perspective of the agent's situation. And this gap works both ways. Each of us is by turns an agent and a spectator, so each of us has not only experienced the inability to understand another fully (which, as a spectator, is not always so distressing) but also experienced the pain of not being understood by others (which is generally far more distressing). As is usually the case in a market-like environment, however, when there is a significant want, people find a way to supply it. In this case, a tool is developed to help facilitate better mutual understanding between agents and spectators, which thereby helps to facilitate mutual sympathy of sentiments. This tool is the impartial spectator. People spontaneously come to judge first their own and then everyone else's conduct not from the perspective of their own position as spectator or agent, but, rather, from the perspective of a knowledgeable but disinterested third party. We find that our best chance to have others sympathize with us is when we do two things. First, we encourage others to view our situation as an impartial spectator would, taking into account all the relevant information, but no more; we do this to engage the spectators' sentiments to a greater degree than that to which they might otherwise be inclined. Second, we discipline ourselves to adopt only those sentiments or actions that an impartial spectator would approve; we do this to temper our own passions, which might otherwise carry us away. The combined effect of these two strategies is to raise spectators' sentiments closer to those of the person principally concerned, and to lower the sentiments of the person principally concerned closer to those of spectators. The goal whose attainment these exercises make more likely is mutual sympathy of sentiments.

Each of us, then, is encouraged by his desire to achieve mutual sympathy to adopt the perspective of the impartial spectator when he judges his own conduct. One asks oneself what an impartial spectator would think about undertaking this or that action or what such a spectator would think about this or that sentiment. When examining one's own conduct, one thus imaginatively divides oneself into two persons, an actor and a spectator. In the capacity of judge of one's own conduct, one tries to position oneself as an impartial spectator disinterestedly reviewing the actions of someone else. From this position, then, one asks what one-as-impartial-judge thinks of the actions of one-as-person-principally-concerned. The purpose of undergoing this imaginative personality-splitting is to get a more accurate idea of what others must think of one's conduct. Other people are not as partial to one as oneself is, so one is more likely to predict what their judgment of one will be if one tries to disconnect oneself from the position one presently occupies and tries to adopt the perspective of an impartial spectator. By making better predictions about others' judgments, one increases one's chances of achieving mutual sympathy of sentiments. Now the habits of behavior one has already formed are good indicators for what the judgment of impartial spectators would be—because they were adopted, after all, on the basis of one's earlier successes and failures at achieving sympathy. The more experiences one has with other people and with their judgments, then, the more refined do one's habits of behavior become. And as one employs these principles and this perspective more and more, the impartial spectator procedure becomes more and more second nature. That is, adopting an impartial spectator's perspective, imagining what one's sentiments would be if one were such a spectator, comparing of those imagined sentiments either with one's own (when one is judging oneself) or with those of the person principally concerned (when one is judging another), and finally pronouncing moral approbation or disapprobation depending on whether an accord or discord between the respective sentiments was discovered—all this becomes the habitual, even unconscious process that informs the judgments we make of persons and actions every day. It is in this way that the voice of the impartial spectator becomes internalized in each of us, and it is this voice that each of us comes to know as his personal conscience.

The general rules of behavior that inform the judgments of the impartial spectator, and hence inform everyone's conscience, are devised and adopted in the same way that behaviors and protocols are devised and adopted in economic marketplaces. They are the result of individuals striving to satisfy their own interests. Over time, people find that they can better satisfy their interests if they cooperate in certain ways, and these methods of cooperation develop into systems of order that in turn influence and direct the actions of individuals. The individuals themselves had no such systems in mind, so we can call the systems of order "unintended." The unintended systems of order then coordinate the efforts of individuals to satisfy their respective interests, and they allow the individuals to serve the interests of other individuals at the same time—whether they are aware of it or not, whether they know the people they serve or not. The general rules of morality that develop in the way described earlier together constitute just such a system of order: they are rules of cooperation by which individuals regulate their own conduct so as to accord with those methods that have proved in the past to allow people to satisfy their interests. Given the nature of peculiarly human interests, the virtues of justice, benevolence, prudence, and self-command, all as adjudged by the impartial spectator, have emerged as the core of mankind's universal system of morality. Similarly, a system of rules has emerged that allows us to satisfy the other principal universal human interest, the desire to better our condition; this system of rules frames our behavior in economic marketplaces. In these arenas, rules about property and contracts are those that have proved to satisfy human interests most efficiently and, consequently, have come to be regarded as inviolable.

Less important protocols of behavior will come and go. Notions about proper attire, proper forms of address, and proper table manners have changed over time and will continue to change. For the more important rules, however, change is infrequent—even, in some cases, nonexistent. For example, proscriptions against murder and incest tend to remain constant and, except in the most extraordinary cases, have been condemned in virtually all times and places. Those general rules that withstand the test of time and place and that get passed on from one generation to the next—principally what Smith calls the rules of justice—begin to take on something of a sacred aura. Their universal acceptance gives them an added authority, which people tend to consider their moral duty. That is, people come to view it as their duty to follow these rules and to view breaches of these rules as breaches of moral duty. When the development reaches the point where people begin to write down these most important rules or to preach them publicly (or both), it is a short step to believing these rules to be sacred. And indeed this step is usually taken: these few privileged rules often come to be considered as embodying or issuing from the will of God. So considered, these rules enjoy an even greater authority, and many people will believe that these rules command absolute obedience because of the authority of their source. And viewing these rules as the will of God has its practical benefit as well: because these rules could only have achieved the status they have if they had proved over long periods of time to be supremely advantageous to the satisfaction of our interests, future satisfaction of interests will also tend to depend on their observation. If they are seen as rules issuing from God's own command, they will receive the obedience that is necessary for them to work in the way they have in the past. Hence the most important rules of social cooperation enjoy the most unforgiving obedience—which bodes well for people's future chances of satisfying their interests.

The process of market-style development of moral standards should not be seen, however, as having no ultimate justification. One might think that because moral rules developed unintentionally as the increasingly efficient means of satisfying people's wants, there is no reason to follow them, no reason to be moral, except insofar as doing so conduces to satisfying one's wants. One might think that there is nothing inherent in the moral rules developed in this way that absolutely or objectively commands one's respect. But that is not true. It is true that the rules of morality formed unintentionally: individuals devised and adopted them because they served their individual interests, not because they conduced to the general welfare of the entire community. But one must ask the question why it is that individuals pursuing their own interests increase every other person's chances of satisfying his interests. Why is it that we have a desire for mutual sympathy of sentiments, which leads them to form societies and to take a sincere interest in others—precisely the two conditions necessary for individuals to achieve true happiness? Why should it be the case that by freely pursuing their private interests in achieving mutual sympathy and bettering their condition we simultaneously enable others to achieve the same? Although we can explain how this process works— we can explain the efficient causes that simultaneously tend to serve individual and others' interests—we have not thereby explained why the elements that initiate this process existed in the first place. That we are equipped with just the necessary features to enable us to achieve psychological well-being and material prosperity only by peaceful, voluntary cooperation with others seems too special a set of circumstances to be left unexplained or to be explained by chance. The reasonable conclusion, instead, is that someone planned it that way. Some great, benevolent intelligence designed the circumstances of the world, including mankind in particular, so that our free activity would tend to produce those conditions in which we can be truly happy. And this great, benevolent intelligence could only be God himself. So we have, then, three reasons to spread human freedom as widely as possible. First, it allows us to seek out, establish, and maintain those interpersonal relationships that are necessary for our psychological well-being; second, it allows us to barter and exchange for our mutual material benefit; and, finally, third, it allows us to achieve the true happiness that those two conditions together constitute—which is the state that God himself has wanted for us to attain.

## II. Two Observations

### Markets and Benevolence

That is Smith's argument. My reconstruction of it points toward the extent to which I think the Adam Smith Problem can be solved, and it points moreover toward the first general comment I want to make about Smith's theory, namely, that Smith's theory shows how a market-like institution actually encourages benevolence to follow on actions motivated by self-interest.

I have argued that a fundamental unity exists between Smith's two books; it centers around Smith's single, constant understanding of the nature of human institutions and associations. Smith understands them to be systems of order that are unintentionally developed by individuals as they strive to satisfy their interests. Large-scale human institutions can then be seen as the unintentional by-products of people aiming to serve their local interests. This model underlies Smith's description of languages, of morals, and of economic markets. Insofar as both TMS and WN are examinations of the nature of certain large-scale human institutions—the system of morality and marketplaces of exchange, respectively—the books are thus consistent: each is an instantiation of a marketplace at work. I have argued, however, that a discrepancy nevertheless seems to exist between the way Smith describes proper or moral motivation in TMS and the way he describes motivation in WN. In the former, Smith argues that the impartial spectator approves of the adoption of four principal virtues—justice, benevolence, prudence, and self-command. The virtuous person, as determined by the impartial spectator, acts with justice at all times, and because a person must have self-command before he will be able to exercise the other virtues, it, too, is required almost universally.[2] The relative degree to which a virtuous person would be motivated by either

---

[2] I say "almost" universally because there will be some occasions on which one's immediate passions already accord with a behavior or sentiment that the impartial spectator endorses, in which case self-command might not be required for one to act virtuously. See TMS, 241.

benevolence or prudence, meaning roughly the degree to which he would act either on other-regarding or self-regarding motives, depends on the nature of the situation under question. The impartial spectator will judge different situations differently in this regard, and he will be guided by what I have called Smith's familiarity principle. The familiarity principle states that one's natural affection for another, which informs the extent to which benevolence will naturally prompt one toward that other, extends in a direct relation with one's familiarity with that other. The more familiar one is with another person, the more natural affection will one have for him, and the more likely will one act out of benevolence when one interacts with him; conversely, the less familiar one is, the less natural affection will one have, and the less likely is one to act out of benevolence. Smith argues that this principle is natural in the sense that we all feel it without reflecting on it, and he argues in addition that the impartial spectator endorses the principle for the most part because it tends to conduce both to the person's psychological well-being and also, when generally adopted, to the community's overall welfare.

Based on the position Smith adopts in TMS, we should expect that he would argue that benevolence is the proper motive to feel in connection with one's family; that a preponderance of benevolence, along with a tincture of self-interest, is the proper motivation with one's friends; that a roughly equal amount of benevolence and self-interest is proper when one deals with one's acquaintances; that a preponderance of self-interest with a tincture of benevolence is proper with distant acquaintances; and that self-interest is proper with strangers. When we discover, then, that in WN Smith speaks only of self-interest, and speaks as if that were the sole motive we feel—never mind what is proper or improper—we might well be dismayed. But a considerable part of what thus seems to be a discrepancy disappears when one realizes that when Smith discusses market relations between, for example, oneself and one's butcher or baker, Smith is thinking of people who are not family or friends. He envisions the marketplaces of exchange to coordinate the mutual satisfaction of interests among people who are largely unaware of and strangers to one another. So although I might in time come to make an acquaintance with my neighborhood butcher, I do not know the farmer who supplies his cattle, or the other farmers who supply the feed for the first farmer's cattle, or the blacksmith who supplies the knives with which the butcher cuts, and so on.[3] In all these relations, we stand to one another, as Smith says, only in our respective capacities as fellow citizens pursuing our material interests in the marketplace. Hence we act on little or no natural benevolence toward one another, and we presume others do the same; we act primarily out of self-interest with one another, and we presume others do the same; and as long as our behavior is within the bounds prescribed by the rules of justice—which is a principal implication of seeing each other as "fellow citizens" (WN, 27)—our behavior meets with the impartial spectator's approval. Although, then, the Adam Smith of WN speaks as though we felt nothing but self-interest for one another, it is a mistake to extrapolate this belief to all areas of life. Smith is speaking only about economic market relations in WN, which, according to the analysis in TMS, are, in fact, properly governed by self-interest within the rules of justice. The Adam Smith of WN and the Adam Smith of TMS are therefore not so far apart as one might at first have believed.

There is, however, the nagging problem that the Adam Smith of WN gives no real indication that there ever was an Adam Smith of TMS. There is no mention in WN of the four cardinal virtues that the impartial spectator endorses, there is no discussion even of the impartial spectator or the impartial spectator procedure, and there is no discussion of the natural human desire that TMS argued was perhaps our most important, the desire for mutual sympathy of sentiments. I discussed in Chapters 4 and 5 how one might account for the apparent discrepancy between the early Adam Smith and the late Adam Smith, but one can still imagine that people reading only Smith's second book might come to some rather unappetizing conclusions not only about Smith but also about the free markets he seems to endorse. Keeping in mind that Smith does not endorse the abolition of all government—he thinks government will be necessary to carry on several functions[4]—he nonetheless advocates the abolition or sharp reduction of tariffs, trade restrictions, and tax duties. When couched

---

[3] See WN, 22–24, for Smith's description of how extensive these relations and dependencies in a commercial society can be. See also WN, 276–78.

[4] See Book 5 of WN, 689–947.

in terms that describe human beings as fundamentally self-interested, Smith's recommendations have been found by some commentators to be distasteful. Some have thought that Smith would seem to see the world as an arena in which it is every man for himself: a world-wide competition of all against all, with only a minority flourishing—and probably at the expense of the rest. It seems to presume a kind of Hobbesian atomistic individuality, where people are separate and utterly independent from all others, where they care only about themselves and nothing about others (except insofar as "caring" about others serves their own self-interest, as Mandeville argued). And many have thought—quite rightly, I believe—that this is, first, not the way the world really is, and, second, not the kind of world one would wish to live in.[5] On the one hand, surely it is obvious that people care about more than only their own personal success and self-aggrandizement—what about concern for family and friends, for example? On the other hand, even if it turns out that many or most people are fundamentally self-interested, many would consider that a bad thing and would wish rather to discourage such behavior than to encourage it through Smithian markets. Marx, for example, criticized the capitalistic order for encouraging selfish behavior that resulted in alienation of each person from everyone else in a deep, almost metaphysical sense.[6] If Smithian markets have the atomizing result of Marxian *Entfremdung*, would we not rather wish to live in a world ruled by benevolence?—and hence should we not militate against the self-interest that actuates Smithian markets?

Without rehearsing the criticisms that have been leveled against markets and the defenses that have been marshaled over the years,[7] I would like to make a more modest claim on behalf of Smith's analysis in particular. Smith has argued that natural affection for others is enabled by familiarity with them, and that the more familiar one is with another, the more likely one is to act toward him out of benevolence.[8] If this is true, then marketplaces can actually enable more

---

[5] For an example of this charge, see Etzioni (1998).

[6] See, for example, Marx (1978), 70–81.

[7] For discussions that run the gamut, see Cohen (1995); Etzioni (1995); and Machan and Rasmussen (1995).

[8] See TMS, 220.

extensive benevolence than other kinds of economic arrangements, more than in premarket societies in particular.[9] Let us assume for a moment a society or community in which no extensive or welfare-state government exists—one, that is, in which there is no regulation of production or exchange, no system for redistribution of wealth, and no state-sponsored relief programs—but in which there do exist measures for the minimal protections of justice a Smithian society would require, namely, protections of people's lives, of private property, and of the obligations and sanctity of voluntary exchanges and contracts. In such a society, people would individually bear responsibility for satisfying their own interests, and the fruits of successful ventures along with the consequences of failed ones would redound upon themselves. Under these circumstances, a Smithian would argue, people would understand that they cannot satisfy their interests in isolation, or at least that the chances of satisfying their interests increase greatly when they cooperate with others. They would thus form communities. If at first the members of these communities do not know one another very well, the bonds that tie them together would be founded largely on each member's self-interest. In time, they would discover that by dividing the necessary duties of survival they could make themselves more efficient; hence a primitive, but ever-growing, division of labor would develop, with people tending to seek out those tasks at which they excel in order to increase their own ability to buy or exchange for the services of others. People always wish to have greater satisfaction of their interests, which will encourage further division of labor, which will mean more efficient production of goods, which, finally— allowing for periodic interruptions of religious or political initiatives, which will slow the progress—will mean greater overall wealth for the community: this is the by-now familiar Smithian story of the evolution of civilization.[10]

One part of Smith's story that does not receive much attention, however, is that in order for individuals to satisfy their interests in a society like the one described earlier, they must be able to produce and

---

[9] This idea was first suggested to me by Henry Hazlitt in his *Foundations of Morality* (1994 [1964]). But the idea has its adumbrations already in Smith: see TMS, 224, for example.

[10] For discussion, see Muller (1993), 117–25.

provide a good or service in which others are interested. If a person cannot find or generate interest in what he produces, then he will go out of business; he will then either have to produce something else or will not succeed in life (excepting, of course, cases of charitable intervention). To be successful, then, one will have to produce something others want, but that means one will have to have some idea of what it is that others do or might want—meaning, in turn, that one will have to take the time to discover what this is or speculate what it might be. In a society enshrining "the obvious and simple system of natural liberty" (WN, 687), therefore, people's desire to satisfy their own interests will lead them to take an interest in others. The successful person will be the one who has sensitive and extensive knowledge of the wants and needs of others, and who combines that with an entrepreneurial willingness to experiment with new ways to better satisfy those wants and needs. Markets thus create incentives to establish and maintain ever more extensive networks of producers and consumers that are founded on mutual interest in, as Smith says, "the fortune of others" (TMS, 9). But on Smith's argument, frequent contact and familiarity with others produces natural affection, which prompts benevolence. I suggest, then, that for Smith open markets will for this reason provide incentives to create conditions in which benevolence can grow, and the effect will be that the more extensive the markets, the more extensive people's natural benevolence. That does not mean that the act of discovering what a person wants in order to sell it to him by itself constitutes benevolence. Rather, my suggestion is that in seeking to find out what another wants one puts oneself in a position where the conditions are ripe for the growth of natural benevolence. Thus in an open market the initial motivation is still self-interest—seeking a profit—but that motivation prompts actions that can in time lead to a greater extension of Smithian natural benevolence than would otherwise exist.

A qualification is required by the fact that in well-developed market-based societies, the commercial relationships are so extensively interdependent, and the people forming those relationships are so numerous, that it is impossible for people to come into any contact with many of the people they nevertheless do business with. The executives of an athletic shoe corporation have never met the vast majority of the people who buy their shoes. Hence the familiarity that engenders affection on Smith's account is absent here, which means that the affection itself is absent. I think two things should be said in this regard, however. First, although the business owners or executives may well not know their customers, they nevertheless will sincerely wish them well—for the obvious and weighty reason that their livelihood depends upon them. No business succeeds without customers, and hence we should expect a genuine desire for the continued prosperity of people generally on the behalf of business owners. Second, owners may not know their ultimate customers, but they will know their more immediate workers, suppliers, business partners, and the like—and their contact with them will create the familiarity that can lead to natural affection. The number of such people with whom a business owner has regular dealings will in a commercial society certainly be greater than what would obtain within societies at earlier stages of development, which is consistent with the contention that a commercial society encourages more extensive natural affection and thence benevolence than is otherwise possible.

The question still remains whether Smith is right in claiming that benevolence extends with familiarity, but the resolution of that issue is not relevant to my argument here. Smith's conception of markets cannot be said to be hostile toward or make no room for benevolence. Indeed, correctly understood, Smithian markets would predict an extension of benevolence beyond what would take place in, for example, precommercial societies. Before extensive division of labor began to take place, individuals or families had to fend largely for themselves. One person or only a few persons would have to provide food, shelter, and clothing for himself or themselves, which would mean that each person would have to assume many different tasks. The predicted result would be, and was in fact, that most persons could not become expert in any single task, and the majority of each person's time was spent procuring the necessities for survival. Little time is left over to find more efficient means of production—not to mention to discover medicines, conduct scientific research, or write philosophy books. If people did not work to increase the efficiency of production, little or no produce was left after their own private consumption; with no surplus, there would be nothing to trade with others, and no markets would develop. Without the chance to exchange goods with others, people would tend not even to associate with many others.

Instead, they would rarely venture beyond the confines of their small group, tribe, or clan. Under these circumstances, their natural affection for others would not extend far; it would almost certainly not extend to people in groups, tribes, or clans other than their own. What Smith's model would predict, then, is what we in fact find in much of early human history: numberless squabbles and fighting between and among these small groups of people, a principal cause of which was mutual suspicion or fear based on mutual ignorance and a lack of mutual affection.

Smith's markets would tend to break down mutual suspicion and fear by creating mutual familiarity—not to mention the fact that peoples who trade or do business with each other want others as customers, which means they will tend not to want to kill or fight with them. People in market-based communities or societies are highly dependent on others to supply various of their needs; specialization and division of labor entail a commensurate level of mutual dependence. Moreover, as I have argued, people cannot succeed in markets unless they take an interest in others, which requires that they spend time getting to know others' needs and wants. Smith's argument suggests that this mutual familiarity will lead to mutual natural affection and hence benevolence. Thus even if benevolence does not play an explicit role in WN, I suggest that Smith's analysis in WN implies the expansion of benevolence by showing the connections between markets, familiarity, and natural affection. Whatever else one thinks about Smith's analysis in WN, then, one cannot accuse Smith of having made no room for benevolence, or of disallowing the possibility that what constitutes a great engine for increasing prosperity—the market—could only function if self-interest were the sole motivation people felt. TMS proves that Smith knew the importance of benevolence in human life, and, when rightly understood, WN provides a blueprint for taking our natural motivation in marketplaces, self-interest, and not only providing material prosperity by means of it but also creating the conditions that would be necessary to extend natural benevolence farther than it had extended before.

## Moral Deviancy

The second general observation I wish to make is to indicate what I consider to be an omission in Smith's theory, at least as he presents it.

Smith does not consider in any systematic fashion the phenomenon of moral deviancy. Smith speaks of vices, not just virtues, and of the crucial role of other people and the impartial spectator in correcting vicious behavior, both of which show that he was aware of human moral failings. But Smith seems to think that whatever morally deviant communities or subcommunities that might initially arise would not survive the competition for members that takes place in the marketplace of human society. He might account for the rare individual person who has no desire for mutual sympathy of sentiments as simply a freak of nature—that is, he could say that by some mistake of nature such people were not equipped with the proper innate gear that is necessary to live a successful human life. But what about those cases in which groups of people adopted, for example, systematically racist codes of morality? What do we make of contemporary inner-city gangs whose members seem to have an absolute dearth of the virtues of justice and benevolence? What about quasi-religious cults whose members eschew self-command and prudence in an effort to maximize their immediate pleasure? Or, to take a specific example, how do we explain the widespread practice among tribes of North American Indians by which the name they had for themselves is best translated as "people" or "human beings"—the implication being that if you were not a member of their tribe you were not truly human, and you could be (and often were) dealt with as with any subhuman beast?[11] The pages of history are suffused with the rapacity of countless leaders and groups of people who preach—and practice—systems of morality that are not consistent with Smith's description of the "universal" core of human morality, at least toward people not members of their own groups. Smith was well-enough versed in history to have been familiar with many such examples, but we find in TMS no explicit attempt to account for their presence. In a work that purports to investigate the actual, historical nature and development of human moral judging, this would seem to be a significant omission.

[11] Many, though not all, tribes' names for themselves are apparently best translated this way, including the names for the often bellicose Apaches and Navajos. See Sturtevant (1978–98). Professor Amy Dahlstrom of the University of Chicago tells me that these Smithsonian volumes contain the most reliable and complete information currently available.

The problem is compounded, I think, by the fact that Smith regards the unintentionally developed system of morality as a manifestation of the (benevolent) will of God. In addition, Smith considers to be innate and universal the various traits of human nature that he argued are necessary for this system of morality to develop. The combination of these two claims seems strongly to imply that a bad or evil system of morality could not develop. Yet systems that most would consider bad or evil have developed. And they were indeed *systems*, meaning that they obtained in communities of people, not just in the lives of scattered perverse individuals; sometimes these communities are quite small, but they are communities nonetheless. Moreover, among some of the members of some of these communities, it seems difficult to find the full package of natural passions and affections that Smith believed was universal. Let me cite an example with which Smith would surely have been familiar. Can one plausibly argue that, despite their often cruel and inhumane behavior, the turn-of-the-millennium Vikings were still endowed with an original aversion to breaches of the rules of justice? Or that they were endowed with an original desire to please and not offend others? The case of the Vikings would seem particularly difficult to account for on Smith's theory for two reasons. One, the system of morality that obtained among those Vikings who conducted the raids was likely the same system of morality that obtained among their family and friends back home, since successful raids were occasions for celebration and accolades for the returning men. Two, the Viking raids were not isolated, temporary events; they were executed along much of the European coastline and interior, particularly against the British, French, and Germanic peoples, for roughly three centuries.[12]

There is some discussion in Smith to which one could turn to address this matter. First, one possibly malignant unintended order

---

[12] One thing Vikings routinely did in their raids was leave infants for dead, often by killing or enslaving their parents. Consider that practice in light of Smith's discussion of infant exposition (TMS, 209–12), which he concludes thus: "There is an obvious reason why custom should never pervert our sentiments with regard to the general style and character of conduct and behaviour, in the same degree as with regard to the propriety or unlawfulness of particular usages. There can never be any such custom. No society could subsist a moment, in which the usual strain of men's conduct and behaviour was of a piece with the horrible practice I have just now mentioned [i.e., infant exposition]" (TMS, 211).

of morality of which Smith is aware is religious fanaticism and enthusiasm. In both TMS and WN Smith speaks of the dangers to which these phenomena can lead. In TMS, for example, Smith writes: "Of all the corrupters of moral sentiments, therefore, faction and fanaticism have always been the greatest" (TMS, 156). Later he writes: "False notions of religion are almost the only causes which can occasion any very gross perversion of our natural sentiments in this way" (TMS, 176).[13] Yet Smith gives no explanation for how such fanaticism can arise; he simply notes their existence and that they can corrupt the moral sentiments. Smith's discussion of the pernicious effects that overzealous religious devotion can have is lengthier in WN, however. One of the few tasks Smith thinks the state ought to undertake—though only partially—is that of providing a basic education for its citizens, one chiefly centering on teaching people to "read, write, and account" (WN, 785).[14] He offers several reasons why the state should attend to this task: having such workers increases efficiency in economic production, education expands the minds of workers who otherwise spend their days on one or a few simple tasks, and these abilities enable workers to better defend their countries in war.[15] An additional reason, however, is that Smith thinks that some education can soften the zealousness of religious sentiments—which he apparently thinks can, if left unchecked, lead to faction and instability.[16] Interestingly, he thinks that religious belief stands the best chance of leading to fanaticism when it is organized hierarchically, with doctrine established and promulgated by authorities and accepted uncritically by inferiors— as in the Catholic church.[17] The way to mitigate the fanaticism and

---

[13] See also TMS, 171, §1, and 176–78.

[14] Smith writes, "The publick can facilitate this acquisition [by its citizens of the abilities to read, write, and account] by establishing in every parish or district a little school, where children may be taught for a reward so moderate, that even a common labourer may afford it; the master being partly, but not wholly paid by the publick; because if he was wholly, or even principally paid by it, he would soon learn to neglect his business" (WN, 785). See also WN, 796, §14. Samuel Fleischacker makes an ambitious, though I think ultimately unconvincing, case that Smith thinks the state should provide a substantially richer education for its citizens than merely teaching them to read, write, and account. See Fleischacker (1999), especially Chapters 6–8. For discussion, see Otteson (forthcoming).

[15] See WN, 781–82.

[16] See WN, 788–814.

[17] See WN, 788–93.

enthusiasm to which this kind of religious organization can lead is twofold: first, by giving citizens an education that includes "the study of science and philosophy," which is "the great antidote to the poison of enthusiasm and superstition" (WN, 796); and second, by allowing a marketplace of religions. The state should take a neutral position with respect to religions, and let various sects compete for parishioners:

> The teachers of each sect, seeing themselves surrounded on all sides with more adversaries than friends, would be obliged to learn that candour and moderation which is so seldom to be found among the teachers of those great sects, whose tenets being supported by the civil magistrate, are held in veneration by almost all the inhabitants of extensive kingdoms and empires, and who therefore see nothing round them but followers, disciples, and humble admirers. (WN, 793)[18]

These discussions show that Smith is aware of groups of people whose codes of morality are shared but nevertheless destructive of other important political ends. Although Smith does not explicitly discuss how such groups could arise on his account of the development of shared moral standards, I think it is nevertheless possible to construct a "Smithian" explanation of them. Recall that a significant factor in the development of a community's system of morality is the external circumstances in which members of that community find themselves. I suggested in Chapter 6 that Smith's analysis of this process of development allows for—even predicts—the development of suborders in which protocols peculiar to smaller groups within the community obtain. These suborders share the central developmental characteristics of the overall order in that they too are constituted by unintentionally developed rules as the pertinent individuals seek to satisfy their interests. What distinguishes the suborders from the overall order and from each other is the narrower scope and unique nature of the interests they unfold to serve. I gave as an example the accepted protocols and practices of college professors in their dealings with their colleagues. Since not everyone is a professor, and since professors have special interests in their capacities as professors, we should expect to find that the protocols governing their interactions would reflect in some way the temperament and circumstances peculiar and unique to

---

[18] For a good discussion of this issue, see Griswold (1997).

professors.[19] And I think this is what we do find: there are various un-written rules about how to dress and not to dress, how to refer to and to address one another, and so on. There are perhaps indefinitely many such subgroups within a large-scale society, each having a share of pro-tocols peculiar to it. Of course, many of these groups will overlap—each of us turns in many circles in society—and hence their peculiar system of protocols will in the main be the same as most others; nonetheless a careful observer could no doubt distinguish many separate groups whose special protocols make their precise characterization unique. The Smithian story that one could tell about moral deviancy would, I think, be spun out of this feature of Smith's theory.

Smith argued that our natural affection for others is dependent on our familiarity with them, and that hence benevolence, which depends on natural affection, is also an extension of this familiarity principle. He also thought that both people and societies are naturally recom-mended to our care and attention to a gradually lessening degree as the persons or societies in question recede from us. Now, although Smith sometimes writes as though our universal desire for mutual sympathy of sentiments is indifferent as to the person with whose sentiments one achieves a sympathy,[20] I think we might instead be warranted in holding that a mutual sympathy with certain people will be more im-portant to us than a mutual sympathy with others. It seems that on Smith's account there would be more superficial and more profound sympathies, depending on the degree to which the spectator is familiar with the full extent of the agent's situation, and the degree to which the agent understands the position from which the spectator judges him. The fuller and more sensitive a spectator's knowledge of an agent's sit-uation, and the fuller and more sensitive the agent's knowledge of his spectator's perspective, the more extensive or the deeper or the more complete will the resultant sympathy be. Perfectly complete sympathy is not possible on Smith's account because the totality of each person's experience is unique and private to him alone; nevertheless, some ac-tual sympathies will be nearer to this ideal than others. One would thus have a better chance of achieving a deeper sympathy when one

---

[19] See TMS, 34.
[20] See TMS, 34, §1; 235, §1; and 237, §6.

is in the company of people with whom one is more familiar, and the relative chance varies directly with the level of familiarity. Given the strength of the desire for mutual sympathy, what seems to follow is that we will tend to concentrate our efforts for the achievement of sympathy on those who mean most to us, probably in most cases our family and friends, leading us to act on and adopt not only the core elements of the universal system of morality but also those finer elements that are peculiar to the groups constituted by our closest compatriots. The people that mean most to us, then, would, of all the external factors, have the largest influence on us.[21]

When one considers the vast number of groups into which people formally and informally organize themselves, it does not seem implausible to think that there might spontaneously arise in some of them bizarre or perverse ideas that could in time develop into bizarre or perverse protocols, practices, or behaviors. These practices would be confined to members of the group in question, but their existence within the group could become self-enforcing, each member of the group acting as an encouragement to the other members. If the members of a particular group become especially fond of one another, which frequent association with one another will foster, they could come to prize sympathy with fellow members above sympathy with others, leading them, in turn, to organize more and more of their lives around the practices of the group. In such a case, the desire for mutual sympathy could act like a centripetal force, pulling members in ever more tightly. In this way a subgroup of a community could gradually splinter off from the rest of the community and come to separate itself not only from the less important details of the community's general system of morality but even, perhaps, from the core of its morality.[22]

---

[21] This goes some way, I think, toward answering Eugene Heath's worries that Smith's reliance on the desire for mutual sympathy of sentiments is not enough to generate common standards of behavior and moral judgment because, as Heath argues, one's efforts would simply be dissipated as one attempted to achieve a mutual sympathy of sentiments with everyone one encountered. See Heath (1995). See also the discussion of Heath in Chapter 3.

[22] This last might conflict, however, with Smith's contention that "the sentiments of moral approbation and disapprobation, are founded on the strongest and most vigorous passions of human nature; and though they may be somewhat warpt, cannot be entirely perverted" (TMS, 200).

The result would be a group possessing a system of morality of its own—a system that developed in the fashion Smith describes but that in time would tend to suppress or redirect certain impulses of human nature (for example, channeling our natural, general abhorrence of injustice to abhorrence of injustice only under certain conditions or only toward certain people). In other words, the result would be a group resembling those I gave as examples earlier.

I suggest that this account constitutes what would be a Smithian explanation of the existence of morally deviant groups. Smith explicitly speaks, for example, of the peculiar "habits of imagination" that people tend to develop, habits that are brought about in accordance with the peculiar circles in which one turns in one's community and that make it difficult for others outside those circles to achieve sympathy with one: "A philosopher is company to a philosopher only; the member of a club, to his own little knot of companions" (TMS, 34); "The objects with which men in the different professions and states of life are conversant, being very different, and habituating them to very different passions, naturally form in them very different characters and manners" (TMS, 201).[23] In addition, Smith's discussion of the virtue that is peculiarly applicable to the "prudent man" (TMS, 212–17), of the virtue that is peculiarly applicable to the "great" man as opposed to that of the "man of inferior rank" (TMS, 50–57), and of the "two different roads" to virtue presented to those in "the superior stations of life" as opposed to those in "the middling and inferior stations of life" (TMS, 61–66) both underscore Smith's appreciation of the fact that one's circumstances affect one's proper behavior in important ways. Finally, his remarks about the notions of justice that obtain among bands of robbers and murderers (TMS, 86) again suggest that he acknowledges not only that there are groups of morally deviant people, but that within those groups there will be peculiar systems of morality determining what is "just" and "unjust."[24] Taken in consideration with the account given earlier of the way Smithian sympathy will operate to create and maintain groups of people who are familiar with one another, I believe that despite the fact that Smith

---

[23] See also TMS, 223–24 and 230.
[24] The case of the robbers' justice is an example of the general abhorrence of injustice having been narrowed to an abhorrence of injustice only within the relevant group.

has no explicit discussion of moral deviancy, his theory nonetheless allows for a plausible story to be told in that regard along the lines I have sketched.

The principal problem that this Smithian account seems unable to resolve is that concerning the length of time some of these groups have survived—even flourished—within their morally deviant systems. The Vikings raided, raped, and pillaged for some 300 years. To be consistent with Smith's theory, the morally deviant systems of morality would presumably have to die out. Smith's argument that the system of morality develops like a market does not, as I am suggesting, preclude the possibility of moral deviancy arising, just as economic markets do not preclude the possibility of people engaging in immoral or fraudulent practices; Smith's argument does imply, however, that marketplaces of both the moral and economic type will in the long run tend to reward or encourage the development and enforcement of rules of behavior that conduce to the ultimate benefit of individuals and society generally, and that they will discourage disutilitarian rules and behavior. The implication is that morally deviant groups, whose codes of morality would presumably not be conducive to overall human happiness in the long run, would eventually lose members and thus die out—whereas morally proper groups would survive and flourish. The question becomes, then, how long is "in the long run"? For most such groups, Smith's prediction that their runs would be short-lived is probably correct. But what about the Vikings? Three hundred years seems like a long time—would Smith argue that it was not enough? Would he argue that we must instead take a five-hundred-year sweep of history? A one-thousand-year sweep? Would his argument assert, then, that no deviant system of morality could last more than one thousand years, that by at least that time such systems will prove to be antagonistic to overall welfare and hence will vanish? This issue now opens up into many questions that we cannot address here.[25] In any case Smith's argument would seem to predict that, though they would no doubt periodically be tried out and would perhaps even gain some ground in an open marketplace of morals, morally deviant systems of

---

[25] Perhaps it is telling that the Vikings eventually settled down, were largely Christianized, and became relatively peaceful farmers and traders by about 1100 A.D. See Jones (1984).

morality—which would not conduce to the overall, long-term utility even of the members of the group in question, let alone to that of the larger community—would not survive in the competition for effective and efficient rules of behavior.

How long this process would take, however, and whether groups like the Vikings constitute counterexamples to Smith's argument are questions that cannot be answered without further investigation, as well as some speculation. It would need to be determined, for example, whether the Vikings (or other groups in question) were in fact happy in Smith's sense, what in fact led to the development of their system of morality, and what in fact led to their ultimate demise. It was for this reason that I said that Smith's not having discussed moral deviancy was a failing of his theory "as he presented it": Smith's own mentioning of the possibility of morally deviant groups indicates his awareness of their existence; and though I have constructed what I think is a plausibly "Smithian" account of them, he should have addressed the matter himself. Its importance makes his failure to do so a significant omission.

## III. Some Suggestive Recent Evidence

There is some recent evidence that suggests that human beings might indeed have some of the innate equipment Smith thought they did, which tends to support at least part of Smith's overall argument. Sociologist James Q. Wilson has recently brought together data from a diverse range of studies that collectively seem to indicate that human beings have what Wilson calls a natural "moral sense."[26] Wilson argues that the evidence he has collected warrants this conclusion:

man has a moral sense, one that emerges as naturally as his sense of beauty or ritual (with which morality has much in common) and that will affect his behavior, though not always and in some cases not obviously. The moral "sense" exists in two meanings of the word: First, virtually everyone, beginning at a very young age, makes moral judgments that, though they may vary greatly in complexity, sophistication, and wisdom, distinguish between actions on the grounds that some are right and others are wrong, and virtually everyone

[26] Wilson (1993). All Wilson citations are to this book, on the page given in parentheses.

recognizes that for these distinctions to be persuasive to others they must be, or at least appear to be, disinterested. Second, virtually everyone, beginning at a very young age, acquires a set of social habits that we ordinarily find pleasing in others and satisfying when we practice them ourselves. (25)

Wilson's argument is that empirical evidence shows that people all over the world and at all times have endorsed certain common virtues, including principally what he calls "sympathy," "fairness," "self-control," and "duty." Though not everyone acts on these virtues, it is nonetheless the case, Wilson argues, that virtually all communities formally endorse them. Because these virtues seem to transcend time and place, Wilson concludes that they cannot plausibly be explained by reference to various communities' environmental or external factors. Rather, one must instead conclude that human beings have a natural or innate predisposition to sentiments and behaviors that reflect these virtues. What is of interest here is that several of the sentiments and behaviors that Wilson claims to be "virtually" universal correspond in significant ways with the virtues that Smith argued were the universal result of the unintended development of the impartial spectator perspective. Let us look at two in particular, Wilson's "sympathy" and "self-control."

Wilson's notion of sympathy comprehends two senses of the word, namely, pity or compassion, on the one hand, and having the same sentiments as another person, on the other. He includes the second sense of sympathy with explicit, favorable reference to Smith and to TMS.[27] Wilson claims that recent evidence suggests that Smith was right to think that we are naturally inclined to take an interest in the fortune of others, if by that we mean that we have a natural "capacity for being affected by the feelings and experiences of others" (30). Studies show, for example, that people tend to feel distress when witnessing the plight of another, and that this distress tends to prompt them to help that other. The motive to help is not universal, however, and it varies with circumstances—when people estimate that the cost of their help will be high, or when they believe that others will provide the necessary assistance, for example, they tend to help less (36–37). Nevertheless, the dozens of studies Wilson cites suggest that human

---

[27] Ibid., 31–34 and passim.

beings are naturally, or innately, or simply without thinking about it, affected to bring the sentiments of others home to themselves, a process that frequently moves them to act.[28] Wilson goes on to argue that the near universality of the human capacity for sympathy suggests that it is biologically innate in us, and he provides a scheme of human evolution by which nature might have selected for humans with this trait because it increased its possessors' fitness and hence chances for survival. I wrote in Chapter 6 that Smith had no notion of natural selection for biological traits, so on that count Wilson's argument goes beyond Smith's. But in important respects, the evidence Wilson presents about a natural capacity for fellow-feeling supports Smith's account. Wilson even cites evidence suggesting that the human ability to sympathize with another is increased or decreased according to one's familiarity with the other in question (46–50)—which, if true, would be a striking confirmation of Smith's familiarity principle.

By "self-control," Wilson tells us he means the everyday notion of controlling one's impulse to pursue an "immediate pleasure" in order to pursue "a more distant one that is of greater value"; he means roughly, he says, what Aristotle meant by "temperance" (80). Wilson argues that the belief that one ought to control immediate impulses— that is, the belief that it is morally good or morally required to do so—is another virtually universal human commonplace. Although researchers have given less attention to the source of this belief than they have, for example, to the sources of sympathy and altruism, Wilson says that the attention paid to people who *lack* this capacity is just as telling. His argument is that the fact that few researchers look into this phenomenon is a symptom of its universal nature; it is such a commonplace that people do not seem even to notice it. On the other hand, researchers do pay a great deal of serious attention to its absence, indicating once again, though indirectly, its universality (85–88). The absence of what researchers call "appropriate" self-control[29] in children, for example, was once called "hyperactivity" and

---

[28] See ibid., Chapter 2.
[29] A Smithian might be inclined to see the work of an impartial spectator, determining the propriety of sentiments and behaviors, implicit in researchers' use of terms like "appropriate" and "inappropriate."

is now called "attention deficit disorder." It has three main characteristics, all of which have been and continue to be thoroughly canvassed
by researchers:

inattention (failing to finish tasks, being easily distracted, not listening, not
concentrating), impulsivity (acting before thinking, not waiting one's turn,
unreasonably shifting from one task to another, requiring constant supervi-
sion), and hyperactivity (fidgeting, running about, restlessness, and difficulty
sitting still). (86)

Batteries of studies have been conducted concerning the suspected
hormonal bases of self-control and attention deficit disorder, on the
kinds of adults that children with "inappropriate" self-control or attention deficit disorder become, of the connections between crime
and lack of self-control, and so on.[30] Wilson argues that the unstated
assumptions on which all these studies operate are that normal adults
are expected to have self-control and that self-control is a good thing.
What is interesting about these assumptions is their normative content, especially in what is often considered "value-free" scientific inquiry. We think of people who are unable to control their appetites
as lacking self-control, and we generally disapprove of this lack. But
why? As Wilson asks, is being thin morally superior to being fat? Similarly, we generally disapprove of people who are sexually promiscuous
as (perhaps among other things) lacking self-control—and we do so
even if we cannot specify why self-control is a good thing. Nevertheless
we believe it is.

Although studies suggest that, owing to the differing natural dispositions people have, self-control is easier for some people than it is for
others, Wilson argues that the preponderance of evidence nevertheless
indicates that being surrounded by people of resolute character is the
best antidote to impulsivity. For example, those hyperactive children
whose parents are "affectionate, consistent, and firm" had the best
statistical chance of all hyperactive children of learning the proper
measure of self-control (90). And the best chance that irresolute or
incontinent adults have of gaining self-control or temperance is being
in the company of people who both manifest those virtues and rebuke

[30] See Wilson (1993), Chapter 4, especially 86–90.

others for their lack of it.[31] As was the case with sympathy, Wilson tells an evolutionary story about why mankind value self-control, and why they seem to approve of self-control instinctively. He suggests that

one might suspect that evolution has selected for people who can take a longer view of their own interests and against those who rush headlong into every situation. Our moral approval of self-control would then reflect the fact that, on the whole, social arrangements are made better if society is composed of people who can keep their appetites under reasonable control. (97–98)

Wilson thinks that the actual evolutionary process was probably more complicated than this—he suspects in particular that impulsivity under certain conditions might well have been selected for in earlier stages in mankind's development—but I do not wish to evaluate the plausibility of his evolutionary argument here. Instead I wish merely to point out how similar his argument is to that of Smith's concerning the process of developing moral standards. Smith's "self-command," which is quite similar to Wilson's "self-control," develops as a result of, on the one hand, one's natural instinct to care most about oneself and one's own desires or interests, and, on the other, the inability of others to enter into one's sentiments when one acts solely out of concern for oneself. According to Smith, the desire for mutual sympathy of sentiments encourages people to temper their concern for themselves, which in practice will mean moderating many of their impulsive passions, so that people who do not have the same passions—who, that is, judge from an impartial perspective—may enter into their sentiments and hence approve of them. In broad outlines, this is the same analysis Wilson gives.

I do not claim that Wilson's study proves that Smith's analysis of sympathy and self-command was right. Indeed, Wilson himself cautions that in most cases the evidence is only suggestive or indicative, not decisive. And in any case many of Wilson's conclusions are controversial. But the amount of contemporary sociological evidence that exists that

---

[31] Compare this passage from Smith: "The mind, therefore, is rarely so disturbed, but that the company of a friend will restore it to some degree of tranquillity and sedateness.... Society and conversation, therefore, are the most powerful remedies for restoring the mind to its tranquillity, if, at any time, it has unfortunately lost it; as well as the best preservatives of that equal and happy temper, which is so necessary to self-satisfaction and enjoyment" (TMS, 22–23). See also TMS, 153–54 and 207.

supports some of Smith's central claims is, I believe, intriguing. The entire second half of Wilson's book, for example, argues that a community's long-standing moral standards—which Wilson, like Smith, believes will always center around a single, universal core of common morality—are the result of a slow, gradual interplay between features innate in human nature and the circumstances in which individuals find themselves. One's family life is the principal external influence on one's moral character and on the content of one's mature moral judgments, Wilson argues (141–63), and the principal fact about human nature that drives the development of moral standards is that man "is by nature a social animal," by which Wilson seems partly to mean that human beings have an innate desire for something like Smith's mutual sympathy of sentiments (123–33). His argument thus occupies the same middle ground that I argued Smith's theory occupied, namely, that which argues that both "nature" and "nurture" are necessary elements in the development of the human system of morality. Moreover, two of the sentiments that Wilson argues are natural, which he calls "fairness" and "duty," together approximate Smith's single virtue of justice: the former encompassing the sense that one must respect the persons and property of others just as one would like them to do for oneself, the latter entailing the sense that one ought to keep one's promises and honor one's obligations. Once again, Wilson gives an evolutionary explanation for why a sense of fairness and a sense of duty are virtually universal features of human communities and individuals, and again his explanation includes both necessary elements of human nature and contingent elements of people's surroundings.

Although Wilson's study lends credence to some of what Smith said, then, I do not pretend that these matters are thereby settled. As Wilson says, much work would still need to be done before the empirical case supporting Wilson's (or Smith's) conception of human nature would be convincing—especially when some deny that there is any such thing as an identifiable human nature at all.[32] But I introduced

---

[32] I should point out that many other people argue similarly for certain innate features of human nature. For a classic account, see Wilson (1978). For more recent accounts, see Hocutt (2000), Waal (1996), and Wright (1994). Another recent study that explicitly draws on Smith is Ridley (1996). See also Khalil (1997, 2000) and Lal (1998).

Wilson's work also for another reason. When studying thinkers of the past, even the great ones, we tend sometimes to see them only as historical figures, and hence we tend to view their work as of only historical interest. But the larger project of a scholar should always be to see what others got right, to see what is true in what they said, so that he can incorporate that into his own view of the world; gaining a correct understanding of what others said is thus only a means, though a necessary one, to that ultimate end. Adam Smith was in many respects one of that small group of people who was able to see farther than the ordinary run of thinkers. He was, as Robert Heilbroner put it, one of the "worldly philosophers."[33] Wilson's work, along with that of many other sociobiologists, underscores that.

## IV. Adam Smith and "Spontaneous" Order

Ronald Hamowy begins his short monograph *The Scottish Enlightenment and the Theory of the Spontaneous Order* in this way: "Perhaps the single most significant sociological contribution made by that group of writers whom we today regard as constituting the Scottish Enlightenment is the notion of spontaneously generated social orders."[34] Of all the Enlightenment thinkers one would include in this group—Hamowy discusses Bernard Mandeville (who was not, strictly speaking, part of the Scottish Enlightenment but did greatly influence it), David Hume, Adam Smith, Adam Ferguson, Lord Kames, Gilbert Stuart, Thomas Reid, John Millar, and Dugald Stewart—this statement is especially true, I believe, of Adam Smith. Each of these thinkers made use to varying extents of the notion that larger systems of order could arise spontaneously or unintentionally as the joint product of the actions or decisions of people whose individual interests concern only local matters. But Smith stands out among them in two respects. First, Smith saw that this conception of the development of certain institutions might constitute an account of human institutions generally. Smith's examination in TMS not only shows that moral standards and the system

---

[33] Heilbroner (1953), 42–74.

[34] Hamowy (1987), 3. An intriguing contemporary account of the genesis and development of "spontaneous" orders is given by University of Michigan computer scientist John Holland (1996).

of morality of which they are a part constitute just such a system of unintended order, but it also, as I have argued, provides a theoretical framework sufficient to extend this conception to every kind of human association and institution. Thus, as I argued in Chapter 7, the marketplace of human institutions is not limited to economic institutions (as it largely is in Mandeville) or to isolated aspects of morality (such as our sense of justice, as in Hume), but rather it is generalized to form the foundational understanding of the overall development and evolution of human social institutions generally. Second, Smith saw the scope of this model's explanatory power before anyone else. Although the notion of unintended order was in existence before TMS's first appearance in 1759, those earlier appearances are not systematic and do not reveal a full understanding of the power of this notion. Adam Ferguson, whose *Essay on the History of Civil Society* appeared just eight years after the first edition of TMS, is perhaps the first person after Smith to apply this notion generally, arguing as he does that human social development is entirely the result of unintended consequences of individual actions.[35] But Ferguson's account is incomplete because it does not contain an analysis of human psychology that could explain why people form the associations they do. Moreover, he provides only a summary account of its workings in specifically economic arenas. Dugald Stewart is probably the only other member of the group who worked out a theory of spontaneous order with thoroughness and care, but his work did not begin to appear until after Smith's death. Thus Smith should, I suggest, be considered the pioneering thinker in the Scottish Enlightenment's important contributions to sociological thought.

I accordingly think Smith's most important contribution to specifically moral philosophy is his idea that moral judgments and moral standards ultimately reflect an evolutionary system of order that was unintentionally created by individuals. In the twentieth century Friedrich Hayek popularized Michael Polanyi's term "spontaneous order" to describe this phenomenon,[36] but as far as I know he does not address specifically moral concerns with his notion of spontaneous

---

[35] Ferguson (1995 [1767]). Smith apparently accused Ferguson of plagiarizing from him. See Rae (1895), 65.

[36] See, for example, Hayek (1960).

order, perhaps because he seems to think that moral truths, like geo-
metrical truths, are transcendent and not subject to an evolutionary
development. This points towards what I think is one of the most
promising features of Smith's moral theory: its union of, on the one
hand, a kind of Burkean conservatism, which tends towards the stability
of society, with, on the other hand, a respect for progressive development, which allows for creativity and innovation in society. An implication of Smith's theory is that it is strongly antirationalist, meaning
principally two things. First, it would deny that moral rules are the products of pure, unaided reason. The rules of morality are instead inductive generalizations on the basis of innumerable particular instances of
behavior and judgment. Second, because of the vast range of human
activity that the moral rules cover, there will inevitably be individual
situations in which no single person can see a rational justification
for the rule that applies—despite the fact that his compliance with
this rule will be expected by everyone familiar with the situation
(including, probably, himself) and that noncompliance would be
roundly criticized. This point indicates what I mean by saying that
Smith's theory contains an element of Burkean conservatism. Because
the general rules of morality are the product of so many people
whose individual experiences are collectively beyond the capacity of
any one of them to know or fully comprehend, these rules, as I argued
in Chapter 6, embody a wisdom necessarily greater than that of any
one individual. Unless there is clear and compelling reason to the
contrary, then, the standing practical rule of good conduct will be to
follow the traditional rules of morality. A community's or society's established moral rules thus enjoy a presumptive authority that cannot
be, or at least ought not to be, trumped merely by an individual's not
understanding why the rule in question exists or by his inability to
construct an a priori argument requiring compliance. I think this is
the essence of Burke's belief that the established customs, protocols,
and mores of a society should be trusted and respected except under
the most extraordinary circumstances.[37]

If Smith is right that moral rules develop by incorporating the
wisdom and experience of many people, then an allegiance to the

---

[37] See Burke (1982 [1757], 1987 [1789–90]). For discussion of Smith's Burkeanism,
see Winch (1978), 24 and passim.

moral traditions of one's community—what one might call a moral conservatism—would seem the reasonable course to follow. But this kind of moral conservatism stands open to the following objection. It would seem that these moral rules would be applicable or relevant only to those people who, first, have the same "nature" as those among whom the rules unintentionally developed, and, second, to those whose environmental or external circumstances are the same as that of those among whom the rules developed. For those people for whom these two assumptions are not true, however, it would seem that their allegiance is properly paid to a different set of rules, namely, those that developed within their own community. Cultural moral relativists like Ruth Benedict have made just such arguments to support their contention that people ought, as it were, to mind their own moral business.[38] Smith's argument responds to this objection by contending that it does not fully understand the nature of human moral standards. Smithian antirationalism and moral conservatism do not imply that a society's established moral rules are absolutely, transcendently true or that they are beyond scrutiny. Indeed, the very notion of these rules *developing* implies rather that they are in constant states of modification or emendation. In this way Smith thinks there is always progress and innovation in human society, though specifically moral progress is slow and gradual. Hence no person or society can claim absolute certainty that its rules are the only correct ones. But that is not the end of the story, as Smith sees it. Human society is in continual progress, but progress toward what? In relation to the development of its moral standards, Smith's answer is toward general human happiness—and this suggests a criterion against which to judge not only our own behavior and practices but also that of others. Do those practices adhere to general rules that conduce to our overall happiness? If they do not, they are immoral; if they do, they are not immoral. A particular community's established practices would enjoy the same presumptive authority as those of any other community, but if one community has already tried out a set of practices and found them inefficient or unproductive of human happiness, or if one community's customs were generally more conducive to its members' happiness, it would be in a

---

[38] See Benedict (1989 [1934]). For philosophical accounts, see Gauthier (1986) and Mackie (1991 [1977]).

position to criticize another community for adopting the set of practices in question. Again, no practices or rules of behavior would be immune from criticism, but with a common ultimate end in mind, relative cross-cultural criticisms would be possible.

Now this argument presupposes something that, as I have mentioned, not everyone is willing to concede: a common human nature. Smith certainly thought that was the case, and recent studies like James Wilson's support his belief; but this is nevertheless a large and controversial question. So perhaps the best we can say here is that Smith's theory is a coherent description of a universal system of morality appropriate to people whose nature is approximated by Smith's plausible descriptions. This is no small accomplishment.

# Bibliography

Anspach, Ralph. "The Implications of the *Theory of Moral Sentiments* for Adam Smith's Economic Thought." *History of Political Economy* 4 (1972): 176–206.

Árdal, P. S. *Passion and Value in Hume's* Treatise. Edinburgh: Edinburgh University Press, 1966.

Benedict, Ruth. *Patterns of Culture* (1934). Boston: Houghton Mifflin, 1989.

Berkeley, George (Bishop). *The Principles of Human Knowledge* (1710). In *Berkeley's Philosophical Writings*, David M. Armstrong, ed. New York: Macmillan, 1965.

Berlin, Isaiah. *Four Essays on Liberty*. Oxford: Oxford University Press, 1969.

Berry, Christopher J. "Adam Smith's *Considerations* on Language." *Journal of the History of Ideas* 35 (1974): 130–38.

–*Social Theory of the Scottish Enlightenment*. Edinburgh: Edinburgh University Press, 1997.

Bethel, Tom. *The Noblest Triumph: Property and Prosperity through the Ages*. New York: St. Martin's, 1998.

Birzer, Bradley J. "Expansive Creative Destruction: Entrepreneurship in the American Wests." *Western Historical Quarterly* 30, 1 (Spring 1999): 45–63.

Blaug, Mark. *Economic Theory in Retrospect*, 5th ed. Cambridge: Cambridge University Press, 1996.

Bonar, James. *Catalogue of Adam Smith's Library* (1894). New York: Augustus M. Kelley, 1966.

Booth, William J. "On the Idea of the Moral Economy." *American Political Science Review* 88, 3 (September 1994): 653–67.

Brown, Vivienne. *Adam Smith's Discourse: Canonicity, Commerce and Conscience*. London: Routledge, 1994.

–"'Mere Inventions of the Imagination': A Survey of Recent Literature on Adam Smith." *Economics and Philosophy* 13 (1997): 281–312.

Brugman, Karl. "Der Nominalgeschlect in den indogermanischen Sprachen." *Internationale Zeitschrift für Allgemeine Sprachwissenschaft* 4 (1888): 101–104.

Burke, Edmund. *Reflections on the Revolution in France* (1789–90). J. G. A. Pocock, ed. Indianapolis: Hackett, 1987.

–*A Vindication of Natural Society* (1757). Frank N. Pagano, ed. Indianapolis: Liberty Classics, 1982.

Campbell, T. D. *Adam Smith's Science of Morals*. London: Allen and Unwin, 1971.

Cannan, Edwin, ed. *Lectures on Justice, Police, Revenue and Arms, delivered in the University of Glasgow by Adam Smith*. Oxford: Oxford University Press, 1896.

Coase, Ronald H. "Adam Smith's View of Man." *Journal of Law and Economics* 19 (1976): 538–39.

Cohen, G. A. *Self-Ownership, Freedom, and Equality*. Cambridge: Cambridge University Press, 1995.

Copley, Stephen, and Sutherland, Kathryn, eds. *Adam Smith and the "Wealth of Nations": New Interdisciplinary Essays*. Manchester: Manchester University Press, 1995.

Cropsey, Joseph. *Polity and Economy: An Interpretation of the Principles of Adam Smith*. Martinus Nijhoff: The Hague, 1957.

Cudworth, Ralph. *A Treatise Concerning Eternal and Immutable Morality* (1731). In *British Moralists 1650–1800*, D. D. Raphael, ed. Indianapolis: Hackett, 1991.

Danford, John W. *David Hume and the Problem of Reason*. New Haven: Yale University Press, 1990.

Dear, I. C. B. *Oxford English*. Oxford: Oxford University Press, 1986.

Den Uyl, Douglas J., and Griswold, Charles L., Jr. "Adam Smith on Friendship and Love." *Review of Metaphysics* 49 (March 1996): 609–37.

Diamond, Jared. *Guns, Germs, and Steel: The Fates of Human Societies*. New York: W. W. Norton, 1997.

Dickey, Laurence. "Historicizing the 'Adam Smith Problem': Conceptual, Historiographical, and Textual Issues." *Journal of Modern History* 58 (September 1986): 579–609.

Dollar, David, and Kraay, Aart. "Growth *Is* Good for the Poor." Washington, DC: World Bank, 2001. Available at http://www.worldbank.org/research/growth/pdfiles/growthgoodforpoor.pdf.

Dupuy, Jean-Pierre. "A Reconsideration of *Das Adam Smith Problem*." *Stanford French Review* 17, 1 (1993): 45–57.

Etzioni, Amitai. *The New Golden Rule: Community and Morality in a Democratic Society*. New York: Basic Books, 1998.

–ed. *New Communitarian Thinking: Persons, Virtues, and Communities*. Charlottesville: University of Virginia Press, 1995.

Ferguson, Adam. *An Essay on the History of Civil Society* (1767). New Brunswick, NJ: Transaction, 1995.

Firth, Roderick. "Ethical Absolutism and the Ideal Observer." *Philosophy and Phenomenological Research* 12, 3 (March 1952): 317–45.

Fitzgibbons, Athol. *Adam Smith's System of Liberty, Wealth, and Virtue: The Moral and Political Foundations of* The Wealth of Nations. Oxford: Oxford University Press, 1995.

Fleischacker, Samuel. "Philosophy in Moral Practice: Kant and Adam Smith." *Kant-Studien* 82 (1991): 249–69.

–*A Third Concept of Liberty: Judgment and Freedom in Kant and Adam Smith.* Princeton, NJ: Princeton University Press, 1999.

Fogel, Robert W. *The Fourth Great Awakening and the Future of Egalitarianism.* Chicago: University of Chicago Press, 2000.

Gauthier, David. *Morals by Agreement.* Oxford: Clarendon Press, 1986.

Griswold, Charles L., Jr. *Adam Smith and the Virtues of Enlightenment.* Cambridge: Cambridge University Press, 1999.

–"Religion and Community: Adam Smith on the Virtues of Liberty." *Journal of the History of Philosophy* 35, 3 (July 1997): 395–419.

Gwartney, J., Lawson, R., and Samida, D. *Economic Freedom of the World.* Victoria, BC: The Fraser Institute, 2000. Available at http://www. freetheworld.com/release.html.

Haakonssen, Knud. *The Cambridge Companion to Adam Smith.* Cambridge: Cambridge University Press, forthcoming.

–*Natural Law and Moral Philosophy: From Grotius to the Scottish Enlightenment.* Cambridge: Cambridge University Press, 1996.

–*The Science of a Legislator: The Natural Jurisprudence of David Hume and Adam Smith.* Cambridge: Cambridge University Press, 1981.

Hamowy, Ronald. *The Scottish Enlightenment and the Theory of Spontaneous Order.* Carbondale, IL: Southern Illinois University Press, 1987.

Hayek, F. A. von. *The Constitution of Liberty.* Chicago: University of Chicago Press, 1960.

–*The Counter-Revolution in Science: Studies on the Abuse of Reason.* Indianapolis: Liberty Press, 1979.

Hazlitt, Henry. *The Foundations of Morality* (1964). Irvington-on-Hudson, NY: Foundation for Economic Education, 1994.

Heath, Eugene. "The Commerce of Sympathy: Adam Smith on the Emergence of Morals." *Journal of the History of Philosophy* 33, 3 (July 1995): 447–66.

Heilbroner, Robert L. *The Worldly Philosophers.* New York: Simon & Schuster, 1953.

Hildebrand, Bruno. *Die Nationalökonomie der Gegenwart und Zukunft.* Jena: G. Fischer, 1848.

Hocutt, Max. *Grounded Ethics: The Empirical Bases of Normative Judgments.* New Brunswick, NJ: Transaction, 2000.

Holland, John. *Hidden Order: How Adaptation Builds Complexity.* New York: Addison-Wesley, 1996.

Hollander, Samuel. *The Economics of Adam Smith.* Toronto: University of Toronto, 1973.

Hull, David. *Science as a Process.* Chicago: University of Chicago Press, 1988.

Hume, David. "Of Commerce." In *Essays, Moral, Political, and Literary,* Eugene F. Miller, ed. Indianapolis: Liberty Press, 1987.

–*Dialogues Concerning Natural Religion* (1779). Richard H. Popkin, ed. 2nd ed. Indianapolis: Hackett, 1998.
–*An Enquiry Concerning Human Understanding* (1748). Eric Steinberg, ed. Indianapolis: Hackett, 1977.
–*An Enquiry Concerning the Principles of Morals* (1751). J. B. Schneewind, ed. Indianapolis: Hackett, 1983.
–*History of England* (1778). Indianapolis: Liberty Classics, 1983.
–"Of the Origin of Government." In *Essays, Moral, Political, and Literary*, Eugene F. Miller, ed. Indianapolis: Liberty Press, 1987.
–"Of the Original Contract." In *Essays, Moral, Political, and Literary*, Eugene F. Miller, ed. Indianapolis: Liberty Press, 1987.
–"Of Taxes." In *Essays, Moral, Political, and Literary*, Eugene F. Miller, ed. Indianapolis: Liberty Press, 1987.
–*A Treatise of Human Nature* (1739–40). L. A. Selby-Bigge, ed. 2nd ed., with rev. text and notes by P. H. Nidditch. Oxford: Oxford University Press, 1978.
Hutcheson, Francis. *Illustrations upon the Moral Sense* (1728). In *British Moralists 1650–1800*, D. D. Raphael, ed. Indianapolis: Hackett, 1991.
–*Inquiry Concerning Moral Good and Evil* (1725). In *British Moralists 1650–1800*, D. D. Raphael, ed. Indianapolis: Hackett, 1991.
Jones, Gwyn. *A History of the Vikings*. Oxford: Oxford University Press, 1984.
Keller, Rudi. *On Language Change: The Invisible Hand in Language*. London and New York: Routledge, 1994.
Khalil, Elias L. "Beyond Natural Selection and Divine Intervention: The Lamarckian Implication of Adam Smith's Invisible Hand." *Journal of Evolutionary Economics* 10 (2000): 373–93.
–"Evolutionary Biology and Evolutionary Economics." *Journal of Interdisciplinary Economics* 8, 4 (1997): 221–44.
Kleer, Richard A. "Final Causes in Adam Smith's *Theory of Moral Sentiments*." *Journal of the History of Philosophy* 33 (April 1995): 275–300.
Knies, Carl G. A. *Die Politische Oekonomie vom Standpunkte der geschichtlichen Methode*. Braunschweig: C. S. Schwetschke, 1853.
Lal, Deepak. *Unintended Consequences*. Cambridge, MA: MIT Press, 1998.
Land, Stephen K. "Adam Smith's 'Considerations concerning the First Formation of Languages.'" *Journal of the History of Ideas* 38 (1977): 677–90.
Landes, David S. *The Wealth and Poverty of Nations: Why Some Are So Rich and Some Are So Poor*. New York: W. W. Norton, 1999.
Livingston, Donald W. *Hume's Philosophy of Common Life*. Chicago: University of Chicago Press, 1984.
Locke, John. *An Essay Concerning Human Understanding* (1700). Peter H. Nidditch, ed. Oxford: Oxford University Press, 1975.
Lux, Kenneth. *Adam Smith's Mistake: How a Moral Philosopher Invented Economics and Ended Morality*. Boston: Shambhala, 1990.
McCawley, James D. "The Biological Side of Otto Jespersen's Linguistic Thought." *Historiographia Linguistica* XIX, 1 (1992): 97–110.
–"Review of 'The Human Language.'" *Language* 71, 3 (1995): 622–29.

Macfarlane, Alan. *The Riddle of the Modern World: Of Liberty, Wealth and Equality.* London: Macmillan, 2000.

Macfie, A. L. *The Individual in Society: Papers on Adam Smith.* London: Allen and Unwin, 1967.

Machan, Tibor R., and Rasmussen, Douglas B., eds. *Liberty for the 21st Century: Contemporary Libertarian Thought.* Lanham, MD: Rowman & Littlefield, 1995.

MacIntyre, Alasdair. *After Virtue.* Rev. 2nd ed. Notre Dame, IN: University of Notre Dame Press, 1984.

Mackie, J. L. *Ethics: Inventing Right and Wrong* (1977). New York: Viking, 1991.

McLuhan, T. C., ed. *Touch the Earth: A Self-Portrait of Indian Existence.* New York: Outerbridge & Dienstfrey, 1971.

Malebranche, Nicolas. *De la recherche de la vérité* (1674–75). In *Malebranche: Philosophical Selections,* Steven Nadler, ed. Indianapolis: Hackett, 1992.

Mandeville, Bernard. *Fable of the Bees: or, Private Vices, Publick Benefits* (1714). F. B. Kaye, ed. Oxford: Oxford University Press, 1924.

Manley, Michael. "Adam Smith Was Right." *New Perspectives Quarterly* 9, 3 (Summer 1992): 46–51.

Martin, Marie A. "Utility and Morality: Adam Smith's Critique of Hume." *Hume Studies* 16, 2 (1990): 107–20.

Marx, Karl. "Estranged Labour." *Economic and Philosophical Manuscripts of 1844.* In *The Marx-Engels Reader,* Robert C. Tucker, ed. New York: W. W. Norton, 1978.

Merton, Robert K. "The Unanticipated Consequences of Purposive Social Action." *American Sociological Review* 1 (1936): 894–904.

Miller, David H. "To Economize on Love: An Alternative Approach to Social Philosophy and Economy." Available at http://www.foresight.org/essays/econlove.html.

Minowitz, Peter. *Profits, Priests and Princes.* Stanford, CA: Stanford University Press, 1993.

Morrow, Glenn R. "Adam Smith: Moralist and Philosopher." In *Adam Smith, 1776–1926: Lectures to Commemorate the Sesquicentennial of the Publication of "The Wealth of Nations,"* John M. Clark et al., eds. Chicago: University of Chicago Press, 1928.

Muller, Jerry Z. *Adam Smith in His Time and Ours: Designing the Decent Society.* New York: The Free Press, 1993.

Nagel, Thomas. *The View from Nowhere.* Oxford: Oxford University Press, 1986.

Norlin, Kurt. "What Is an Ideal Observer Theory of Ethics?" Unpublished manuscript: University of California at Irvine, 1995.

Nozick, Robert. *Anarchy, State, and Utopia.* New York: Basic Books, 1974.

Oncken, August. "The Consistency of Adam Smith." *Economic Journal of London* vii (1897): 443–50.

Otteson, James R. "Adam Smith on the Emergence of Morals: A Reply to Eugene Heath." *British Journal for the History of Philosophy* 8, 3 (October 2000): 545–51.

–"Adam Smith's First Market: The Development of Language." *History of Philosophy Quarterly* 19, 1 (January 2002): 65–86.

–"Limits on Our Obligation to Give." *Public Affairs Quarterly* 14, 3 (July 2000): 183–203.

–"Private Judgment, Individual Liberty, and the Role of the State." *Journal of Social Philosophy* (forthcoming).

–Review of Charles L. Griswold, Jr., *Adam Smith and the Virtues of Enlightenment.* *Philosophy and Phenomenological Research* LXI, 3 (November 2000): 714–18.

–Review of Samuel Fleischacker, *A Third Concept of Liberty: Judgment and Freedom in Kant and Adam Smith. Journal of Social Philosophy* 54, 2 (December 2000): 426–28.

Pinker, Steven. *The Language Instinct: How the Mind Creates Language.* New York: HarperCollins, 1994.

Plato. *Republic.* G. M. A. Grube, trans. Indianapolis: Hackett, 1992.

Rae, John. *Life of Adam Smith.* London: Macmillan, 1895.

Raphael, D. D. *Adam Smith.* Oxford: Oxford University Press, 1985.

–*British Moralists 1650–1800.* Indianapolis: Hackett, 1991.

–"The Impartial Spectator." In *Essays on Adam Smith,* Andrew S. Skinner and Thomas Wilson, eds. Oxford: Clarendon Press, 1975.

Reid, Thomas. *Essay on the Active Powers of Man* (1788). In *British Moralists 1650–1800,* D. D. Raphael, ed. Indianapolis: Hackett, 1991.

Ridley, Matt. *The Origins of Virtue: Human Instincts and the Evolution of Cooperation.* New York: Viking, 1996.

Robbins, Lionel. *The Theory of Economic Policy.* London: Macmillan, 1952.

Robertson, H. M., and Taylor, W. L. "Adam Smith's Approach to the Theory of Value." *Economic Journal* LXVII, 266 (June 1957): 182–98.

Rosenberg, Nathan. "Adam Smith and the Stock of Moral Capital." *History of Political Economy* 22, 1 (1990): 1–17.

–and Birdzell, L. E., Jr. *How the West Grew Rich: The Economic Transformation of the Industrial World.* New York: Basic Books, 1986.

Ross, I. S. *The Life of Adam Smith.* Oxford: Oxford University Press, 1995.

Rothschild, Emma. "Adam Smith and the Invisible Hand." *American Economic Review* 84, no 2 (May 1994): 319–22.

–*Economic Sentiments: Adam Smith, Condorcet, and the Enlightenment.* Cambridge, MA: Harvard University Press, 2001.

Rousseau, Jean-Jacques. *Discourse on the Origin of Inequality* (1754). In *Jean-Jacques Rousseau: The Basic Political Writings,* Donald A. Cress, ed. Indianapolis: Hackett, 1987.

Skarzynski, Witold von. *Adam Smith als Moralphilosoph und Schoepfer der Nationaloekonomie.* Berlin: Theobald Grieben, 1878.

Smith, Adam. *Correspondence of Adam Smith.* Rev. ed. E. C. Mossner and I. S. Ross, eds. Oxford: Oxford University Press, 1987.

–*Essays on Philosophical Subjects.* W. L. D. Wightman, ed. Oxford: Oxford University Press, 1980.

–*An Inquiry into the Nature and Causes of the Wealth of Nations* (1776). R. H. Campbell, A. S. Skinner, and W. B. Todd, eds. Oxford: Oxford University Press, 1976.

–*Lectures on Jurisprudence* (1762–63, 1766). R. L. Meek, D. D. Raphael, and P. G. Stein, eds. Oxford: Oxford University Press, 1978.

–*Lectures on Rhetoric and Belles Lettres.* J. C. Bryce, ed. Oxford: Oxford University Press, 1983.

–*The Theory of Moral Sentiments* (1759). D. D. Raphael and A. L. Macfie, eds. Oxford: Oxford University Press, 1976.

Stewart, Dugald. *Biographical Memoir of Adam Smith, L.L.D.* (1793). New York: Augustus M. Kelley, 1966.

Stigler, George J. "The Division of Labor Is Limited by the Extent of the Market." *Journal of Political Economy* LIX, 3 (June 1951): 185–93.

Sturtevant, William C., gen. ed. *Handbook of North American Indians.* 12 vols. Washington, DC: Smithsonian Institution, 1978–98.

Swabey, William C. *Ethical Theory from Hobbes to Kant.* New York: Philosophical Library, 1961.

Teichgraeber, Richard F., III. *"Free Trade" and Moral Philosophy: Rethinking the Sources of Adam Smith's* Wealth of Nations. Durham, NC: Duke University Press, 1986.

–"Rethinking *Das Adam Smith Problem.*" *Journal of British Studies* 20 (1981): 106–23.

Terry, Richard. "Literature, Aesthetics, and Canonicity in the Eighteenth Century." *Eighteenth-Century Life* 21 (1997): 80–101.

Ullmann-Margalit, Edna. "Invisible-Hand Explanations." *Synthese* 39 (1978): 263–91.

Viner, Jacob. "Adam Smith and Laissez Faire." In *Adam Smith, 1776–1926: Lectures to Commemorate the Sesquicentennial of the Publication of "The Wealth of Nations,"* John M. Clark et al., eds. Chicago: University of Chicago Press, 1928.

Waal, Franz de. *Good Natured: The Origins of Right and Wrong in Humans and Other Animals.* Cambridge, MA: Harvard University Press, 1996.

Way, K. Brad. "Invisible Hands and the Success of Science." *Philosophy of Science* 67 (March 2000): 163–75.

Winch, Donald. *Adam Smith's Politics.* Cambridge: Cambridge University Press, 1978.

Wilson, E. O. *On Human Nature.* Cambridge, MA: Harvard University Press, 1978.

Wilson, James Q. *The Moral Sense.* New York: The Free Press, 1993.

Wright, Robert. *The Moral Animal: Evolutionary Psychology and Everyday Life.* New York: Pantheon Books, 1994.

# Index